C Programming: Just the FAQs

C PROGRAMMING: JUST THE FAQS

Paul S. R. Chisholm
David Hanley
Michael Jones
Michael Lindner
Lloyd Work

SAMS
PUBLISHING

201 West 103rd Street
Indianapolis, Indiana 46290

Trademarks

Overview

Contents

Introduction

What is a *FAQ*? It's a Frequently Asked Question. You can see FAQs just about everywhere in the online community. They originated in the USENET groups on the Internet as a way to answer users' most common questions regarding the groups. The FAQs files were efficient. Instead of answering the same questions over and over, one file was written that contained all the frequently asked questions and answers to those questions.

This book is a comprehensive list of FAQs, assembled by a group of professional C programmers. This book contains the FAQs most often posed by our readers over our many years of publishing programming books. You won't find a FAQ list that goes into as much detail as this book does. (Have you ever seen a 400-page FAQ list?)

Our team of expert programmers has tackled the toughest topics, including variables and data storage, sorting data, pointers and memory allocation, tables and arrays, debugging, portability, ANSI standards, and Windows concerns. If something in C is stumping you, odds are you'll find an answer in this book. In addition, the extensive cross referencing in this book will help you find the answer you need—even if you start out looking in the wrong spot.

CHAPTER

The C Language

This chapter focuses on some basic elements of the C programming language. When you begin programming in C, you probably will find yourself coming up with basic questions regarding the conventions, keywords, and terms used with the C language. This chapter attempts to answer some of the most frequently asked questions regarding these subjects.

For instance, one of the most commonly used constructs of the C language is the `switch` statement. This chapter includes three frequently asked questions regarding this powerful language element. This chapter also covers several other topics such as loops, branching, operator precedence, and blocking guidelines. When reading this chapter, pay close attention to the questions regarding the `switch` statement and operator precedence, because these elements of the C language sometimes can be confusing for the beginning C programmer.

I.1: What is a local block?
Answer:

A local block is any portion of a C program that is enclosed by the left brace (`{`) and the right brace (`}`). A C function contains left and right braces, and therefore anything between the two braces is contained in a local block. An `if` statement or a `switch` statement can also contain braces, so the portion of code between these two braces would be considered a local block. Additionally, you might want to create your own local block without the aid of a C function or keyword construct. This is perfectly legal. Variables can be declared within local blocks, but they must be declared only at the *beginning* of a local block. Variables declared in this manner are visible only within the local block. Duplicate variable names declared within a local block take precedence over variables with the same name declared outside the local block. Here is an example of a program that uses local blocks:

```c
#include <stdio.h>

void main(void);

void main()
{
    /* Begin local block for function main() */

    int test_var = 10;

    printf("Test variable before the if statement: %d\n", test_var);

    if (test_var > 5)
    {
        /* Begin local block for "if" statement */

        int test_var = 5;

        printf("Test variable within the if statement: %d\n",
            test_var);

        {
            /* Begin independent local block (not tied to
               any function or keyword) */

            int test_var = 0;

            printf(
            "Test variable within the independent local block:%d\n",
            test_var);

        }

        /* End independent local block */

    }

    /* End local block for "if" statement */

    printf("Test variable after the if statement: %d\n", test_var);

}

/* End local block for function main() */
```

This example program produces the following output:

```
Test variable before the if statement: 10
Test variable within the if statement: 5
```

```
Test variable within the independent local block: 0
Test variable after the if statement: 10
```

Notice that as each `test_var` was defined, it took precedence over the previously defined `test_var`. Also notice that when the `if` statement local block had ended, the program had reentered the scope of the original `test_var`, and its value was 10.

Cross Reference:

I.2: Should variables be stored in local blocks?

I.2: Should variables be stored in local blocks?

Answer:

The use of local blocks for storing variables is unusual and therefore should be avoided, with only rare exceptions. One of these exceptions would be for debugging purposes, when you might want to declare a local instance of a global variable to test within your function. You also might want to use a local block when you want to make your program more readable in the current context. Sometimes having the variable declared closer to where it is used makes your program more readable. However, well-written programs usually do not have to resort to declaring variables in this manner, and you should avoid using local blocks.

Cross Reference:

I.1: What is a local block?

I.3: When is a *switch* statement better than multiple *if* statements?

Answer:

A `switch` statement is generally best to use when you have more than two conditional expressions based on a single variable of *numeric* type. For instance, rather than the code

```
if (x == 1)
    printf("x is equal to one.\n");
else if (x == 2)
    printf("x is equal to two.\n");
else if (x == 3)
    printf("x is equal to three.\n");
else
    printf("x is not equal to one, two, or three.\n");
```

the following code is easier to read and maintain:

```
switch (x)
{
    case 1:    printf("x is equal to one.\n");
```

```
                      break;
       case 2:   printf("x is equal to two.\n");
                      break;
       case 3:   printf("x is equal to three.\n");
                      break;
       default:  printf("x is not equal to one, two, or three.\n");
                      break;
}
```

Notice that for this method to work, the conditional expression must be based on a variable of *numeric* type in order to use the switch statement. Also, the conditional expression must be based on a single variable. For instance, even though the following if statement contains more than two conditions, it is not a candidate for using a switch statement because it is based on string comparisons and not numeric comparisons:

```
char* name = "Lupto";

if (!stricmp(name, "Isaac"))
    printf("Your name means 'Laughter'.\n");
else if (!stricmp(name, "Amy"))
    printf("Your name means 'Beloved'.\n ");
else if (!stricmp(name, "Lloyd"))
    printf("Your name means 'Mysterious'.\n ");
else
    printf("I haven't a clue as to what your name means.\n");
```

Cross Reference:

I.4: Is a default case necessary in a switch statement?

I.5: Can the last case of a switch statement skip including the break?

I.4: Is a default case necessary in a *switch* statement?

Answer:

No, but it is not a bad idea to put default statements in switch statements for error- or logic-checking purposes. For instance, the following switch statement is perfectly normal:

```
switch (char_code)
{
    case 'Y':
    case 'y': printf("You answered YES!\n");
              break;
    case 'N':
    case 'n': printf("You answered NO!\n");
              break;
}
```

Consider, however, what would happen if an unknown character code were passed to this switch statement. The program would not print anything. It would be a good idea, therefore, to insert a default case where this condition would be taken care of:

```
...
    default:  printf("Unknown response: %d\n", char_code);
              break;
...
```

Additionally, default cases come in handy for logic checking. For instance, if your switch statement handled a fixed number of conditions and you considered any value *outside* those conditions to be a logic error, you could insert a default case which would flag that condition. Consider the following example:

```c
void move_cursor(int direction)
{
    switch (direction)
    {
        case UP:     cursor_up();
                     break;
        case DOWN:   cursor_down();
                     break;
        case LEFT:   cursor_left();
                     break;
        case RIGHT:  cursor_right();
                     break;
        default:     printf("Logic error on line number %ld!!!\n",
                            __LINE__);
                     break;
    }
}
```

Cross Reference:

I.3: When is a switch statement better than multiple if statements?

I.5: Can the last case of a switch statement skip including the break?

I.5: Can the last case of a *switch* statement skip including the *break*?

Answer:

Even though the last case of a switch statement does not require a break statement at the end, you should add break statements to all cases of the switch statement, including the last case. You should do so primarily because your program has a strong chance of being maintained by someone other than you who might add cases but neglect to notice that the last case has no break statement. This oversight would cause what would formerly be the last case statement to "fall through" to the new statements added to the bottom of the switch statement. Putting a break after each case statement would prevent this possible mishap and make your program more "bulletproof." Besides, most of today's optimizing compilers will *optimize out* the last break, so there will be no performance degradation if you add it.

Cross Reference:

I.3: When is a switch statement better than multiple if statements?

I.4: Is a default case necessary in a switch statement?

I.6: Other than in a *for* statement, when is the comma operator used?

Answer:

The comma operator is commonly used to separate variable declarations, function arguments, and expressions, as well as the elements of a for statement. Look closely at the following program, which shows some of the many ways a comma can be used:

```c
#include <stdio.h>
#include <stdlib.h>

void main(void);

void main()
{
    /* Here, the comma operator is used to separate
       three variable declarations. */

    int i, j, k;

    /* Notice how you can use the comma operator to perform
       multiple initializations on the same line. */

    i = 0, j = 1, k = 2;

    printf("i = %d, j = %d, k = %d\n", i, j, k);

    /* Here, the comma operator is used to execute three expressions
       in one line: assign k to i, increment j, and increment k.
       The value that i receives is always the rightmost expression. */

    i = (j++, k++);

    printf("i = %d, j = %d, k = %d\n", i, j, k);

    /* Here, the while statement uses the comma operator to
       assign the value of i as well as test it. */

    while (i = (rand() % 100), i != 50)
        printf("i is %d, trying again...\n", i);

    printf("\nGuess what? i is 50!\n");

}
```

Notice the line that reads

```c
i = (j++, k++);
```

This line actually performs three actions at once. These are the three actions, in order:

1. Assigns the value of k to i. This happens because the left value (lvalue) always evaluates to the rightmost argument. In this case, it evaluates to k. Notice that it does not evaluate to k++, because k++ is a postfix incremental expression, and k is not incremented until the assignment of k to i is made. If the expression had read ++k, the value of ++k would be assigned to i because it is a prefix incremental expression, and it is incremented before the assignment is made.

2. Increments j.

3. Increments k.

Also, notice the strange-looking while statement:

```
while (i = (rand() % 100), i != 50)
    printf("i is %d, trying again...\n");
```

Here, the comma operator separates two expressions, each of which is evaluated for each iteration of the while statement. The first expression, to the left of the comma, assigns i to a random number from 0 to 99. The second expression, which is more commonly found in a while statement, is a conditional expression that tests to see whether i is not equal to 50. For each iteration of the while statement, i is assigned a new random number, and the value of i is checked to see that it is not 50. Eventually, i is randomly assigned the value 50, and the while statement terminates.

Cross Reference:

I.12: Is left-to-right or right-to-left order guaranteed for operator precedence?

I.13: What is the difference between ++var and var++?

I.7: How can you tell whether a loop ended prematurely?
Answer:

Generally, loops are dependent on one or more variables. Your program can check those variables outside the loop to ensure that the loop executed properly. For instance, consider the following example:

```
#define REQUESTED_BLOCKS 512

int x;
char* cp[REQUESTED_BLOCKS];

/* Attempt (in vain, I must add...) to
   allocate 512 10KB blocks in memory. */


for (x=0; x< REQUESTED_BLOCKS; x++)
{

    cp[x] = (char*) malloc(10000, 1);

    if (cp[x] == (char*) NULL)
        break;

}
```

```
/* If x is less than REQUESTED_BLOCKS,
   the loop has ended prematurely. */

if (x < REQUESTED_BLOCKS)
    printf("Bummer! My loop ended prematurely!\n");
```

Notice that for the loop to execute successfully, it would have had to iterate through 512 times. Immediately following the loop, this condition is tested to see whether the loop ended prematurely. If the variable x is anything less than 512, some error has occurred.

Cross Reference:

None.

I.8: What is the difference between *goto* and *longjmp()* and *setjmp()*?

Answer:

A goto statement implements a *local* jump of program execution, and the longjmp() and setjmp() functions implement a *nonlocal,* or far, jump of program execution. Generally, a jump in execution of any kind should be avoided because it is not considered good programming practice to use such statements as goto and longjmp in your program.

A goto statement simply bypasses code in your program and jumps to a predefined position. To use the goto statement, you give it a labeled position to jump to. This predefined position must be within the same function. You cannot implement gotos between functions. Here is an example of a goto statement:

```
void bad_programmers_function(void)
{
    int x;

    printf("Excuse me while I count to 5000...\n");

    x = 1;

    while (1)
    {
        printf("%d\n", x);

        if (x == 5000)
            goto all_done;
        else
            x = x + 1;
    }

all_done:

    printf("Whew! That wasn't so bad, was it?\n");

}
```

This example could have been written much better, avoiding the use of a goto statement. Here is an example of an improved implementation:

```c
void better_function(void)
{

    int x;

    printf("Excuse me while I count to 5000...\n");

    for (x=1; x<=5000; x++)
        printf("%d\n", x);

    printf("Whew! That wasn't so bad, was it?\n");

}
```

As previously mentioned, the longjmp() and setjmp() functions implement a nonlocal goto. When your program calls setjmp(), the current state of your program is saved in a structure of type jmp_buf. Later, your program can call the longjmp() function to restore the program's state as it was when you called setjmp(). Unlike the goto statement, the longjmp() and setjmp() functions do not need to be implemented in the same function. However, there is a major drawback to using these functions: your program, when restored to its previously saved state, will lose its references to any dynamically allocated memory between the longjmp() and the setjmp(). This means you will waste memory for every malloc() or calloc() you have implemented between your longjmp() and setjmp(), and your program will be horribly inefficient. It is highly recommended that you avoid using functions such as longjmp() and setjmp() because they, like the goto statement, are quite often an indication of poor programming practice.

Here is an example of the longjmp() and setjmp() functions:

```c
#include <stdio.h>
#include <setjmp.h>

jmp_buf saved_state;

void main(void);
void call_longjmp(void);

void main(void)
{

    int ret_code;

    printf("The current state of the program is being saved...\n");

    ret_code = setjmp(saved_state);

    if (ret_code == 1)
    {
        printf("The longjmp function has been called.\n");
        printf("The program's previous state has been restored.\n");
        exit(0);
    }
```

```
        printf("I am about to call longjmp and\n");
        printf("return to the previous program state...\n");

        call_longjmp();

}

void call_longjmp(void)
{

        longjmp(saved_state, 1);

}
```

Cross Reference:

None.

I.9: What is an lvalue?
Answer:

An lvalue is an expression to which a value can be assigned. The lvalue expression is located on the *left side* of an assignment statement, whereas an rvalue (see FAQ I.11) is located on the *right side* of an assignment statement. Each assignment statement must have an lvalue and an rvalue. The lvalue expression must reference a storable variable in memory. It cannot be a constant. For instance, the following lines show a few examples of lvalues:

```
int x;
int* p_int;

x = 1;
*p_int = 5;
```

The variable x is an integer, which is a storable location in memory. Therefore, the statement x = 1 qualifies x to be an lvalue. Notice the second assignment statement, *p_int = 5. By using the * modifier to reference the area of memory that p_int points to, *p_int is qualified as an lvalue. In contrast, here are a few examples of what would not be considered lvalues:

```
#define CONST_VAL 10

int x;

/* example 1 */
1 = x;

/* example 2 */
CONST_VAL = 5;
```

In both statements, the left side of the statement evaluates to a constant value that cannot be changed because constants do not represent storable locations in memory. Therefore, these two assignment statements *do not* contain lvalues and will be flagged by your compiler as errors.

Cross Reference:

I.10: Can an array be an lvalue?

I.11: What is an rvalue?

I.10: Can an array be an lvalue?

Answer:

In FAQ I.9, an lvalue was defined as an expression to which a value can be assigned. Is an array an expression to which we can assign a value? The answer to this question is no, because an array is composed of several separate *array elements* that cannot be treated as a whole for assignment purposes. The following statement is therefore illegal:

```
int x[5], y[5];

x = y;
```

You could, however, use a for loop to iterate through each element of the array and assign values individually, such as in this example:

```
int i;
int x[5];
int y[5];

...
for (i=0; i<5; i++)
    x[i] = y[i]
...
```

Additionally, you might want to copy the whole array all at once. You can do so using a library function such as the memcpy() function, which is shown here:

```
memcpy(x, y, sizeof(y));
```

It should be noted here that unlike arrays, structures *can* be treated as lvalues. Thus, you can assign one structure variable to another structure variable of the same type, such as this:

```
typedef struct t_name
{
    char last_name[25];
    char first_name[15];
    char middle_init[2];
} NAME;

...

NAME my_name, your_name;

...

your_name = my_name;

...
```

In the preceding example, the entire contents of the my_name structure were copied into the your_name structure. This is essentially the same as the following line:

```
memcpy(your_name, my_name, sizeof(your_name));
```

Cross Reference:

I.9: What is an lvalue?

I.11: What is an rvalue?

I.11: What is an rvalue?

Answer:

In FAQ I.9, an lvalue was defined as an expression to which a value can be assigned. It was also explained that an lvalue appears on the *left side* of an assignment statement. Therefore, an rvalue can be defined as an expression that can be assigned to an lvalue. The rvalue appears on the *right side* of an assignment statement. Unlike an lvalue, an rvalue can be a constant or an expression, as shown here:

```
int x, y;

x = 1;              /* 1 is an rvalue; x is an lvalue */

y = (x + 1);        /* (x + 1) is an rvalue; y is an lvalue */
```

As stated in FAQ I.9, an assignment statement must have both an lvalue and an rvalue. Therefore, the following statement would not compile because it is missing an rvalue:

```
int x;

x = void_function_call()  /* the function void_function_call()
                             returns nothing */
```

If the function had returned an integer, it would be considered an rvalue because it evaluates into something that the lvalue, x, can store.

Cross Reference:

I.9: What is an lvalue?

I.10: Can an array be an lvalue?

I.12: Is left-to-right or right-to-left order guaranteed for operator precedence?

Answer:

The simple answer to this question is neither. The C language does not always evaluate left-to-right or right-to-left. Generally, function calls are evaluated first, followed by complex expressions and then simple expressions. Additionally, most of today's popular C compilers often rearrange the order in which the expression is evaluated in order to get better optimized code. You therefore should *always* implicitly define your operator precedence by using parentheses.

For example, consider the following expression:

```
a = b + c/d / function_call() * 5
```

The way this expression is to be evaluated is totally ambiguous, and you probably will not get the results you want. Instead, try writing it by using implicit operator precedence:

```
a = b + (((c/d) / function_call()) * 5)
```

Using this method, you can be assured that your expression will be evaluated properly and that the compiler will not rearrange operators for optimization purposes.

Cross Reference:

None.

I.13: What is the difference between ++*var* and *var*++?

Answer:

The ++ operator is called the increment operator. When the operator is placed *before* the variable (++var), the variable is incremented by 1 before it is used in the expression. When the operator is placed *after* the variable (var++), the expression is evaluated, and then the variable is incremented by 1. The same holds true for the decrement operator (--). When the operator is placed before the variable, you are said to have a prefix operation. When the operator is placed after the variable, you are said to have a postfix operation.

For instance, consider the following example of postfix incrementation:

```
int x, y;

x = 1;
y = (x++ * 5);
```

In this example, postfix incrementation is used, and x is not incremented until after the evaluation of the expression is done. Therefore, y evaluates to 1 times 5, or 5. After the evaluation, x is incremented to 2.

Now look at an example using prefix incrementation:

```
int x, y;

x = 1;
y = (++x * 5);
```

This example is the same as the first one, except that this example uses prefix incrementation rather than postfix. Therefore, x is incremented before the expression is evaluated, making it 2. Hence, y evaluates to 2 times 5, or 10.

Cross Reference:

None.

I.14: What does the modulus operator do?

Answer:

The modulus operator (%) gives the *remainder* of two divided numbers. For instance, consider the following portion of code:

```
x = 15/7
```

If x were an integer, the resulting value of x would be 2. However, consider what would happen if you were to apply the modulus operator to the same equation:

```
x = 15%7
```

The result of this expression would be the remainder of 15 divided by 7, or 1. This is to say that 15 divided by 7 is 2 with a remainder of 1.

The modulus operator is commonly used to determine whether one number is evenly divisible into another. For instance, if you wanted to print every third letter of the alphabet, you would use the following code:

```
int x;

for (x=1; x<=26; x++)
    if ((x%3) == 0)
        printf("%c", x+64);
```

The preceding example would output the string "cfilorux", which represents every third letter in the alphabet.

Cross Reference:

None.

CHAPTER

◆

Variables and Data Storage

One of the C language's strengths is its flexibility in defining data storage. There are two aspects that can be controlled in C: scope and lifetime. Scope refers to the places in the code from which the variable can be accessed. Lifetime refers to the points in time at which the variable can be accessed.

Three scopes are available to the programmer:

extern   This is the default for variables declared outside any function. The scope of variables with extern scope is all the code in the entire program.

static   The scope of a variable declared static outside any function is the rest of the code in that source file. The scope of a variable declared static inside a function is the rest of the local block.

auto   This is the default for variables declared inside a function. The scope of an auto variable is the rest of the local block.

Three lifetimes are available to the programmer. They do not have predefined keywords for names as scopes do. The first is the lifetime of extern and static variables, whose lifetime is from before main() is called until the program exits. The second is the lifetime of function arguments and automatics, which is from the time the function is called until it returns. The third lifetime is that of dynamically allocated data. It starts when the program calls malloc() or calloc() to allocate space for the data and ends when the program calls free() or when it exits, whichever comes first.

II.1: Where in memory are my variables stored?

Answer:

Variables can be stored in several places in memory, depending on their lifetime. Variables that are defined outside any function (whether of global or file `static` scope), and variables that are defined inside a function as `static` variables, exist for the lifetime of the program's execution. These variables are stored in the "data segment." The data segment is a fixed-size area in memory set aside for these variables. The data segment is subdivided into two parts, one for initialized variables and another for uninitialized variables.

Variables that are defined inside a function as `auto` variables (that are not defined with the keyword `static`) come into existence when the program begins executing the block of code (delimited by curly braces `{}`) containing them, and they cease to exist when the program leaves that block of code. Variables that are the arguments to functions exist only during the call to that function. These variables are stored on the "stack." The stack is an area of memory that starts out small and grows automatically up to some predefined limit. In DOS and other systems without virtual memory, the limit is set either when the program is compiled or when it begins executing. In UNIX and other systems with virtual memory, the limit is set by the system, and it is usually so large that it can be ignored by the programmer. For a discussion on what virtual memory is, see FAQ II.3.

The third and final area doesn't actually store variables but can be used to store data pointed to by variables. Pointer variables that are assigned to the result of a call to the `malloc()` function contain the address of a dynamically allocated area of memory. This memory is in an area called the "heap." The heap is another area that starts out small and grows, but it grows only when the programmer explicitly calls `malloc()` or other memory allocation functions, such as `calloc()`. The heap can share a memory segment with either the data segment or the stack, or it can have its own segment. It all depends on the compiler options and operating system. The heap, like the stack, has a limit on how much it can grow, and the same rules apply as to how that limit is determined.

Cross Reference:

I.1: What is a local block?

II.2: Do variables need to be initialized?

II.3: What is page thrashing?

VII.20: What is the stack?

VII.21: What is the heap?

II.2: Do variables need to be initialized?

Answer:

No. All variables should be given a value before they are used, and a good compiler will help you find variables that are used before they are set to a value. Variables need not be initialized, however. Variables defined outside a function or defined inside a function with the `static` keyword (those defined in the data segment discussed in the preceding FAQ) are already initialized to 0 for you if you do not explicitly initialize them.

Automatic variables are variables defined inside a function or block of code without the `static` keyword. These variables have undefined values if you don't explicitly initialize them. If you don't initialize an automatic variable, you must make sure you assign to it before using the value.

Space on the heap allocated by calling `malloc()` contains undefined data as well and must be set to a known value before being used. Space allocated by calling `calloc()` is set to 0 for you when it is allocated.

Cross Reference:

I.1: What is a local block?

VII.20: What is the stack?

VII.21: What is the heap?

II.3: What is page thrashing?
Answer:

Some operating systems (such as UNIX or Windows in enhanced mode) use virtual memory. Virtual memory is a technique for making a machine behave as if it had more memory than it really has, by using disk space to simulate RAM (random-access memory). In the 80386 and higher Intel CPU chips, and in most other modern microprocessors (such as the Motorola 68030, Sparc, and Power PC), exists a piece of hardware called the Memory Management Unit, or MMU.

The MMU treats memory as if it were composed of a series of "pages." A page of memory is a block of contiguous bytes of a certain size, usually 4096 or 8192 bytes. The operating system sets up and maintains a table for each running program called the Process Memory Map, or PMM. This is a table of all the pages of memory that program can access and where each is really located.

Every time your program accesses any portion of memory, the address (called a "virtual address") is processed by the MMU. The MMU looks in the PMM to find out where the memory is really located (called the "physical address"). The physical address can be any location in memory or on disk that the operating system has assigned for it. If the location the program wants to access is on disk, the page containing it must be read from disk into memory, and the PMM must be updated to reflect this action (this is called a "page fault").

Hope you're still with me, because here's the tricky part. Because accessing the disk is so much slower than accessing RAM, the operating system tries to keep as much of the virtual memory as possible in RAM. If you're running a large enough program (or several small programs at once), there might not be enough RAM to hold all the memory used by the programs, so some of it must be moved out of RAM and onto disk (this action is called "paging out").

The operating system tries to guess which areas of memory aren't likely to be used for a while (usually based on how the memory has been used in the past). If it guesses wrong, or if your programs are accessing lots of memory in lots of places, many page faults will occur in order to read in the pages that were paged out. Because all of RAM is being used, for each page read in to be accessed, another page must be paged out. This can lead to more page faults, because now a different page of memory has been moved to disk. The problem of many page faults occurring in a short time, called "page thrashing," can drastically cut the performance of a system.

Programs that frequently access many widely separated locations in memory are more likely to cause page thrashing on a system. So is running many small programs that all continue to run even when you are not actively using them. To reduce page thrashing, you can run fewer programs simultaneously. Or you can try changing the way a large program works to maximize the capability of the operating system to guess which pages won't be needed. You can achieve this effect by caching values or changing lookup algorithms in large data structures, or sometimes by changing to a memory allocation library which provides an implementation of `malloc()` that allocates memory more efficiently. Finally, you might consider adding more RAM to the system to reduce the need to page out.

Cross Reference:

VII.17: How do you declare an array that will hold more than 64KB of data?

VII.21: What is the heap?

XVIII.14: How can I get more than 640KB of memory available to my DOS program?

XXI.31: How is memory organized in Windows?

II.4: What is a *const* pointer?

Answer:

The access modifier keyword `const` is a promise the programmer makes to the compiler that the value of a variable will not be changed after it is initialized. The compiler will enforce that promise as best it can by not enabling the programmer to write code which modifies a variable that has been declared `const`.

A "const pointer," or more correctly, a "pointer to const," is a pointer which points to data that is `const` (constant, or unchanging). A pointer to `const` is declared by putting the word `const` at the beginning of the pointer declaration. This declares a pointer which points to data that can't be modified. The pointer itself can be modified. The following example illustrates some legal and illegal uses of a `const` pointer:

```
const char  *str = "hello";
char  c = *str     /* legal */
str++;             /* legal */
*str = 'a';        /* illegal */
str[1] = 'b';      /* illegal */
```

The first two statements here are legal because they do not modify the data that `str` points to. The next two statements are illegal because they modify the data pointed to by `str`.

Pointers to `const` are most often used in declaring function parameters. For instance, a function that counted the number of characters in a string would not need to change the contents of the string, and it might be written this way:

```
my_strlen(const char *str)
{
        int count = 0;
        while (*str++)
        {
```

```
        count++;
    }
    return count;
}
```

Note that non-const pointers are implicitly converted to const pointers when needed, but const pointers are not converted to non-const pointers. This means that my_strlen() could be called with either a const or a non-const character pointer.

Cross Reference:

II.7: Can a variable be both const and volatile?

II.8: When should the const modifier be used?

II.14: When should a type cast not be used?

II.18: What is the benefit of using const for declaring constants?

II.5: When should the register modifier be used? Does it really help?

Answer:

The register modifier hints to the compiler that the variable will be heavily used and should be kept in the CPU's registers, if possible, so that it can be accessed faster. There are several restrictions on the use of the register modifier.

First, the variable must be of a type that can be held in the CPU's register. This usually means a single value of a size less than or equal to the size of an integer. Some machines have registers that can hold floating-point numbers as well.

Second, because the variable might not be stored in memory, its address cannot be taken with the unary & operator. An attempt to do so is flagged as an error by the compiler.

Some additional rules affect how useful the register modifier is. Because the number of registers is limited, and because some registers can hold only certain types of data (such as pointers or floating-point numbers), the number and types of register modifiers that will actually have any effect are dependent on what machine the program will run on. Any additional register modifiers are silently ignored by the compiler.

Also, in some cases, it might actually be slower to keep a variable in a register because that register then becomes unavailable for other purposes or because the variable isn't used enough to justify the overhead of loading and storing it.

So when should the register modifier be used? The answer is never, with most modern compilers. Early C compilers did not keep any variables in registers unless directed to do so, and the register modifier was a valuable addition to the language. C compiler design has advanced to the point, however, where the compiler will usually make better decisions than the programmer about which variables should be stored in registers. In fact, many compilers actually ignore the register modifier, which is perfectly legal, because it is only a hint and not a directive.

In the rare event that a program is too slow, and you know that the problem is due to a variable being stored in memory, you might try adding the register modifier as a last resort, but don't be surprised if this action doesn't change the speed of the program.

Cross Reference:

II.6: When should the volatile modifier be used?

II.6: When should the *volatile* modifier be used?

Answer:

The volatile modifier is a directive to the compiler's optimizer that operations involving this variable should not be optimized in certain ways. There are two special cases in which use of the volatile modifier is desirable. The first case involves memory-mapped hardware (a device such as a graphics adaptor that appears to the computer's hardware as if it were part of the computer's memory), and the second involves shared memory (memory used by two or more programs running simultaneously).

Most computers have a set of registers that can be accessed faster than the computer's main memory. A good compiler will perform a kind of optimization called "redundant load and store removal." The compiler looks for places in the code where it can either remove an instruction to load data from memory because the value is already in a register, or remove an instruction to store data to memory because the value can stay in a register until it is changed again anyway.

If a variable is a pointer to something other than normal memory, such as memory-mapped ports on a peripheral, redundant load and store optimizations might be detrimental. For instance, here's a piece of code that might be used to time some operation:

```
time_t time_addition(volatile const struct timer *t, int a)
{
        int     n;
        int     x;
        time_t  then;
        x = 0;
        then = t->value;
        for (n = 0; n < 1000; n++)
        {
                x = x + a;
        }

        return t->value - then;
}
```

In this code, the variable t->value is actually a hardware counter that is being incremented as time passes. The function adds the value of a to x 1000 times, and it returns the amount the timer was incremented by while the 1000 additions were being performed.

Without the volatile modifier, a clever optimizer might assume that the value of t does not change during the execution of the function, because there is no statement that explicitly changes it. In that case, there's no need to read it from memory a second time and subtract it, because the answer will always be 0. The compiler might therefore "optimize" the function by making it always return 0.

If a variable points to data in shared memory, you also don't want the compiler to perform redundant load and store optimizations. Shared memory is normally used to enable two programs to communicate with each other by having one program store data in the shared portion of memory and the other program read the same portion of memory. If the compiler optimizes away a load or store of shared memory, communication between the two programs will be affected.

Cross Reference:

II.7: Can a variable be both `const` and `volatile`?

II.14: When should a type cast not be used?

II.7: Can a variable be both *const* and *volatile*?
Answer:

Yes. The `const` modifier means that this code cannot change the value of the variable, but that does not mean that the value cannot be changed by means outside this code. For instance, in the example in FAQ II.6, the timer structure was accessed through a `volatile const` pointer. The function itself did not change the value of the timer, so it was declared `const`. However, the value was changed by hardware on the computer, so it was declared `volatile`. If a variable is both `const` and `volatile`, the two modifiers can appear in either order.

Cross Reference:

II.6: When should the `volatile` modifier be used?

II.8: When should the `const` modifier be used?

II.14: When should a type cast not be used?

II.8: When should the *const* modifier be used?
Answer:

There are several reasons to use `const` pointers. First, it allows the compiler to catch errors in which code accidentally changes the value of a variable, as in

```
while (*str = 0) /* programmer meant to write *str != 0 */
{
    /* some code here */
    str++;
}
```

in which the = sign is a typographical error. Without the `const` in the declaration of `str`, the program would compile but not run properly.

Another reason is efficiency. The compiler might be able to make certain optimizations to the code generated if it knows that a variable will not be changed.

Any function parameter which points to data that is not modified by the function or by any function it calls should declare the pointer a pointer to const. Function parameters that are passed by value (rather than through a pointer) can be declared const if neither the function nor any function it calls modifies the data. In practice, however, such parameters are usually declared const only if it might be more efficient for the compiler to access the data through a pointer than by copying it.

Cross Reference:

II.7: Can a variable be both const and volatile?

II.14: When should a type cast not be used?

II.18: What is the benefit of using const for declaring constants?

II.9: How reliable are floating-point comparisons?
Answer:

Floating-point numbers are the "black art" of computer programming. One reason why this is so is that there is no optimal way to represent an arbitrary number. The Institute of Electrical and Electronic Engineers (IEEE) has developed a standard for the representation of floating-point numbers, but you cannot guarantee that every machine you use will conform to the standard.

Even if your machine does conform to the standard, there are deeper issues. It can be shown mathematically that there are an infinite number of "real" numbers between any two numbers. For the computer to distinguish between two numbers, the bits that represent them must differ. To represent an infinite number of different bit patterns would take an infinite number of bits. Because the computer must represent a large range of numbers in a small number of bits (usually 32 to 64 bits), it has to make approximate representations of most numbers.

Because floating-point numbers are so tricky to deal with, it's generally bad practice to compare a floating-point number for equality with anything. Inequalities are much safer. If, for instance, you want to step through a range of numbers in small increments, you might write this:

```
#include <stdio.h>
const float first = 0.0;
const float last = 70.0;
const float small = 0.007;
main()
{
        float   f;
        for (f = first; f != last && f < last + 1.0; f += small)
                ;
        printf("f is now %g\n", f);
}
```

However, rounding errors and small differences in the representation of the variable small might cause f to never be equal to last (it might go from being just under it to being just over it). Thus, the loop would go past the value last. The inequality f < last + 1.0 has been added to prevent the program from running on for a very long time if this happens. If you run this program and the value printed for f is 71 or more, this is what has happened.

A safer way to write this loop is to use the inequality f < last to test for the loop ending, as in this example:

```
float   f;
for (f = first; f < last; f += small)
        ;
```

You could even precompute the number of times the loop should be executed and use an integer to count iterations of the loop, as in this example:

```
float   f;
int     count = (last - first) / small;
for (f = first; count-- > 0; f += small)
        ;
```

Cross Reference:

II.11: Are there any problems with performing mathematical operations on different variable types?

II.10: How can you determine the maximum value that a numeric variable can hold?

Answer:

The easiest way to find out how large or small a number that a particular type can hold is to use the values defined in the ANSI standard header file limits.h. This file contains many useful constants defining the values that can be held by various types, including these:

Value	Description
CHAR_BIT	Number of bits in a char
CHAR_MAX	Maximum decimal integer value of a char
CHAR_MIN	Minimum decimal integer value of a char
MB_LEN_MAX	Maximum number of bytes in a multibyte character
INT_MAX	Maximum decimal value of an int
INT_MIN	Minimum decimal value of an int
LONG_MAX	Maximum decimal value of a long
LONG_MIN	Minimum decimal value of a long
SCHAR_MAX	Maximum decimal integer value of a signed char
SCHAR_MIN	Minimum decimal integer value of a signed char
SHRT_MAX	Maximum decimal value of a short
SHRT_MIN	Minimum decimal value of a short
UCHAR_MAX	Maximum decimal integer value of unsigned char

continues

Value	Description
UINT_MAX	Maximum decimal value of an unsigned integer
ULONG_MAX	Maximum decimal value of an unsigned long int
USHRT_MAX	Maximum decimal value of an unsigned short int

For integral types, on a machine that uses two's complement arithmetic (which is just about any machine you're likely to use), a signed type can hold numbers from $-2^{(number\ of\ bits - 1)}$ to $+2^{(number\ of\ bits - 1)} - 1$. An unsigned type can hold values from 0 to $+2^{(number\ of\ bits)} - 1$. For instance, a 16-bit signed integer can hold numbers from -2^{15} (−32768) to $+2^{15} - 1$ (32767).

Cross Reference:

X.1: What is the most efficient way to store flag values?

X.2: What is meant by "bit masking"?

X.6: How are 16- and 32-bit numbers stored?

II.11: Are there any problems with performing mathematical operations on different variable types?

Answer:

C has three categories of built-in data types: pointer types, integral types, and floating-point types.

Pointer types are the most restrictive in terms of the operations that can be performed on them. They are limited to

- subtraction of two pointers, valid only when both pointers point to elements in the same array. The result is the same as subtracting the integer subscripts corresponding to the two pointers.

+ addition of a pointer and an integral type. The result is a pointer that points to the element which would be selected by that integer.

Floating-point types consist of the built-in types float, double, and long double. Integral types consist of char, unsigned char, short, unsigned short, int, unsigned int, long, and unsigned long. All of these types can have the following arithmetic operations performed on them:

+	Addition
-	Subtraction
*	Multiplication
/	Division

Integral types also can have those four operations performed on them, as well as the following operations:

%	Modulo or remainder of division
<<	Shift left
>>	Shift right
&	Bitwise AND operation
¦	Bitwise OR operation

    ^   Bitwise exclusive OR operation
    !   Logical negative operation
    ~   Bitwise "one's complement" operation

Although C permits "mixed mode" expressions (an arithmetic expression involving different types), it actually converts the types to be the same type before performing the operations (except for the case of pointer arithmetic described previously). The process of automatic type conversion is called "operator promotion." Operator promotion is explained in FAQ II.12.

Cross Reference:

II.12: What is operator promotion?

II.12: What is operator promotion?
Answer:

If an operation is specified with operands of two different types, they are converted to the smallest type that can hold both values. The result has the same type as the two operands wind up having. To interpret the rules, read the following table from the top down, and stop at the first rule that applies.

If Either Operand Is	*And the Other Is*	*Change Them To*
long double	any other type	long double
double	any smaller type	double
float	any smaller type	float
unsigned long	any integral type	unsigned long
long	unsigned > LONG_MAX	unsigned long
long	any smaller type	long
unsigned	any signed type	unsigned

The following example code illustrates some cases of operator promotion. The variable f1 is set to 3 / 4. Because both 3 and 4 are integers, integer division is performed, and the result is the integer 0. The variable f2 is set to 3 / 4.0. Because 4.0 is a float, the number 3 is converted to a float as well, and the result is the float 0.75.

```
#include <stdio.h>
main()
{
        float f1 = 3 / 4;
        float f2 = 3 / 4.0;
        printf("3 / 4 == %g or %g depending on the type used.\n",
               f1, f2);
}
```

Cross Reference:

II.11: Are there any problems with performing mathematical operations on different variable types?

II.13: When should a type cast be used?

II.13: When should a type cast be used?

Answer:

There are two situations in which to use a type cast. The first use is to change the type of an operand to an arithmetic operation so that the operation will be performed properly. If you have read FAQ II.12, the following listing should look familiar. The variable f1 is set to the result of dividing the integer i by the integer j. The result is 0, because integer division is used. The variable f2 is set to the result of dividing i by j as well. However, the (float) type cast causes i to be converted to a float. That in turn causes floating-point division to be used (see FAQ II.11) and gives the result 0.75.

```
#include <stdio.h>
main()
{
        int     i = 3;
        int     j = 4;
        float f1 = i / j;
        float f2 = (float) i / j;
        printf("3 / 4 == %g or %g depending on the type used.\n",
                f1, f2);
}
```

The second case is to cast pointer types to and from void * in order to interface with functions that expect or return void pointers. For example, the following line type casts the return value of the call to malloc() to be a pointer to a foo structure.

```
struct foo      *p = (struct foo *) malloc(sizeof(struct foo));
```

Cross Reference:

II.6: When should the volatile modifier be used?

II.8: When should the const modifier be used?

II.11: Are there any problems with performing mathematical operations on different variable types?

II.12: What is operator promotion?

II.14: When should a type cast not be used?

VII.5: What is a void pointer?

VII.6: When is a void pointer used?

VII.21: What is the heap?

VII.27: Can math operations be performed on a void pointer?

II.14: When should a type cast not be used?

Answer:

A type cast should not be used to override a `const` or `volatile` declaration. Overriding these type modifiers can cause the program to fail to run correctly.

A type cast should not be used to turn a pointer to one type of structure or data type into another. In the rare events in which this action is beneficial, using a union to hold the values makes the programmer's intentions clearer.

Cross Reference:

II.6: When should the `volatile` modifier be used?

II.8: When should the `const` modifier be used?

II.15: Is it acceptable to declare/define a variable in a C header?

Answer:

A global variable that must be accessed from more than one file can and should be declared in a header file. In addition, such a variable must be defined in one source file. Variables should not be defined in header files, because the header file can be included in multiple source files, which would cause multiple definitions of the variable. The ANSI C standard will allow multiple external definitions, provided that there is only one initialization. But because there's really no advantage to using this feature, it's probably best to avoid it and maintain a higher level of portability.

 NOTE

Don't confuse declaring and defining variables. FAQ II.16 states the differences between these two actions.

"Global" variables that do not have to be accessed from more than one file should be declared `static` and should not appear in a header file.

Cross Reference:

II.16: What is the difference between declaring a variable and defining a variable?

II.17: Can `static` variables be declared in a header file?

II.16: What is the difference between declaring a variable and defining a variable?

Answer:

Declaring a variable means describing its type to the compiler but not allocating any space for it. Defining a variable means declaring it and also allocating space to hold the variable. You can also initialize a variable at the time it is defined. Here is a declaration of a variable and a structure, and two variable definitions, one with initialization:

```
extern int     decl1;   /* this is a declaration */
struct decl2 {
       int member;
}; /* this just declares the type--no variable mentioned */
int    def1 = 8;      /* this is a definition */
int    def2;          /* this is a definition */
```

To put it another way, a declaration says to the compiler, "Somewhere in my program will be a variable with this name, and this is what type it is." A definition says, "Right here is this variable with this name and this type."

> **NOTE**
>
> One way to remember what each term means is to remember that the Declaration of Independence didn't actually make the United States independent (the Revolutionary War did that); it just stated that it was independent.

A variable can be declared many times, but it must be defined exactly once. For this reason, definitions do not belong in header files, where they might get #included into more than one place in your program.

Cross Reference:

II.17: Can static variables be declared in a header file?

II.17: Can *static* variables be declared in a header file?

Answer:

You can't declare a static variable without defining it as well (this is because the storage class modifiers static and extern are mutually exclusive). A static variable can be defined in a header file, but this would cause each source file that included the header file to have its own private copy of the variable, which is probably not what was intended.

Cross Reference:

II.16: What is the difference between declaring a variable and defining a variable?

II.18: What is the benefit of using *const* for declaring constants?

Answer:

The benefit of using the const keyword is that the compiler might be able to make optimizations based on the knowledge that the value of the variable will not change. In addition, the compiler will try to ensure that the values won't be changed inadvertently.

Of course, the same benefits apply to #defined constants. The reason to use const rather than #define to define a constant is that a const variable can be of any type (such as a struct, which can't be represented by a #defined constant). Also, because a const variable is a real variable, it has an address that can be used, if needed, and it resides in only one place in memory (some compilers make a new copy of a #defined character string each time it is used—see FAQ IX.9).

Cross Reference:

II.7: Can a variable be both const and volatile?

II.8: When should the const modifier be used?

II.14: When should a type cast not be used?

IX.9: What is the difference between a string and an array?

CHAPTER

◆

Sorting and Searching Data

Few problems in computer science have been studied as much as sorting. Many good books are available that cover the subject in great depth. This chapter serves merely as an introduction, with an emphasis on practical applications in C.

Sorting

Five basic kinds of sorting algorithms are available to the programmer:

- ◆ Insertion sorts
- ◆ Exchange sorts
- ◆ Selection sorts
- ◆ Merge sorts
- ◆ Distribution sorts

An easy way to visualize how each sorting algorithm works is to think about how to sort a shuffled deck of cards lying on the table using each method. The cards are to be sorted by suit (clubs, diamonds, hearts, and spades) as well as by rank (2 through ace). You might have seen some of these algorithms in action at your last bridge game.

In an insertion sort, you pick up the cards one at a time, starting with the top card in the pile, and insert them into the correct position in your hand. When you have picked up all the cards, they are sorted.

In an exchange sort, you pick up the top two cards. If the one on the left belongs after the one on the right, you exchange the two cards' positions. Then you pick up the next card and perform the compare on the two rightmost cards and (if needed) exchange their positions. You repeat the process until all the cards are in your hand. If you didn't have to exchange any cards, the deck is sorted. Otherwise, you put down the deck and repeat the entire procedure until the deck is sorted.

In a selection sort, you search the deck for the lowest card and pick it up. You repeat the process until you are holding all the cards.

To perform a merge sort, you deal the deck into 52 piles of one card each. Because each pile is ordered (remember, there's only one card in it), if you merge adjacent piles, keeping cards in order, you will have 26 ordered piles of 2 cards each. You repeat so that you have 13 piles of 4 cards, then 7 piles (6 piles of 8 cards and 1 pile of 4 cards), until you have 1 pile of 52 cards.

In a distribution (or radix) sort, you deal the cards into 13 piles, placing each rank on its own pile. You then pick up all the piles in order and deal the cards into 4 piles, placing each suit on its own pile. You put the four piles together, and the deck is sorted.

There are several terms you should be aware of when examining sorting algorithms. The first is *natural*. A sort is said to be natural if it works faster (does less work) on data that is already sorted, and works slower (does more work) on data that is more mixed up. It is important to know whether a sort is natural if the data you're working with is already close to being sorted.

A sort is said to be *stable* if it preserves the ordering of data that are considered equal by the algorithm. Consider the following list:

> Mary Jones
> Mary Smith
> Tom Jones
> Susie Queue

If this list is sorted by last name using a stable sort, "Mary Jones" will remain before "Tom Jones" in the sorted list because they have the same last name. A stable sort can be used to sort data on a primary and secondary key, such as first and last names (in other words, sorted primarily by last name, but sorted by first name for entries with the same last name). This action is accomplished by sorting first on the secondary key, then on the primary key with a stable sort.

A sort that operates on data kept entirely in RAM is an *internal* sort. If a sort operates on data on disk, tape, or other secondary storage, it is called an *external* sort.

Searching

Searching algorithms have been studied nearly as much as sorting algorithms. The two are related in that many searching algorithms rely on the ordering of the data being searched. There are four basic kinds of searching algorithms:

◆ Sequential searching

◆ Comparison searching

◆ Radix searching

◆ Hashing

Each of these methods can be described using the same deck of cards example that was used for sorting.

In sequential searching, you go through the deck from top to bottom, looking at each card until you find the card you are looking for.

In comparison searching (also called binary searching), you start with an already sorted deck. You pick a card from the exact middle of the deck and compare it to the card you want. If it matches, you're done. Otherwise, if it's lower, you try the same search again in the first half of the deck. If it's higher, you try again in the second half of the deck.

In radix searching, you deal the deck into the 13 piles as described in radix *sorting*. To find a desired card, you choose the pile corresponding to the desired rank and search for the card you want in that pile using any search method. Or you could deal the deck into 4 piles based on suit as described in radix *sorting*. You could then pick the pile according to the desired suit and search there for the card you want.

In hashing, you make space for some number of piles on the table, and you choose a function that maps cards into a particular pile based on rank and suit (called a *hash* function). You then deal all the cards into the piles, using the hash function to decide where to put each card. To find a desired card, you use the hash function to find out which pile the desired card should be in. Then you search for the card in that pile.

For instance, you might make 16 piles and pick a hash function like `pile = rank + suit`. If `rank` is a card's rank treated as a number (ace = 1, 2 = 2, all the way up to king = 13), and `suit` is a card's suit treated as a number (clubs = 0, diamonds = 1, hearts = 2, spades = 3), then for each card you can compute a `pile` number that will be from 1 to 16, indicating which pile the card belongs in. This technique sounds crazy, but it's a very powerful searching method. All sorts of programs, from compression programs (such as Stacker) to disk caching programs (such as SmartDrive) use hashing to speed up searches for data.

Performance of Sorting or Searching

One of the chief concerns in searching and sorting is speed. Often, this concern is misguided, because the sort or search takes negligible time compared to the rest of the program. For most sorting and searching applications, you should use the easiest method available (see FAQs III.1 and III.4). If you later find that the program is too slow because of the searching or sorting algorithm used, you can substitute another method easily. By starting with a simple method, you haven't invested much time and effort on code that has to be replaced.

One measure of the speed of a sorting or searching algorithm is the number of operations that must be performed in the best, average, and worst cases (sometimes called the algorithm's *complexity*). This is described by a mathematical expression based on the number of elements in the data set to be sorted or searched. This expression shows how fast the execution time of the algorithm grows as the number of elements increases. It does not tell how fast the algorithm is for a given size data set, because that rate depends on the exact implementation and hardware used to run the program.

The fastest algorithm is one whose complexity is $O(1)$ (which is read as "order 1"). This means that the number of operations is not related to the number of elements in the data set. Another common complexity for algorithms is $O(N)$ (N is commonly used to refer to the number of elements in the data set). This means that the number of operations is directly related to the number of elements in the data set. An algorithm with complexity $O(\log N)$ is somewhere between the two in speed. The $O(\log N)$ means that the number of operations is related to the logarithm of the number of elements in the data set.

NOTE

If you're unfamiliar with the term, you can think of a *log N* as the number of digits needed to write the number *N*. Thus, the *log 34* is 2, and the *log 900* is 3 (actually, *log 10* is 2 and *log 100* is 3— *log 34* is a number between 2 and 3).

If you're still with me, I'll add another concept. A logarithm has a particular base. The logarithms described in the preceding paragraph are base 10 logarithms (written as *log10 N*), meaning that if *N* gets 10 times as big, *log N* gets bigger by 1. The base can be any number. If you are comparing two algorithms, both of which have complexity *O(log N)*, the one with the larger base would be faster. No matter what the base is, *log N* is always a smaller number than *N*.

An algorithm with complexity *O(N log N)* (*N* times *log N*) is slower than one of complexity *O(N)*, and an algorithm of complexity *O(N²)* is slower still. So why don't they just come up with one algorithm with the lowest complexity number and use only that one? Because the complexity number only describes how the program will slow down as *N* gets larger.

The complexity does not indicate which algorithm is faster for any particular value of *N*. That depends on many factors, including the type of data in the set, the language the algorithm is written in, and the machine and compiler used. What the complexity number does communicate is that as *N* gets bigger, there will be a point at which an algorithm with a lower order complexity will be faster than one of a higher order complexity.

Table 3.1 shows the complexity of all the algorithms listed in this chapter. The best and worst cases are given for the sorting routines. Depending on the original order of the data, the performance of these algorithms will vary between best and worst case. The average case is for randomly ordered data. The average case complexity for searching algorithms is given. The best case for all searching algorithms (which is if the data happens to be in the first place searched) is obviously *O(1)*. The worst case (which is if the data being searching for doesn't exist) is generally the same as the average case.

Table 3.1. The relative complexity of all the algorithms presented in this chapter.

Algorithm	Best	Average	Worst
Quick sort	*O(N log N)*	*O(N log N)*	*O(N²)*
Merge sort	*O(N)*	*O(N log N)*	*O(N log N)*
Radix sort	*O(N)*	*O(N)*	*O(N)*
Linear search		*O(N)*	
Binary search		*O(log N)*	
Hashing		*O(N/M)**	
Digital trie		*O(1)***	

  * *M* is the size of hash table
 ** Actually, equivalent to a hash table with 2^{32} entries

To illustrate the difference between the complexity of an algorithm and its actual running time, Table 3.2 shows execution time for all the sample programs listed in this chapter. Each program was compiled with the GNU C Compiler (gcc) Version 2.6.0 under the Linux operating system on a 90 MHz Pentium computer. Different computer systems should provide execution times that are proportional to these times.

Table 3.2. The execution times of all the programs presented in this chapter.

Program	Algorithm	2000	4000	6000	8000	10000
3_1	qsort()	0.02	0.05	0.07	0.11	0.13
3_2a	quick sort	0.02	0.06	0.13	0.18	0.20
3_2b	merge sort	0.03	0.08	0.14	0.18	0.26
3_2c	radix sort	0.07	0.15	0.23	0.30	0.39
3_4	bsearch()	0.37	0.39	0.39	0.40	0.41
3_5	binary search	0.32	0.34	0.34	0.36	0.36
3_6	linear search	9.67	20.68	28.71	36.31	45.51
3_7	trie search	0.27	0.28	0.29	0.29	0.30
3_8	hash search	0.25	0.26	0.28	0.29	0.28

NOTE

All times are in seconds. Times are normalized, by counting only the time for the program to perform the sort or search.

The 2000–10000 columns indicate the number of elements in the data set to be sorted or searched. Data elements were words chosen at random from the file /usr/man/man1/gcc.1 (documentation for the GNU C compiler).

For the search algorithms, the data searched for were words chosen at random from the file /usr/man/man1/g++.1 (documentation for the GNU C++ compiler).

qsort() and bsearch() are standard library implementations of quick sort and binary search, respectively. The rest of the programs are developed from scratch in this chapter.

This information should give you a taste of what issues are involved in deciding which algorithm is appropriate for sorting and searching in different situations. The book *The Art of Computer Programming, Volume 3, Sorting and Searching,* by Donald E. Knuth, is entirely devoted to algorithms for sorting and searching, with much more information on complexity and complexity theory as well as many more algorithms than are described here.

Some Code to Get Started With

This chapter includes several code examples that are complete enough to actually compile and run. To avoid duplicating the code that is common to several examples, the code is shown at the end of this chapter.

III.1: What is the easiest sorting method to use?

Answer:

The answer is the standard library function qsort(). It's the easiest sort by far for several reasons:

It is already written.

It is already debugged.

It has been optimized as much as possible (usually).

The algorithm used by qsort() is generally the quick sort algorithm, developed by C. A. R. Hoare in 1962. Here is the prototype for qsort():

```
void qsort(void *buf, size_t num, size_t size,
           int (*comp)(const void *ele1, const void *ele2));
```

The qsort() function takes a pointer to an array of user-defined data (buf). The array has num elements in it, and each element is size bytes long. Decisions about sort order are made by calling comp, which is a pointer to a function that compares two elements of buf and returns a value that is less than, equal to, or greater than 0 according to whether the ele1 is less than, equal to, or greater than ele2.

For instance, say you want to sort an array of strings in alphabetical order. The array is terminated by a NULL pointer. Listing III.1 shows the function sortStrings(), which sorts a NULL-terminated array of character strings using the qsort() function. You can compile this example into a working program using the code found at the end of this chapter.

Listing III.1. An example of using qsort().

```
 1: #include        <stdlib.h>
 2:
 3: /*
 4:  * This routine is used only by sortStrings(), to provide a
 5:  * string comparison function to pass to qsort().
 6:  */
 7: static int comp(const void *ele1, const void *ele2)
 8: {
 9:         return strcmp(*(const char **) ele1,
10:                 *(const char **) ele2);
11: }
12:
13: /* Sort strings using the library function qsort() */
14: void sortStrings(const char *array[])
15: {
16:         /* First, determine the length of the array */
17:         int     num;
18:
```

```
19:          for (num = 0; array[num]; num++)
20:              ;
21:          qsort(array, num, sizeof(*array), comp);
22: }
```

The for loop on lines 19 and 20 simply counts the number of elements in the array so that the count can be passed to qsort(). The only "tricky" part about this code is the comp() function. Its sole purpose is to bridge the gap between the types that qsort() passes to it (const void *) and the types expected by strcmp() (const char *). Because qsort() works with pointers to elements, and the elements are themselves pointers, the correct type to cast ele1 and ele2 to is const char **. The result of the cast is then dereferenced (by putting the * in front of it) to get the const char * type that strcmp() expects.

Given that qsort() exists, why would a C programmer ever write another sort program? There are several reasons. First, there are pathological cases in which qsort() performs very slowly and other algorithms perform better. Second, some overhead is associated with qsort() because it is general purpose. For instance, each comparison involves an indirect function call through the function pointer provided by the user. Also, because the size of an element is a runtime parameter, the code to move elements in the array isn't optimized for a single size of element. If these performance considerations are important, writing a sort routine might be worth it.

Besides the drawbacks mentioned, the qsort() implementation assumes that all the data is in one array. This might be inconvenient or impossible given the size or nature of the data. Lastly, qsort() implementations are usually not "stable" sorts.

Cross Reference:

III.2: What is the quickest sorting method to use?

III.3: How can I sort things that are too large to bring into memory?

III.7: How can I sort a linked list?

VII.1: What is indirection?

VII.2: How many levels of pointers can you have?

VII.5: What is a void pointer?

VII.6: When is a void pointer used?

III.2: What is the quickest sorting method to use?

Answer:

The answer depends on what you mean by quickest. For most sorting problems, it just doesn't matter how quick the sort is because it is done infrequently or other operations take significantly more time anyway. Even in cases in which sorting speed is of the essence, there is no one answer. It depends on not only the size and nature of the data, but also the likely order. No algorithm is best in all cases.

There are three sorting methods in this author's "toolbox" that are all very fast and that are useful in different situations. Those methods are quick sort, merge sort, and radix sort.

The Quick Sort

The quick sort algorithm is of the "divide and conquer" type. That means it works by reducing a sorting problem into several easier sorting problems and solving each of them. A "dividing" value is chosen from the input data, and the data is partitioned into three sets: elements that belong before the dividing value, the value itself, and elements that come after the dividing value. The partitioning is performed by exchanging elements that are in the first set but belong in the third with elements that are in the third set but belong in the first. Elements that are equal to the dividing element can be put in any of the three sets—the algorithm will still work properly.

After the three sets are formed, the middle set (the dividing element itself) is already sorted, so quick sort is applied to the first and third sets, recursively. At some point, the set being sorting becomes too small for quick sort. Obviously, a set of two or fewer elements cannot be divided into three sets. At this point, some other sorting method is used. The cutoff point at which a different method of sorting is applied is up to the person implementing the sort. This cutoff point can dramatically affect the efficiency of the sort, because there are methods that are faster than quick sort for relatively small sets of data.

The string sorting example (from FAQ III.1) will be rewritten using a quick sort. Excuse the preprocessor trickery, but the goal is to make the code readable and fast. Listing III.2a shows myQsort(), an implementation of the quick sort algorithm from scratch. You can compile this example into a working program using the code at the end of this chapter.

The function myQsort() sorts an array of strings into ascending order. First it checks for the simplest cases. On line 17 it checks for the case of zero or one element in the array, in which case it can return—the array is already sorted. Line 19 checks for the case of an array of two elements, because this is too small an array to be handled by the rest of the function. If there are two elements, either the array is sorted or the two elements are exchanged to make the array sorted.

Line 28 selects the middle element of the array as the one to use to partition the data. It moves that element to the beginning of the array and begins partitioning the data into two sets. Lines 37–39 find the first element in the array that belongs in the second set, and lines 45–47 find the last element in the array that belongs in the first set.

Line 49 checks whether the first element that belongs in the second set is after the last element that belongs in the first set. If this is the case, *all* the elements in the first set come before the elements in the second set, so the data are partitioned. Otherwise, the algorithm swaps the two elements so that they will be in the proper set, and then continues.

After the array has been properly partitioned into two sets, line 55 puts the middle element back into its proper place between the two sets, which turns out to be its correct position in the sorted array. Lines 57 and 58 sort each of the two sets by calling myQsort() recursively. When each set is sorted, the entire array is sorted.

Listing III.2a. An implementation of quick sort that doesn't use the qsort() function.

```
1: #include        <stdlib.h>
2:
3: #define exchange(A, B, T)      ((T) = (A), (A) = (B), \
4:                                            (B) = (T))
5:
```

```
 6: /* Sorts an array of strings using quick sort algorithm */
 7: static void myQsort(const char *array[], size_t num)
 8: {
 9:         const char      *temp;
10:         size_t  i, j;
11:
12:         /*
13:          * Check the simple cases first:
14:          * If fewer than 2 elements, already sorted
15:          * If exactly 2 elements, just swap them (if needed).
16:          */
17:         if (num < 2)
18:                 return;
19:         else if (num == 2)
20:         {
21:                 if (strcmp(array[0], array[1]) > 0)
22:                         exchange(array[0], array[1], temp);
23:         }
24:         /*
25:          * Partition the array using the middle (num / 2)
26:          * element as the dividing element.
27:          */
28:         exchange(array[0], array[num / 2], temp);
29:         i = 1;
30:         j = num;
31:         for ( ; ; )
32:         {
33:                 /*
34:                  * Sweep forward until an element is found that
35:                  * belongs in the second partition.
36:                  */
37:                 while (i < j && strcmp(array[i], array[0])
38:                                                         <= 0)
39:                         i++;
40:                 /*
41:                  * Then sweep backward until an element
42:                  * is found that belongs in the first
43:                  * partition.
44:                  */
45:                 while (i < j && strcmp(array[j - 1], array[0])
46:                                                         >= 0)
47:                         j--;
48:                 /* If no out-of-place elements, you're done */
49:                 if (i >= j)
50:                         break;
51:                 /* Else, swap the two out-of-place elements */
52:                 exchange(array[i], array[j - 1], temp);
53:         }
54:         /* Restore dividing element */
55:         exchange(array[0], array[i - 1], temp);
56:         /* Now apply quick sort to each partition */
57:         myQsort(array, i - 1);
58:         myQsort(array + i, num - i);
59: }
60:
61: /* Sort strings using your own implementation of quick sort */
62: void sortStrings(const char *array[])
```

continues

Listing III.2a. continued

```
63: {
64:         /* First, determine the length of the array */
65:         int     num;
66:
67:         for (num = 0; array[num]; num++)
68:                 ;
69:         myQsort((void *) array, num);
70: }
```

The Merge Sort

The merge sort is a "divide and conquer" sort as well. It works by considering the data to be sorted as a sequence of already-sorted lists (in the worst case, each list is one element long). Adjacent sorted lists are merged into larger sorted lists until there is a single sorted list containing all the elements. The merge sort is good at sorting lists and other data structures that are not in arrays, and it can be used to sort things that don't fit into memory. It also can be implemented as a stable sort. The merge sort was suggested by John von Neumann in 1945!

Listing III.2b shows an implementation of the merge sort algorithm. To make things more interesting, the strings will be put into a linked list structure rather than an array. In fact, the algorithm works better on data that is organized as lists, because elements in an array cannot be merged in place (some extra storage is required). You can compile this example into a working program using the code at the end of this chapter. The code for (and a description of) the list_t type and the functions that operate on list_ts are also at the end of this chapter.

There are four functions that together implement merge sort. The function split() takes a list of strings and turns it into a list of lists of strings, in which each list of strings is sorted. For instance, if the original list was ("the" "quick" "brown" "fox"), split() would return a list of three lists—("the"), ("quick"), and ("brown" "fox")—because the strings "brown" and "fox" are already in the correct order. The algorithm would work just as well if split() made lists of one element each, but splitting the list into already-sorted chunks makes the algorithm natural by reducing the amount of work left to do if the list is nearly sorted already (see the introduction to this chapter for a definition of natural sorts). In the listing, the loop on lines 14–24 keeps processing as long as there are elements on the input list. Each time through the loop, line 16 makes a new list, and the loop on lines 17–22 keeps moving elements from the input list onto this list as long as they are in the correct order. When the loop runs out of elements on the input list or encounters two elements out of order, line 23 appends the current list to the output list of lists.

The function merge() takes two lists that are already sorted and merges them into a single sorted list. The loop on lines 37–45 executes as long as there is something on both lists. The if statement on line 40 selects the smaller first element of the two lists and moves it to the output list. When one of the lists becomes empty, all the elements of the other list must be appended to the output list. Lines 46 and 47 concatenate the output list with the empty list and the non-empty list to complete the merge.

The function mergePairs() takes a list of lists of strings and calls merge() on each pair of lists of strings, replacing the original pair with the single merged list. The loop on lines 61–77 executes as long as there is something in the input list. The if statement on line 63 checks whether there are at least two lists of strings on the input list. If not, line 76 appends the odd list to the output list. If so, lines 65 and 66 remove the two lists, which are merged on lines 68 and 69. The new list is appended to the output list on line 72, and all the intermediate list nodes that were allocated are freed on lines 70, 71, and 73. Lines 72 and 73 remove the two lists that were merged from the input list.

The last function is sortStrings(), which performs the merge sort on an array of strings. Lines 88 and 89 put the strings into a list. Line 90 calls split() to break up the original list of strings into a list of lists of strings. The loop on lines 91 and 92 calls mergePairs() until there is only one list of strings on the list of lists of strings. Line 93 checks to ensure that the list isn't empty (which is the case if the array has 0 elements in it to begin with) before removing the sorted list from the list of lists. Finally, lines 95 and 96 put the sorted strings back into the array. Note that sortStrings() does not free all the memory if allocated.

Listing III.2b. An implementation of a merge sort.

```
 1: #include       <stdlib.h>
 2: #include       "list.h"
 3:
 4: /*
 5:  * Splits a list of strings into a list of lists of strings
 6:  * in which each list of strings is sorted.
 7:  */
 8: static list_t split(list_t in)
 9: {
10:         list_t  out;
11:         list_t  *curr;
12:         out.head = out.tail = NULL;
13:
14:         while (in.head)
15:         {
16:                 curr = newList();
17:                 do
18:                 {
19:                         appendNode(curr, removeHead(&in));
20:                 }
21:                 while (in.head && strcmp(curr->tail->u.str,
22:                                 in.head->u.str) <= 0);
23:                 appendNode(&out, newNode(curr));
24:         }
25:         return out;
26: }
27:
28: /*
29:  * Merge two sorted lists into a third sorted list,
30:  * which is then returned.
31:  */
32: static list_t merge(list_t first, list_t second)
33: {
34:         list_t  out;
35:         out.head = out.tail = NULL;
36:
37:         while (first.head && second.head)
38:         {
39:                 listnode_t      *temp;
40:                 if (strcmp(first.head->u.str,
41:                                 second.head->u.str) <= 0)
```

continues

Listing III.2b. continued

```
42:                                appendNode(&out, removeHead(&first));
43:                    else
44:                                appendNode(&out, removeHead(&second));
45:            }
46:        concatList(&out, &first);
47:        concatList(&out, &second);
48:        return out;
49: }
50:
51: /*
52:  * Takes a list of lists of strings and merges each pair of
53:  * lists into a single list. The resulting list has 1/2 as
54:  * many lists as the original.
55:  */
56: static list_t mergePairs(list_t in)
57: {
58:        list_t  out;
59:        out.head = out.tail = NULL;
60:
61:        while (in.head)
62:        {
63:                if (in.head->next)
64:                {
65:                        list_t *first = in.head->u.list;
66:                        list_t *second =
67:                                        in.head->next->u.list;
68:                        in.head->u.list = copyOf(merge(*first,
69:                                                *second));
70:                        free(first);
71:                        free(second);
72:                        appendNode(&out, removeHead(&in));
73:                        free(removeHead(&in));
74:                }
75:                else
76:                        appendNode(&out, removeHead(&in));
77:        }
78:        return out;
79: }
80:
81: /* Sort strings using merge sort */
82: void sortStrings(const char *array[])
83: {
84:        int     i;
85:        list_t  out;
86:        out.head = out.tail = NULL;
87:
88:        for (i = 0; array[i]; i++)
89:                appendNode(&out, newNode((void *) array[i]));
90:        out = split(out);
91:        while (out.head != out.tail)
92:                out = mergePairs(out);
93:        if (out.head)
94:                out = *out.head->u.list;
95:        for (i = 0; array[i]; i++)
96:                array[i] = removeHead(&out)->u.str;
97: }
```

The Radix Sort

The radix sort shown in Listing III.2c takes a list of integers and puts each element on a smaller list, depending on the value of its least significant byte. Then the small lists are concatenated, and the process is repeated for each more significant byte until the list is sorted. The radix sort is simpler to implement on fixed-length data such as ints, but it is illustrated here using strings. You can compile this example into a working program using the code at the end of this chapter.

Two functions perform the radix sort. The function radixSort() performs one pass through the data, performing a partial sort. Line 12 ensures that all the lists in table are empty. The loop on lines 13–24 executes as long as there is something on the input list. Lines 15–22 select which position in the table to put the next string on, based on the value of the character in the string specified by whichByte. If the string has fewer characters than whichByte calls for, the position is 0 (which ensures that the string "an" comes before the string "and"). Finally, lines 25 and 26 concatenate all the elements of table into one big list in table[0].

The function sortStrings() sorts an array of strings by calling radixSort() several times to perform partial sorts. Lines 39–46 create the original list of strings, keeping track of the length of the longest string (because that's how many times it needs to call radixSort()). Lines 47 and 48 call radixSort() for each byte in the longest string in the list. Finally, lines 49 and 50 put all the strings in the sorted list back into the array. Note that sortStrings() doesn't free all the memory it allocates.

Listing III.2c. An implementation of a radix sort.

```
 1: #include       <stdlib.h>
 2: #include       <limits.h>
 3: #include       <memory.h>
 4: #include       "list.h"
 5:
 6: /* Partially sort list using radix sort */
 7: static list_t radixSort(list_t in, int whichByte)
 8: {
 9:         int     i;
10:         list_t  table[UCHAR_MAX + 1];
11:
12:         memset(table, 0, sizeof(table));
13:         while (in.head)
14:         {
15:                 int     len = strlen(in.head->u.str);
16:                 int     pos;
17:
18:                 if (len > whichByte)
19:                         pos = (unsigned char)
20:                                 in.head->u.str[whichByte];
21:                 else
22:                         pos = 0;
23:                 appendNode(&table[pos], removeHead(&in));
24:         }
25:         for (i = 1; i < UCHAR_MAX + 1; i++)
26:                 concatList(&table[0], &table[i]);
27:         return table[0];
28: }
29:
```

continues

Listing III.2c. continued

```
30: /* Sort strings using radix sort */
31: void sortStrings(const char *array[])
32: {
33:         int     i;
34:         int     len;
35:         int     maxLen = 0;
36:         list_t  list;
37:
38:         list.head = list.tail = NULL;
39:         for (i = 0; array[i]; i++)
40:         {
41:                 appendNode(&list,
42:                         newNode((void *) array[i]));
43:                 len = strlen(array[i]);
44:                 if (len > maxLen)
45:                         maxLen = len;
46:         }
47:         for (i = maxLen - 1; i >= 0; i--)
48:                 list = radixSort(list, i);
49:         for (i = 0; array[i]; i++)
50:                 array[i] = removeHead(&list)->u.str;
51: }
```

Cross Reference:

III.1: What is the easiest sorting method to use?

III.3: How can I sort things that are too large to bring into memory?

III.7: How can I sort a linked list?

III.3: How can I sort things that are too large to bring into memory?

Answer:

A sorting program that sorts items that are on secondary storage (disk or tape) rather than primary storage (memory) is called an *external* sort. Exactly how to sort large data depends on what is meant by "too large to fit in memory." If the items to be sorted are themselves too large to fit in memory (such as images), but there aren't many items, you can keep in memory only the sort key and a value indicating the data's location on disk. After the key/value pairs are sorted, the data is rearranged on disk into the correct order.

If "too large to fit in memory" means that there are too many items to fit into memory at one time, the data can be sorted in groups that will fit into memory, and then the resulting files can be merged. A sort such as a radix sort can also be used as an external sort, by making each bucket in the sort a file.

Even the quick sort can be an external sort. The data can be partitioned by writing it to two smaller files. When the partitions are small enough to fit, they are sorted in memory and concatenated to form the sorted file.

The example in Listing III.3 is an external sort. It sorts data in groups of 10,000 strings and writes them to files, which are then merged. If you compare this listing to the listing of the merge sort (Listing III.2b), you will notice many similarities.

Any of the four sort programs introduced so far in this chapter can be used as the in-memory sort algorithm (the makefile given at the end of the chapter specifies using qsort() as shown in Listing III.1). The functions myfgets() and myfputs() simply handle inserting and removing the newline ('\n') characters at the ends of lines. The openFile() function handles error conditions during the opening of files, and fileName() generates temporary filenames.

The function split() reads in up to 10,000 lines from the input file on lines 69–74, sorts them in memory on line 76, and writes them to a temporary file on lines 77–80. The function merge() takes two files that are already sorted and merges them into a third file in exactly the same way that the merge() routine in Listing III.2b merged two lists. The function mergePairs() goes through all the temporary files and calls merge() to combine pairs of files into single files, just as mergePairs() in Listing III.2b combines lists. Finally, main() invokes split() on the original file, then calls mergePairs() until all the files are combined into one big file. It then replaces the original unsorted file with the new, sorted file.

Listing III.3. An example of an external sorting algorithm.

```
 1: #include        <stdlib.h>
 2: #include        <string.h>
 3: #include        <stdio.h>
 4: #include        <stdio.h>
 5:
 6: #define LINES_PER_FILE  10000
 7:
 8: /* Just like fgets(), but removes trailing '\n'. */
 9: char*
10: myfgets(char *buf, size_t size, FILE *fp)
11: {
12:         char    *s = fgets(buf, size, fp);
13:         if (s)
14:                 s[strlen(s) - 1] = '\0';
15:         return s;
16: }
17:
18: /* Just like fputs(), but adds trailing '\n'. */
19: void
20: myfputs(char *s, FILE *fp)
21: {
22:         int     n = strlen(s);
23:         s[n] = '\n';
24:         fwrite(s, 1, n + 1, fp);
25:         s[n] = '\0';
26: }
27:
28: /* Just like fopen(), but prints message and dies if error. */
29: FILE*
30: openFile(const char *name, const char *mode)
31: {
32:         FILE    *fp = fopen(name, mode);
33:
34:         if (fp == NULL)
```

continues

Listing III.3. continued

```
35:             {
36:                     perror(name);
37:                     exit(1);
38:             }
39:         return fp;
40: }
41:
42: /* Takes a number and generates a filename from it. */
43: const char*
44: fileName(int n)
45: {
46:         static char     name[16];
47:
48:         sprintf(name, "temp%d", n);
49:         return name;
50: }
51:
52: /*
53:  * Splits input file into sorted files with no more
54:  * than LINES_PER_FILE lines each.
55:  */
56: int
57: split(FILE *infp)
58: {
59:         int     nfiles = 0;
60:         int     line;
61:
62:         for (line = LINES_PER_FILE; line == LINES_PER_FILE; )
63:         {
64:                 char    *array[LINES_PER_FILE + 1];
65:                 char    buf[1024];
66:                 int     i;
67:                 FILE    *fp;
68:
69:                     for (line = 0; line < LINES_PER_FILE; line++)
70:                     {
71:                             if (!myfgets(buf, sizeof(buf), infp))
72:                                     break;
72:                             array[line] = strdup(buf);
74:                     }
75:                     array[line] = NULL;
76:                     sortStrings(array);
77:                     fp = openFile(fileName(nfiles++), "w");
78:                     for (i = 0; i < line; i++)
79:                             myfputs(array[i], fp);
80:                     fclose(fp);
81:         }
82:         return nfiles;
83: }
84:
85: /*
86:  * Merges two sorted input files into
87:  * one sorted output file.
88:  */
89: void
90: merge(FILE *outfp, FILE *fp1, FILE *fp2)
```

```
 91: {
 92:         char    buf1[1024];
 93:         char    buf2[1024];
 94:         char    *first;
 95:         char    *second;
 96:
 97:         first = myfgets(buf1, sizeof(buf1), fp1);
 98:         second = myfgets(buf2, sizeof(buf2), fp2);
 99:         while (first && second)
100:         {
101:                 if (strcmp(first, second) > 0)
102:                 {
103:                         myfputs(second, outfp);
104:                         second = myfgets(buf2, sizeof(buf2),
105:                                                         fp2);
106:                 }
107:                 else
108:                 {
109:                         myfputs(first, outfp);
110:                         first = myfgets(buf1, sizeof(buf1),
111:                                                         fp1);
112:                 }
113:         }
114:         while (first)
115:         {
116:                 myfputs(first, outfp);
117:                 first = myfgets(buf1, sizeof(buf1), fp1);
118:         }
119:         while (second)
120:         {
121:                 myfputs(second, outfp);
122:                 second = myfgets(buf2, sizeof(buf2), fp2);
123:         }
124: }
125:
126: /*
127:  * Takes nfiles files and merges pairs of them.
128:  * Returns new number of files.
129:  */
130: int
131: mergePairs(int nfiles)
132: {
133:         int     i;
134:         int     out = 0;
135:
136:         for (i = 0; i < nfiles - 1; i += 2)
137:         {
138:                 FILE    *temp;
139:                 FILE    *fp1;
140:                 FILE    *fp2;
141:                 const char      *first;
142:                 const char      *second;
143:
144:                 temp = openFile("temp", "w");
145:                 fp1 = openFile(fileName(i), "r");
146:                 fp2 = openFile(fileName(i + 1), "r");
147:                 merge(temp, fp1, fp2);
148:                 fclose(fp1);
```

continues

Listing III.3. continued

```
149:                    fclose(fp2);
150:                    fclose(temp);
151:                    unlink(fileName(i));
152:                    unlink(fileName(i + 1));
153:                    rename("temp", fileName(out++));
154:            }
155:            if (i < nfiles)
156:            {
157:                    char    *tmp = strdup(fileName(i));
158:                    rename(tmp, fileName(out++));
159:                    free(tmp);
160:            }
161:            return out;
162: }
163:
164: int
165: main(int argc, char **argv)
166: {
167:            char    buf2[1024];
168:            int     nfiles;
169:            int     line;
170:            int     in;
171:            int     out;
172:            FILE    *infp;
173:
174:            if (argc != 2)
175:            {
176:                    fprintf(stderr, "usage: %s file\n", argv[0]);
177:                    exit(1);
178:            }
179:            infp = openFile(argv[1], "r");
180:            nfiles = split(infp);
181:            fclose(infp);
182:            while (nfiles > 1)
183:                    nfiles = mergePairs(nfiles);
184:            rename(fileName(0), argv[1]);
185:            return 0;
186: }
```

Cross Reference:

III.1: What is the easiest sorting method to use?

III.2: What is the quickest sorting method to use?

III.7: How can I sort a linked list?

III.4: What is the easiest searching method to use?
Answer:

Just as qsort() was the easiest sorting method, because it is part of the standard library, bsearch() is the easiest searching method to use.

Following is the prototype for bsearch():

```
void *bsearch(const void *key, const void *buf, size_t num, size_t size,
              int (*comp)(const void *, const void *));
```

The bsearch() function performs a binary search on an array of sorted data elements. A binary search is another "divide and conquer" algorithm. The key is compared with the middle element of the array. If it is equal, the search is done. If it is less than the middle element, the item searched for must be in the first half of the array, so a binary search is performed on just the first half of the array. If the key is greater than the middle element, the item searched for must be in the second half of the array, so a binary search is performed on just the second half of the array. Listing III.4a shows a simple function that calls the bsearch() function. This listing borrows the function comp() from Listing III.1, which used qsort(). Listing III.4b shows a binary search, performed without calling bsearch(), for a string in a sorted array of strings. You can make both examples into working programs by combining them with code at the end of this chapter.

Listing III.4a. An example of how to use bsearch().

```
 1: #include        <stdlib.h>
 2:
 3: static int comp(const void *ele1, const void *ele2)
 4: {
 5:         return strcmp(*(const char **) ele1,
 6:                 *(const char **) ele2);
 7: }
 8:
 9: const char *search(const char *key, const char **array,
10:                                         size_t num)
11: {
12:         char    **p = bsearch(&key, array, num,
13:                                 sizeof(*array), comp);
14:         return p ? *p : NULL;
15: }
```

Listing III.4b. An implementation of a binary search.

```
 1: #include        <stdlib.h>
 2:
 3: const char *search(const char *key, const char **array,
 4:                                         size_t num)
 5: {
 6:         int     low = 0;
 7:         int     high = num - 1;
 8:
 9:         while (low <= high)
10:         {
11:                 int     mid = (low + high) / 2;
12:                 int     n = strcmp(key, array[mid]);
13:
14:                 if (n < 0)
15:                         high = mid - 1;
16:                 else if (n > 0)
17:                         low = mid + 1;
```

continues

Listing III.4b. continued

```
18:                else
19:                    return array[mid];
20:        }
21:        return 0;
22: }
```

Another simple searching method is a linear search. A linear search is not as fast as bsearch() for searching among a large number of items, but it is adequate for many purposes. A linear search might be the only method available, if the data isn't sorted or can't be accessed randomly. A linear search starts at the beginning and sequentially compares the key to each element in the data set. Listing III.4c shows a linear search. As with all the examples in this chapter, you can make it into a working program by combining it with code at the end of the chapter.

Listing III.4c. An implementation of linear searching.

```
1: #include        <stdlib.h>
2:
3: const char *search(const char *key, const char **array,
4:                                        size_t num)
5: {
6:        int     i;
7:
8:        for (i = 0; i < num; i++)
9:        {
10:                if (strcmp(key, array[i]) == 0)
11:                        return array[i];
12:        }
13:        return 0;
14: }
```

Cross Reference:

III.5: What is the quickest searching method to use?

III.6: What is hashing?

III.8: How can I search for data in a linked list?

III.5: What is the quickest searching method to use?

Answer:

A binary search, such as bsearch() performs, is much faster than a linear search. A hashing algorithm can provide even faster searching. One particularly interesting and fast method for searching is to keep the data in a "digital trie." A digital trie offers the prospect of being able to search for an item in essentially a constant amount of time, independent of how many items are in the data set.

A digital trie combines aspects of binary searching, radix searching, and hashing. The term "digital trie" refers to the data structure used to hold the items to be searched. It is a multilevel data structure that branches N ways at each level (in the example that follows, each level branches from 0 to 16 ways). The subject of treelike data structures and searching is too broad to describe fully here, but a good book on data structures or algorithms can teach you the concepts involved.

Listing III.5 shows a program implementing digital trie searching. You can combine this example with code at the end of the chapter to produce a working program. The concept is not too hard. Suppose that you use a hash function that maps to a full 32-bit integer. The hash value can also be considered to be a concatenation of eight 4-bit hash values. You can use the first 4-bit hash value to index into a 16-entry hash table.

Naturally, there will be many collisions, with only 16 entries. Collisions are resolved by having the table entry point to a second 16-entry hash table, in which the next 4-bit hash value is used as an index.

The tree of hash tables can be up to eight levels deep, after which you run out of hash values and have to search through all the entries that collided. However, such a collision should be very rare because it occurs only when all 32 bits of the hash value are identical, so most searches require only one comparison.

The binary searching aspect of the digital trie is that it is organized as a 16-way tree that is traversed to find the data. The radix search aspect is that successive 4-bit chunks of the hash value are examined at each level in the tree. The hashing aspect is that it is conceptually a hash table with 2^{32} entries.

Listing III.5. An implementation of digital trie searching.

```
 1: #include      <stdlib.h>
 2: #include      <string.h>
 3: #include      "list.h"
 4: #include      "hash.h"
 5:
 6: /*
 7:  * NOTE: This code makes several assumptions about the
 8:  * compiler and machine it is run on. It assumes that
 9:  *
10:  * 1. The value NULL consists of all "0" bits.
11:  *
12:  *      If not, the calloc() call must be changed to
13:  *      explicitly initialize the pointers allocated.
14:  *
15:  * 2. An unsigned and a pointer are the same size.
16:  *
17:  *      If not, the use of a union might be incorrect, because
18:  *      it is assumed that the least significant bit of the
19:  *      pointer and unsigned members of the union are the
20:  *      same bit.
21:  *
22:  * 3. The least significant bit of a valid pointer
23:  *      to an object allocated on the heap is always 0.
24:  *
25:  *      If not, that bit can't be used as a flag to determine
26:  *      what type of data the union really holds.
27:  */
28:
29: /* number of bits examined at each level of the trie */
```

continues

Listing III.5. continued

```
30: #define TRIE_BITS        4
31:
32: /* number of subtries at each level of the trie */
33: #define TRIE_FANOUT     (1 << TRIE_BITS)
34:
35: /* mask to get lowest TRIE_BITS bits of the hash */
36: #define TRIE_MASK       (TRIE_FANOUT - 1)
37:
38: /*
39:  * A trie can be either a linked list of elements or
40:  * a pointer to an array of TRIE_FANOUT tries. The num
41:  * element is used to test whether the pointer is even
42:  * or odd.
43:  */
44: typedef union trie_u {
45:         unsigned        num;
46:         listnode_t      *list;  /* if "num" is even */
47:         union trie_u    *node;          /* if "num" is odd */
48: } trie_t;
49:
50: /*
51:  * Inserts an element into a trie and returns the resulting
52:  * new trie. For internal use by trieInsert() only.
53:  */
54: static trie_t eleInsert(trie_t t, listnode_t *ele, unsigned h,
55:                                                     int depth)
56: {
57:         /*
58:          * If the trie is an array of tries, insert the
59:          * element into the proper subtrie.
60:          */
61:         if (t.num & 1)
62:         {
63:                 /*
64:                  * nxtNode is used to hold the pointer into
65:                  * the array. The reason for using a trie
66:                  * as a temporary instead of a pointer is
67:                  * it's easier to remove the "odd" flag.
68:                  */
69:                 trie_t  nxtNode = t;
70:
71:                 nxtNode.num &= ~1;
72:                 nxtNode.node += (h >> depth) & TRIE_MASK;
73:                 *nxtNode.node =
74:                         eleInsert(*nxtNode.node,
75:                                 ele, h, depth + TRIE_BITS);
76:         }
77:         /*
78:          * Since t wasn't an array of tries, it must be a
79:          * list of elements. If it is empty, just add this
80:          * element.
81:          */
82:         else if (t.list == NULL)
83:                 t.list = ele;
84:         /*
85:          * Since the list is not empty, check whether the
86:          * element belongs on this list or whether you should
```

```
 87:            * make several lists in an array of subtries.
 88:            */
 89:          else if (h == hash(t.list->u.str))
 90:          {
 91:                  ele->next = t.list;
 92:                  t.list = ele;
 93:          }
 94:          else
 95:          {
 96:                  /*
 97:                   * You're making the list into an array or
 98:                   * subtries. Save the current list, replace
 99:                   * this entry with an array of TRIE_FANOUT
100:                   * subtries, and insert both the element and
101:                   * the list in the subtries.
102:                   */
103:                  listnode_t   *lp = t.list;
104:
105:                  /*
106:                   * Calling calloc() rather than malloc()
107:                   * ensures that the elements are initialized
108:                   * to NULL.
109:                   */
110:                  t.node = (trie_t *) calloc(TRIE_FANOUT,
111:                                  sizeof(trie_t));
112:                  t.num |= 1;
113:                  t = eleInsert(t, lp, hash(lp->u.str),
114:                          depth);
115:                  t = eleInsert(t, ele, h, depth);
116:          }
117:          return t;
118: }
119:
120: /*
121:  * Finds an element in a trie and returns the resulting
122:  * string, or NULL. For internal use by search() only.
123:  */
124: static const char * eleSearch(trie_t t, const char * string,
125:                                  unsigned h, int depth)
126: {
127:          /*
128:           * If the trie is an array of subtries, look for the
129:           * element in the proper subtree.
130:           */
131:          if (t.num & 1)
132:          {
133:                  trie_t  nxtNode = t;
134:                  nxtNode.num &= ~1;
135:                  nxtNode.node += (h >> depth) & TRIE_MASK;
136:                  return eleSearch(*nxtNode.node,
137:                          string, h, depth + TRIE_BITS);
138:          }
139:          /*
140:           * Otherwise, the trie is a list. Perform a linear
141:           * search for the desired element.
142:           */
143:          else
```

continues

Listing III.5. continued

```
144:             {
145:                     listnode_t    *lp = t.list;
146:
147:                     while (lp)
148:                     {
149:                             if (strcmp(lp->u.str, string) == 0)
150:                                     return lp->u.str;
151:                             lp = lp->next;
152:                     }
153:             }
154:         return NULL;
155: }
156:
157: /* Test function to print the structure of a trie */
158: void triePrint(trie_t t, int depth)
159: {
160:         if (t.num & 1)
161:         {
162:                 int     i;
163:                 trie_t  nxtNode = t;
164:                 nxtNode.num &= ~1;
165:                 if (depth)
166:                         printf("\n");
167:                 for (i = 0; i < TRIE_FANOUT; i++)
168:                 {
169:                         if (nxtNode.node[i].num == 0)
170:                                 continue;
171:                         printf("%*s[%d]", depth, "", i);
172:                         triePrint(nxtNode.node[i], depth + 8);
173:                 }
174:         }
175:         else
176:         {
177:                 listnode_t    *lp = t.list;
178:                 while (lp)
179:                 {
180:                         printf("\t'%s'", lp->u.str);
181:                         lp = lp->next;
182:                 }
183:                 putchar('\n');
184:         }
185: }
186:
187: static trie_t    t;
188:
189: void insert(const char *s)
190: {
191:         t = eleInsert(t, newNode((void *) s), hash(s), 0);
192: }
193:
194: void print(void)
195: {
196:         triePrint(t, 0);
197: }
```

```
198:
199: const char *search(const char *s)
200: {
201:         return eleSearch(t, s, hash(s), 0);
202: }
```

Cross Reference:

III.4: What is the easiest searching method to use?

III.6: What is hashing?

III.8: How can I search for data in a linked list?

III.6: What is hashing?

Answer:

To hash means to grind up, and that's essentially what hashing is all about. The heart of a hashing algorithm is a hash function that takes your nice, neat data and grinds it into some random-looking integer.

The idea behind hashing is that some data either has no inherent ordering (such as images) or is expensive to compare (such as images). If the data has no inherent ordering, you can't perform comparison searches. If the data is expensive to compare, the number of comparisons used even by a binary search might be too many. So instead of looking at the data themselves, you'll condense (hash) the data to an integer (its hash value) and keep all the data with the same hash value in the same place. This task is carried out by using the hash value as an index into an array.

To search for an item, you simply hash it and look at all the data whose hash values match that of the data you're looking for. This technique greatly lessens the number of items you have to look at. If the parameters are set up with care and enough storage is available for the hash table, the number of comparisons needed to find an item can be made arbitrarily close to one. Listing III.6 shows a simple hashing algorithm. You can combine this example with code at the end of this chapter to produce a working program.

One aspect that affects the efficiency of a hashing implementation is the hash function itself. It should ideally distribute data randomly throughout the entire hash table, to reduce the likelihood of collisions. Collisions occur when two different keys have the same hash value. There are two ways to resolve this problem. In "open addressing," the collision is resolved by the choosing of another position in the hash table for the element inserted later. When the hash table is searched, if the entry is not found at its hashed position in the table, the search continues checking until either the element is found or an empty position in the table is found.

The second method of resolving a hash collision is called "chaining." In this method, a "bucket" or linked list holds all the elements whose keys hash to the same value. When the hash table is searched, the list must be searched linearly.

Listing III.6. A simple example of a hash algorithm.

```
 1: #include        <stdlib.h>
 2: #include        <string.h>
 3: #include        "list.h"
 4: #include        "hash.h"
 5:
 6: #define HASH_SIZE       1024
 7:
 8: static  listnode_t      *hashTable[HASH_SIZE];
 9:
10: void insert(const char *s)
11: {
12:         listnode_t      *ele = newNode((void *) s);
13:         unsigned int    h = hash(s) % HASH_SIZE;
14:
15:         ele->next = hashTable[h];
16:         hashTable[h] = ele;
17: }
18:
19: void print(void)
20: {
21:         int     h;
22:
23:         for (h = 0; h < HASH_SIZE; h++)
24:         {
25:                 listnode_t      *lp = hashTable[h];
26:
27:                 if (lp == NULL)
28:                         continue;
29:                 printf("[%d]", h);
30:                 while (lp)
31:                 {
32:                         printf("\t'%s'", lp->u.str);
33:                         lp = lp->next;
34:                 }
35:                 putchar('\n');
36:         }
37: }
38:
39: const char *search(const char *s)
40: {
41:         unsigned int    h = hash(s) % HASH_SIZE;
42:         listnode_t      *lp = hashTable[h];
43:
44:         while (lp)
45:         {
46:                 if (!strcmp(s, lp->u.str))
47:                         return lp->u.str;
48:                 lp = lp->next;
49:         }
50:         return NULL;
51: }
```

Cross Reference:

III.4: What is the easiest searching method to use?

III.5: What is the quickest searching method to use?

III.8: How can I search for data in a linked list?

III.7: How can I sort a linked list?
Answer:

Both the merge sort and the radix sort shown in FAQ III.2 (see Listings III.2b and III.2c for code) are good sorting algorithms to use for linked lists.

Cross Reference:

III.1: What is the easiest sorting method to use?

III.2: What is the quickest sorting method to use?

III.3: How can I sort things that are too large to bring into memory?

III.8: How can I search for data in a linked list?
Answer:

Unfortunately, the only way to search a linked list is with a linear search, because the only way a linked list's members can be accessed is sequentially. Sometimes it is quicker to take the data from a linked list and store it in a different data structure so that searches can be more efficient.

Cross Reference:

III.4: What is the easiest searching method to use?

III.5: What is the quickest searching method to use?

III.6: What is hashing?

Sample Code

You can combine the following code with the code from each of the listings in this chapter to form a working program you can compile and run. Each example has been compiled and run on the same data set, and the results are compared in the introduction section of this chapter entitled "Performance of Sorting and Searching."

The first listing is a makefile, which can be used with a make utility to compile each program. Because some make utilites don't understand this format, and because not everyone has a make utility, you can use the information in this makefile yourself. Each nonblank line lists the name of an example followed by a colon and the source files needed to build it. The actual compiler commands will depend on which brand of compiler you have and which options (such as memory model) you want to use. Following the makefile are source files for the main driver programs and the linked list code used by some of the algorithms.

The code in driver1.c (Listing III.9a) sorts all of its command-line arguments, as strings, using whatever sorting algorithm it is built with, and prints the sorted arguments. The code in driver2.c (Listing III.9b) generates a table of the first 10,000 prime numbers, then searches for each of its command-line arguments (which are numbers) in that table.

Because the algorithm in Listing III.6 does not search items in an array, it has its own main procedure. It reads lines of input until it gets to the end-of-file, and then it prints the entire trie data structure. Then it searches for each of its command-line arguments in the trie and prints the results.

Listing III.9. A makefile with rules to build the programs in this chapter.

```
3_1:      3_1.c driver1.c

3_2a:     3_2a.c driver1.c

3_2b:     3_2b.c list.c driver1.c

3_2c:     3_2c.c list.c driver1.c

3_3:      3_3.c 3_1.c

3_4:      3_4.c 3_1.c driver2.c

3_5:      3_5.c 3_1.c driver2.c

3_6:      3_6.c 3_1.c driver2.c

3_7:      3_7.c list.c hash.c driver3.c

3_8:      3_8.c list.c hash.c driver3.c
```

Listing III.9a. The driver1.c driver for all the sorting algorithms except the external sort algorithm.

```c
#include        <stdio.h>

extern void sortStrings(const char **);

/* Sorts its arguments and prints them, one per line */
int
main(int argc, const char *argv[])
{
        int     i;

        sortStrings(argv + 1);
        for (i = 1; i < argc; i++)
                puts(argv[i]);
        return 0;
}
```

Listing III.9b. The driver2.c driver for the searching algorithms using bsearch(), binary, and linear search algorithms.

```
#include        <stdio.h>
#include        <string.h>

extern const char       *search(const char *, const char **,
                                                size_t);

static int      size;
static const char       **array;

static void initArray(int limit)
{
        char    buf[1000];

        array = (const char **) calloc(limit, sizeof(char *));
        for (size = 0; size < limit; size++)
        {
                if (gets(buf) == NULL)
                        break;
                array[size] = strdup(buf);
        }
        sortStrings(array, size);
}

int main(int argc, char **argv)
{
        int     i;
        int     limit;

        if (argc < 2)
        {
                fprintf(stderr, "usage: %s size [lookups]\n",
                                                argv[0]);
                exit(1);
        }
        limit = atoi(argv[1]);
        initArray(limit);
        for (i = 2; i < argc; i++)
        {
                const char      *s;

                if (s = search(argv[i], array, limit))
                        printf("%s -> %s\n", argv[i], s);
                else
                        printf("%s not found\n", argv[i]);
        }
        return 0;
}
```

Listing III.9c. The driver3.c driver for the trie and hash search programs.

```c
#include        <stdio.h>
#include        <string.h>

extern void     insert(const char *);
extern void     print(void);
extern const char       *search(const char *);

int
main(int argc, char *argv[])
{
        int     i;
        int     limit;
        char    buf[1000];

        if (argc < 2)
        {
                fprintf(stderr, "usage: %s size [lookups]\n",
                                                argv[0]);
                exit(1);
        }
        limit = atoi(argv[1]);
        for (i = 0; i < limit; i++)
        {
                if (gets(buf) == NULL)
                        break;
                insert(strdup(buf));
        }
        print();
        for (i = 2; i < argc; i++)
        {
                const char      *p = search(argv[i]);
                if (p)
                        printf("%s -> %s\n", argv[i], p);
                else
                        printf("%s not found\n", argv[i]);
        }
        return 0;
}
```

Listing III.9d. The list.h header file, which provides a simple linked list type.

```c
/*
 * Generic linked list node structure--can hold either
 * a character string or another list as data.
 */
typedef struct listnode_s {
        struct listnode_s       *next;
        union {
                void    *data;
                struct list_s   *list;
                const char      *str;
        } u;
} listnode_t;
```

```
typedef struct list_s {
        listnode_t      *head;
        listnode_t      *tail;
} list_t;

extern void appendNode(list_t *, listnode_t *);
extern listnode_t *removeHead(list_t *);
extern void concatList(list_t *, list_t *);
extern list_t *copyOf(list_t);
extern listnode_t *newNode(void *);
extern list_t *newList();
```

Listing III.9e. The list.c source file, which provides a simple linked list type.

```
#include         <malloc.h>
#include         "list.h"

/* Appends a listnode_t to a list_t. */
void appendNode(list_t *list, listnode_t *node)
{
        node->next = NULL;
        if (list->head)
        {
                list->tail->next = node;
                list->tail = node;
        }
        else
                list->head = list->tail = node;
}

/* Removes the first node from a list_t and returns it. */
listnode_t *removeHead(list_t *list)
{
        listnode_t      *node = 0;
        if (list->head)
        {
                node = list->head;
                list->head = list->head->next;
                if (list->head == NULL)
                        list->tail = NULL;
                node->next = NULL;
        }
        return node;
}

/* Concatenates two lists into the first list. */
void concatList(list_t *first, list_t *second)
{
        if (first->head)
        {
                if (second->head)
                {
                        first->tail->next = second->head;
                        first->tail = second->tail;
                }
        }
```

continues

Listing III.9e. continued

```
        else
                *first = *second;
        second->head = second->tail = NULL;
}

/* Returns a copy of a list_t from the heap. */
list_t *copyOf(list_t list)
{
        list_t  *new = (list_t *) malloc(sizeof(list_t));
        *new = list;
        return new;
}

/* Allocates a new listnode_t from the heap. */
listnode_t *newNode(void *data)
{
        listnode_t      *new = (listnode_t *)
                                malloc(sizeof(listnode_t));
        new->next = NULL;
        new->u.data = data;
        return new;
}

/* Allocates an empty list_t from the heap. */
list_t *newList()
{
        list_t  *new = (list_t *) malloc(sizeof(list_t));
        new->head = new->tail = NULL;
        return new;
}
```

Listing III.9f. The hash.h header file, which provides a simple character string hash function.

```
unsigned int    hash(const char *);
```

Listing III.9g. The hash.c source file, which provides a simple character string hash function.

```
#include        "hash.h"

/* This is a simple string hash function */
unsigned int hash(const char *string)
{
        unsigned h = 0;

        while (*string)
                h = 17 * h + *string++;
        return h;
}
```

CHAPTER

◆

Data Files

This chapter focuses on one of C's strongest assets: disk input and output. For many years, the fastest and leanest professional programs have been developed in C and have benefited from the language's optimized file I/O routines.

File manipulation can be a difficult task sometimes, and this chapter presents some of the most frequently asked questions regarding data files. Subjects such as streams, file modes (text and binary), file and directory manipulation, and file sharing are addressed. Most of today's professional programs are network-aware, so pay close attention to those questions at the end of the chapter that deal with file sharing and concurrency control topics. In addition, some diverse file-related topics, such as file handles in DOS and installing a hardware error handling routine, are covered in this chapter. Enjoy!

IV.1: If *errno* contains a nonzero number, is there an error?

Answer:

The global variable errno is used by many standard C library functions to pass back to your program an error code that denotes specifically which error occurred. However, your program *should not* check the value of errno to determine whether an error occurred. Usually, the standard C library function you are calling returns with a return code which denotes that an error has occurred and that the value of errno has been set to a specific error number. If no error has occurred or if you are using a library function that does not reference errno, there is a good chance that errno will contain an erroneous value. For performance enhancement, the errno variable is sometimes not cleared by the functions that use it.

You should *never* rely on the value of errno alone; always check the return code from the function you are calling to see whether errno should be referenced. Refer to your compiler's library documentation for references to functions that utilize the errno global variable and for a list of valid values for errno.

Cross Reference:

None.

IV.2: What is a stream?

Answer:

A stream is a continuous series of bytes that flow into or out of your program. Input and output from devices such as the mouse, keyboard, disk, screen, modem, and printer are all handled with streams. In C, all streams appear as files—not physical disk files necessarily, but rather *logical* files that refer to an input/output source. The C language provides five "standard" streams that are always available to your program. These streams do not have to be opened or closed. These are the five standard streams:

Name	Description	Example
stdin	Standard Input	Keyboard
stdout	Standard Output	Screen
stderr	Standard Error	Screen
stdprn	Standard Printer	LPT1: port
stdaux	Standard Auxiliary	COM1: port

Note that the stdprn and stdaux streams are not always defined. This is because LPT1: and COM1: have no meaning under certain operating systems. However, stdin, stdout, and stderr are always defined. Also, note that the stdin stream does not have to come from the keyboard; it can come from a disk file or some other device through what is called redirection. In the same manner, the stdout stream does not have to appear on-screen; it too can be redirected to a disk file or some other device. See the next FAQ for an explanation of redirection.

Cross Reference:

IV.3: How do you redirect a standard stream?

IV.4: How can you restore a redirected standard stream?

IV.5: Can stdout be forced to print somewhere other than the screen?

IV.3: How do you redirect a standard stream?

Answer:

Most operating systems, including DOS, provide a means to redirect program input and output to and from different devices. This means that rather than your program output (stdout) going to the screen, it can be redirected to a file or printer port. Similarly, your program's input (stdin) can come from a file rather than the keyboard. In DOS, this task is accomplished using the redirection characters, < and >. For example, if you wanted a program named PRINTIT.EXE to receive its input (stdin) from a file named STRINGS.TXT, you would enter the following command at the DOS prompt:

```
C:>PRINTIT < STRINGS.TXT
```

Notice that the name of the executable file always comes first. The less-than sign (<) tells DOS to take the strings contained in STRINGS.TXT and use them as input for the PRINTIT program. See FAQ IV.5 for an example of redirecting the stdout standard stream.

Redirection of standard streams does not always have to occur at the operating system. You can redirect a standard stream from *within your program* by using the standard C library function named freopen(). For example, if you wanted to redirect the stdout standard stream within your program to a file named OUTPUT.TXT, you would implement the freopen() function as shown here:

```
...
freopen("output.txt", "w", stdout);
...
```

Now, every output statement (printf(), puts(), putch(), and so on) in your program will appear in the file OUTPUT.TXT.

Cross Reference:

IV.2: What is a stream?

IV.4: How can you restore a redirected standard stream?

IV.5: Can stdout be forced to print somewhere other than the screen?

IV.4: How can you restore a redirected standard stream?

Answer:

The preceding example showed how you can redirect a standard stream from within your program. But what if later in your program you wanted to restore the standard stream to its *original* state? By using the standard C library functions named dup() and fdopen(), you can restore a standard stream such as stdout to its original state.

The dup() function duplicates a file handle. You can use the dup() function to save the file handle corresponding to the stdout standard stream. The fdopen() function opens a stream that has been duplicated with the dup() function. Thus, as shown in the following example, you can redirect standard streams and restore them:

```
#include <stdio.h>
```

```
void main(void);

void main(void)
{

    int orig_stdout;

    /* Duplicate the stdout file handle and store it in orig_stdout. */

    orig_stdout = dup(fileno(stdout));

    /* This text appears on-screen. */

    printf("Writing to original stdout...\n");

    /* Reopen stdout and redirect it to the "redir.txt" file. */

    freopen("redir.txt", "w", stdout);

    /* This text appears in the "redir.txt" file. */

    printf("Writing to redirected stdout...\n");

    /* Close the redirected stdout. */

    fclose(stdout);

    /* Restore the original stdout and print to the screen again. */

    fdopen(orig_stdout, "w");

    printf("I'm back writing to the original stdout.\n");

}
```

Cross Reference:

IV.2: What is a stream?

IV.3: How do you redirect a standard stream?

IV.5: Can stdout be forced to print somewhere other than the screen?

IV.5: Can *stdout* be forced to print somewhere other than the screen?

Answer:

Although the stdout standard stream defaults to the screen, you can force it to print to another device using something called *redirection* (see FAQ IV.3 for an explanation of redirection). For instance, consider the following program:

```
/* redir.c */

#include <stdio.h>

void main(void);

void main(void)
{

    printf("Let's get redirected!\n");

}
```

At the DOS prompt, instead of entering just the executable name, follow it with the redirection character >, and thus redirect what normally would appear on-screen to some other device. The following example would redirect the program's output to the prn device, usually the printer attached on LPT1:

```
C:>REDIR > PRN
```

Alternatively, you might want to redirect the program's output to a file, as the following example shows:

```
C:>REDIR > REDIR.OUT
```

In this example, all output that would have normally appeared on-screen will be written to the file REDIR.OUT.

Refer to FAQ IV.3 for an example of how you can redirect standard streams from *within* your program.

Cross Reference:

IV.2: What is a stream?

IV.3: How do you redirect a standard stream?

IV.4: How can you restore a redirected standard stream?

IV.6: What is the difference between text and binary modes?
Answer:

Streams can be classified into two types: *text* streams and *binary* streams. Text streams are interpreted, with a maximum length of 255 characters. With text streams, carriage return/line feed combinations are translated to the newline \n character and vice versa. Binary streams are uninterpreted and are treated one byte at a time with no translation of characters. Typically, a text stream would be used for reading and writing standard text files, printing output to the screen or printer, or receiving input from the keyboard. A binary text stream would typically be used for reading and writing binary files such as graphics or word processing documents, reading mouse input, or reading and writing to the modem.

Cross Reference:

IV.18: How can I read and write comma-delimited text?

IV.7: How do you determine whether to use a stream function or a low-level function?

Answer:

Stream functions such as fread() and fwrite() are buffered and are more efficient when reading and writing text or binary data to files. You generally gain better performance by using stream functions rather than their unbuffered low-level counterparts such as read() and write().

In multiuser environments, however, when files are typically shared and portions of files are continuously being locked, read from, written to, and unlocked, the stream functions do not perform as well as the low-level functions. This is because it is hard to buffer a shared file whose contents are constantly changing.

Generally, you should always use buffered stream functions when accessing nonshared files, and you should always use the low-level functions when accessing shared files.

Cross Reference:

None.

IV.8: How do you list files in a directory?

Answer:

Unfortunately, there is no built-in function provided in the C language such as dir_list() that would easily provide you with a list of all files in a particular directory. By utilizing some of C's built-in directory functions, however, you can write your own dir_list() function.

First of all, the include file dos.h defines a structure named find_t, which represents the structure of the DOS file entry block. This structure holds the name, time, date, size, and attributes of a file. Second, your C compiler library contains the functions _dos_findfirst() and _dos_findnext(), which can be used to find the first or next file in a directory.

The _dos_findfirst() function requires three arguments. The first argument is the file mask for the directory list. A mask of *.* would be used to list all files in the directory. The second argument is an attribute mask, defining which file attributes to search for. For instance, you might want to list only files with the Hidden or Directory attributes. See FAQ IV.11 for a more detailed explanation of file attributes. The last argument of the _dos_findfirst() function is a pointer to the variable that is to hold the directory information (the find_t structure variable).

The second function you will use is the _dos_findnext() function. Its only argument is a pointer to the find_t structure variable that you used in the _dos_findfirst() function. Using these two functions and the find_t structure, you can iterate through the directory on a disk and list each file in the directory. Here is the code to perform this task:

```
#include <stdio.h>
#include <direct.h>
```

```
#include <dos.h>
#include <malloc.h>
#include <memory.h>
#include <string.h>

typedef struct find_t FILE_BLOCK;

void main(void);

void main(void)
{
    FILE_BLOCK f_block;      /* Define the find_t structure variable */
    int ret_code;     /* Define a variable to store the return codes */

    printf("\nDirectory listing of all files in this directory:\n\n");

    /* Use the "*.*" file mask and the 0xFF attribute mask to list
       all files in the directory, including system files, hidden
       files, and subdirectory names. */

    ret_code = _dos_findfirst("*.*", 0xFF, &f_block);

    /* The _dos_findfirst() function returns a 0 when it is successful
       and has found a valid filename in the directory. */

    while (ret_code == 0)
    {

        /* Print the file's name */

        printf("%-12s\n", f_block.name);

        /* Use the _dos_findnext() function to look
           for the next file in the directory. */

        ret_code = _dos_findnext(&f_block);

    }

    printf("\nEnd of directory listing.\n");

}
```

Cross Reference:

IV.9: How do you list a file's date and time?

IV.10: How do you sort filenames in a directory?

IV.11: How do you determine a file's attributes?

IV.9: How do you list a file's date and time?

Answer:

A file's date and time are stored in the find_t structure returned from the _dos_findfirst() and _dos_findnext() functions (see FAQ IV.8). Using the example from IV.8, the source code can be modified slightly so that the date and time stamp of each file, as well as its name, is printed.

The date and time stamp of the file is stored in the find_t.wr_date and find_t.wr_time structure members. The file date is stored in a two-byte unsigned integer as shown here:

Element	Offset	Range
Seconds	5 bits	0–9 (multiply by 2 to get the seconds value)
Minutes	6 bits	0–59
Hours	5 bits	0–23

Similarly, the file time is stored in a two-byte unsigned integer, as shown here:

Element	Offset	Range
Day	5 bits	1–31
Month	4 bits	1–12
Year	7 bits	0–127 (add the value "1980" to get the year value)

Because DOS stores a file's seconds in *two-second* intervals, only the values 0 to 29 are needed. You simply multiply the value by 2 to get the file's true seconds value. Also, because DOS came into existence in 1980, no files can have a time stamp prior to that year. Therefore, you must add the value "1980" to get the file's true year value.

The following example program shows how you can get a directory listing along with each file's date and time stamp:

```c
#include <stdio.h>
#include <direct.h>
#include <dos.h>
#include <malloc.h>
#include <memory.h>
#include <string.h>

typedef struct find_t FILE_BLOCK;

void main(void);

void main(void)
{
    FILE_BLOCK f_block;    /* Define the find_t structure variable */
    int ret_code;          /* Define a variable to store return codes */
    int hour;              /* We're going to use a 12-hour clock! */
    char* am_pm;           /* Used to print "am" or "pm" */

    printf("\nDirectory listing of all files in this directory:\n\n");
```

```
    /* Use the "*.*" file mask and the 0xFF attribute mask to list
       all files in the directory, including system files, hidden
       files, and subdirectory names. */

    ret_code = _dos_findfirst("*.*", 0xFF, &f_block);

    /* The _dos_findfirst() function returns a 0 when it is successful
       and has found a valid filename in the directory. */

    while (ret_code == 0)
    {
        /* Convert from a 24-hour format to a 12-hour format. */

        hour = (f_block.wr_time >> 11);

        if (hour > 12)
        {
            hour = hour - 12;
            am_pm = "pm";
        }
        else
            am_pm = "am";

        /* Print the file's name, date stamp, and time stamp. */

        printf("%-12s  %02d/%02d/%4d  %02d:%02d:%02d %s\n",
                f_block.name,                    /* name   */
                (f_block.wr_date >> 5) & 0x0F,   /* month */
                (f_block.wr_date) & 0x1F,        /* day    */
                (f_block.wr_date >> 9) + 1980,   /* year   */
                hour,                            /* hour   */
                (f_block.wr_time >> 5) & 0x3F,   /* minute  */
                (f_block.wr_time & 0x1F) * 2,    /* seconds */
                am_pm);

        /* Use the _dos_findnext() function to look
           for the next file in the directory. */

        ret_code = _dos_findnext(&f_block);

    }

    printf("\nEnd of directory listing.\n");

}
```

Notice that a lot of bit-shifting and bit-manipulating had to be done to get the elements of the time variable and the elements of the date variable. If you happen to suffer from *bitshiftophobia* (fear of shifting bits), you can optionally code the preceding example by forming a union between the find_t structure and your own user-defined structure, such as this:

```
/* This is the find_t structure as defined by ANSI C. */

struct find_t
{
    char reserved[21];
    char attrib;
```

```
        unsigned wr_time;
        unsigned wr_date;
        long size;
        char name[13];
}

/* This is a custom find_t structure where we
   separate out the bits used for date and time. */

struct my_find_t
{
    char reserved[21];
    char attrib;
    unsigned seconds:5;
    unsigned minutes:6;
    unsigned hours:5;
    unsigned day:5;
    unsigned month:4;
    unsigned year:7;
    long size;
    char name[13];
}

/* Now, create a union between these two structures
   so that we can more easily access the elements of
   wr_date and wr_time. */

union file_info
{
    struct find_t ft;
    struct my_find_t mft;
}
```

Using the preceding technique, instead of using bit-shifting and bit-manipulating, you can now extract date and time elements like this:

```
...
file_info my_file;
...

printf("%-12s  %02d/%02d/%4d  %02d:%02d:%02d %s\n",
        my_file.mft.name,             /* name    */
        my_file.mft.month,            /* month   */
        my_file.mft.day,              /* day     */
        (my_file.mft.year + 1980),    /* year    */
        my_file.mft.hours,            /* hour    */
        my_file.mft.minutes,          /* minute  */
        (my_file.mft.seconds * 2),    /* seconds */
        am_pm);
```

Cross Reference:

IV.8: How do you list files in a directory?

IV.10: How do you sort filenames in a directory?

IV.11: How do you determine a file's attributes?

IV.10: How do you sort filenames in a directory?

Answer:

The example in FAQ IV.8 shows how to get a list of files one at a time. The example uses the _dos_findfirst() and _dos_findnext() functions to walk through the directory structure. As each filename is found, it is printed to the screen.

When you are sorting the filenames in a directory, the one-at-a-time approach does not work. You need some way to *store* the filenames and then sort them when all filenames have been obtained. This task can be accomplished by creating an array of pointers to find_t structures for each filename that is found. As each filename is found in the directory, memory is allocated to hold the find_t entry for that file. When all filenames have been found, the qsort() function is used to sort the array of find_t structures by filename.

The qsort() function can be found in your compiler's library. This function takes four parameters: a pointer to the array you are sorting, the number of elements to sort, the size of each element, and a pointer to a function that compares two elements of the array you are sorting. The comparison function is a user-defined function that you supply. It returns a value less than zero if the first element is less than the second element, greater than zero if the first element is greater than the second element, or zero if the two elements are equal. Consider the following example:

```
#include <stdio.h>
#include <direct.h>
#include <dos.h>
#include <malloc.h>
#include <memory.h>
#include <string.h>

typedef struct find_t FILE_BLOCK;

int  sort_files(FILE_BLOCK**, FILE_BLOCK**);
void main(void);

void main(void)
{
    FILE_BLOCK f_block;        /* Define the find_t structure variable */
    int ret_code;              /* Define a variable to store the return
                                  codes */
    FILE_BLOCK** file_list;    /* Used to sort the files */
    int file_count;            /* Used to count the files */
    int x;                     /* Counter variable */

    file_count = -1;

    /* Allocate room to hold up to 512 directory entries. */

    file_list = (FILE_BLOCK**) malloc(sizeof(FILE_BLOCK*) * 512);

    printf("\nDirectory listing of all files in this directory:\n\n");

    /* Use the "*.*" file mask and the 0xFF attribute mask to list
       all files in the directory, including system files, hidden
       files, and subdirectory names. */
```

```
        ret_code = _dos_findfirst("*.*", 0xFF, &f_block);

        /* The _dos_findfirst() function returns a 0 when it is successful
           and has found a valid filename in the directory. */

        while (ret_code == 0 && file_count < 512)
        {
            /* Add this filename to the file list */

            file_list[++file_count] =
                (FILE_BLOCK*) malloc(sizeof(FILE_BLOCK));

            *file_list[file_count] = f_block;

            /* Use the _dos_findnext() function to look
               for the next file in the directory. */

            ret_code = _dos_findnext(&f_block);

        }

        /* Sort the files */

        qsort(file_list, file_count, sizeof(FILE_BLOCK*), sort_files);

        /* Now, iterate through the sorted array of filenames and
           print each entry. */

        for (x=0; x<file_count; x++)
        {
            printf("%-12s\n", file_list[x]->name);

        }

        printf("\nEnd of directory listing.\n");

}

int sort_files(FILE_BLOCK** a, FILE_BLOCK** b)
{
        return (strcmp((*a)->name, (*b)->name));

}
```

This example uses the user-defined function named sort_files() to compare two filenames and return the appropriate value based on the return value from the standard C library function strcmp(). Using this same technique, you can easily modify the program to sort by date, time, extension, or size by changing the element on which the sort_files() function operates.

Cross Reference:

IV.8: How do you list files in a directory?

IV.9: How do you list a file's date and time?

IV.11: How do you determine a file's attributes?

IV.11: How do you determine a file's attributes?

Answer:

The file attributes are stored in the find_t.attrib structure member (see FAQ IV.8). This structure member is a single character, and each file attribute is represented by a single bit. Here is a list of the valid DOS file attributes:

Value	Description	Constant
0x00	Normal	(none)
0x01	Read Only	FA_RDONLY
0x02	Hidden File	FA_HIDDEN
0x04	System File	FA_SYSTEM
0x08	Volume Label	FA_LABEL
0x10	Subdirectory	FA_DIREC
0x20	Archive File	FA_ARCHIVE

To determine the file's attributes, you check which bits are turned on and map them corresponding to the preceding table. For example, a read-only hidden system file will have the first, second, and third bits turned on. A "normal" file will have none of the bits turned on. To determine whether a particular bit is turned on, you do a bit-wise AND with the bit's constant representation.

The following program uses this technique to print a file's attributes:

```
#include <stdio.h>
#include <direct.h>
#include <dos.h>
#include <malloc.h>
#include <memory.h>
#include <string.h>

typedef struct find_t FILE_BLOCK;

void main(void);

void main(void)
{

    FILE_BLOCK f_block;  /* Define the find_t structure variable */
    int ret_code;        /* Define a variable to store the return codes */

    printf("\nDirectory listing of all files in this directory:\n\n");

    /* Use the "*.*" file mask and the 0xFF attribute mask to list
       all files in the directory, including system files, hidden
       files, and subdirectory names. */

    ret_code = _dos_findfirst("*.*", 0xFF, &f_block);

    /* The _dos_findfirst() function returns a 0 when
       it is successful and has found a valid filename
       in the directory. */
```

```
while (ret_code == 0)
{
    /* Print the file's name */

    printf("%-12s  ", f_block.name);

    /* Print the read-only attribute */

    printf("%s ", (f_block.attrib & FA_RDONLY) ? "R" : ".");

    /* Print the hidden attribute */

    printf("%s ", (f_block.attrib & FA_HIDDEN) ? "H" : ".");

    /* Print the system attribute */

    printf("%s ", (f_block.attrib & FA_SYSTEM) ? "S" : ".");

    /* Print the directory attribute */

    printf("%s ", (f_block.attrib & FA_DIREC)  ? "D" : ".");

    /* Print the archive attribute */

    printf("%s\n", (f_block.attrib & FA_ARCH)  ? "A" : ".");

    /* Use the _dos_findnext() function to look
       for the next file in the directory. */

    ret_code = _dos_findnext(&f_block);

}

printf("\nEnd of directory listing.\n");

}
```

Cross Reference:

IV.8: How do you list files in a directory?

IV.9: How do you list a file's date and time?

IV.10: How do you sort filenames in a directory?

IV.12: How do you view the *PATH*?

Answer:

Your C compiler library contains a function called getenv() that can retrieve any specified environment variable. It has one argument, which is a pointer to a string containing the environment variable you want to retrieve. It returns a pointer to the desired environment string on successful completion. If the function cannot find your environment variable, it returns NULL.

The following example program shows how to obtain the PATH environment variable and print it on-screen:

```
#include <stdio.h>
#include <stdlib.h>

void main(void);

void main(void)
{

    char* env_string;

    env_string = getenv("PATH");

    if (env_string == (char*) NULL)
        printf("\nYou have no PATH!\n");
    else
        printf("\nYour PATH is: %s\n", env_string);

}
```

Cross Reference:

None.

IV.13: How can I open a file so that other programs can update it at the same time?

Answer:

Your C compiler library contains a *low-level* file function called sopen() that can be used to open a file in shared mode. Beginning with DOS 3.0, files could be opened in shared mode by loading a special program named SHARE.EXE. Shared mode, as the name implies, allows a file to be shared with other programs as well as your own. Using this function, you can allow other programs that are running to update the same file you are updating.

The sopen() function takes four parameters: a pointer to the filename you want to open, the operational mode you want to open the file in, the file sharing mode to use, and, if you are creating a file, the mode to create the file in. The second parameter of the sopen() function, usually referred to as the "operation flag" parameter, can have the following values assigned to it:

Constant	Description
O_APPEND	Appends all writes to the end of the file
O_BINARY	Opens the file in binary (untranslated) mode
O_CREAT	If the file does not exist, it is created
O_EXCL	If the O_CREAT flag is used and the file exists, returns an error
O_RDONLY	Opens the file in read-only mode
O_RDWR	Opens the file for reading and writing

Constant	Description
O_TEXT	Opens the file in text (translated) mode
O_TRUNC	Opens an existing file and writes over its contents
O_WRONLY	Opens the file in write-only mode

The third parameter of the sopen() function, usually referred to as the "sharing flag," can have the following values assigned to it:

Constant	Description
SH_COMPAT	No other program can access the file
SH_DENYRW	No other program can read from or write to the file
SH_DENYWR	No other program can write to the file
SH_DENYRD	No other program can read from the file
SH_DENYNO	Any program can read from or write to the file

If the sopen() function is successful, it returns a non-negative number that is the file's handle. If an error occurs, −1 is returned, and the global variable errno is set to one of the following values:

Constant	Description
ENOENT	File or path not found
EMFILE	No more file handles are available
EACCES	Permission denied to access file
EINVACC	Invalid access code

The following example shows how to open a file in shared mode:

```
#include <stdio.h>
#include <fcntl.h>
#include <sys\stat.h>
#include <io.h>
#include <share.h>

void main(void);

void main(void)
{

    int file_handle;

    /* Note that sopen() is not ANSI compliant */

    file_handle = sopen("C:\\DATA\\TEST.DAT", O_RDWR, SH_DENYNO);

    close(file_handle);

}
```

Whenever you are sharing a file's contents with other programs, you should be sure to use the standard C library function named locking() to lock a portion of your file when you are updating it. See FAQ IV.15 for an explanation of the locking() function.

Cross Reference:

IV.14: How can I make sure that my program is the only one accessing a file?

IV.15: How can I prevent another program from modifying part of a file that I am modifying?

IV.14: How can I make sure that my program is the only one accessing a file?

Answer:

By using the sopen() function (see FAQ IV.13), you can open a file in shared mode and explicitly deny reading and writing permissions to any other program but yours. This task is accomplished by using the SH_DENYWR shared flag to denote that your program is going to deny any writing or reading attempts by other programs. For example, the following snippet of code shows a file being opened in shared mode, denying access to all other files:

```
/* Note that the sopen() function is not ANSI compliant... */

fileHandle = sopen("C:\\DATA\\SETUP.DAT", O_RDWR, SH_DENYWR);
```

By issuing this statement, all other programs are denied access to the SETUP.DAT file. If another program were to try to open SETUP.DAT for reading or writing, it would receive an EACCES error code, denoting that access is denied to the file.

Cross Reference:

IV.13: How can I open a file so that other programs can update it at the same time?

IV.15: How can I prevent another program from modifying part of a file that I am modifying?

IV.15: How can I prevent another program from modifying part of a file that I am modifying?

Answer:

Under DOS 3.0 and later, file sharing can be implemented by using the SHARE.EXE program (see FAQ IV.13). Your C compiler library comes with a function named locking() that can be used to lock and unlock portions of shared files.

The locking function takes three arguments: a handle to the shared file you are going to lock or unlock, the operation you want to perform on the file, and the number of bytes you want to lock. The file lock is placed relative to the current position of the file pointer, so if you are going to lock bytes located anywhere but at the beginning of the file, you need to reposition the file pointer by using the lseek() function.

The following example shows how a binary index file named SONGS.DAT can be locked and unlocked:

```c
#include <stdio.h>
#include <io.h>
#include <fcntl.h>
#include <process.h>
#include <string.h>
#include <share.h>
#include <sys\locking.h>

void main(void);

void main(void)
{

    int     file_handle, ret_code;
    char* song_name = "Six Months In A Leaky Boat";
    char  rec_buffer[50];

    file_handle = sopen("C:\\DATA\\SONGS.DAT", O_RDWR, SH_DENYNO);

    /* Assuming a record size of 50 bytes, position the file
       pointer to the 10th record. */

    lseek(file_handle, 450, SEEK_SET);

    /* Lock the 50-byte record. */

    ret_code = locking(file_handle, LK_LOCK, 50);

    /* Write the data and close the file. */

    memset(rec_buffer, '\0', sizeof(rec_buffer));

    sprintf(rec_buffer, "%s", song_name);

    write(file_handle, rec_buffer, sizeof(rec_buffer));

    lseek(file_handle, 450, SEEK_SET);

    locking(file_handle, LK_UNLCK, 50);

    close(file_handle);

}
```

Notice that before the record is locked, the record pointer is positioned to the 10th record (450th byte) by using the lseek() function. Also notice that to write the record to the file, the record pointer has to be repositioned to the beginning of the record before unlocking the record.

Cross Reference:

IV.13: How can I open a file so that other programs can update it at the same time?

IV.14: How can I make sure that my program is the only one accessing a file?

IV.16: How can I have more than 20 files open at once?

Answer:

The DOS configuration file, CONFIG.SYS, usually contains a FILES entry that tells DOS how many file handles to allocate for your programs to use. By default, DOS allows 20 files to be open at once. In many cases, especially if you are a user of Microsoft Windows or a database program, 20 file handles is not nearly enough. Fortunately, there is an easy way to allocate more file handles to the system. To do this, replace your FILES= statement in your CONFIG.SYS file with the number of file handles you want to allocate. If your CONFIG.SYS file does not contain a FILES entry, you can append such an entry to the end of the file. For example, the following statement in your CONFIG.SYS file will allocate 100 file handles to be available for system use:

```
FILES=100
```

On most systems, 100 file handles is sufficient. If you happen to be encountering erratic program crashes, you might have too few file handles allocated to your system, and you might want to try allocating more file handles. Note that each file handle takes up memory, so there is a cost in having a lot of file handles; the more file handles you allocate, the less memory your system will have to run programs. Also, note that file handles not only are allocated for data files, but also are applicable to binary files such as executable programs.

Cross Reference:

None.

IV.17: How can I avoid the *Abort, Retry, Fail* messages?

Answer:

When DOS encounters a critical error, it issues a call to *interrupt 24,* the critical error handler. Your C compiler library contains a function named harderr() that takes over the handling of calls to interrupt 24. The harderr() function takes one argument, a pointer to a function that is called if there is a hardware error.

Your user-defined hardware error-handling function is passed information regarding the specifics of the hardware error that occurred. In your function, you can display a user-defined message to avoid the ugly Abort, Retry, Fail message. This way, your program can elegantly handle such simple user errors as your not inserting the disk when prompted to do so.

When a hardware error is encountered and your function is called, you can either call the C library function hardretn() to return control to your application or call the C library function hardresume() to return control to DOS. Typically, disk errors can be trapped and your program can continue by using the hardresume() function. Other device errors, such as a bat FAT (file allocation table) error, are somewhat fatal, and your application should handle them by using the hardretn() function. Consider the following example, which uses the harderr() function to trap for critical errors and notifies the user when such an error occurs:

```
#include <stdio.h>
#include <dos.h>
#include <fcntl.h>
```

```c
#include <ctype.h>

void main(void);
void far error_handler(unsigned, unsigned, unsigned far*);

void main(void)
{
    int file_handle, ret_code;

    /* Install the custom error-handling routine. */

    _harderr(error_handler);

    printf("\nEnsure that the A: drive is empty, \n");
    printf("then press any key.\n\n");

    getch();

    printf("Trying to write to the A: drive...\n\n");

    /* Attempt to access an empty A: drive... */

    ret_code = _dos_open("A:FILE.TMP", O_RDONLY, &file_handle);

    /* If the A: drive was empty, the error_handler() function was
       called. Notify the user of the result of that function. */

    switch (ret_code)
    {
        case 100:    printf("Unknown device error!\n");
                        break;

        case 2:      printf("FILE.TMP was not found on drive A!\n");
                        break;

        case 0:      printf("FILE.TMP was found on drive A!\n");
                        break;

        default:     printf("Unknown error occurred!\n");
                        break;

    }

}

void far error_handler(unsigned device_error, unsigned error_val,
                                    unsigned far* device_header)
{
    long x;

    /* This condition will be true only if a nondisk error occurred. */

    if (device_error & 0x8000)
        _hardretn(100);

    /* Pause one second. */
```

```
    for (x=0; x<2000000; x++);

    /* Retry to access the drive. */

    _hardresume(_HARDERR_RETRY);

}
```

In this example, a custom hardware error handler is installed named error_handler(). When the program attempts to access the A: drive and no disk is found there, the error_handler() function is called. The error_handler() function first checks to ensure that the problem is a disk error. If the problem is *not* a disk error, it returns 100 by using the hardretn() function. Next, the program pauses for one second and issues a hardresume() call to retry accessing the A: drive.

Cross Reference:

None.

IV.18: How can I read and write comma-delimited text?

Answer:

Many of today's popular programs use comma-delimited text as a means of transferring data from one program to another, such as the exported data from a spreadsheet program that is to be imported by a database program. Comma-delimited means that all data (with the exception of numeric data) is surrounded by double quotation marks (" ") followed by a comma. Numeric data appears as-is, *with no surrounding double quotation marks.* At the end of each line of text, the comma is omitted and a newline is used.

To read and write the text to a file, you would use the fprintf() and fscanf() standard C library functions. The following example shows how a program can write out comma-delimited text and then read it back in.

```c
#include <stdio.h>
#include <string.h>

typedef struct name_str
{
    char        first_name[15];
    char        nick_name[30];
    unsigned years_known;
} NICKNAME;

NICKNAME nick_names[5];

void main(void);
void set_name(unsigned, char*, char*, unsigned);

void main(void)
{

    FILE*       name_file;
    int         x;
    NICKNAME tmp_name;
```

```c
printf("\nWriting data to NICKNAME.DAT, one moment please...\n");

/* Initialize the data with some values... */

set_name(0,    "Sheryl",    "Basset",     26);
set_name(1,    "Joel",      "Elkinator",   1);
set_name(2,    "Cliff",     "Shayface",   12);
set_name(3,    "Lloyd",     "Lloydage",   28);
set_name(4,    "Scott",     "Pie",         9);

/* Open the NICKNAME.DAT file for output in text mode. */

name_file = fopen("NICKNAME.DAT", "wt");

/* Iterate through all the data and use the fprintf() function
   to write the data to a file. */

for (x=0; x<5; x++)
{

    fprintf(name_file, "\"%s\", \"%s\", %u\n",
                nick_names[x].first_name,
                nick_names[x].nick_name,
                nick_names[x].years_known);

}

/* Close the file and reopen it for input. */

fclose(name_file);

printf("\nClosed NICKNAME.DAT, reopening for input...\n");

name_file = fopen("NICKNAME.DAT", "rt");

printf("\nContents of the file NICKNAME.DAT:\n\n");

/* Read each line in the file using the scanf() function
   and print the file's contents. */

while (1)
{

    fscanf(name_file, "%s %s %u",
                tmp_name.first_name,
                tmp_name.nick_name,
                &tmp_name.years_known);

    if (feof(name_file))
        break;

    printf("%-15s %-30s %u\n",
                tmp_name.first_name,
                tmp_name.nick_name,
                tmp_name.years_known);

}
```

```
        fclose(name_file);

}

void set_name(unsigned name_num, char* f_name,
              char* n_name, unsigned years)
{

    strcpy(nick_names[name_num].first_name, f_name);
    strcpy(nick_names[name_num].nick_name,  n_name);

    nick_names[name_num].years_known = years;

}
```

Cross Reference:

IV.6: What is the difference between text and binary modes?

IV.7: How do you determine whether to use a stream function or a low-level function?

CHAPTER

V

Working with the Preprocessor

This chapter focuses on questions pertaining to the preprocessor. The preprocessor is the program that is run before your program gets passed on to the compiler. You might never have seen this program before, because it is usually run "behind the scenes" and is hidden from the programmer. Nevertheless, its function is important.

The preprocessor is used to modify your program according to the *preprocessor directives* in your source code. Preprocessor directives (such as #define) give the preprocessor specific instructions on how to modify your source code. The preprocessor reads in all of your include files and the source code you are compiling and creates a preprocessed version of your source code. This preprocessed version has all of its macros and constant symbols replaced by their corresponding code and value assignments. If your source code contains any conditional preprocessor directives (such as #if), the preprocessor evaluates the condition and modifies your source code accordingly.

The preprocessor contains many features that are powerful to use, such as creating macros, performing conditional compilation, inserting predefined environment variables into your code, and turning compiler features on and off. For the professional programmer, in-depth knowledge of the features of the preprocessor can be one of the keys to creating fast, efficient programs.

As you read through the frequently asked questions in this chapter, keep in mind the techniques presented (as well as some of the common traps) so that you can tap into the full power behind the preprocessor and use its features effectively in your development cycle.

V.1: What is a macro, and how do you use it?
Answer:

A macro is a preprocessor directive that provides a mechanism for token replacement in your source code. Macros are created by using the #define statement. Here is an example of a macro:

```
#define VERSION_STAMP "1.02"
```

The macro being defined in this example is commonly referred to as a *symbol*. The symbol VERSION_STAMP is simply a physical representation of the string "1.02". When the *preprocessor* is invoked (see FAQ V.2), every occurrence of the VERSION_STAMP symbol is replaced with the literal string "1.02".

Here is another example of a macro:

```
#define CUBE(x) ((x) * (x) * (x))
```

The macro being defined here is named CUBE, and it takes one argument, x. The rest of the code on the line represents the body of the CUBE macro. Thus, the simplistic macro CUBE(x) will represent the more complex expression ((x) * (x) * (x)). When the preprocessor is invoked, every instance of the macro CUBE(x) in your program is replaced with the code ((x) * (x) * (x)).

Macros can save you many keystrokes when you are coding your program. They can also make your program much more readable and reliable, because you enter a macro in one place and use it in potentially several places. There is no overhead associated with macros, because the code that the macro represents is expanded in-place, and no jump in your program is invoked. Additionally, the arguments are not type-sensitive, so you don't have to worry about what data type you are passing to the macro.

Note that there must be *no white space* between your macro name and the parentheses containing the argument definition. Also, you should enclose the body of the macro in parentheses to avoid possible ambiguity regarding the translation of the macro. For instance, the following example shows the CUBE macro defined incorrectly:

```
#define CUBE (x) x * x * x
```

You also should be careful with what is passed to a macro. For instance, a very common mistake is to pass an incremented variable to a macro, as in the following example:

```
#include <stdio.h>

#define CUBE(x) (x*x*x)

void main(void);

void main(void)
{
    int x, y;

    x = 5;
    y = CUBE(++x);

    printf("y is %d\n", y);

}
```

What will y be equal to? You might be surprised to find out that y is *not* equal to 125 (the cubed value of 5) and *not* equal to 336 (6 * 7 * 8), but rather is 512. This is because the variable x is incremented while being passed as a parameter to the macro. Thus, the expanded CUBE macro in the preceding example actually appears as follows:

```
y = ((++x) * (++x) * (++x));
```

Each time x is referenced, it is incremented, so you wind up with a very different result from what you had intended. Because x is referenced three times and you are using a prefix increment operator, x is actually 8 when the code is expanded. Thus, you wind up with the cubed value of 8 rather than 5. This common mistake is one you should take note of because tracking down such bugs in your software can be a very frustrating experience. I personally have seen this mistake made by people with many years of C programming under their belts. I recommend that you type the example program and see for yourself how surprising the resulting value (512) is.

Macros can also utilize special operators such as the *stringizing* operator (#) and the *concatenation* operator (##). The stringizing operator can be used to convert macro parameters to quoted strings, as in the following example:

```
#define DEBUG_VALUE(v) printf(#v " is equal to %d.\n", v)
```

In your program, you can check the value of a variable by invoking the DEBUG_VALUE macro:

```
...

int x = 20;

DEBUG_VALUE(x);

...
```

The preceding code prints "x is equal to 20." on-screen. This example shows that the stringizing operator used with macros can be a very handy debugging tool.

The concatenation operator (##) is used to concatenate (combine) two separate strings into one single string. See FAQ V.16 for a detailed explanation of how to use the concatenation operator.

Cross Reference:

V.10: Is it better to use a macro or a function?

V.16: What is the concatenation operator?

V.17: How can type-insensitive macros be created?

V.18: What are the standard predefined macros?

V.31: How do you override a defined macro?

V.2: What will the preprocessor do for a program?

Answer:

The C preprocessor is used to modify your program according to the *preprocessor directives* in your source code. A preprocessor directive is a statement (such as #define) that gives the preprocessor specific instructions on how to modify your source code. The preprocessor is invoked as the first part of your compiler program's compilation step. It is usually hidden from the programmer because it is run automatically by the compiler.

The preprocessor reads in all of your include files and the source code you are compiling and creates a preprocessed version of your source code. This preprocessed version has all of its macros and constant symbols replaced by their corresponding code and value assignments. If your source code contains any conditional preprocessor directives (such as #if), the preprocessor evaluates the condition and modifies your source code accordingly.

Here is an example of a program that uses the preprocessor extensively:

```
#include <stdio.h>

#define TRUE                    1
#define FALSE                   (!TRUE)

#define GREATER(a,b)    ((a) > (b) ? (TRUE) : (FALSE))

#define PIG_LATIN       FALSE

void main(void);

void main(void)
{

    int x, y;

#if PIG_LATIN
    printf("Easeplay enternay ethay aluevay orfay xnay: ");
    scanf("%d", &x);
    printf("Easeplay enternay ethay aluevay orfay ynay: ");
    scanf("%d", &y);
#else
    printf("Please enter the value for x: ");
    scanf("%d", &x);
    printf("Please enter the value for y: ");
    scanf("%d", &y);
#endif

    if (GREATER(x,y) == TRUE)
    {

#if PIG_LATIN
        printf("xnay islay eatergray anthay ynay!\n");
#else
        printf("x is greater than y!\n");
#endif

    }
    else
    {
```

```
#if PIG_LATIN
        printf("xnay islay otnay eatergray anthay ynay!\n");
#else
        printf("x is not greater than y!\n");
#endif

    }

}
```

This program uses preprocessor directives to define symbolic constants (such as TRUE, FALSE, and PIG_LATIN), a macro (such as GREATER(a,b)), and conditional compilation (by using the #if statement). When the preprocessor is invoked on this source code, it reads in the stdio.h file and interprets its preprocessor directives, then it replaces all symbolic constants and macros in your program with the corresponding values and code. Next, it evaluates whether PIG_LATIN is set to TRUE and includes either the pig latin text or the plain English text.

If PIG_LATIN is set to FALSE, as in the preceding example, a preprocessed version of the source code would look like this:

```
/* Here is where all the include files
   would be expanded. */

void main(void)
{

    int x, y;

    printf("Please enter the value for x: ");
    scanf("%d", &x);
    printf("Please enter the value for y: ");
    scanf("%d", &y);

    if (((x) > (y) ? (1) : (!1)) == 1)
    {

        printf("x is greater than y!\n");

    }
    else
    {

        printf("x is not greater than y!\n");

    }

}
```

This preprocessed version of the source code can then be passed on to the compiler. If you want to see a preprocessed version of a program, most compilers have a command-line option or a standalone preprocessor program to invoke only the preprocessor and save the preprocessed version of your source code to a file. This capability can sometimes be handy in debugging strange errors with macros and other preprocessor directives, because it shows your source code *after* it has been run through the preprocessor.

Cross Reference:

V.3: How can you avoid including a header more than once?

V.4: Can a file other than a .h file be included with #include?

V.12: What is the difference between #include <file> and #include "file"?

V.22: What is a pragma?

V.23: What is #line used for?

V.3: How can you avoid including a header more than once?

Answer:

One easy technique to avoid multiple inclusions of the same header is to use the #ifndef and #define preprocessor directives. When you create a header for your program, you can #define a symbolic name that is unique to that header. You can use the conditional preprocessor directive named #ifndef to check whether that symbolic name has already been assigned. If it is assigned, you should not include the header, because it has already been preprocessed. If it is not defined, you should define it to avoid any further inclusions of the header. The following header illustrates this technique:

```
#ifndef _FILENAME_H
#define _FILENAME_H

#define VER_NUM       "1.00.00"
#define REL_DATE      "08/01/94"

#if _ _WINDOWS_ _
#define OS_VER         "WINDOWS"
#else
#define OS_VER         "DOS"
#endif

#endif
```

When the preprocessor encounters this header, it first checks to see whether _FILENAME_H has been defined. If it hasn't been defined, the header has not been included yet, and the _FILENAME_H symbolic name is defined. Then, the rest of the header is parsed until the last #endif is encountered, signaling the end of the conditional #ifndef _FILENAME_H statement. Substitute the actual name of the header file for "FILENAME" in the preceding example to make it applicable for your programs.

Cross Reference:

V.4: Can a file other than a .h file be included with #include?

V.12: What is the difference between #include <file> and #include "file"?

V.14: Can include files be nested?

V.15: How many levels deep can include files be nested?

V.4: Can a file other than a .h file be included with *#include*?

Answer:

The preprocessor will include whatever file you specify in your #include statement. Therefore, if you have the line

```
#include <macros.inc>
```

in your program, the file macros.inc will be included in your precompiled program.

It is, however, unusual programming practice to put any file that does not have a .h or .hpp extension in an #include statement. You should always put a .h extension on any of your C files you are going to include. This method makes it easier for you and others to identify which files are being used for preprocessing purposes. For instance, someone modifying or debugging your program might not know to look at the macros.inc file for macro definitions. That person might try in vain by searching all files with .h extensions and come up empty. If your file had been named macros.h, the search would have included the macros.h file, and the searcher would have been able to see what macros you defined in it.

Cross Reference:

V.3: How can you avoid including a header more than once?

V.12: What is the difference between #include <file> and #include "file"?

V.14: Can include files be nested?

V.15: How many levels deep can include files be nested?

V.5: What is the benefit of using *#define* to declare a constant?

Answer:

Using the #define method of declaring a constant enables you to declare a constant in one place and use it throughout your program. This helps make your programs more maintainable, because you need to maintain only the #define statement and not several instances of individual constants throughout your program. For instance, if your program used the value of pi (approximately 3.14159) several times, you might want to declare a constant for pi as follows:

```
#define PI 3.14159
```

This way, if you wanted to expand the precision of pi for more accuracy, you could change it in one place rather than several places. Usually, it is best to put #define statements in an include file so that several modules can use the same constant value.

Using the #define method of declaring a constant is probably the most familiar way of declaring constants to traditional C programmers. Besides being the most common method of declaring constants, it also takes up the least memory. Constants defined in this manner are simply placed directly into your source code, with no variable space allocated in memory. Unfortunately, this is one reason why most debuggers cannot inspect constants created using the #define method.

Constants defined with the #define method can also be overridden using the #undef preprocessor directive. This means that if a symbol such as NULL is not defined the way you would like to see it defined, you can remove the previous definition of NULL and instantiate your own custom definition. See FAQ V.31 for a more detailed explanation of how this can be done.

Cross Reference:

V.6: What is the benefit of using enum to declare a constant?

V.7: What is the benefit of using an enum rather than a #define constant?

V.31: How do you override a defined macro?

V.6: What is the benefit of using *enum* to declare a constant?

Answer:

Using the enum keyword to define a constant can have several benefits. First, constants declared with enum are automatically generated by the compiler, thereby relieving the programmer of manually assigning unique values to each constant. Also, constants declared with enum tend to be more readable to the programmer, because there is usually an enumerated type identifier associated with the constant's definition.

Additionally, enumerated constants can usually be inspected during a debugging session. This can be an enormous benefit, especially when the alternative is having to manually look up the constant's value in a header file. Unfortunately, using the enum method of declaring constants takes up slightly more memory space than using the #define method of declaring constants, because a memory location must be set up to store the constant.

Here is an example of an enumerated constant used for tracking errors in your program:

```
enum Error_Code
{
    OUT_OF_MEMORY,
    INSUFFICIENT_DISK_SPACE,
    LOGIC_ERROR,
    FILE_NOT_FOUND
};
```

See FAQ V.7 for a more detailed look at the benefits of using the enum method compared with using the #define method of declaring constants.

Cross Reference:

V.5: What is the benefit of using #define to declare a constant?

V.7: What is the benefit of using an enum rather than a #define constant?

V.7: What is the benefit of using an *enum* rather than a *#define* constant?

Answer:

The use of an *enumeration constant* (enum) has many advantages over using the traditional *symbolic constant* style of #define. These advantages include a lower maintenance requirement, improved program readability, and better debugging capability. The first advantage is that enumerated constants are generated automatically by the compiler. Conversely, symbolic constants must be manually assigned values by the programmer. For instance, if you had an enumerated constant type for error codes that could occur in your program, your enum definition could look something like this:

```
enum Error_Code
{
    OUT_OF_MEMORY,
    INSUFFICIENT_DISK_SPACE,
    LOGIC_ERROR,
    FILE_NOT_FOUND
};
```

In the preceding example, OUT_OF_MEMORY is automatically assigned the value of 0 (zero) by the compiler because it appears first in the definition. The compiler then continues to automatically assign numbers to the enumerated constants, making INSUFFICIENT_DISK_SPACE equal to 1, LOGIC_ERROR equal to 2, and so on. If you were to approach the same example by using symbolic constants, your code would look something like this:

```
#define OUT_OF_MEMORY            0
#define INSUFFICIENT_DISK_SPACE  1
#define LOGIC_ERROR              2
#define FILE_NOT_FOUND           3
```

Each of the two methods arrives at the same result: four constants assigned numeric values to represent error codes. Consider the maintenance required, however, if you were to add two constants to represent the error codes DRIVE_NOT_READY and CORRUPT_FILE. Using the enumeration constant method, you simply would put these two constants anywhere in the enum definition. The compiler would generate two *unique* values for these constants. Using the symbolic constant method, you would have to *manually* assign two new numbers to these constants. Additionally, you would want to ensure that the numbers you assign to these constants are unique. Because you don't have to worry about the actual values, defining your constants using the enumerated method is easier than using the symbolic constant method. The enumerated method also helps prevent accidentally reusing the same number for different constants.

Another advantage of using the enumeration constant method is that your programs are more readable and thus can be understood better by others who might have to update your program later. For instance, consider the following piece of code:

```
void copy_file(char* source_file_name, char* dest_file_name)
{
    ...
    Error_Code err;
    ...
```

```
        if (drive_ready() != TRUE)
            err = DRIVE_NOT_READY;
    ...
}
```

Looking at this example, you can derive from the definition of the variable err that err should be assigned only numbers of the enumerated type Error_Code. Hence, if another programmer were to modify or add functionality to this program, the programmer would know from the definition of Error_Code what constants are valid for assigning to err.

Conversely, if the same example were to be applied using the symbolic constant method, the code would look like this:

```
void copy_file(char* source_file, char* dest_file)
{
    ...
    int err;
    ...
    if (drive_ready() != TRUE)
        err = DRIVE_NOT_READY;
    ...
}
```

Looking at the preceding example, a programmer modifying or adding functionality to the copy_file() function would not immediately know what values are valid for assigning to the err variable. The programmer would need to search for the #define DRIVE_NOT_READY statement and hope that all relevant constants are defined in the same header file. This could make maintenance more difficult than it needs to be and make your programs harder to understand.

 NOTE

> Simply defining your variable to be of an enumerated type does not ensure that only valid values of that enumerated type will be assigned to that variable. In the preceding example, the compiler will not require that only values found in the enumerated type Error_Code be assigned to err; it is up to the programmer to ensure that only valid values found in the Error_Code type definition are used.

A third advantage to using enumeration constants is that some symbolic debuggers can print the value of an enumeration constant. Conversely, most symbolic debuggers cannot print the value of a symbolic constant. This can be an enormous help in debugging your program, because if your program is stopped at a line that uses an enum, you can simply inspect that constant and instantly know its value. On the other hand, because most debuggers cannot print #define values, you would most likely have to search for that value by manually looking it up in a header file.

Cross Reference:

V.5: What is the benefit of using #define to declare a constant?

V.6: What is the benefit of using enum to declare a constant?

V.8: How are portions of a program disabled in demo versions?

Answer:

If you are distributing a demo version of your program, the preprocessor can be used to enable or disable portions of your program. The following portion of code shows how this task is accomplished, using the preprocessor directives #if and #endif:

```
int save_document(char* doc_name)
{

#if DEMO_VERSION
    printf("Sorry! You can't save documents using the DEMO version of
    ➥this program!\n");
    return(0);
#endif

    ...

}
```

When you are compiling the demo version of your program, insert the line #define DEMO_VERSION and the preprocessor will include the conditional code that you specified in the save_document() function. This action prevents the users of your demo program from saving their documents.

As a better alternative, you could define DEMO_VERSION in your compiler options when compiling and avoid having to change the source code for the program.

This technique can be applied to many different situations. For instance, you might be writing a program that will support several operating systems or operating environments. You can create macros such as WINDOWS_VER, UNIX_VER, and DOS_VER that direct the preprocessor as to what code to include in your program depending on what operating system you are compiling for.

Cross Reference:

V.32: How can you check to see whether a symbol is defined?

V.9: When should you use a macro rather than a function?

Answer:

See the answer to FAQ V.10.

Cross Reference:

V.1: What is a macro, and how do you use it?

V.10: Is it better to use a macro or a function?

V.17: How can type-insensitive macros be created?

V.10: Is it better to use a macro or a function?
Answer:

The answer depends on the situation you are writing code for. Macros have the distinct advantage of being more efficient (and faster) than functions, because their corresponding code is inserted directly into your source code at the point where the macro is called. There is no overhead involved in using a macro like there is in placing a call to a function. However, macros are generally small and cannot handle large, complex coding constructs. A function is more suited for this type of situation. Additionally, macros are expanded inline, which means that the code is replicated for each occurrence of a macro. Your code therefore could be somewhat larger when you use macros than if you were to use functions.

Thus, the choice between using a macro and using a function is one of deciding between the tradeoff of faster program speed versus smaller program size. Generally, you should use macros to replace small, repeatable code sections, and you should use functions for larger coding tasks that might require several lines of code.

Cross Reference:

V.1: What is a macro, and how do you use it?

V.17: How can type-insensitive macros be created?

V.11: What is the best way to comment out a section of code that contains comments?
Answer:

Most C compilers offer two ways of putting comments in your program. The first method is to use the /* and */ symbols to denote the beginning and end of a comment. Everything from the /* symbol to the */ symbol is considered a comment and is omitted from the compiled version of the program. This method is best for commenting out sections of code that contain many comments. For instance, you can comment out a paragraph containing comments like this:

```
/*
This portion of the program contains
a comment that is several lines long
and is not included in the compiled
version of the program.
*/
```

The other way to put comments in your program is to use the // symbol. Everything from the // symbol to the end of the current line is omitted from the compiled version of the program. This method is best for one-line comments, because the // symbol must be replicated for each line that you want to add a comment to. The preceding example, which contains four lines of comments, would not be a good candidate for this method of commenting, as demonstrated here:

```
// This portion of the program contains
// a comment that is several lines long
// and is not included in the compiled
```

```
// version of the program.
```

You should consider using the /* and */ method of commenting rather than the // method, because the // method of commenting is not ANSI compatible. Many older compilers might not support the // comments.

Cross Reference:

V.8: How are portions of a program disabled in demo versions?

V.12: What is the difference between *#include <file>* and *#include "file"*?

Answer:

When writing your C program, you can include files in two ways. The first way is to surround the file you want to include with the angled brackets < and >. This method of inclusion tells the preprocessor to look for the file in the predefined default location. This predefined default location is often an INCLUDE environment variable that denotes the path to your include files. For instance, given the INCLUDE variable

```
INCLUDE=C:\COMPILER\INCLUDE;S:\SOURCE\HEADERS;
```

using the #include <file> version of file inclusion, the compiler first checks the C:\COMPILER\INCLUDE directory for the specified file. If the file is not found there, the compiler then checks the S:\SOURCE\HEADERS directory. If the file is still not found, the preprocessor checks the current directory.

The second way to include files is to surround the file you want to include with double quotation marks. This method of inclusion tells the preprocessor to look for the file in the current directory first, then look for it in the predefined locations you have set up. Using the #include "file" version of file inclusion and applying it to the preceding example, the preprocessor first checks the current directory for the specified file. If the file is not found in the current directory, the C:\COMPILER\INCLUDE directory is searched. If the file is still not found, the preprocessor checks the S:\SOURCE\HEADERS directory.

The #include <file> method of file inclusion is often used to include *standard* headers such as stdio.h or stdlib.h. This is because these headers are rarely (if ever) modified, and they should always be read from your compiler's standard include file directory. The #include "file" method of file inclusion is often used to include *nonstandard* header files that you have created for use in your program. This is because these headers are often modified in the current directory, and you will want the preprocessor to use your newly modified version of the header rather than the older, unmodified version.

Cross Reference:

V.3: How can you avoid including a header more than once?

V.4: Can a file other than a .h file be included with #include?

V.14: Can include files be nested?

V.15: How many levels deep can include files be nested?

V.13: Can you define which header file to include at compile time?

Answer:

Yes. This can be done by using the #if, #else, and #endif preprocessor directives. For example, certain compilers use different names for header files. One such case is between Borland C++, which uses the header file alloc.h, and Microsoft C++, which uses the header file malloc.h. Both of these headers serve the same purpose, and each contains roughly the same definitions. If, however, you are writing a program that is to support Borland C++ and Microsoft C++, you must define which header to include at compile time. The following example shows how this can be done:

```
#ifdef __BORLANDC__
#include <alloc.h>
#else
#include <malloc.h>
#endif
```

When you compile your program with Borland C++, the __BORLANDC__ symbolic name is automatically defined by the compiler. You can use this predefined symbolic name to determine whether your program is being compiled with Borland C++. If it is, you must include the alloc.h file rather than the malloc.h file.

Cross Reference:

V.21: How can you tell whether a program was compiled using C versus C++?

V.32: How can you check to see whether a symbol is defined?

V.14: Can include files be nested?

Answer:

Yes. Include files can be nested any number of times. As long as you use precautionary measures (see FAQ V.3), you can avoid including the same file twice.

In the past, nesting header files was seen as bad programming practice, because it complicates the dependency tracking function of the MAKE program and thus slows down compilation. Many of today's popular compilers make up for this difficulty by implementing a concept called *precompiled headers,* in which all headers and associated dependencies are stored in a precompiled state.

Many programmers like to create a custom header file that has #include statements for every header needed for each module. This is perfectly acceptable and can help avoid potential problems relating to #include files, such as accidentally omitting an #include file in a module.

Cross Reference:

V.3: How can you avoid including a header more than once?

V.4: Can a file other than a .h file be included with #include?

V.15: How many levels deep can include files be nested?
Answer:

Even though there is no limit to the number of levels of nested include files you can have, your compiler might run out of stack space while trying to include an inordinately high number of files. This number varies according to your hardware configuration and possibly your compiler.

In practice, although nesting include files is perfectly legal, you should avoid getting nest-crazy and purposely implementing a large number of include levels. You should create an include level only where it makes sense, such as creating one include file that has an #include statement for each header required by the module you are working with.

Cross Reference:

V.3: How can you avoid including a header more than once?

V.4: Can a file other than a .h file be included with #include?

V.12: What is the difference between #include <file> and #include "file"?

V.14: Can include files be nested?

V.16: What is the concatenation operator?
Answer:

The concatenation operator (##) is used to concatenate (combine) two separate strings into one single string. The concatenation operator is often used in C macros, as the following program demonstrates:

```
#include <stdio.h>

#define SORT(x) sort_function ## x

void main(void);

void main(void)
{
    char* array;
    int   elements, element_size;

    ...

    SORT(3)(array, elements, element_size);

    ...

}
```

In the preceding example, the SORT macro uses the concatenation operator to combine the strings sort_function and whatever is passed in the parameter x. This means that the line

```
SORT(3)(array, elements, element_size);
```

is run through the preprocessor and is translated into the following line:

```
sort_function3(array, elements, element_size);
```

As you can see, the concatenation operator can come in handy when you do not know what function to call until runtime. Using the concatenation operator, you can dynamically construct the name of the function you want to call, as was done with the SORT macro.

Cross Reference:

V.1: What is a macro, and how do you use it?

V.17: How can type-insensitive macros be created?

V.17: How can type-insensitive macros be created?
Answer:

A type-insensitive macro is a macro that performs the same basic operation on different data types. This task can be accomplished by using the concatenation operator to create a call to a type-sensitive function based on the parameter passed to the macro. The following program provides an example:

```
#include <stdio.h>

#define SORT(data_type) sort_ ## data_type

void sort_int(int** i);
void sort_long(long** l);
void sort_float(float** f);
void sort_string(char** s);
void main(void);

void main(void)
{

    int** ip;
    long** lp;
    float** fp;
    char** cp;

    ...

    sort(int)(ip);
    sort(long)(lp);
    sort(float)(fp);
    sort(char)(cp);

    ...

}
```

This program contains four functions to sort four different data types: `int`, `long`, `float`, and `string` (notice that only the function prototypes are included for brevity). A macro named `SORT` was created to take the data type passed to the macro and combine it with the `sort_` string to form a valid function call that is appropriate for the data type being sorted. Thus, the string

```
sort(int)(ip);
```

translates into

```
sort_int(ip);
```

after being run through the preprocessor.

Cross Reference:

V.1: What is a macro, and how do you use it?

V.16: What is the concatenation operator?

V.18: What are the standard predefined macros?
Answer:

The ANSI C standard defines six predefined macros for use in the C language:

Macro Name	Purpose
`__LINE__`	Inserts the current source code line number in your code.
`__FILE__`	Inserts the current source code filename in your code.
`__DATE__`	Inserts the current date of compilation in your code.
`__TIME__`	Inserts the current time of compilation in your code.
`__STDC__`	Is set to 1 if you are enforcing strict ANSI C conformity.
`__cplusplus`	Is defined if you are compiling a C++ program.

The `__LINE__` and `__FILE__` symbols are commonly used for debugging purposes (see FAQs V.19 and V.20). The `__DATE__` and `__TIME__` symbols are commonly used to put a time stamp on your compiled program for version tracking purposes (see FAQ V.28). The `__STDC__` symbol is set to 1 only if you are forcing your compiler to conform to strict ANSI C standards (see FAQ V.30). The `__cplusplus` symbol is defined only when you are compiling your program using the C++ compiler (see FAQ V.21).

Cross Reference:

V.1: What is a macro, and how do you use it?

V.24: What is the `__FILE__` preprocessor command?

V.26: What is the `__LINE__` preprocessor command?

V.28: What are the `__DATE__` and `__TIME__` preprocessor commands?

V.19: How can a program be made to print the line number where an error occurs?

Answer:

The ANSI C standard includes a predefined macro named _ _LINE_ _ that can be used to insert the current source code line number in your program. This can be a very valuable macro when it comes to debugging your program and checking for logic errors. For instance, consider the following portion of code:

```c
int print_document(char* doc_name, int destination)
{
    switch (destination)
    {
        case TO_FILE:

            print_to_file(doc_name);
            break;

        case TO_SCREEN:

            print_preview(doc_name);
            break;

        case TO_PRINTER:

            print_to_printer(doc_name);
            break;

        default:

            printf("Logic error on line number %d!\n", _ _LINE_ _);
            exit(1);

    }

}
```

If the function named print_document() is passed an erroneous argument for the destination parameter (something other than TO_FILE, TO_SCREEN, and TO_PRINTER), the default case in the switch statement traps this logic error and prints the line number in which it occurred. This capability can be a tremendous help when you are trying to debug your program and track down what could be a very bad logic error.

Cross Reference:

V.18: What are the standard predefined macros?

V.20: How can a program be made to print the name of a source file where an error occurs?

V.21: How can you tell whether a program was compiled using C versus C++?

V.28: What are the _ _DATE_ _ and _ _TIME_ _ preprocessor commands?

V.20: How can a program be made to print the name of a source file where an error occurs?

Answer:

The ANSI C standard includes a predefined macro named _ _FILE_ _ that can be used to insert the current source code filename in your program. This macro, like the _ _LINE_ _ macro (explained in FAQ V.19), can be very valuable when it comes to debugging your program and checking for logic errors. For instance, the following code builds on the example for FAQ V.19 by including the filename as well as the line number when logic errors are trapped:

```c
int print_document(char* doc_name, int destination)
{

    switch (destination)
    {
        case TO_FILE:

            print_to_file(doc_name);
            break;

        case TO_SCREEN:

            print_preview(doc_name);
            break;

        case TO_PRINTER:

            print_to_printer(doc_name);
            break;

        default:

            printf("Logic error on line number %d in the file %s!\n",
                    __LINE__, __FILE__);
            exit(1);

    }
}
```

Now, any erroneous values for the destination parameter can be trapped, and the offending source file and line number can be printed.

Cross Reference:

V.18: What are the standard predefined macros?

V.19: How can a program be made to print the line number where an error occurs?

V.21: How can you tell whether a program was compiled using C versus C++?

V.28: What are the _ _DATE_ _ and _ _TIME_ _ preprocessor commands?

V.21: How can you tell whether a program was compiled using C versus C++?

Answer:

The ANSI standard for the C language defines a symbol named _ _cplusplus that is defined only when you are compiling a C++ program. If you are compiling a C program, the _ _cplusplus symbol is undefined. Therefore, you can check to see whether the C++ compiler has been invoked with the following method:

```
#ifdef _ _cplusplus              /* Is _ _cplusplus defined? */
#define  USING_C FALSE           /* Yes, we are not using C */
#else
#define  USING_C TRUE            /* No, we are using C */
#endif
```

When the preprocessor is invoked, it sets USING_C to FALSE if the _ _cplusplus symbol is defined. Otherwise, if _ _cplusplus is undefined, it sets USING_C to TRUE. Later in your program, you can check the value of the USING_C constant to determine whether the C++ compiler is being used.

Cross Reference:

V.18: What are the standard predefined macros?

V.19: How can a program be made to print the line number where an error occurs?

V.20: How can a program be made to print the name of a source file where an error occurs?

V.28: What are the _ _DATE_ _ and _ _TIME_ _ preprocessor commands?

V.22: What is a pragma?

Answer:

The #pragma preprocessor directive allows each compiler to implement compiler-specific features that can be turned on and off with the #pragma statement. For instance, your compiler might support a feature called *loop optimization*. This feature can be invoked as a command-line option or as a #pragma directive. To implement this option using the #pragma directive, you would put the following line into your code:

```
#pragma loop_opt(on)
```

Conversely, you can turn off loop optimization by inserting the following line into your code:

```
#pragma loop_opt(off)
```

Sometimes you might have a certain function that causes your compiler to produce a warning such as Parameter xxx is never used in function yyy or some other warning that you are well aware of but choose to ignore. You can temporarily disable this warning message on some compilers by using a #pragma directive to turn off the warning message before the function and use another #pragma directive to turn it back on after the function. For instance, consider the following example, in which the function named insert_record() generates a warning message that has the unique ID of 100. You can temporarily disable this warning as shown here:

```
#pragma warn -100     /* Turn off the warning message for warning #100 */

int insert_record(REC* r)   /* Body of the function insert_record() */
{

    /* insert_rec() function statements go here... */

}

#pragma warn +100 /* Turn the warning message for warning #100 back on */
```

Check your compiler's documentation for a list of #pragma directives. As stated earlier, each compiler's implementation of this feature is different, and what works on one compiler almost certainly won't work on another. Nevertheless, the #pragma directives can come in very handy when you're turning on and off some of your compiler's favorite (or most annoying) features.

Cross Reference:

V.2: What will the preprocessor do for a program?

V.23: What is #line used for?

V.23: What is *line* used for?
Answer:

The #line preprocessor directive is used to reset the values of the _ _LINE_ _ and _ _FILE_ _ symbols, respectively. This directive is commonly used in fourth-generation languages that generate C language source files. For instance, if you are using a fourth-generation language named "X," the 4GL compiler will generate C source code routines for compilation based on your 4GL source code. If errors are present in your 4GL code, they can be mapped back to your 4GL source code by using the #line directive. The 4GL code generator simply inserts a line like this into the generated C source:

```
#line 752, "XSOURCE.X"

void generated_code(void)
{

...

}
```

Now, if an error is detected anywhere in the generated_code() function, it can be mapped back to the original 4GL source file named XSOURCE.X. This way, the 4GL compiler can report the 4GL source code line that has the error in it.

When the #line directive is used, the _ _LINE_ _ symbol is reset to the first argument after the #line keyword (in the preceding example, 752), and the _ _FILE_ _ symbol is reset to the second argument after the #line keyword (in the preceding example, "XSOURCE.X"). All references hereafter to the _ _LINE_ _ and _ _FILE_ _ symbols will reflect the reset values and not the original values of _ _LINE_ _ and _ _FILE_ _.

Cross Reference:

V.2: What will the preprocessor do for a program?

V.22: What is a pragma?

V.24: What is the _ _*FILE*_ _ preprocessor command?
Answer:

See the answer to FAQ V.20.

Cross Reference:

V.18: What are the standard predefined macros?

V.19: How can a program be made to print the line number where an error occurs?

V.20: How can a program be made to print the name of a source file where an error occurs?

V.21: How can you tell whether a program was compiled using C versus C++?

V.28: What are the _ _DATE_ _ and _ _TIME_ _ preprocessor commands?

V.25: How can I print the name of the source file in a program?
Answer:

See the answer to FAQ V.20.

Cross Reference:

V.18: What are the standard predefined macros?

V.19: How can a program be made to print the line number where an error occurs?

V.20: How can a program be made to print the name of a source file where an error occurs?

V.21: How can you tell whether a program was compiled using C versus C++?

V.28: What are the _ _DATE_ _ and _ _TIME_ _ preprocessor commands?

V.26: What is the _ _*LINE*_ _ preprocessor command?
Answer:

See the answer to FAQ V.19.

Cross Reference:

V.18: What are the standard predefined macros?

V.19: How can a program be made to print the line number where an error occurs?

V.20: How can a program be made to print the name of a source file where an error occurs?

V.21: How can you tell whether a program was compiled using C versus C++?

V.28: What are the _ _DATE_ _ and _ _TIME_ _ preprocessor commands?

V.27: How can I print the current line number of the source file in a program?

Answer:

See the answer to FAQ V.19.

Cross Reference:

V.18: What are the standard predefined macros?

V.19: How can a program be made to print the line number where an error occurs?

V.20: How can a program be made to print the name of a source file where an error occurs?

V.21: How can you tell whether a program was compiled using C versus C++?

V.28: What are the _ _DATE_ _ and _ _TIME_ _ preprocessor commands?

V.28: What are the _ _*DATE*_ _ and _ _*TIME*_ _ preprocessor commands?

Answer:

The _ _DATE_ _ macro is used to insert the current compilation date in the form "mm dd yyyy" into your program. Similarly, the _ _TIME_ _ macro is used to insert the current compilation time in the form "hh:mm:ss" into your program. This date-and-time-stamp feature should not be confused with the *current* system date and time. Rather, these two macros enable you to keep track of the date and time your program was last *compiled*. This feature can come in very handy when you are trying to track different versions of your program. For instance, many programmers like to put a function in their programs that gives compilation information as to when the current module was compiled. This task can be performed as shown here:

```
#include <stdio.h>

void main(void);
void print_version_info(void);

void main(void)
{
```

```
        print_version_info();

}

void print_version_info(void)
{

    printf("Date Compiled: %s\n", __DATE__);
    printf("Time Compiled: %s\n", __TIME__);

}
```

In this example, the function print_version_info() is used to show the date and time stamp of the last time this module was compiled.

Cross Reference:

V.18: What are the standard predefined macros?

V.19: How can a program be made to print the line number where an error occurs?

V.20: How can a program be made to print the name of a source file where an error occurs?

V.21: How can you tell whether a program was compiled using C versus C++?

V.29: How can I print the compile date and time in a program?
Answer:

See the answer to FAQ V.28.

Cross Reference:

V.18: What are the standard predefined macros?

V.19: How can a program be made to print the line number where an error occurs?

V.20: How can a program be made to print the name of a source file where an error occurs?

V.21: How can you tell whether a program was compiled using C versus C++?

V.28: What are the __DATE__ and __TIME__ preprocessor commands?

V.30: How can you be sure that a program follows the ANSI C standard?
Answer:

The ANSI C standard provides a predefined symbol named __STDC__ that is set to 1 when the compiler is enforcing strict ANSI standard conformance. If you want your programs to be 100 percent ANSI conformant, you should ensure that the __STDC__ symbol is defined. If the program is being compiled with non-ANSI options, the _ _STDC_ _ symbol is undefined. The following code segment shows how this symbol can be checked:

```
...

#ifdef _ _STDC_ _
    printf("Congratulations! You are conforming perfectly to the ANSI
    ➥standards!\n");
#else
    printf("Shame on you, you nonconformist anti-ANSI rabble-rousing
    ➥programmer!\n");
#endif

...
```

Cross Reference:

V.1: What is a macro?

V.24: What is the _ _FILE_ _ preprocessor command?

V.26: What is the _ _LINE_ _ preprocessor command?

V.28: What are the _ _DATE_ _ and _ _TIME_ _ preprocessor commands?

V.31: How do you override a defined macro?
Answer:

You can use the #undef preprocessor directive to undefine (override) a previously defined macro. Many programmers like to ensure that their applications are using their own terms when defining symbols such as TRUE and FALSE. Your program can check to see whether these symbols have been defined already, and if they have, you can override them with your own definitions of TRUE and FALSE. The following portion of code shows how this task can be accomplished:

```
...

#ifdef TRUE         /* Check to see if TRUE has been defined yet */
#undef TRUE         /* If so, undefine it */
#endif

#define TRUE 1      /* Define TRUE the way we want it defined */

#ifdef FALSE        /* Check to see if FALSE has been defined yet */
#undef FALSE        /* If so, undefine it */
#endif

#define FALSE !TRUE  /* Define FALSE the way we want it defined */

...
```

In the preceding example, the symbols TRUE and FALSE are checked to see whether they have been defined yet. If so, they are undefined, or overridden, using the #undef preprocessor directive, and they are redefined in the desired manner. If you were to eliminate the #undef statements in the preceding example, the compiler would warn you that you have multiple definitions of the same symbol. By using this technique, you can avoid this warning and ensure that your programs are using valid symbol definitions.

Cross Reference:

V.1: What is a macro, and how do you use it?

V.10: Is it better to use a macro or a function?

V.16: What is the concatenation operator?

V.17: How can type-insensitive macros be created?

V.18: What are the standard predefined macros?

V.31: How do you override a defined macro?

V.32: How can you check to see whether a symbol is defined?
Answer:

You can use the `#ifdef` and `#ifndef` preprocessor directives to check whether a symbol has been defined (`#ifdef`) or whether it has not been defined (`#ifndef`). Many programmers like to ensure that their own version of NULL is defined, not someone else's. This task can be accomplished as shown here:

```
#ifdef NULL
#undef NULL
#endif

#define NULL (void*) 0
```

The first line, `#ifdef NULL`, checks to see whether the NULL symbol has been defined. If so, it is undefined using `#undef NULL` (see FAQ V.31), and the new definition of NULL is defined.

To check whether a symbol has not been defined yet, you would use the `#ifndef` preprocessor directive. See FAQ V.3 for an example of how you can use `#ifndef` to determine whether you have already included a particular header file in your program.

Cross Reference:

V.3: How can you avoid including a header more than once?

V.8: How are portions of a program disabled in demo versions?

V.33: What common macros are available?
Answer:

See the answer to FAQ V.18.

Cross Reference:

V.1: What is a macro, and how do you use it?

V.18: What are the standard predefined macros?

V.24: What is the _ _FILE_ _ preprocessor command?

V.26: What is the _ _LINE_ _ preprocessor command?

V.28: What are the _ _DATE_ _ and _ _TIME_ _ preprocessor commands?

CHAPTER VI

◆

Working with Strings

This chapter focuses on manipulating strings—copying strings, copying portions of strings, performing string comparisons, right-justifying, removing trailing and leading spaces, executing string conversions, and more. The standard C library provides many functions that aid in string manipulation, and several of these functions will be covered in this chapter.

You will probably find yourself using string manipulation techniques often when writing your C programs. The examples in this chapter are provided to help you get a jump-start on utilizing the functions you need in order to be productive right away. Pay close attention to the examples provided here—several of them could save you valuable time when you're writing your programs.

VI.1: What is the difference between a string copy (*strcpy*) and a memory copy (*memcpy*)? When should each be used?

Answer:

The strcpy() function is designed to work exclusively with strings. It copies each byte of the source string to the destination string and stops when the terminating *null character*

(\0) has been moved. On the other hand, the memcpy() function is designed to work with any type of data. Because not all data ends with a null character, you must provide the memcpy() function with the number of bytes you want to copy from the source to the destination. The following program shows examples of both the strcpy() and the memcpy() functions:

```c
#include <stdio.h>
#include <string.h>

typedef struct cust_str {
    int   id;
    char last_name[20];
    char first_name[15];
} CUSTREC;

void main(void);

void main(void)
{

    char*   src_string = "This is the source string";
    char    dest_string[50];
    CUSTREC src_cust;
    CUSTREC dest_cust;

    printf("Hello!  I'm going to copy src_string into dest_string!\n");

    /* Copy src_string into dest_string. Notice that the destination
       string is the first argument. Notice also that the strcpy()
       function returns a pointer to the destination string. */

    printf("Done! dest_string is: %s\n",
            strcpy(dest_string, src_string));

    printf("Encore! Let's copy one CUSTREC to another.\n");
    printf("I'll copy src_cust into dest_cust.\n");

    /* First, initialize the src_cust data members. */

    src_cust.id = 1;

    strcpy(src_cust.last_name, "Strahan");
    strcpy(src_cust.first_name, "Troy");

    /* Now, use the memcpy() function to copy the src_cust structure to
       the dest_cust structure. Notice that, just as with strcpy(), the
       destination comes first. */

    memcpy(&dest_cust, &src_cust, sizeof(CUSTREC));

    printf("Done! I just copied customer number #%d (%s %s).",
            dest_cust.id, dest_cust.first_name, dest_cust.last_name);

}
```

When dealing with strings, you generally should use the strcpy() function, because it is easier to use with strings. When dealing with abstract data other than strings (such as structures), you should use the memcpy() function.

Cross Reference:

VI.6: How can I copy just a portion of a string?

VI.9: How do you print only part of a string?

VI.2: How can I remove the trailing spaces from a string?

Answer:

The C language does not provide a standard function that removes trailing spaces from a string. It is easy, however, to build your own function to do just this. The following program uses a custom function named rtrim() to remove the trailing spaces from a string. It carries out this action by iterating through the string backward, starting at the character before the terminating null character (\0) and ending when it finds the first nonspace character. When the program finds a nonspace character, it sets the next character in the string to the terminating null character (\0), thereby effectively eliminating all the trailing blanks. Here is how this task is performed:

```c
#include <stdio.h>
#include <string.h>

void main(void);
char* rtrim(char*);

void main(void)
{

    char* trail_str = "This string has trailing spaces in it.              ";

    /* Show the status of the string before calling the rtrim()
       function. */

    printf("Before calling rtrim(), trail_str is '%s'\n", trail_str);
    printf("and has a length of %d.\n", strlen(trail_str));

    /* Call the rtrim() function to remove the trailing blanks. */

    rtrim(trail_str);

    /* Show the status of the string
       after calling the rtrim() function. */

    printf("After calling rtrim(), trail_str is '%s'\n", trail_str);
    printf("and has a length of %d.\n", strlen(trail_str));

}

/* The rtrim() function removes trailing spaces from a string. */

char* rtrim(char* str)
{
```

```
        int n = strlen(str) - 1;      /* Start at the character BEFORE
                                         the null character (\0). */

        while (n>0)                /* Make sure we don't go out of bounds... */
        {
            if (*(str+n) != ' ')      /*  If we find a nonspace character: */
            {
                *(str+n+1) = '\0'; /* Put the null character at one
                                      character past our current
                                      position. */
                break;                /* Break out of the loop. */
            }
            else      /* Otherwise, keep moving backward in the string. */
                n--;
        }

        return str;                   /* Return a pointer to the string. */

}
```

Notice that the rtrim() function works because in C, strings are terminated by the null character. With the insertion of a null character after the last nonspace character, the string is considered terminated at that point, and all characters beyond the null character are ignored.

Cross Reference:

VI.3: How can I remove the leading spaces from a string?

VI.5: How can I pad a string to a known length?

VI.3: How can I remove the leading spaces from a string?
Answer:

The C language does not provide a standard function that removes leading spaces from a string. It is easy, however, to build your own function to do just this. Using the example from FAQ VI.2, you can easily construct a custom function that uses the rtrim() function in conjunction with the standard C library function strrev() to remove the leading spaces from a string. Look at how this task is performed:

```
#include <stdio.h>
#include <string.h>

void main(void);
char* ltrim(char*);
char* rtrim(char*);

void main(void)
{
    char* lead_str = "            This string has leading spaces in it.";

    /* Show the status of the string before calling the ltrim()
       function. */
```

```
        printf("Before calling ltrim(), lead_str is '%s'\n", lead_str);
        printf("and has a length of %d.\n", strlen(lead_str));

        /* Call the ltrim() function to remove the leading blanks. */

        ltrim(lead_str);

        /* Show the status of the string
           after calling the ltrim() function. */

        printf("After calling ltrim(), lead_str is '%s'\n", lead_str);
        printf("and has a length of %d.\n", strlen(lead_str));

}

/* The ltrim() function removes leading spaces from a string. */

char* ltrim(char* str)
{

        strrev(str);    /* Call strrev() to reverse the string. */

        rtrim(str);     /* Call rtrim() to remove the "trailing" spaces. */

        strrev(str);    /* Restore the string's original order. */

        return str;     /* Return a pointer to the string. */

}

/* The rtrim() function removes trailing spaces from a string. */

char* rtrim(char* str)
{

        int n = strlen(str) - 1;    /* Start at the character BEFORE
                                       the null character (\0). */

        while (n>0)             /* Make sure we don't go out of bounds... */
        {
            if (*(str+n) != ' ')    /* If we find a nonspace character: */
            {
                *(str+n+1) = '\0'; /* Put the null character at one
                                       character past our current
                                       position. */
                break;              /* Break out of the loop. */
            }
            else        /* Otherwise, keep moving backward in the string. */
                n--;
        }

        return str;                 /* Return a pointer to the string. */

}
```

Notice that the ltrim() function performs the following tasks: First, it calls the standard C library function strrev(), which reverses the string that is passed to it. This action puts the original string in reverse order, thereby creating "trailing spaces" rather than leading spaces. Now, the rtrim() function (that was created in the example from FAQ VI.2) is used to remove the "trailing spaces" from the string. After this task is done, the `strrev()` function is called again to "reverse" the string, thereby putting it back in its original order. See FAQ VI.2 for an explanation of the `rtrim()` function.

Cross Reference:

VI.2: How can I remove the trailing spaces from a string?

VI.5: How can I pad a string to a known length?

VI.4: How can I right-justify a string?
Answer:

Even though the C language does not provide a standard function that right-justifies a string, you can easily build your own function to perform this action. Using the `rtrim()` function (introduced in the example for FAQ VI.2), you can create your own function to take a string and right-justify it. Here is how this task is accomplished:

```c
#include <stdio.h>
#include <string.h>
#include <malloc.h>

void main(void);
char* rjust(char*);
char* rtrim(char*);

void main(void)
{
    char* rjust_str = "This string is not right-justified.          ";

    /* Show the status of the string before calling the rjust()
       function. */

    printf("Before calling rjust(), rjust_str is '%s'\n.", rjust_str);

    /* Call the rjust() function to right-justify this string. */

    rjust(rjust_str);

    /* Show the status of the string
       after calling the rjust() function. */

    printf("After calling rjust(), rjust_str is '%s'\n.", rjust_str);

}
/* The rjust() function right-justifies a string. */

char* rjust(char* str)
{
    int n = strlen(str);    /* Save the original length of the string. */
    char* dup_str;
```

```
    dup_str = strdup(str);  /* Make an exact duplicate of the string. */

    rtrim(dup_str);          /* Trim off the trailing spaces. */

    /* Call sprintf() to do a virtual "printf" back into the original
       string. By passing sprintf() the length of the original string,
       we force the output to be the same size as the original, and by
       default the sprintf() right-justifies the output. The sprintf()
       function fills the beginning of the string with spaces to make
       it the same size as the original string. */

    sprintf(str, "%*.*s", n, n, dup_str);

    free(dup_str);    /* Free the memory taken by
                         the duplicated string. */

    return str;       /* Return a pointer to the string. */

}

/* The rtrim() function removes trailing spaces from a string. */

char* rtrim(char* str)
{
    int n = strlen(str) - 1;  /* Start at the character BEFORE the null
                                 character (\0). */

    while (n>0)               /* Make sure we don't go out of bounds... */
    {
        if (*(str+n) != ' ')    /* If we find a nonspace character: */
        {
            *(str+n+1) = '\0'; /* Put the null character at one
                                  character past our current
                                  position. */
            break;              /* Break out of the loop. */
        }
        else       /* Otherwise, keep moving backward in the string. */
            n--;
    }

    return str;                 /* Return a pointer to the string. */

}
```

The rjust() function first saves the length of the original string in a variable named n. This step is needed because the output string must be the same length as the input string. Next, the rjust() function calls the standard C library function named strdup() to create a duplicate of the original string. A duplicate of the string is required because the original version of the string is going to be overwritten with a right-justified version. After the duplicate string is created, a call to the rtrim() function is invoked (using the duplicate string, not the original), which eliminates all trailing spaces from the duplicate string.

Next, the standard C library function sprintf() is called to rewrite the new string to its original place in memory. The sprintf() function is passed the original length of the string (stored in n), thereby forcing the output string to be the same length as the original. Because sprintf() by default right-justifies string output, the output string is filled with leading spaces to make it the same size as the original string. This has the effect of right-justifying the input string. Finally, because the strdup() function dynamically allocates memory, the free() function is called to free up the memory taken by the duplicate string.

Cross Reference:

VI.5: How can I pad a string to a known length?

VI.5: How can I pad a string to a known length?
Answer:

Padding strings to a fixed length can be handy when you are printing fixed-length data such as tables or spreadsheets. You can easily perform this task using the printf() function. The following example program shows how to accomplish this task:

```c
#include <stdio.h>

char *data[25] = {
     "REGION", "--Q1--",    "--Q2--",   "--Q3--", "   --Q4--",
     "North", "10090.50", "12200.10", "26653.12", "62634.32",
     "South", "21662.37", "95843.23", "23788.23", "48279.28",
     "East", "23889.38", "23789.05", "89432.84", "29874.48",
     "West", "85933.82", "74373.23", "78457.23", "28799.84" };

void main(void);

void main(void)
{

    int x;

    for (x=0; x<25; x++)
    {

        if ((x % 5) == 0 && (x != 0))
            printf("\n");

        printf("%-10.10s", data[x]);

    }

}
```

In this example, a character array (char* data[]) is filled with this year's sales data for four regions. Of course, you would want to print this data in an orderly fashion, not just print one figure after the other with no formatting. This being the case, the following statement is used to print the data:

```c
printf("%-10.10s", data[x]);
```

The "%-10.10s" argument tells the printf() function that you are printing a string and you want to force it to be 10 characters long. By default, the string is right-justified, but by including the minus sign (–) before the first 10, you tell the printf() function to left-justify your string. This action forces the printf() function to pad the string with spaces to make it 10 characters long. The result is a clean, formatted spreadsheet-like output:

```
REGION      --Q1--    --Q2--     --Q3--    --Q4--
North      10090.50  12200.10   26653.12  62634.32
South      21662.37  95843.23   23788.23  48279.28
East       23889.38  23789.05   89432.84  29874.48
West       85933.82  74373.23   78457.23  28799.84
```

Cross Reference:

VI.4: How can I right-justify a string?

VI.6: How can I copy just a portion of a string?
Answer:

You can use the standard C library function strncpy() to copy one portion of a string into another string. The strncpy() function takes three arguments: the first argument is the destination string, the second argument is the source string, and the third argument is an integer representing the number of characters you want to copy from the source string to the destination string. For example, consider the following program, which uses the strncpy() function to copy portions of one string to another:

```c
#include <stdio.h>
#include <string.h>

void main(void);

void main(void)
{
    char* source_str = "THIS IS THE SOURCE STRING";
    char dest_str1[40] = {0}, dest_str2[40] = {0};

    /* Use strncpy() to copy only the first 11 characters. */

    strncpy(dest_str1, source_str, 11);

    printf("How about that! dest_str1 is now: '%s'!!!\n", dest_str1);

    /* Now, use strncpy() to copy only the last 13 characters. */

    strncpy(dest_str2, source_str + (strlen(source_str) - 13), 13);

    printf("Whoa! dest_str2 is now: '%s'!!!\n", dest_str2);

}
```

The first call to strncpy() in this example program copies the first 11 characters of the source string into dest_str1. This example is fairly straightforward, one you might use often. The second call is a bit more complicated and deserves some explanation. In the second argument to the strncpy() function call, the total length of the source_str string is calculated (using the strlen() function). Then, 13 (the number of characters you want to print) is subtracted from the total length of source_str. This gives the number of remaining characters in source_str. This number is then added to the address of source_str to give a pointer to an address in the source string that is 13 characters from the end of source_str. Then, for the last argument, the number 13 is specified to denote that 13 characters are to be copied out of the string. The combination of these three arguments in the second call to strncpy() sets dest_str2 equal to the last 13 characters of source_str.

The example program prints the following output:

```
How about that! dest_str1 is now: 'THIS IS THE'!!!
Whoa! dest_str2 is now: 'SOURCE STRING'!!!
```

Notice that before source_str was copied to dest_str1 and dest_st2, dest_str1 and dest_str2 had to be initialized to null characters (\0). This is because the strncpy() function does not automatically append a null character to the string you are copying to. Therefore, you must ensure that you have put the null character after the string you have copied, or else you might wind up with garbage being printed.

Cross Reference:

VI.1: What is the difference between a string copy (strcpy) and a memory copy (memcpy)? When should each be used?

VI.9: How do you print only part of a string?

VI.7: How can I convert a number to a string?
Answer:

The standard C library provides several functions for converting numbers of all formats (integers, longs, floats, and so on) to strings and vice versa. One of these functions, itoa(), is used here to illustrate how an integer is converted to a string:

```c
#include <stdio.h>
#include <stdlib.h>

void main(void);

void main(void)
{
    int num = 100;
    char str[25];

    itoa(num, str, 10);

    printf("The number 'num' is %d and the string 'str' is %s.\n",
            num, str);

}
```

Notice that the itoa() function takes three arguments: the first argument is the number you want to convert to the string, the second is the destination string to put the converted number into, and the third is the base, or radix, to be used when converting the number. The preceding example uses the common base 10 to convert the number to the string.

The following functions can be used to convert integers to strings:

Function Name	Purpose
itoa()	Converts an integer value to a string.
ltoa()	Converts a long integer value to a string.
ultoa()	Converts an unsigned long integer value to a string.

Note that the itoa(), ltoa(), and ultoa() functions are not ANSI compatible. An alternative way to convert an integer to a string (that is ANSI compatible) is to use the sprintf() function, as in the following example:

```
#include <stdio.h>
#include <stdlib.h>

void main(void);

void main(void)
{

    int num = 100;
    char str[25];

    sprintf(str, "%d", num);

    printf("The number 'num' is %d and the string 'str' is %s.\n",
            num, str);

}
```

When floating-point numbers are being converted, a different set of functions must be used. Here is an example of a program that uses the standard C library function fcvt() to convert a floating-point value to a string:

```
#include <stdio.h>
#include <stdlib.h>

void main(void);

void main(void)
{

    double num = 12345.678;
    char* str;
    int dec_pl, sign, ndigits = 3;     /* Keep 3 digits of precision. */

    str = fcvt(num, ndigits, &dec_pl, &sign);  /* Convert the float
                                                   to a string. */

    printf("Original number:  %f\n", num);     /* Print the original
                                                   floating-point
                                                   value. */
    printf("Converted string: %s\n", str);     /* Print the converted
```

```
                                                  string's value. */
        printf("Decimal place:    %d\n", dec_pl);  /* Print the location of
                                                      the decimal point. */
        printf("Sign:             %d\n", sign);    /* Print the sign.
                                                      0 = positive,
                                                      1 = negative. */

}
```

Notice that the fcvt() function is quite different from the itoa() function used previously. The fcvt() function takes four arguments. The first argument is the floating-point value you want to convert. The second argument is the number of digits to be stored to the right of the decimal point. The third argument is a pointer to an integer that is used to return the position of the decimal point in the converted string. The fourth argument is a pointer to an integer that is used to return the sign of the converted number (0 is positive, 1 is negative).

Note that the converted string does not contain the actual decimal point. Instead, the fcvt() returns the *position* of the decimal point as it would have been if it were in the string. In the preceding example, the dec_pl integer variable contains the number 5 because the decimal point is located after the fifth digit in the resulting string. If you wanted the resulting string to include the decimal point, you could use the gcvt() function (described in the following table).

The following functions can be used to convert floating-point values to strings:

Function Name	Purpose
ecvt()	Converts a double-precision floating-point value to a string without an embedded decimal point.
fcvt()	Same as ecvt(), but forces the precision to a specified number of digits.
gcvt()	Converts a double-precision floating-point value to a string with an embedded decimal point.

See FAQ VI.8 for an explanation of how you can convert strings to numbers.

Cross Reference:

VI.8: How can I convert a string to a number?

VI.8: How can I convert a string to a number?
Answer:

The standard C library provides several functions for converting strings to numbers of all formats (integers, longs, floats, and so on) and vice versa. One of these functions, atoi(), is used here to illustrate how a string is converted to an integer:

```
#include <stdio.h>
#include <stdlib.h>

void main(void);
```

```
void main(void)
{

    int num;
    char* str = "100";

    num = atoi(str);

    printf("The string 'str' is %s and the number 'num' is %d.\n",
              str, num);

}
```

To use the atoi() function, you simply pass it the string containing the number you want to convert. The return value from the atoi() function is the converted integer value.

The following functions can be used to convert strings to numbers:

Function Name	Purpose
atof()	Converts a string to a double-precision floating-point value.
atoi()	Converts a string to an integer.
atol()	Converts a string to a long integer.
strtod()	Converts a string to a double-precision floating-point value and reports any "leftover" numbers that could not be converted.
strtol()	Converts a string to a long integer and reports any "leftover" numbers that could not be converted.
strtoul()	Converts a string to an unsigned long integer and reports any "leftover" numbers that could not be converted.

Sometimes, you might want to trap overflow errors that can occur when converting a string to a number that results in an overflow condition. The following program shows an example of the strtoul() function, which traps this overflow condition:

```
#include <stdio.h>
#include <stdlib.h>
#include <limits.h>

void main(void);

void main(void)
{

    char* str  = "12345678910111213141516171819920";
    unsigned long num;
    char* leftover;

    num = strtoul(str, &leftover, 10);

    printf("Original string:     %s\n", str);
    printf("Converted number:    %lu\n", num);
    printf("Leftover characters: %s\n", leftover);

}
```

In this example, the string to be converted is much too large to fit into an unsigned long integer variable. The strtoul() function therefore returns ULONG_MAX (4294967295) and sets the char* leftover to point to the character in the string that caused it to overflow. It also sets the global variable errno to ERANGE to notify the caller of the function that an overflow condition has occurred. The strtod() and strtol() functions work exactly the same way as the strtoul() function shown above. Refer to your C compiler documentation for more information regarding the syntax of these functions.

Cross Reference:

VI.7: How can I convert a number to a string?

VI.9: How do you print only part of a string?
Answer:

FAQ VI.6 showed you how to copy only part of a string. But how do you *print* a portion of a string? The answer is to use some of the same techniques as in the example for FAQ VI.6, except this time, rather than the strncpy() function, the printf() function is used. The following program is a modified version of the example from FAQ VI.6 that shows how to print only part of a string using the printf() function:

```c
#include <stdio.h>
#include <string.h>

void main(void);

void main(void)
{

    char* source_str = "THIS IS THE SOURCE STRING";

    /* Use printf() to print the first 11 characters of source_str. */

    printf("First 11 characters: '%11.11s'\n", source_str);

    /* Use printf() to print only the
       last 13 characters of source_str. */

    printf("Last 13 characters: '%13.13s'\n",
                source_str + (strlen(source_str) - 13));

}
```

This example program produces the following output:

```
First 11 characters: 'THIS IS THE'
Last 13 characters: 'SOURCE STRING'
```

The first call to printf() uses the argument "%11.11s" to force the printf() function to make the output exactly 11 characters long. Because the source string is longer than 11 characters, it is truncated, and only the first 11 characters are printed. The second call to printf() is a bit more tricky. The total length of the source_str string is calculated (using the strlen() function). Then, 13 (the number of characters you want to print) is subtracted from the total length of source_str. This gives the number of remaining characters in source_str. This number is then added to the address of source_str to give a pointer to an address in the source string that is 13 characters from the end of source_str. By using the argument "%13.13s", the program forces the output to be exactly 13 characters long, and thus the last 13 characters of the string are printed.

See FAQ VI.6 for a similar example of extracting a portion of a string using the strncpy() function rather than the printf() function.

Cross Reference:

VI.1: What is the difference between a string copy (strcpy) and a memory copy (memcpy)? When should each be used?

VI.6: How can I copy just a portion of a string?

VI.10: How do you remove spaces from the end of a string?
Answer:

See the answer to FAQ VI.2.

Cross Reference:

VI.2: How can I remove the trailing spaces from a string?

VI.11: How can you tell whether two strings are the same?
Answer:

The standard C library provides several functions to compare two strings to see whether they are the same. One of these functions, strcmp(), is used here to show how this task is accomplished:

```c
#include <stdio.h>
#include <string.h>

void main(void);

void main(void)
{
    char* str_1 = "abc";
    char* str_2 = "abc";
    char* str_3 = "ABC";

    if (strcmp(str_1, str_2) == 0)
        printf("str_1 is equal to str_2.\n");
    else
        printf("str_1 is not equal to str_2.\n");
```

```
    if (strcmp(str_1, str_3) == 0)
        printf("str_1 is equal to str_3.\n");
    else
        printf("str_1 is not equal to str_3.\n");

}
```

This program produces the following output:

```
str_1 is equal to str_2.
str_1 is not equal to str_3.
```

Notice that the strcmp() function is passed two arguments that correspond to the two strings you want to compare. It performs a case-sensitive lexicographic comparison of the two strings and returns one of the following values:

Return Value	Meaning
< 0	The first string is less than the second string.
0	The two strings are equal.
> 0	The first string is greater than the second string.

In the preceding example code, strcmp() returns 0 when comparing str_1 (which is "abc") and str_2 (which is "abc"). However, when comparing str_1 (which is "abc") with str_3 (which is "ABC"), strcmp() returns a value greater than 0, because the string "ABC" is greater than (in ASCII order) the string "abc".

Many variations of the strcmp() function perform the same basic function (comparing two strings), but with slight differences. The following table lists some of the functions available that are similar to strcmp():

Function Name	Description
strcmp()	Case-sensitive comparison of two strings
strcmpi()	Case-insensitive comparison of two strings
stricmp()	Same as strcmpi()
strncmp()	Case-sensitive comparison of a portion of two strings
strnicmp()	Case-insensitive comparison of a portion of two strings

Looking at the example provided previously, if you were to replace the call to strcmp() with a call to strcmpi() (a case-insensitive version of strcmp()), the two strings "abc" and "ABC" would be reported as being equal.

Cross Reference:

VI.1: What is the difference between a string copy (strcpy) and a memory copy (memcpy)? When should each be used?

CHAPTER VII

Pointers and Memory Allocation

Pointers are the double-edged swords of C programming. Using them, you can cut through to the heart of a problem. Your code can be efficient, terse, and elegant. Pointers can also slice your program to shreds.

With a pointer, you can write data anywhere. That's the point. If you have a "wild" pointer that points in the wrong place, none of your data is safe. The data you put on the heap can get damaged. The data structures used to manage the heap can be corrupted. Even operating-system information can be modified. Maybe all three.

What happens next? That depends on how badly mangled everything has gotten, and how much more the damaged parts of memory are used. At some point, maybe right away, maybe later, some function runs into real trouble. It could be one of the allocation functions, or one of your functions, or a library function.

The program might die with an error message. It might hang. It might go into an infinite loop. It might produce bad results. Or maybe, this time, nothing essential gets damaged, and the program seems to be just fine.

The exciting part is that the program might not fail visibly until long after the root problem has happened. It might not fail at all when you test it, only when users run it.

In C programs, any wild pointer or out-of-bounds array subscript can bring the house down this way. So can "double deallocation" (see FAQ VII.22). Did you ever wonder why some C programmers earn big bucks? Now you know part of the answer.

There are memory allocation tools that can help find leaks (see FAQ VII.21), double deallocations, some wild pointers and subscripts, and other problems. Such tools are not portable; they work only with specific operating systems, or even specific brands of compilers. If you can find such a tool, get it and use it; it can save you a lot of time and improve the quality of your software.

Pointer arithmetic is unique to C (and its derivatives, such as C++). Assembler language enables you to perform arithmetic on addresses, but all notion of data typing is lost. Most high-level languages don't enable you to do anything with pointers except see what they point to. C is different.

C does arithmetic on pointers the way a person might do arithmetic on street addresses. Say you live in a town where, on every block, all the street addresses are used. One side of the street uses consecutive even addresses; the other, consecutive odd addresses. If you wanted to know the address of the house five doors north of 158 River Rd., you wouldn't add 5 and look for number 163. You would multiply 5 (the number of houses you want to advance) by 2 (the "distance" between houses), add that number to 158, and head for 168 River Rd. Similarly, if you had a pointer to a two-byte short at address 158 (decimal) and added 5, the result would be a pointer to a short at address 168 (decimal). See FAQs VII.7 and VII.8 for details on adding and subtracting from pointers.

Street addresses work only within a given block. Pointer arithmetic works only within an array. In practice, that's not a limitation; an array is the only place pointer arithmetic makes sense. An array, in this case, doesn't need to be the contents of an array variable. `malloc()` and `calloc()` return a pointer to an array allocated off the heap. (What's the difference? See FAQ VII.16.)

Pointer declarations are hard to read. A declaration such as

```
char *p;
```

means that `*p` is a `char`. (The "star," or asterisk, is known as the indirection operator; when a program "goes indirect on a pointer," it refers to the pointed-to data.)

For most kinds of computers, a pointer is a pointer. Some have different pointers to data and to functions, or to bytes (`char*`s and `void*`s) and to words (everything else). If you use `sizeof`, you're unlikely to have a problem. Some C programs and programmers assume that any pointer can be stored in an `int`, or at least a `long`. That's not guaranteed. This isn't a big deal—unless your programs have to run on IBM-compatible PCs.

 NOTE

Macintosh and UNIX programmers are excused from the following discussion.

The original IBM PC used a processor that couldn't efficiently use pointers that were more than 16 bits long. (This point can be argued, preferably over a few beers. The 16-bit "pointers" are offsets; see the discussion of base/offset pointers in FAQ IX.3.) With some contortions, the original IBM PC could use pointers that were effectively 20 bits long. Ever since, all sorts of software for IBM compatibles have been fighting that limit.

To get 20-bit pointers to data, you need to tell your compiler to use the right memory model, perhaps compact. Twenty-bit function pointers come with the medium memory model. The large and huge memory models use 20-bit pointers for both data and functions. Either way, you might need to specify `far` pointers (see FAQs VII.18 and VII.19).

The 286-based systems could break through the 20-bit ceiling, but not easily. Starting with the 386, PC compatibles have been able to use true 32-bit addresses. MS-DOS hasn't. Operating systems such as MS-Windows and OS/2 are catching up.

If you run out of conventional memory in an MS-DOS program, you might need to allocate from expanded or extended memory. Various C compilers and libraries enable you to do this in different ways.

All this is grossly unportable. Some of it works for most or all MS-DOS and MS-Windows C compilers. Some is specific to particular compilers. Some works only with a given add-on library. If you already have such a product, check its documentation for details. If you don't, sleep easy tonight, and dream of the fun that awaits you.

VII.1: What is indirection?

Answer:

If you declare a variable, its name is a direct reference to its value. If you have a pointer to a variable, or any other object in memory, you have an indirect reference to its value. If p is a pointer, the value of p is the address of the object. *p means "apply the indirection operator to p"; its value is the value of the object that p points to. (Some people would read it as "Go indirect on p.")

*p is an lvalue; like a variable, it can go on the left side of an assignment operator, to change the value. If p is a pointer to a constant, *p is not a modifiable lvalue; it can't go on the left side of an assignment. (See FAQ II.4 and the discussion at the beginning of this chapter.) Consider the following program. It shows that when p points to i, *p can appear wherever i can.

Listing VII.1. An example of indirection.

```
#include <stdio.h>
int
main()
{
        int i;
        int *p;
        i = 5;
        p = & i;      /* now *p == i */
        /* %P is described in FAQ VII.28 */
        printf("i=%d, p=%P, *p=%d\n", i, p, *p);
        *p = 6;       /* same as i = 6 */
        printf("i=%d, p=%P, *p=%d\n", i, p, *p);
        return 0; /* see FAQ XVI.4 */
}
```

After p points to i (p = &i), you can print i or *p and get the same thing. You can even assign to *p, and the result is the same as if you had assigned to i.

Cross Reference:

II.4: What is a const pointer?

VII.2: How many levels of pointers can you have?

Answer:

The answer depends on what you mean by "levels of pointers." If you mean "How many levels of indirection can you have in a single declaration?" the answer is "At least 12."

```
int     i = 0;
int     *ip01 = & i;
int     **ip02 = & ip01;
int     ***ip03 = & ip02;
int     ****ip04 = & ip03;
int     *****ip05 = & ip04;
int     ******ip06 = & ip05;
int     *******ip07 = & ip06;
int     ********ip08 = & ip07;
int     *********ip09 = & ip08;
int     **********ip10 = & ip09;
int     ***********ip11 = & ip10;
int     ************ip12 = & ip11;
************ip12 = 1;    /* i = 1 */
```

> **NOTE**
>
> The ANSI C standard says all compilers must handle at least 12 levels. Your compiler might support more.

If you mean "How many levels of pointer can you use before the program gets hard to read," that's a matter of taste, but there is a limit. Having two levels of indirection (a pointer to a pointer to something) is common. Any more than that gets a bit harder to think about easily; don't do it unless the alternative would be worse.

If you mean "How many levels of pointer indirection can you have at runtime," there's no limit. This point is particularly important for circular lists, in which each node points to the next. Your program can follow the pointers forever. Consider the following (rather dumb) example in Listing VII.2.

Listing VII.2. A circular list that uses infinite indirection.

```
/* Would run forever if you didn't limit it to MAX */
#include <stdio.h>
struct circ_list
{
        char    value[ 3 ];     /* e.g., "st" (incl '\0') */
        struct circ_list        *next;
};
struct circ_list    suffixes[] = {
        "th", & suffixes[ 1 ], /* 0th */
        "st", & suffixes[ 2 ], /* 1st */
        "nd", & suffixes[ 3 ], /* 2nd */
        "rd", & suffixes[ 4 ], /* 3rd */
        "th", & suffixes[ 5 ], /* 4th */
        "th", & suffixes[ 6 ], /* 5th */
        "th", & suffixes[ 7 ], /* 6th */
        "th", & suffixes[ 8 ], /* 7th */
```

```
            "th", & suffixes[ 9 ], /* 8th */
            "th", & suffixes[ 0 ], /* 9th */
};
#define MAX 20
main()
{
    int i = 0;
    struct circ_list    *p = suffixes;
    while (i <= MAX) {
            printf( "%d%s\n", i, p->value );
            ++i;
            p = p->next;
    }
```

Each element in suffixes has one suffix (two characters plus the terminating NUL character) and a pointer to the next element. next is a pointer to something that has a pointer, to something that has a pointer, ad infinitum.

The example is dumb because the number of elements in suffixes is fixed. It would be simpler to have an array of suffixes and to use the i%10'th element. In general, circular lists can grow and shrink; they're much more interesting than suffixes in Listing VII.2.

Cross Reference:

VII.1: What is indirection?

VII.3: What is a null pointer?
Answer:

There are times (see FAQ VII.4) when it's necessary to have a pointer that doesn't point to anything. The macro NULL, defined in <stddef.h>, has a value that's guaranteed to be different from any valid pointer. NULL is a literal zero, possibly cast to void* or char*. Some people, notably C++ programmers, prefer to use 0 rather than NULL.

You can't use an integer when a pointer is required. The exception is that a literal zero value can be used as the null pointer. (It doesn't have to be a literal zero, but that's the only useful case. Any expression that can be evaluated at compile time, and that is zero, will do. It's not good enough to have an integer variable that might be zero at runtime.)

NOTE

The null pointer might not be stored as a zero; see FAQ VII.10.

WARNING

You should never go indirect on a null pointer. If you do, your program might get garbage, get a value that's all zeros, or halt gracelessly.

Cross Reference:

VII.4: When is a null pointer used?

VII.10: Is NULL always equal to 0?

VII.24: What is a "null pointer assignment" error? What are bus errors, memory faults, and core dumps?

VII.4: When is a null pointer used?
Answer:

The null pointer is used in three ways:

To stop indirection in a recursive data structure
As an error value
As a sentinel value

Using a Null Pointer to Stop Indirection or Recursion

Recursion is when one thing is defined in terms of itself. A recursive function calls itself. The following factorial function calls itself and therefore is considered recursive:

```
/* Dumb implementation; should use a loop */
unsigned factorial( unsigned i )
{
    if ( i == 0 || i == 1 )
    {
        return 1;
    }
    else
    {
        return i * factorial( i - 1 );
    }
}
```

A recursive data structure is defined in terms of itself. The simplest and most common case is a (singularly) linked list. Each element of the list has some value, and a pointer to the next element in the list:

```
struct string_list
{
    char    *str;   /* string (in this case) */
    struct string_list    *next;
};
```

There are also doubly linked lists (which also have a pointer to the preceding element) and trees and hash tables and lots of other neat stuff. You'll find them described in any good book on data structures.

You refer to a linked list with a pointer to its first element. That's where the list starts; where does it stop? This is where the null pointer comes in. In the last element in the list, the next field is set to NULL when there is no following element. To visit all the elements in a list, start at the beginning and go indirect on the next pointer as long as it's not null:

```
while ( p != NULL )
{
    /* do something with p->str */
    p = p->next;
}
```

Notice that this technique works even if p starts as the null pointer.

Using a Null Pointer As an Error Value

The second way the null pointer can be used is as an error value. Many C functions return a pointer to some object. If so, the common convention is to return a null pointer as an error code:

```
if ( setlocale( cat, loc_p ) == NULL )
{
    /* setlocale() failed; do something */
    /* ... */
}
```

This can be a little confusing. Functions that return pointers almost always return a valid pointer (one that doesn't compare equal to zero) on success, and a null pointer (one that compares equal to zero) pointer on failure. Other functions return an int to show success or failure; typically, zero is success and nonzero is failure. That way, a "true" return value means "do some error handling":

```
if ( raise( sig ) != 0 ) {
        /* raise() failed; do something */
        /* ... */
}
```

The success and failure return values make sense one way for functions that return ints, and another for functions that return pointers. Other functions might return a count on success, and either zero or some negative value on failure. As with taking medicine, you should read the instructions first.

Using a Null Pointer As a Sentinel Value

The third way a null pointer can be used is as a "sentinel" value. A sentinel value is a special value that marks the end of something. For example, in main(), argv is an array of pointers. The last element in the array (argv[argc]) is always a null pointer. That's a good way to run quickly through all the elements:

```
/*
A simple program that prints all its arguments.
It doesn't use argc ("argument count"); instead,
it takes advantage of the fact that the last
value in argv ("argument vector") is a null pointer.
*/
#include <stdio.h>
#include <assert.h>
int
main( int argc, char **argv)
{
        int i;
        printf("program name = \"%s\"\n", argv[0]);
        for (i=1; argv[i] != NULL; ++i)
                printf("argv[%d] = \"%s\"\n",
                    i, argv[i]);
```

```
            assert(i == argc);    /* see FAQ XI.5 */
            return 0; /* see FAQ XVI.4 */
    }
```

Cross Reference:

VII.3: What is a null pointer?

VII.10: Is NULL always equal to 0?

XX.2: Should programs always assume that command-line parameters can be used?

VII.5: What is a *void* pointer?
Answer:

A void pointer is a C convention for "a raw address." The compiler has no idea what type of object a void pointer "really points to." If you write

```
int     *ip;
```

ip points to an int. If you write

```
void    *p;
```

p doesn't point to a void!

In C and C++, any time you need a void pointer, you can use another pointer type. For example, if you have a char*, you can pass it to a function that expects a void*. You don't even need to cast it. In C (but not in C++), you can use a void* any time you need any kind of pointer, without casting. (In C++, you need to cast it.)

Cross Reference:

VII.6: When is a void pointer used?

VII.27: Can math operations be performed on a void pointer?

XV.2: What is the difference between C++ and C?

VII.6: When is a *void* pointer used?
Answer:

A void pointer is used for working with raw memory or for passing a pointer to an unspecified type.

Some C code operates on raw memory. When C was first invented, character pointers (char *) were used for that. Then people started getting confused about when a character pointer was a string, when it was a character array, and when it was raw memory.

For example, strcpy() is used to copy data from one string to another, and strncpy() is used to copy at most a certain length string to another:

```
char  *strcpy( char *str1, const char *str2 );
char  *strncpy( char *str1, const char *str2, size_t n );
```

memcpy() is used to move data from one location to another:

```
void  *memcpy( void *addr1, void *addr2, size_t n );
```

void pointers are used to mean that this is raw memory being copied. NUL characters (zero bytes) aren't significant, and just about anything can be copied. Consider the following code:

```
#include "thingie.h"    /* defines struct thingie */
struct thingie  *p_src, *p_dest;
/* ... */
memcpy( p_dest, p_src, sizeof( struct thingie) * numThingies );
```

This program is manipulating some sort of object stored in a struct thingie. p1 and p2 point to arrays, or parts of arrays, of struct thingies. The program wants to copy numThingies of these, starting at the one pointed to by p_src, to the part of the array beginning at the element pointed to by p_dest. memcpy() treats p_src and p_dest as pointers to raw memory; sizeof(struct thingie) * numThingies is the number of bytes to be copied.

The keyword void had been invented to mean "no value," so void* was adopted to mean "a pointer to some thing, I don't know what exactly." void pointers are often used with function pointers.

Cross Reference:

VII.5: What is a void pointer?

VII.14: When would you use a pointer to a function?

VII.7: Can you subtract pointers from each other? Why would you?

Answer:

If you have two pointers into the same array, you can subtract them. The answer is the number of elements between the two elements.

Consider the street address analogy presented in the introduction of this chapter. Say that I live at 118 Fifth Avenue and that my neighbor lives at 124 Fifth Avenue. The "size of a house" is two (on my side of the street, sequential even numbers are used), so my neighbor is (124–118)/2 (or 3) houses up from me. (There are two houses between us, 120 and 122; my neighbor is the third.) You might do this subtraction if you're going back and forth between indices and pointers.

You might also do it if you're doing a binary search. If p points to an element that's before what you're looking for, and q points to an element that's after it, then (q-p)/2+p points to an element between p and q. If that element is before what you want, look between it and q. If it's after what you want, look between p and it.

(If it's what you're looking for, stop looking.)

You can't subtract arbitrary pointers and get meaningful answers. Someone might live at 110 Main Street, but I can't subtract 110 Main from 118 Fifth (and divide by 2) and say that he or she is four houses away! If each block starts a new hundred, I can't even subtract 120 Fifth Avenue from 204 Fifth Avenue. They're on the same street, but in different blocks of houses (different arrays).

C won't stop you from subtracting pointers inappropriately. It won't cut you any slack, though, if you use the meaningless answer in a way that might get you into trouble.

When you subtract pointers, you get a value of some integer type. The ANSI C standard defines a typedef, ptrdiff_t, for this type. (It's in <stddef.h>.) Different compilers might use different types (int or long or whatever), but they all define ptrdiff_t appropriately.

Listing VII.7 is a simple program that demonstrates this point. The program has an array of structures, each 16 bytes long. The difference between array[0] and array[8] is 8 when you subtract struct stuff pointers, but 128 (hex 0x80) when you cast the pointers to raw addresses and then subtract.

 NOTE

Pointers are usually cast to "raw addresses" by casting to void*. The example casts to char*, because void*s can't be subtracted; see FAQ VII.27.

If you subtract 8 from a pointer to array[8], you don't get something 8 bytes earlier; you get something 8 *elements* earlier.

Listing VII.7. Pointer arithmetic.

```
#include <stdio.h>
#include <stddef.h>
struct stuff {
        char    name[16];
        /* other stuff could go here, too */
};
struct stuff array[] = {
        { "The" },
        { "quick" },
        { "brown" },
        { "fox" },
        { "jumped" },
        { "over" },
        { "the" },
        { "lazy" },
        { "dog." },
        /*
        an empty string signifies the end;
        not used in this program,
        but without it, there'd be no way
        to find the end (see FAQ IX.4)
        */
        { "" }
};
main()
{
```

```
            struct stuff    *p0 = & array[0];
            struct stuff    *p8 = & array[8];
            ptrdiff_t       diff = p8 - p0;
            ptrdiff_t       addr_diff = (char*) p8 - (char*) p0;
            /*
            cast the struct stuff pointers to void*
            (which we know printf() can handle; see FAQ VII.28)
            */
            printf("& array[0] = p0 = %P\n", (void*) p0);
            printf("& array[8] = p8 = %P\n", (void*) p8);
            /*
            cast the ptrdiff_t's to long's
            (which we know printf() can handle)
            */
            printf("The difference of pointers is %ld\n",
              (long) diff);
            printf("The difference of addresses is %ld\n",
              (long) addr_diff);
            printf("p8 - 8 = %P\n", (void*) (p8 - 8));
            /* example for FAQ VII.8 */
            printf("p0 + 8 = %P (same as p8)\n", (void*) (p0 + 8));
            return 0;    /* see FAQ XVI.4 */
        }
```

Cross Reference:

VII.8: When you add a value to a pointer, what is really added?

VII.12: Can you add pointers together? Why would you?

VII.27: Can math operations be performed on a void pointer?

VII.8: When you add a value to a pointer, what is really added?
Answer:

If you think only in terms of raw addresses, what's "really" added is the value times the size of the thing being pointed to...and you're missing the point of how C pointers work. When you add an integer and a pointer, the sum points that many elements away, not just that many bytes away.

Look at the end of Listing VII.7. When you add 8 to & array[0], you don't get something eight bytes away. You get & array[8], which is eight *elements* away.

Think about the street-address analogy presented in this chapter's introduction. You live on the even-numbered side of Oak Street, at number 744. There are no gaps in the even numbers. The "size of a house" is 2. If someone wants to know the address of the place three doors up from you, he multiplies the size (2) times 3, and thus adds 6; the address is 750. The house one door down is 744 + (−1)*2, or 742.

Street-address arithmetic works only within a given block; pointer arithmetic works only within a given array. If you try to calculate the address 400 blocks south of you, you'll get −56 Oak Street; fine, but that doesn't mean anything. If your program uses a meaningless address, it'll probably blow up.

Cross Reference:

VII.7: Can you subtract pointers from each other? Why would you?

VII.12: Can you add pointers together? Why would you?

VII.27: Can math operations be performed on a void pointer?

VII.9: Is *NULL* always defined as 0?
Answer:

NULL is defined as either 0 or (void*)0. These values are almost identical; either a literal zero or a void pointer is converted automatically to any kind of pointer, as necessary, whenever a pointer is needed (although the compiler can't always tell when a pointer is needed).

Cross Reference:

VII.10: Is NULL always equal to 0?

VII.10: Is *NULL* always equal to 0?
Answer:

The answer depends on what you mean by "equal to." If you mean "compares equal to," such as

```
if ( /* ... */ )
{
    p = NULL;
}
else
{
    p = /* something else */;
}
/* ... */
if ( p == 0 )
```

then yes, NULL is always equal to 0. That's the whole point of the definition of a null pointer.

If you mean "is stored the same way as an integer zero," the answer is no, not necessarily. That's the most common way to store a null pointer. On some machines, a different representation is used.

The only way you're likely to tell that a null pointer isn't stored the same way as zero is by displaying a pointer in a debugger, or printing it. (If you cast a null pointer to an integer type, that might also show a nonzero value.)

Cross Reference:

VII.9: Is NULL always defined as 0?

VII.28: How do you print an address?

VII.11: What does it mean when a pointer is used in an *if* statement?

Answer:

Any time a pointer is used as a condition, it means "Is this a non-null pointer?" A pointer can be used in an `if`, `while`, `for`, or `do/while` statement, or in a conditional expression. It sounds a little complicated, but it's not.

Take this simple case:

```
if ( p )
{
    /* do something */
}
else
{
    /* do something else */
}
```

An `if` statement does the "then" (first) part when its expression compares unequal to zero. That is,

```
if ( /* something */ )
```

is always exactly the same as this:

```
if ( /* something */ != 0 )
```

That means the previous simple example is the same thing as this:

```
if ( p != 0 )
{
    /* do something (not a null pointer) */
}
else
{
    /* do something else (a null pointer) */
}
```

This style of coding is a little obscure. It's very common in existing C code; you don't have to write code that way, but you need to recognize such code when you see it.

Cross Reference:

VII.3: What is a null pointer?

VII.12: Can you add pointers together? Why would you?

Answer:

No, you can't add pointers together. If you live at 1332 Lakeview Drive, and your neighbor lives at 1364 Lakeview, what's 1332+1364? It's a number, but it doesn't mean anything. If you try to perform this type of calculation with pointers in a C program, your compiler will complain.

The only time the addition of pointers might come up is if you try to add a pointer and the difference of two pointers:

```
p = p + p2 - p1;
```

which is the same thing as this:

```
p = (p + p2) - p1.
```

Here's a correct way of saying this:

```
p = p + ( p2 - p1 );
```

Or even better in this case would be this example:

```
p += p2 - p1;
```

Cross Reference

VII.7: Can you subtract pointers from each other? Why would you?

VII.13: How do you use a pointer to a function?
Answer:

The hardest part about using a pointer-to-function is declaring it. Consider an example. You want to create a pointer, pf, that points to the strcmp() function. The strcmp() function is declared in this way:

```
int strcmp( const char *, const char * )
```

To set up pf to point to the strcmp() function, you want a declaration that looks just like the strcmp() function's declaration, but that has *pf rather than strcmp:

```
int     (*pf)( const char *, const char * );
```

Notice that you need to put parentheses around *pf. If you don't include parentheses, as in

```
int *pf( const char *, const char * );   /* wrong */
```

you'll get the same thing as this:

```
(int *) pf( const char *, const char * );   /* wrong */
```

That is, you'll have a declaration of a function that returns int*.

NOTE

For what it's worth, even experienced C programmers sometimes get this wrong. The simplest thing to do is remember where you can find an example declaration and copy it when you need to.

After you've gotten the declaration of pf, you can #include <string.h> and assign the address of strcmp() to pf:

```
pf = strcmp;
```

or

```
pf = & strcmp;   /* redundant & */
```

You don't need to go indirect on pf to call it:

```
if ( pf( str1, str2 ) > 0 )     /* ... */
```

Cross Reference:

VII.14: When would you use a pointer to a function?

VII.14: When would you use a pointer to a function?
Answer:

Pointers to functions are interesting when you pass them to other functions. A function that takes function pointers says, in effect, "Part of what I do can be customized. Give me a pointer to a function, and I'll call it when that part of the job needs to be done. That function can do its part for me." This is known as a "callback." It's used a lot in graphical user interface libraries, in which the style of a display is built into the library but the contents of the display are part of the application.

As a simpler example, say you have an array of character pointers (char*s), and you want to sort it by the value of the strings the character pointers point to. The standard qsort() function uses function pointers to perform that task. (For more on sorting, see Chapter III, "Sorting and Searching Data.") qsort() takes four arguments,

- ◆ a pointer to the beginning of the array,
- ◆ the number of elements in the array,
- ◆ the size of each array element, and
- ◆ a comparison function,

and returns an int.

The comparison function takes two arguments, each a pointer to an element. The function returns 0 if the pointed-to elements compare equal, some negative value if the first element is less than the second, and some positive value if the first element is greater than the second. A comparison function for integers might look like this:

```
int icmp( const int *p1, const int *p2 )
{
     return *p1 - *p2;
}
```

The sorting algorithm is part of qsort(). So is the exchange algorithm; it just copies bytes, possibly by calling memcpy() or memmove(). qsort() doesn't know what it's sorting, so it can't know how to compare them. That part is provided by the function pointer.

You can't use strcmp() as the comparison function for this example, for two reasons. The first reason is that strcmp()'s type is wrong; more on that a little later. The second reason is that it won't work. strcmp() takes two pointers to char and treats them as the first characters of two strings. The example deals with an array of character pointers (char*s), so the comparison function must take two pointers to character pointers (char*s). In this case, the following code might be an example of a good comparison function:

```
int strpcmp( const void *p1, const void *p2 )
{
    char * const *sp1 = (char * const *) p1;
    char * const *sp2 = (char * const *) p2;
    return strcmp( *sp1, *sp2 );
}
```

The call to qsort() might look something like this:

```
qsort( array, numElements, sizeof( char * ), pf2 );
```

qsort() will call strpcmp() every time it needs to compare two character pointers (char*s).

Why can't strcmp() be passed to qsort(), and why were the arguments of strpcmp() what they were? A function pointer's type depends on the return type of the pointed-to function, as well as the number and types of all its arguments. qsort() expects a function that takes two constant void pointers:

```
void qsort( void *base,
            size_t numElements,
            size_t sizeOfElement,
            int (*compFunct)( const void *, const void * ) );
```

Because qsort() doesn't really know what it's sorting, it uses a void pointer in its argument (base) and in the arguments to the comparison function. qsort()'s void* argument is easy; any pointer can be converted to a void* without even needing a cast. The function pointer is harder.

For an array of character arrays, strcmp() would have the right algorithm but the wrong argument types. The simplest, safest way to handle this situation is to pass a function that takes the right argument types for qsort() and then casts them to the right argument types. That's what strpcmp() does.

If you have a function that takes a char*, and you know that a char* and a void* are the same in every environment your program might ever work in, you might cast the function pointer, rather than the pointed-to function's arguments, in this way:

```
char    table[ NUM_ELEMENTS ][ ELEMENT_SIZE ];
/* ... */
/* passing strcmp() to qsort for array of array of char */
qsort( table, NUM_ELEMENTS, ELEMENT_SIZE,
  ( int (*)( const void *, const void * ) ) strcmp );
```

Casting the arguments and casting the function pointer both can be error prone. In practice, casting the function pointer is more dangerous.

The basic problem here is using void* when you have a pointer to an unknown type. C++ programs sometime solve this problem with templates.

Cross Reference:

VII.5: What is a void pointer?

VII.6: When is a void pointer used?

VII.13: How do you use a pointer to a function?

VII.15: Can the size of an array be declared at runtime?
Answer:

No. In an array declaration, the size must be known at compile time. You can't specify a size that's known only at runtime. For example, if i is a variable, you can't write code like this:

```
char    array[i];     /* not valid C */
```

Some languages provide this latitude. C doesn't. If it did, the stack (see FAQ VII.20) would be more complicated, function calls would be more expensive, and programs would run a lot slower.

If you know that you have an array but you won't know until runtime how big it will be, declare a pointer to it and use malloc() or calloc() to allocate the array from the heap.

If you know at compile time how big an array is, you can declare its size at compile time. Even if the size is some complicated expression, as long as it can be evaluated at compile time, it can be used.

Listing VII.15 shows an example. It's a program that copies the argv array passed to main().

Listing VII.15. Arrays with runtime size, using pointers and malloc().

```
/*
A silly program that copies the argv array and all the pointed-to
strings. Just for fun, it also deallocates all the copies.
*/
#include <stdlib.h>
#include <string.h>
int
main(int argc, char** argv)
{
    char** new_argv;
    int i;
    /*
    Since argv[0] through argv[argc] are all valid, the
    program needs to allocate room for argc+1 pointers.
    */
    new_argv = (char**) calloc(argc+1, sizeof (char*));
    /* or malloc((argc+1) * sizeof (char*)) */
    printf("allocated room for %d pointers starting at %P\n",
      argc+1, new_argv);
    /*
    now copy all the strings themselves
    (argv[0] through argv[argc-1])
    */
    for (i = 0; i < argc; ++i) {
        /* make room for '\0' at end, too */
```

continues

Listing VII.15. continued

```
        new_argv[i] = (char*) malloc(strlen(argv[i]) + 1);
        strcpy(new_argv[i], argv[i]);
        printf("allocated %d bytes for new_argv[%d] at %P, "
        "copied \"%s\"\n",
          strlen(argv[i]) + 1, i, new_argv[i], new_argv[i]);
    }
    new_argv[argc] = NULL;
    /*
    To deallocate everything, get rid of the strings (in any
    order), then the array of pointers. If you free the array
    of pointers first, you lose all reference to the copied
    strings.
    */
    for (i = 0; i < argc; ++i) {
        free(new_argv[i]);
        printf("freed new_argv[%d] at %P\n", i, new_argv[i]);
        argv[i] = NULL;     /* paranoia; see note */
    }
    free(new_argv);
    printf("freed new_argv itself at %P\n", new_argv);
    return 0; /* see FAQ XVI.4 */
}
```

NOTE

Why does the program in Listing VII.15 assign NULL to the elements in new_argv after freeing them? This is paranoia based on long experience. After a pointer has been freed, you can no longer use the pointed-to data. The pointer is said to "dangle"; it doesn't point at anything useful. If you "NULL out" or "zero out" a pointer immediately after freeing it, your program can no longer get in trouble by using that pointer. True, you might go indirect on the null pointer instead, but that's something your debugger might be able to help you with immediately. Also, there still might be copies of the pointer that refer to the memory that has been deallocated; that's the nature of C. Zeroing out pointers after freeing them won't solve all problems; it can solve some. See FAQ VII.22 for a related discussion.

Cross Reference:

VII.16: Is it better to use malloc() or calloc()?

VII.20: What is the stack?

VII.21: What is the heap?

VII.22: What happens if you free a pointer twice?

IX.8: Why can't constant values be used to define an array's initial size?

VII.16: Is it better to use *malloc()* or *calloc()*?

Answer:

Both the `malloc()` and the `calloc()` functions are used to allocate dynamic memory. Each operates slightly different from the other. `malloc()` takes a size and returns a pointer to a chunk of memory at least that big:

```
void    *malloc( size_t size );
```

`calloc()` takes a number of elements, and the size of each, and returns a pointer to a chunk of memory at least big enough to hold them all:

```
void    *calloc( size_t numElements, size_t sizeOfElement );
```

There's one major difference and one minor difference between the two functions. The major difference is that `malloc()` doesn't initialize the allocated memory. The first time `malloc()` gives you a particular chunk of memory, the memory might be full of zeros. If memory has been allocated, freed, and reallocated, it probably has whatever junk was left in it. That means, unfortunately, that a program might run in simple cases (when memory is never reallocated) but break when used harder (and when memory is reused).

`calloc()` fills the allocated memory with all zero bits. That means that anything there you're going to use as a `char` or an `int` of any length, `signed` or `unsigned`, is guaranteed to be zero. Anything you're going to use as a pointer is set to all zero bits. That's usually a null pointer, but it's not guaranteed. (See FAQ VII.10.) Anything you're going to use as a `float` or `double` is set to all zero bits; that's a floating-point zero on some types of machines, but not on all.

The minor difference between the two is that `calloc()` returns an array of objects; `malloc()` returns one object. Some people use `calloc()` to make clear that they want an array. Other than initialization, most C programmers don't distinguish between

```
calloc( numElements, sizeOfElement)
```

and

```
malloc( numElements * sizeOfElement)
```

There's a nit, though. `malloc()` doesn't give you a pointer to an array. In theory (according to the ANSI C standard), pointer arithmetic works only within a single array. In practice, if any C compiler or interpreter were to enforce that theory, lots of existing C code would break. (There wouldn't be much use for `realloc()`, either, which also doesn't guarantee a pointer to an array.)

Don't worry about the array-ness of `calloc()`. If you want initialization to zeros, use `calloc()`; if not, use `malloc()`.

Cross Reference:

VII.7: Can you subtract pointers from each other? Why would you?

VII.8: When you add a value to a pointer, what is really added?

VII.10: Is NULL always equal to 0?

VII.17: How do you declare an array that will hold more than 64KB of data?

Answer:

The coward's answer is, you can't, portably. The ANSI/ISO C standard requires compilers to handle only single objects as large as (32KB − 1) bytes long.

Why is 64KB magic? It's the biggest number that needs more than 16 bits to represent it.

For some environments, to get an array that big, you just declare it. It works, no trouble. For others, you can't declare such an array, but you can allocate one off the heap, just by calling `malloc()` or `calloc()`.

On a PC compatible, the same limitations apply, and more. You need to use at least a large data model. (See the discussion at the beginning of the chapter.) You might also need to call "far" variants of `malloc()` or `calloc()`. For example, with Borland C and C++ compilers, you could write

```
far char *buffer = farmalloc(70000L);
```

Or with Microsoft C and C++ compilers, you could write

```
far char *buffer = fmalloc(70000L);
```

to allocate 70,000 bytes of memory into a buffer. (The `L` in `70000L` forces a `long` constant. An `int` constant might be only 15 bits long plus a sign bit, not big enough to store the value 70,000.)

Cross Reference:

VII.18: What is the difference between `far` and `near`?

VII.21: What is the heap?

IX.3: Why worry about the addresses of the elements beyond the end of an array?

VII.18: What is the difference between *far* and *near*?

Answer:

As described at the beginning of this chapter, some compilers for PC compatibles use two types of pointers. `near` pointers are 16 bits long and can address a 64KB range. `far` pointers are 32 bits long and can address a 1MB range.

`near` pointers operate within a 64KB segment. There's one segment for function addresses and one segment for data.

`far` pointers have a 16-bit base (the segment address) and a 16-bit offset. The base is multiplied by 16, so a `far` pointer is effectively 20 bits long. For example, if a `far` pointer had a segment of `0x7000` and an offset of `0x1224`, the pointer would refer to address `0x71224`. A `far` pointer with a segment of `0x7122` and an offset of `0x0004` would refer to the same address.

Before you compile your code, you must tell the compiler which memory model to use. If you use a small-code memory model, near pointers are used by default for function addresses. That means that all the functions need to fit in one 64KB segment. With a large-code model, the default is to use far function addresses. You'll get near pointers with a small data model, and far pointers with a large data model. These are just the defaults; you can declare variables and functions as explicitly near or far.

far pointers are a little slower. Whenever one is used, the code or data segment register needs to be swapped out. far pointers also have odd semantics for arithmetic and comparison. For example, the two far pointers in the preceding example point to the same address, but they would compare as different! If your program fits in a small-data, small-code memory model, your life will be easier. If it doesn't, there's not much you can do.

If it sounds confusing, it is. There are some additional, compiler-specific wrinkles. Check your compiler manuals for details.

Cross Reference:

VII.19: When should a far pointer be used?

VII.19: When should a *far* pointer be used?
Answer:

Sometimes you can get away with using a small memory model in most of a given program. (See FAQ VII.18.) There might be just a few things that don't fit in your small data and code segments.

When that happens, you can use explicit far pointers and function declarations to get at the rest of memory. A far function can be outside the 64KB segment most functions are shoehorned into for a small-code model. (Often, libraries are declared explicitly far, so they'll work no matter what code model the program uses.) A far pointer can refer to information outside the 64KB data segment. Typically, such pointers are used with farmalloc() and such, to manage a heap separate from where all the rest of the data lives.

If you use a small-data, large-code model, you should explicitly make your function pointers far.

Cross Reference:

VII.18: What is the difference between far and near?
VII.21: What is the heap?

VII.20: What is the stack?
Answer:

The stack is where all the functions' local (auto) variables are created. The stack also contains some information used to call and return from functions.

A "stack trace" is a list of which functions have been called, based on this information. When you start using a debugger, one of the first things you should learn is how to get a stack trace.

The stack is very inflexible about allocating memory; everything must be deallocated in exactly the reverse order it was allocated in. For implementing function calls, that is all that's needed. Allocating memory off the stack is extremely efficient. One of the reasons C compilers generate such good code is their heavy use of a simple stack.

There used to be a C function that any programmer could use for allocating memory off the stack. The memory was automatically deallocated when the calling function returned. This was a dangerous function to call; it's not available anymore.

Cross Reference:

VII.15: Can the size of an array be declared at runtime?

VII.21: What is the heap?

VII.21: What is the heap?

Answer:

The heap is where `malloc()`, `calloc()`, and `realloc()` get memory.

Getting memory from the heap is much slower than getting it from the stack. On the other hand, the heap is much more flexible than the stack. Memory can be allocated at any time and deallocated in any order. Such memory isn't deallocated automatically; you have to call `free()`.

Recursive data structures are almost always implemented with memory from the heap. Strings often come from there too, especially strings that could be very long at runtime.

If you can keep data in a local variable (and allocate it from the stack), your code will run faster than if you put the data on the heap. Sometimes you can use a better algorithm if you use the heap—faster, or more robust, or more flexible. It's a tradeoff.

If memory is allocated from the heap, it's available until the program ends. That's great if you remember to deallocate it when you're done. If you forget, it's a problem. A "memory leak" is some allocated memory that's no longer needed but isn't deallocated. If you have a memory leak inside a loop, you can use up all the memory on the heap and not be able to get any more. (When that happens, the allocation functions return a null pointer.) In some environments, if a program doesn't deallocate everything it allocated, memory stays unavailable even after the program ends.

 NOTE

Memory leaks are hard to debug. Memory allocation tools can help find them.

Some programming languages don't make you deallocate memory from the heap. Instead, such memory is "garbage collected" automatically. This maneuver leads to some very serious performance issues. It's also a lot harder to implement. That's an issue for the people who develop compilers, not the people who buy them.

(Except that software that's harder to implement often costs more.) There are some garbage collection libraries for C, but they're at the bleeding edge of the state of the art.

Cross Reference:

VII.4: When is a null pointer used?

VII.20: What is the stack?

VII.22: What happens if you free a pointer twice?

Answer:

If you free a pointer, use it to allocate memory again, and free it again, of course it's safe.

 NOTE

> To be precise and accurate, the pointed-to memory, not the pointer itself, has been freed. Nothing about the pointer has changed. However, C programmers in a hurry (that's all of us, right?) will talk about "a freed pointer" to mean a pointer to freed memory.

If you free a pointer, the memory you freed might be reallocated. If that happens, you might get that pointer back. In this case, freeing the pointer twice is OK, but only because you've been lucky. The following example is silly, but safe:

```
#include <stdlib.h>

int
main(int argc, char** argv)
{
        char** new_argv1;
        char** new_argv2;
        new_argv1 = calloc(argc+1, sizeof(char*));
        free(new_argv1);    /* freed once */
        new_argv2 = (char**) calloc(argc+1, sizeof(char*));
        if (new_argv1 == new_argv2) {
                /*
                new_argv1 accidentally points to freeable memory
                */
                free(new_argv1);    /* freed twice */
        } else {
                free(new_argv2);
        }
        new_argv1 = calloc(argc+1, sizeof(char*));
        free(new_argv1);    /* freed once again */
        return 0;
}
```

In the preceding program, new_argv1 is pointed to a chunk of memory big enough to copy the argv array, which is immediately freed. Then a chunk the same size is allocated, and its address is assigned to new_argv2. Because the first chunk was available again, calloc might have returned it again; in that case, new_argv1 and new_argv2 have the same value, and it doesn't matter which variable you use. (Remember, it's the pointed-to memory that's freed, not the pointer variable.) Just for fun, new_argv1 is pointed to allocated memory again, which is again freed. You can free a pointer as many times as you want; it's the memory you have to be careful about.

What if you free allocated memory, don't get it allocated back to you, and then free it again? Something like this:

```
void caller( ... )
{
        void *p;
        /* ... */
        callee( p );
        free( p );
}
void callee( void* p )
{
        /* ... */
        free( p );
        return;
}
```

In this example, the caller() function is passing p to the callee() function and then freeing p. Unfortunately, callee() is also freeing p. Thus, the memory that p points to is being freed twice. The ANSI/ISO C standard says this is undefined. Anything can happen. Usually, something very bad happens.

The memory allocation and deallocation functions could be written to keep track of what has been used and what has been freed. Typically, they aren't. If you free() a pointer, the pointed-to memory is assumed to have been allocated by malloc() or calloc() but not deallocated since then. free() calculates how big that chunk of memory was (see FAQ VII.26) and updates the data structures in the memory "arena." Even if the memory has been freed already, free() will assume that it wasn't, and it will blindly update the arena. This action is much faster than it would have been if free() had checked to see whether the pointer was OK to deallocate.

If something doesn't work right, your program is now in trouble. When free() updates the arena, it will probably write some information in a wrong place. You now have the fun of dealing with a wild pointer; see the description at the beginning of the chapter.

How can you avoid double deallocation? Write your code carefully, use memory allocation tools, or (preferably) do both.

Cross Reference:

VII.21: What is the heap?

VII.24: What is a "null pointer assignment" error? What are bus errors, memory faults, and core dumps?

VII.26: How does free() know how much memory to release?

VII.23: What is the difference between *NULL* and *NUL*?

Answer:

NULL is a macro defined in <stddef.h> for the null pointer.

NUL is the name of the first character in the ASCII character set. It corresponds to a zero value. There's no standard macro NUL in C, but some people like to define it.

> NOTE
>
> The digit 0 corresponds to a value of 80, decimal. Don't confuse the digit 0 with the value of '\0' (NUL)!

NULL can be defined as ((void*)0), NUL as '\0'. Both can also be defined simply as 0. If they're defined that way, they can be used interchangeably. That's a bad way to write C code. One is meant to be used as a pointer; the other, as a character. If you write your code so that the difference is obvious, the next person who has to read and change your code will have an easier job. If you write obscurely, the next person might have problems. Hint: Typically, the "next person" is the person who originally wrote the code. The time you save might be your own.

Cross Reference:

VII.3: What is a null pointer?

VII.24: What is a "null pointer assignment" error? What are bus errors, memory faults, and core dumps?

Answer:

These are all serious errors, symptoms of a wild pointer or subscript.

Null pointer assignment is a message you might get when an MS-DOS program finishes executing. Some such programs can arrange for a small amount of memory to be available "where the NULL pointer points to" (so to speak). If the program tries to write to that area, it will overwrite the data put there by the compiler. When the program is done, code generated by the compiler examines that area. If that data has been changed, the compiler-generated code complains with null pointer assignment.

This message carries only enough information to get you worried. There's no way to tell, just from a null pointer assignment message, what part of your program is responsible for the error. Some debuggers, and some compilers, can give you more help in finding the problem.

`Bus error: core dumped` and `Memory fault: core dumped` are messages you might see from a program running under UNIX. They're more programmer friendly. Both mean that a pointer or an array subscript was wildly out of bounds. You can get these messages on a read or on a write. They aren't restricted to null pointer problems.

The `core dumped` part of the message is telling you about a file, called `core`, that has just been written in your current directory. This is a dump of everything on the stack and in the heap at the time the program was running. With the help of a debugger, you can use the core dump to find where the bad pointer was used. That might not tell you why the pointer was bad, but it's a step in the right direction. If you don't have write permission in the current directory, you won't get a core file, or the `core dumped` message.

NOTE

> Why "core"? The first UNIX systems ran on hardware that used magnetic cores, not silicon chips, for random access memory.

The same tools that help find memory allocation bugs can help find some wild pointers and subscripts, sometimes. The best such tools can find almost all occurrences of this kind of problem.

Cross Reference:

VII.3: What is a null pointer?

VII.25: How can you determine the size of an allocated portion of memory?

Answer:

You can't, really. `free()` can (see FAQ VII.26), but there's no way for your program to know the trick `free()` uses. Even if you disassemble the library and discover the trick, there's no guarantee the trick won't change with the next release of the compiler. Trying to second guess the compiler this way isn't just tricky, it's crazy.

Cross Reference:

VII.26: How does `free()` know how much memory to release?

VII.26: How does *free()* know how much memory to release?

Answer:

I could tell you, but then I'd have to kill you.

Seriously? There's no standard way. It can vary from compiler to compiler, even from version to version of the same compiler. `free()`, `malloc()`, `calloc()`, and `realloc()` are functions; as long as they all work the same way, they can work any way that works.

Most implementations take advantage of the same trick, though. When `malloc()` (or one of the other allocation functions) allocates a block of memory, it grabs a little more than it was asked to grab. `malloc()` doesn't return the address of the beginning of this block. Instead, it returns a pointer a little bit after that. At the very beginning of the block, before the address returned, `malloc()` stores some information, such as how big the block is. (If this information gets overwritten, you'll have wild pointer problems when you free the memory.)

There's no guarantee `free()` works this way. It could use a table of allocated addresses and their lengths. It could store the data at the end of the block (beyond the length requested by the call to `malloc()`). It could store a pointer rather than a count.

If you're desperate to hack a memory allocation library, write your own.

Cross Reference:

VII.25: How can you determine the size of an allocated portion of memory?

VII.27: Can math operations be performed on a *void* pointer?
Answer:

No. Pointer addition and subtraction are based on advancing the pointer by a number of elements. By definition, if you have a `void` pointer, you don't know what it's pointing to, so you don't know the size of what it's pointing to.

If you want pointer arithmetic to work on raw addresses, use character pointers.

NOTE

You can cast your `void*` to a `char*`, do the arithmetic, and cast it back to a `void*`.

Cross Reference:

VII.7: Can you subtract pointers from each other? Why would you?

VII.8: When you add a value to a pointer, what is really added?

VII.28: How do you print an address?
Answer:

The safest way is to use `printf()` (or `fprintf()` or `sprintf()`) with the `%P` specification. That prints a void pointer (`void*`). Different compilers might print a pointer with different formats. Your compiler will pick a format that's right for your environment.

If you have some other kind of pointer (not a `void*`) and you want to be very safe, cast the pointer to a `void*`:

```
printf( "%P\n", (void*) buffer );
```

There's no guarantee any integer type is big enough to store a pointer. With most compilers, an `unsigned long` is big enough. The second safest way to print an address (the value of a pointer) is to cast it to an `unsigned long`, then print that.

Cross Reference:

None.

VIII

Functions

The focus of this chapter is functions—when to declare them, how to declare them, and different techniques for using them. Functions are the building blocks of the C language, and mastering functions is one of the key elements needed to be a successful C programmer.

When you read this chapter, keep in mind the functions you have written and whether or not you are squeezing every bit of efficiency out of them. If you aren't doing so, you should apply some of the techniques presented in this chapter to make your programs faster and more efficient. Also, keep in mind some of the tips presented here regarding good programming practice—perhaps you can improve your function-writing skills by examining some of the examples provided.

VIII.1: When should I declare a function?

Answer:

Functions that are used only in the current source file should be declared as `static` (see FAQ VIII.4), and the function's declaration should appear in the current source file along with the definition of the function. Functions used outside of the current source file should have their declarations put in a *header file*, which can be included in whatever source file is going to use that function. For instance, if a function named `stat_func()` is used only in the source file stat.c, it should be declared as shown here:

```
/* stat.c */

#include <stdio.h>

static int stat_func(int, int);  /* static declaration of stat_func() */
►void main(void);

void main(void)
{

    ...

    rc = stat_func(1, 2);

    ...

}

/* definition (body) of stat_func() */

static int stat_func(int arg1, int arg2)
{

    ...

    return rc;

}
```

In this example, the function named `stat_func()` is never used outside of the source file stat.c. There is therefore no reason for the prototype (or declaration) of the function to be visible outside of the stat.c source file. Thus, to avoid any confusion with other functions that might have the same name, the declaration of `stat_func()` should be put in the same source file as the declaration of `stat_func()`.

In the following example, the function `glob_func()` is declared and used in the source file global.c and is used in the source file extern.c. Because `glob_func()` is used outside of the source file in which it's declared, the declaration of `glob_func()` should be put in a header file (in this example, named proto.h) to be included in both the global.c and the extern.c source files. This is how it's done:

File: proto.h

```
/* proto.h */

int glob_func(int, int);  /* declaration of the glob_func() function */
```

File: global.c

```
/* global.c */

#include <stdio.h>
#include "proto.h"    /* include this file for the declaration of
                         glob_func() */

void main(void);

void main(void)
```

```
{

    ...

    rc = glob_func(1, 2);

    ...

}

/* definition (body) of the glob_func() function */

int glob_func(int arg1, int arg2)
{

    ...

    return rc;

}
```

File: extern.c

```
/* extern.c */

#include <stdio.h>
#include "proto.h"    /* include this file for the declaration of
                         glob_func() */

void ext_func(void);

void ext_func(void)
{

    ...

    /* call glob_func(), which is defined in the global.c source file */

    rc = glob_func(10, 20);

    ...

}
```

In the preceding example, the declaration of glob_func() is put in the header file named proto.h because glob_func() is used in both the global.c and the extern.c source files. Now, whenever glob_func() is going to be used, you simply need to include the proto.h header file, and you will automatically have the function's declaration. This will help your compiler when it is checking parameters and return values from global functions you are using in your programs. Notice that your function declarations should always appear *before the first function declaration in your source file.*

In general, if you think your function might be of some use outside of the current source file, you should put its declaration in a header file so that other modules can access it. Otherwise, if you are sure your function will never be used outside of the current source file, you should declare the function as static and include the declaration only in the current source file.

Cross Reference:

VIII.2: Why should I prototype a function?

VIII.3: How many parameters should a function have?

VIII.4: What is a static function?

VIII.2: Why should I prototype a function?

Answer:

A function prototype tells the compiler what kind of arguments a function is looking to receive and what kind of return value a function is going to give back. This approach helps the compiler ensure that calls to a function are made correctly and that no erroneous type conversions are taking place. For instance, consider the following prototype:

```
int some_func(int, char*, long);
```

Looking at this prototype, the compiler can check all references (including the definition of some_func()) to ensure that three parameters are used (an integer, a character pointer, and then a long integer) and that a return value of type integer is received. If the compiler finds differences between the prototype and calls to the function or the definition of the function, an error or a warning can be generated to avoid errors in your source code. For instance, the following examples would be flagged as incorrect, given the preceding prototype of some_func():

```
x = some_func(1);                        /* not enough arguments passed */

x = some_func("HELLO!", 1, "DUDE!"); /* wrong type of arguments used */

x = some_func(1, str, 2879, "T");    /* too many arguments passed */
```

In the following example, the return value expected from some_func() is not an integer:

```
long* lValue;

lValue = some_func(1, str, 2879);    /* some_func() returns an int,
                                          not a long* */
```

Using prototypes, the compiler can also ensure that the function definition, or body, is correct and correlates with the prototype. For instance, the following definition of some_func() is not the same as its prototype, and it therefore would be flagged by the compiler:

```
int some_func(char* string, long lValue, int iValue)  /* wrong order of
                                                           parameters */
{

    ...

}
```

The bottom line on prototypes is that you should always include them in your source code because they provide a good error-checking mechanism to ensure that your functions are being used correctly. Besides, many of today's popular compilers give you warnings when compiling if they can't find a prototype for a function that is being referenced.

Cross Reference:

VIII.1: When should I declare a function?

VIII.3: How many parameters should a function have?

VIII.4: What is a static function?

VIII.3: How many parameters should a function have?
Answer:

There is no set number or "guideline" limit to the number of parameters your functions can have. However, it is considered bad programming style for your functions to contain an inordinately high (eight or more) number of parameters. The number of parameters a function has also directly affects the speed at which it is called—the more parameters, the slower the function call. Therefore, if possible, you should minimize the number of parameters you use in a function. If you are using more than four parameters, you might want to rethink your function design and calling conventions.

One technique that can be helpful if you find yourself with a large number of function parameters is to put your function parameters in a structure. Consider the following program, which contains a function named `print_report()` that uses 10 parameters. Instead of making an enormous function declaration and proto-type, the `print_report()` function uses a structure to get its parameters:

```
#include <stdio.h>

typedef struct
{
    int        orientation;
    char       rpt_name[25];
    char       rpt_path[40];
    int        destination;
    char       output_file[25];
    int        starting_page;
    int        ending_page;
    char       db_name[25];
    char       db_path[40];
    int        draft_quality;
} RPT_PARMS;

void main(void);
int print_report(RPT_PARMS*);

void main(void)
{
    RPT_PARMS rpt_parm; /* define the report parameter
                           structure variable */

    ...

    /* set up the report parameter structure variable to pass to the
    print_report() function */
```

```
        rpt_parm.orientation = ORIENT_LANDSCAPE;
        rpt_parm.rpt_name = "QSALES.RPT";
        rpt_parm.rpt_path = "C:\REPORTS";
        rpt_parm.destination = DEST_FILE;
        rpt_parm.output_file = "QSALES.TXT";
        rpt_parm.starting_page = 1;
        rpt_parm.ending_page = RPT_END;
        rpt_parm.db_name = "SALES.DB";
        rpt_parm.db_path = "C:\DATA";
        rpt_parm.draft_quality = TRUE;

    /* Call the print_report() function, passing it a pointer to the
       parameters instead of passing it a long list of 10 separate
       parameters. */

    ret_code = print_report(&rpt_parm);

    ...

}

int print_report(RPT_PARMS* p)
{

    int rc;

    ...

    /* access the report parameters passed to the print_report()
       function */

    orient_printer(p->orientation);

    set_printer_quality((p->draft_quality == TRUE) ? DRAFT : NORMAL);

    ...

    return rc;

}
```

The preceding example avoided a large, messy function prototype and definition by setting up a predefined structure of type RPT_PARMS to hold the 10 parameters that were needed by the print_report() function. The only possible disadvantage to this approach is that by removing the parameters from the function definition, you are bypassing the compiler's capability to type-check each of the parameters for validity during the compile stage.

Generally, you should keep your functions small and focused, with as few parameters as possible to help with execution speed. If you find yourself writing lengthy functions with many parameters, maybe you should rethink your function design or consider using the structure-passing technique presented here. Additionally, keeping your functions small and focused will help when you are trying to isolate and fix bugs in your programs.

Cross Reference:

VIII.4: What is a static function?
Answer:

A *static* function is a function whose *scope* is limited to the current source file. Scope refers to the visibility of a function or variable. If the function or variable is visible outside of the current source file, it is said to have global, or external, scope. If the function or variable is not visible outside of the current source file, it is said to have local, or static, scope.

A static function therefore can be seen and used only by other functions within the current source file. When you have a function that you know will not be used outside of the current source file or if you have a function that you do not want being used outside of the current source file, you should declare it as static. Declaring local functions as static is considered good programming practice. You should use static functions often to avoid possible conflicts with external functions that might have the same name.

For instance, consider the following example program, which contains two functions. The first function, open_customer_table(), is a global function that can be called by any module. The second function, open_customer_indexes(), is a local function that will never be called by another module. This is because you can't have the customer's index files open without first having the customer table open. Here is the code:

```
#include <stdio.h>

int open_customer_table(void);        /* global function, callable from
                                         any module */
static int open_customer_indexes(void); /* local function, used only in
                                            this module */

int open_customer_table(void)
{
    int ret_code;

    /* open the customer table */

    ...

    if (ret_code == OK)
    {
        ret_code = open_customer_indexes();
    }

    return ret_code;

}
```

```
static int open_customer_indexes(void)
{

    int ret_code;

    /* open the index files used for this table */

    ...

    return ret_code;

}
```

Generally, if the function you are writing will not be used outside of the current source file, you should declare it as static.

Cross Reference:

VIII.1: When should I declare a function?

VIII.2: Why should I prototype a function?

VIII.3: How many parameters should a function have?

VIII.5: Should a function contain a *return* statement if it does not return a value?

Answer:

In C, *void* functions (those that do not return a value to the calling function) are not required to include a return statement. Therefore, it is not necessary to include a return statement in your functions declared as being void.

In some cases, your function might trigger some critical error, and an immediate exit from the function might be necessary. In this case, it is perfectly acceptable to use a return statement to bypass the rest of the function's code. However, keep in mind that it is not considered good programming practice to litter your functions with return statements—generally, you should keep your function's exit point as focused and clean as possible.

Cross Reference:

VIII.8: What does a function declared as PASCAL do differently?

VIII.9: Is using exit() the same as using return?

VIII.6: How can you pass an array to a function by value?

Answer:

An array can be passed to a function by value by declaring in the called function the array name with square brackets ([and]) attached to the end. When calling the function, simply pass the address of the array (that is, the array's name) to the called function. For instance, the following program passes the array x[] to the function named byval_func() by value:

```
#include <stdio.h>

void byval_func(int[]);       /* the byval_func() function is passed an
                                 integer array by value */

void main(void);

void main(void)
{
    int x[10];
    int y;

    /* Set up the integer array. */

    for (y=0; y<10; y++)
        x[y] = y;

    /* Call byval_func(), passing the x array by value. */

    byval_func(x);

}

/* The byval_function receives an integer array by value. */

void byval_func(int i[])
{
    int y;

    /* Print the contents of the integer array. */

    for (y=0; y<10; y++)
        printf("%d\n", i[y]);

}
```

In this example program, an integer array named x is defined and initialized with 10 values. The function byval_func() is declared as follows:

```
int byval_func(int[]);
```

The int[] parameter tells the compiler that the byval_func() function will take one argument—an array of integers. When the byval_func() function is called, you pass the address of the array to byval_func():

```
byval_func(x);
```

Because the array is being passed by value, an exact copy of the array is made and placed on the stack. The called function then receives this copy of the array and can print it. Because the array passed to byval_func() is a copy of the original array, modifying the array within the byval_func() function has no effect on the original array.

Passing arrays of any kind to functions can be very costly in several ways. First, this approach is very inefficient because an entire copy of the array must be made and placed on the stack. This takes up valuable program time, and your program execution time is degraded. Second, because a copy of the array is made, more memory (stack) space is required. Third, copying the array requires more code generated by the compiler, so your program is larger.

Instead of passing arrays to functions by value, you should consider passing arrays to functions by reference: this means including a pointer to the original array. When you use this method, no copy of the array is made. Your programs are therefore smaller and more efficient, and they take up less stack space. To pass an array by reference, you simply declare in the called function prototype a pointer to the data type you are holding in the array.

Consider the following program, which passes the same array (x) to a function:

```c
#include <stdio.h>

void const_func(const int*);
void main(void);

void main(void)
{
    int x[10];
    int y;

    /* Set up the integer array. */

    for (y=0; y<10; y++)
        x[y] = y;

    /* Call const_func(), passing the x array by reference. */

    const_func(x);

}

/* The const_function receives an integer array by reference.
   Notice that the pointer is declared as const, which renders
   it unmodifiable by the const_func() function. */

void const_func(const int* i)
{
    int y;

    /* Print the contents of the integer array. */
```

```
    for (y=0; y<10; y++)
        printf("%d\n", *(i+y));
}
```

In the preceding example program, an integer array named x is defined and initialized with 10 values. The function const_func() is declared as follows:

```
int const_func(const int*);
```

The const int* parameter tells the compiler that the const_func() function will take one argument—a constant pointer to an integer. When the const_func() function is called, you pass the address of the array to const_func():

```
const_func(x);
```

Because the array is being passed by reference, no copy of the array is made and placed on the stack. The called function receives simply a constant pointer to an integer. The called function must be coded to be smart enough to know that what it is really receiving is a constant pointer to an array of integers. The const modifier is used to prevent the const_func() from accidentally modifying any elements of the original array.

The only possible drawback to this alternative method of passing arrays is that the called function must be coded correctly to access the array—it is not readily apparent by the const_func() function prototype or definition that it is being passed a reference to an array of integers. You will find, however, that this method is much quicker and more efficient, and it is recommended when speed is of utmost importance.

Cross Reference:

VIII.8: What does a function declared as PASCAL do differently?

VIII.7: Is it possible to execute code even after the program exits the *main()* function?

Answer:

The standard C library provides a function named atexit() that can be used to perform "cleanup" operations when your program terminates. You can set up a set of functions you want to perform automatically when your program exits by passing function pointers to the atexit() function. Here's an example of a program that uses the atexit() function:

```
#include <stdio.h>
#include <stdlib.h>

void close_files(void);
void print_registration_message(void);
int main(int, char**);

int main(int argc, char** argv)
{
```

```
    ...

    atexit(print_registration_message);
    atexit(close_files);

    while (rec_count < max_records)
    {

        process_one_record();

    }

    exit(0);

}
```

This example program uses the atexit() function to signify that the close_files() function and the print_registration_message() function need to be called automatically when the program exits. When the main() function ends, these two functions will be called to close the files and print the registration message.

There are two things that should be noted regarding the atexit() function. First, the functions you specify to execute at program termination must be declared as void functions that take no parameters. Second, the functions you designate with the atexit() function are stacked in the order in which they are called with atexit(), and therefore they are executed in a last-in, first-out (LIFO) method. Keep this information in mind when using the atexit() function. In the preceding example, the atexit() function is stacked as shown here:

```
atexit(print_registration_message);
atexit(close_files);
```

Because the LIFO method is used, the close_files() function will be called first, and then the print_registration_message() function will be called.

The atexit() function can come in handy when you want to ensure that certain functions (such as closing your program's data files) are performed before your program terminates.

Cross Reference:

VIII.9: Is using exit() the same as using return?

VIII.8: What does a function declared as *PASCAL* do differently?

Answer:

A C function declared as PASCAL uses a different *calling convention* than a "regular" C function. Normally, C function parameters are passed right to left; with the PASCAL calling convention, the parameters are passed left to right.

Consider the following function, which is declared normally in a C program:

```
int regular_func(int, char*, long);
```

Using the standard C calling convention, the parameters are pushed on the stack from right to left. This means that when the `regular_func()` function is called in C, the stack will contain the following parameters:

```
long
char*
int
```

The function calling `regular_func()` is responsible for restoring the stack when `regular_func()` returns. When the PASCAL calling convention is being used, the parameters are pushed on the stack from left to right.

Consider the following function, which is declared as using the PASCAL calling convention:

```
int PASCAL pascal_func(int, char*, long);
```

When the function `pascal_func()` is called in C, the stack will contain the following parameters:

```
int
char*
long
```

The function being called is responsible for restoring the stack pointer. Why does this matter? Is there any benefit to using PASCAL functions?

Functions that use the PASCAL calling convention are more efficient than regular C functions—the function calls tend to be slightly faster. Microsoft Windows is an example of an operating environment that uses the PASCAL calling convention. The Windows SDK (Software Development Kit) contains hundreds of functions declared as PASCAL.

When Windows was first designed and written in the late 1980s, using the PASCAL modifier tended to make a noticeable difference in program execution speed. In today's world of fast machinery, the PASCAL modifier is much less of a catalyst when it comes to the speed of your programs. In fact, Microsoft has abandoned the PASCAL calling convention style for the Windows NT operating system.

In your world of programming, if milliseconds make a big difference in your programs, you might want to use the PASCAL modifier when declaring your functions. Most of the time, however, the difference in speed is hardly noticeable, and you would do just fine to use C's regular calling convention.

Cross Reference:

VIII.6: How can you pass an array to a function by value?

VIII.9: Is using *exit()* the same as using *return*?
Answer:

No. The `exit()` function is used to exit your program and return control to the operating system. The `return` statement is used to return from a function and return control to the calling function. If you issue a return from the `main()` function, you are essentially returning control to the calling function, which is the operating system. In this case, the `return` statement and `exit()` function are similar. Here is an example of a program that uses the `exit()` function and `return` statement:

```
#include <stdio.h>
#include <stdlib.h>

int main(int, char**);
```

```
int do_processing(void);
int do_something_daring();

int main(int argc, char** argv)
{
    int ret_code;

    if (argc < 3)
    {
        printf("Wrong number of arguments used!\n");

        /* return 1 to the operating system */

        exit(1);

    }

    ret_code = do_processing();

    ...

    /* return 0 to the operating system */

    exit(0);

}

int do_processing(void)
{
    int rc;

    rc = do_something_daring();

    if (rc == ERROR)
    {
        printf("Something fishy is going on around here..."\n);

        /* return rc to the operating system */

        exit(rc);

    }

    /* return 0 to the calling function */

    return 0;

}
```

In the main() function, the program is exited if the argument count (argc) is less than 3. The statement

```
exit(1);
```

tells the program to exit and return the number 1 to the operating system. The operating system can then decide what to do based on the return value of the program. For instance, many DOS batch files check the environment variable named ERRORLEVEL for the return value of executable programs.

Cross Reference:

VIII.5: Should a function contain a return statement if it does not return a value?

CHAPTER IX

◆

Arrays

A big part of C's popularity is due to the way it handles arrays. C handles arrays very efficiently for three reasons.

First, except for some interpreters that are helpfully paranoid, array subscripting is done at a very low level. There's not enough information at runtime to tell how long an array is, or whether a subscript is valid. The language of the ANSI/ISO C standard says that if you use an invalid subscript, the behavior is undefined. That means that your program can (a) work correctly, maybe, (b) halt or crash dramatically, (c) continue running but get the wrong answer, or (d) none of the above. You don't know what your program will do. This is a Bad Thing. Some people use this weakness as justification to criticize C as merely a high-level assembler language. Certainly, when C programs fail, they can fail spectacularly. But when they're written and tested well, they run fast.

Second, arrays and pointers work very well together. When used in an expression, the value of an array is the same as a pointer to its first element. That makes pointers and arrays almost interchangeable. Using pointers can be twice as fast as using array subscripts. (See FAQ IX.5 for an example.)

Third, when an array is passed as a parameter to a function, it's exactly as if a pointer to the first element was passed. There's no feature built into the C language for copying the contents of arrays ("call by value"). (Structures that contain arrays are copied, which might seem inconsistent.) Just the address ("call by reference") is much faster than call by value. C++ and ANSI C have the const keyword, which allows call by reference to be as safe as call by value. For details, see FAQ II.4 and the beginning of Chapter VII, "Pointers and Memory Allocation."

The equivalence of array and pointer parameters causes some confusion. A function defined as

```
void  f( char a[ MAX ] )
{
      /* ... */
}
```

(in which MAX is a #defined "manifest constant" or some other value known at compile time) is *exactly* the same as this:

```
void  f( char *a )
{
      /* ... */
}
```

This equivalence is the third advantage described previously. Most C programmers learn it early. It's confusing because it's the *only* case in which pointers and arrays mean exactly the same thing. If you write (anywhere but in the declaration of a function parameter)

```
char    a[ MAX ];
```

then space is made for MAX characters. If you write

```
char    *a;
```

instead, then space is made for a char pointer, which is probably only as big as two or four chars. This can be a real disaster if you define

```
char    a[ MAX ];
```

in a source file but declare

```
extern  char    *a;
```

in a header file. The best way to check this is to always have the declaration visible (by #includeing the appropriate header file) when making a definition.

If you define

```
char    a[ MAX ];
```

in a source file, you can declare

```
extern  char    a[];
```

in the appropriate header file. This tells any #includeing files that a is an array, not a pointer. It doesn't say how long a is. This is called an "incomplete" type. Using incomplete types this way is a common practice, and a good one.

IX.1: Do array subscripts always start with zero?
Answer:

Yes. If you have an array a[MAX] (in which MAX is some value known at compile time), the first element is a[0], and the last element is a[MAX-1]. This arrangement is different from what you would find in some other languages. In some languages, such as some versions of BASIC, the elements would be a[1] through a[MAX], and in other languages, such as Pascal, you can have it either way.

> ◈ WARNING
>
> a[MAX] is a valid address, but the value there is not an element of array a (see FAQ IX.2).

This variance can lead to some confusion. The "first element" in non-technical terms is the "zero'th" element according to its array index. If you're using spoken words, use "first" as the opposite of "last." If that's not precise enough, use pseudo-C. You might say, "The elements a sub one through a sub eight," or, "The second through ninth elements of a."

There's something you can do to try to fake array subscripts that start with one. Don't do it. The technique is described here only so that you'll know why not to use it.

Because pointers and arrays are almost identical, you might consider creating a pointer that would refer to the same elements as an array but would use indices that start with one. For example:

```
/* don't do this!!! */
int     a0[ MAX ];
int     *a1 = a0 - 1;   /* & a[ -1 ] */
```

Thus, the first element of a0 (if this worked, which it might not) would be the same as a1[1]. The last element of a0, a0[MAX-1], would be the same as a1[MAX]. There are two reasons why you shouldn't do this.

The first reason is that it might not work. According to the ANSI/ISO standard, it's undefined (which is a Bad Thing). The problem is that &a[-1] might not be a valid address; see FAQ IX.3. Your program might work all the time with some compilers, and some of the time with all compilers. Is that good enough?

The second reason not to do this is that it's not C-like. Part of learning C is to learn how array indices work. Part of reading (and maintaining) someone else's C code is being able to recognize common C idioms. If you do weird stuff like this, it'll be harder for people to understand your code. (It'll be harder for you to understand your own code, six months later.)

Cross Reference:

IX.2: Is it valid to address one element beyond the end of an array?

IX.3: Why worry about the addresses of the elements beyond the end of an array?

IX.2: Is it valid to address one element beyond the end of an array?

Answer:

It's valid to address it, but not to see what's there. (The really short answer is, "Yes, so don't worry about it.")

With most compilers, if you say

```
int     i, a[MAX], j;
```

then either i or j is at the part of memory just after the last element of the array. The way to see whether i or j follows the array is to compare their addresses with that of the element following the array. The way to say this in C is that either

```
& i == & a[ MAX ]
```

is true or

```
& a[ MAX ] == & j
```

is true. This isn't guaranteed; it's just the way it usually works.

The point is, if you store something in a[MAX], you'll usually clobber something outside the a array. Even looking at the value of a[MAX] is technically against the rules, although it's not usually a problem.

Why would you ever want to say &a[MAX]? There's a common idiom of going through every member of a loop using a pointer (see FAQ IX.5). Instead of

```
for ( i = 0; i < MAX; ++i )
{
        /* do something */;
}
```

C programmers often write this:

```
for ( p = a; p < & a[ MAX ]; ++p )
{
        /* do something */;
}
```

The kind of loop shown here is so common in existing C code that the C standard says it must work.

Cross Reference:

IX.3: Why worry about the addresses of the elements beyond the end of an array?

IX.5: Is it better to use a pointer to navigate an array of values, or is it better to use a subscripted array name?

IX.3: Why worry about the addresses of the elements beyond the end of an array?

Answer:

If your programs ran only on nice machines on which the addresses were always between 0x00000000 and 0xFFFFFFFF (or something similar), you wouldn't need to worry. But life isn't always that simple.

Sometimes addresses are composed of two parts. The first part (often called the "base") is a pointer to the beginning of some chunk of memory; the second part is an offset from the beginning of that chunk. The most notorious example of this is the Intel 8086, which is the basis for all MS-DOS programs. (Your shiny new

Pentium chip runs most MS-DOS applications in 8086 compatibility mode.) This is called a "segmented architecture." Even nice RISC chips with linear address spaces have register indexing, in which one register points to the beginning of a chunk, and the second is an offset. Subroutine calls are usually implemented with an offset from a stack pointer.

What if your program was using base/offset addresses, and some array a0 was the first thing in the chunk of memory being pointed to? (More formally, what if the base pointer was the same as & a0[0]?) The point is, because the base can't be changed (efficiently) and the offset can't be negative, there might not be a valid way of saying "the element before a0[0]." The ANSI C standard specifically says attempts to get at this element are undefined. That's why the idea discussed in FAQ IX.1 might not work.

The only other time there could be a problem with the address of the element beyond the end of an array is if the array is the last thing that fits in memory (or in the current memory segment). If the last element of a (that is, a[MAX-1]) is at the last address in memory, what's the address of the element after it? There isn't one. The compiler must complain that there's not enough room for the array, if that's what it takes to ensure that &a[MAX] is valid.

You can say you'll only ever write programs for Windows or UNIX or Macintoshes. The people who defined the C programming language don't have that luxury. They had to define C so that it would work in weird environments, such as microprocessor-controlled toasters and anti-lock braking systems and MS-DOS. They defined it so that programs written strictly by the rules can be compiled and run for almost anything. Whether you want to break the strict rules sometimes is between you, your compiler, and your customers.

Cross Reference:

IX.1: Do array subscripts always start with zero?

IX.2: Is it valid to address one element beyond the end of an array?

IX.4: Can the *sizeof* operator be used to tell the size of an array passed to a function?

Answer:

No. There's no way to tell, at runtime, how many elements are in an array parameter just by looking at the array parameter itself. Remember, passing an array to a function is exactly the same as passing a pointer to the first element. This is a Good Thing. It means that passing pointers and arrays to C functions is very efficient.

It also means that the programmer must use some mechanism to tell how big such an array is. There are two common ways to do that. The first method is to pass a count along with the array. This is what memcpy() does, for example:

```
char    source[ MAX ], dest[ MAX ];
/* ... */
memcpy( dest, source, MAX );
```

The second method is to have some convention about when the array ends. For example, a C "string" is just a pointer to the first character; the string is terminated by an ASCII NUL (`'\0'`) character. This is also commonly done when you have an array of pointers; the last is the null pointer. Consider the following function, which takes an array of char*s. The last char* in the array is NULL; that's how the function knows when to stop.

```
void printMany( char *strings[] )
{
        int     i;
        i = 0;
        while ( strings[ i ] != NULL )
        {
            puts( strings[ i ] );
            ++i;
        }
}
```

Most C programmers would write this code a little more cryptically:

```
void  printMany( char *strings[] )
{
        while ( *strings )
        {
                puts( *strings++ );
        }
}
```

As discussed in FAQ IX.5, C programmers often use pointers rather than indices. You can't change the value of an array tag, but because strings is an array parameter, it's really the same as a pointer (see FAQ IX.6). That's why you can increment strings. Also,

```
while ( *strings )
```

means the same thing as

```
while ( *strings != NULL )
```

and the increment can be moved up into the call to puts().

If you document a function (if you write comments at the beginning, or if you write a "manual page" or a design document), it's important to describe how the function "knows" the size of the arrays passed to it. This description can be something simple, such as "null terminated," or "elephants has numElephants elements." (Or "arr should have 13 elements," if your code is written that way. Using hard coded numbers such as 13 or 64 or 1024 is not a great way to write C code, though.)

Cross Reference:

IX.5: Is it better to use a pointer to navigate an array of values, or is it better to use a subscripted array name?

IX.6: Can you assign a different address to an array tag?

IX.5: Is it better to use a pointer to navigate an array of values, or is it better to use a subscripted array name?

Answer:

It's easier for a C compiler to generate good code for pointers than for subscripts.

Say that you have this:

```
/* X is some type */
X       a[ MAX ];        /* array */
X       *p;     /* pointer */
X       x;      /* element */
int     i;      /* index */
```

Here's one way to loop through all elements:

```
/* version (a) */
for ( i = 0; i < MAX; ++i )
{
        x = a[ i ];
        /* do something with x */
}
```

On the other hand, you could write the loop this way:

```
/* version (b) */
for ( p = a; p < & a[ MAX ]; ++p )
{
        x = *p;
        /* do something with x */
}
```

What's different between these two versions? The initialization and increment in the loop are the same. The comparison is about the same; more on that in a moment. The difference is between x=a[i] and x=*p. The first has to find the address of a[i]; to do that, it needs to multiply i by the size of an X and add it to the address of the first element of a. The second just has to go indirect on the p pointer. Indirection is fast; multiplication is relatively slow.

This is "micro efficiency." It might matter, it might not. If you're adding the elements of an array, or simply moving information from one place to another, much of the time in the loop will be spent just using the array index. If you do any I/O, or even call a function, each time through the loop, the relative cost of indexing will be insignificant.

Some multiplications are less expensive than others. If the size of an X is 1, the multiplication can be optimized away (1 times anything is the original anything). If the size of an X is a power of 2 (and it usually is if X is any of the built-in types), the multiplication can be optimized into a left shift. (It's like multiplying by 10 in base 10.)

What about computing &a[MAX] every time though the loop? That's part of the comparison in the pointer version. Isn't it as expensive computing a[i] each time? It's not, because &a[MAX] doesn't change during the loop. Any decent compiler will compute that, once, at the beginning of the loop, and use the same value each time. It's as if you had written this:

```
/* how the compiler implements version (b) */
X       *temp = & a[ MAX ];      /* optimization */
for ( p = a; p < temp; ++p )
{
        x = *p;
        /* do something with x */
}
```

This works only if the compiler can tell that a and MAX can't change in the middle of the loop.

There are two other versions; both count down rather than up. That's no help for a task such as printing the elements of an array in order. It's fine for adding the values or something similar. The index version presumes that it's cheaper to compare a value with zero than to compare it with some arbitrary value:

```
/* version (c) */
for ( i = MAX - 1; i >= 0; --i )
{
        x = a[ i ];
        /* do something with x */
}
```

The pointer version makes the comparison simpler:

```
/* version (d) */
for ( p = & a[ MAX - 1 ]; p >= a; --p )
{
        x = *p;
        /* do something with x */
}
```

Code similar to that in version (d) is common, but not necessarily right. The loop ends only when p is less than a. That might not be possible, as described in FAQ IX.3.

The common wisdom would finish by saying, "Any decent optimizing compiler would generate the same code for all four versions." Unfortunately, there seems to be a lack of decent optimizing compilers in the world. A test program (in which the size of an X was not a power of 2 and in which the "do something" was trivial) was built with four very different compilers. Version (b) always ran much faster than version (a), sometimes twice as fast. Using pointers rather than indices made a big difference. (Clearly, all four compilers optimize &a[MAX] out of the loop.)

How about counting down rather than counting up? With two compilers, versions (c) and (d) were about the same as version (a); version (b) was the clear winner. (Maybe the comparison is cheaper, but decrementing is slower than incrementing?) With the other two compilers, version (c) was about the same as version (a) (indices are slow), but version (d) was slightly faster than version (b).

So if you want to write portable efficient code to navigate an array of values, using a pointer is faster than using subscripts. Use version (b); version (d) might not work, and even if it does, it might be compiled into slower code.

Most of the time, though, this is micro-optimizing. The "do something" in the loop is where most of the time is spent, usually. Too many C programmers are like half-sloppy carpenters; they sweep up the sawdust but leave a bunch of two-by-fours lying around.

Cross Reference:

IX.2: Is it valid to address one element beyond the end of an array?

IX.3: Why worry about the addresses of the elements beyond the end of an array?

IX.6: Can you assign a different address to an array tag?
Answer:

No, although in one common special case, it looks as if you can.

An array tag is not something you can put on the left side of an assignment operator. (It's not an "lvalue," let alone a "modifiable lvalue.") An array is an object; the array tag is a pointer to the first element in that object.

For an external or static array, the array tag is a constant value known at link time. You can no more change the value of such an array tag than you can change the value of 7.

Assigning to an array tag would be missing the point. An array tag is not a pointer. A pointer says, "Here's one element; there might be others before or after it." An array tag says, "Here's the first element of an array; there's nothing before it, and you should use an index to find anything after it." If you want a pointer, use a pointer.

In one special case, it looks as if you can change an array tag:

```
void  f( char a[ 12 ] )
{
        ++a;     /* legal! */
}
```

The trick here is that array parameters aren't really arrays. They're really pointers. The preceding example is equivalent to this:

```
void  f( char *a )
{
        ++a;     /* certainly legal */
}
```

You can write this function so that the array tag can't be modified. Oddly enough, you need to use pointer syntax:

```
void  f( char * const a )
{
        ++a;     /* illegal */
}
```

Here, the parameter is an lvalue, but the const keyword means it's not modifiable.

Cross Reference:

IX.4: Can the `sizeof` operator be used to tell the size of an array passed to a function?

IX.7: What is the difference between *array_name* and *&array_name*?
Answer:

One is a pointer to the first element in the array; the other is a pointer to the array as a whole.

> **NOTE**
>
> It's strongly suggested that you put this book down for a minute and write the declaration of a variable that points to an array of MAX characters. Hint: Use parentheses. If you botch this assignment, what do you get instead? Playing around like this is the only way to learn the arcane syntax C uses for pointers to complicated things. The solution is at the end of this answer.

An array is a type. It has a base type (what it's an array of), a size (unless it's an "incomplete" array), and a value (the value of the whole array). You can get a pointer to this value:

```
char     a[ MAX ];          /* array of MAX characters */
char     *p;                /* pointer to one character */
/* pa is declared below */
pa = & a;
p = a;   /* = & a[ 0 ] */
```

After running that code fragment, you might find that p and pa would be printed as the same value; they both point to the same address. They point to different types of MAX characters.

The wrong answer is

```
char *( ap[ MAX ] );
```

which is the same as this:

```
char *ap[ MAX ];
```

This code reads, "ap is an array of MAX pointers to characters."

Cross Reference:

None.

IX.8: Why can't constant values be used to define an array's initial size?

Answer:

There are times when constant values can be used and there are times when they can't. A C program can use what C considers to be constant expressions, but not everything C++ would accept.

When defining the size of an array, you need to use a constant expression. A constant expression will always have the same value, no matter what happens at runtime, and it's easy for the compiler to figure out what that value is. It might be a simple numeric literal:

```
char    a[ 512 ];
```

Or it might be a "manifest constant" defined by the preprocessor:

```
#define MAX       512
/* ... */
char    a[ MAX ];
```

Or it might be a `sizeof`:

```
char    a[ sizeof( struct cacheObject ) ];
```

Or it might be an expression built up of constant expressions:

```
char    buf[ sizeof( struct cacheObject ) * MAX ];
```

Enumerations are allowed too.

An initialized `const int` variable is not a constant expression in C:

```
int     max = 512;      /* not a constant expression in C */
char    buffer[ max ];  /* not valid C */
```

Using `const int`s as array sizes is perfectly legal in C++; it's even recommended. That puts a burden on C++ compilers (to keep track of the values of `const int` variables) that C compilers don't need to worry about. On the other hand, it frees C++ programs from using the C preprocessor quite so much.

Cross Reference:

XV.1: Should C++ additions to a compiler be used in a C program?

XV.2: What is the difference between C++ and C?

IX.9: What is the difference between a string and an array?

Answer:

An array is an array of anything. A string is a specific kind of an array with a well-known convention to determine its length.

There are two kinds of programming languages: those in which a string is just an array of characters, and those in which it's a special type. In C, a string is just an array of characters (type char), with one wrinkle: a C string always ends with a NUL character. The "value" of an array is the same as the address of (or a pointer to) the first element; so, frequently, a C string and a pointer to char are used to mean the same thing.

An array can be any length. If it's passed to a function, there's no way the function can tell how long the array is supposed to be, unless some convention is used. The convention for strings is NUL termination; the last character is an ASCII NUL ('\0') character.

In C, you can have a literal for an integer, such as the value of 42; for a character, such as the value of '*'; or for a floating-point number, such as the value of 4.2e1 for a float or double.

> **NOTE**
>
> Actually, what looks like a type char literal is just a type int literal with a funny syntax. 42 and '*' are exactly the same value. This isn't the case for C++, which has true char literals and function parameters, and which generally distinguishes more carefully between a char and an int.

There's no such thing as a literal for an array of integers, or an arbitrary array of characters. It would be very hard to write a program without string literals, though, so C provides them. Remember, C strings conventionally end with a NUL character, so C string literals do as well. "six times nine" is 15 characters long (including the NUL terminator), not just the 14 characters you can see.

There's a little-known, but very useful, rule about string literals. If you have two or more string literals, one after the other, the compiler treats them as if they were one big string literal. There's only one terminating NUL character. That means that "Hello, " "world" is the same as "Hello, world", and that

```
char    message[] =
  "This is an extremely long prompt\n"
  "How long is it?\n"
  "It's so long,\n"
  "It wouldn't fit on one line\n";
```

is exactly the same as some code that wouldn't fit on this page of the book.

When defining a string variable, you need to have either an array that's long enough or a pointer to some area that's long enough. Make sure that you leave room for the NUL terminator. The following example code has a problem:

```
char greeting[ 12 ];
strcpy( greeting, "Hello, world" );    /* trouble */
```

There's a problem because greeting has room for only 12 characters, and "Hello, world" is 13 characters long (including the terminating NUL character). The NUL character will be copied to someplace beyond the greeting array, probably trashing something else nearby in memory. On the other hand,

```
char    greeting[ 12 ] = "Hello, world";  /* not a string */
```

is OK if you treat greeting as a char array, not a string. Because there wasn't room for the NUL terminator, the NUL is not part of greeting. A better way to do this is to write

```
char    greeting[] = "Hello, world";
```

to make the compiler figure out how much room is needed for everything, including the terminating NUL character.

String literals are arrays of characters (type char), not arrays of constant characters (type const char). The ANSI C committee could have redefined them to be arrays of const char, but millions of lines of code would have screamed in terror and suddenly not compiled. The compiler won't stop you from trying to modify the contents of a string literal. You shouldn't do it, though. A compiler can choose to put string literals in some part of memory that can't be modified—in ROM, or somewhere the memory mapping registers will forbid writes. Even if string literals are someplace where they could be modified, the compiler can make them shared. For example, if you write

```
char    *p = "message";
char    *q = "message";
p[ 4 ] = '\0';   /* p now points to "mess" */
```

(and the literals are modifiable), the compiler can take one of two actions. It can create two separate string constants, or it can create just one (that both p and q point to). Depending on what the compiler did, q might still be a message, or it might just be a mess.

NOTE

This is "C humor." Now you know why so few programmers quit their day jobs for stand-up comedy.

Cross Reference:

IX.1: Do array subscripts always start with zero?

CHAPTER

◆

Bits and Bytes

A bit is the smallest unit of information there is. It is a single digit in the binary number system, with the value "0" or "1". Two aspects of a bit make it useful. First, a bit's value can be interpreted as anything at all by the computer. That single bit might represent "yes" or "no," or the presence or absence of a disk, or whether a mouse button is pressed. Second, the values of several bits can be concatenated to represent more complex data. Each bit that's tacked on doubles the number of possible values that can be represented.

In other words, one bit can hold two possible values, "0" or "1". Two bits can hold 2×2, or four, possible values, "00", "01", "10", or "11". Likewise, three bits can hold 2×2×2, or eight, possible values, and so on. This characteristic is both the greatest strength and the greatest limitation of computers. It is a strength because very complex data (such as this book) can be stored by breaking down the information to its representation in bits. It is a weakness because many things in real life have inexact values, which cannot be represented in a finite number of bits.

Programmers must be constantly aware of how many bits must be used to hold each data item. Because a bit is such a small unit, most computers are designed to handle them in more convenient chunks called bytes. A byte is the smallest addressable unit of information on most computers. That means that the computer assigns an address to each byte of information, and it can retrieve or store information only a byte at a time. The number of bits in a byte is arbitrary and can be different on different machines. The most common value is eight bits per byte, which can be store up to 256 different values. Eight bits is a convenient size for storing data that represents characters in ASCII (the American Standard Code for Information Interchange).

The following program displays the ASCII character set, starting with the space character and continuing up through the graphics character set of the PC. Note that the variable ctr must be an int and not a char because a char consists of 8 bits and thus can hold only the values 0 through 255 (or −128 to 127 for signed chars). If ctr were a char, it could never hold a value of 256 or greater, so the program would never end. If you run this program on a machine other than a PC, note that the non-ASCII characters this program prints might result in a garbled screen.

```c
#include <stdio.h>

void main(void);

void main()
{
   /*  Display ASCII char set */

   unsigned char space = ' ';      /*  Start with SPACE
                                        char = 8 bits only */

   int ctr = 0;

   printf("ASCII Characters\n");
   printf("================\n");
   for (ctr = 0; ctr + space < 256; ctr++)
      printf("%c", ctr + space);

   printf("\n");
}
```

Because the computer works in chunks of bytes, most programs work this way as well. Sometimes it becomes necessary to conserve memory space because of either the number of items to be stored or the time it takes to move each bit of information. In this case, we would like to use less than one byte for storing information that has only a few possible values. That's what this chapter is all about.

X.1: What is the most efficient way to store flag values?

Answer:

A flag is a value used to make a decision between two or more options in the execution of a program. For instance, the /w flag on the MS-DOS dir command causes the command to display filenames in several columns across the screen instead of displaying them one per line. Another example of a flag can be seen in the answer to FAQ III.5, in which a flag is used to indicate which of two possible types is held in a union. Because a flag has a small number of values (often only two), it is tempting to save memory space by not storing each flag in its own int or char.

Efficiency in this case is a tradeoff between size and speed. The most memory-space efficient way to store a flag value is as single bits or groups of bits just large enough to hold all the possible values. This is because most computers cannot address individual bits in memory, so the bit or bits of interest must be extracted from the bytes that contain it.

The most time-efficient way to store flag values is to keep each in its own integer variable. Unfortunately, this method can waste up to 31 bits of a 32-bit variable, which can lead to very inefficient use of memory.

If there are only a few flags, it doesn't matter how they are stored. If there are many flags, it might be advantageous to store them packed in an array of characters or integers. They must then be extracted by a process called bit masking, in which unwanted bits are removed from the ones of interest.

Sometimes it is possible to combine a flag with another value to save space. It might be possible to use high-order bits of integers that have values smaller than what an integer can hold. Another possibility is that some data is always a multiple of 2 or 4, so the low-order bits can be used to store a flag. For instance, in FAQ III.5, the low-order bit of a pointer is used to hold a flag that identifies which of two possible types the pointer points to.

Cross Reference:

X.2: What is meant by "bit masking"?

X.3: Are bit fields portable?

X.4: Is it better to bitshift a value than to multiply by 2?

X.2: What is meant by "bit masking"?
Answer:

Bit masking means selecting only certain bits from byte(s) that might have many bits set. To examine some bits of a byte, the byte is bitwise "ANDed" with a mask that is a number consisting of only those bits of interest. For instance, to look at the one's digit (rightmost digit) of the variable flags, you bitwise AND it with a mask of one (the bitwise AND operator in C is &):

```
flags & 1;
```

To set the bits of interest, the number is bitwise "ORed" with the bit mask (the bitwise OR operator in C is ¦). For instance, you could set the one's digit of flags like so:

```
flags = flags ¦ 1;
```

Or, equivalently, you could set it like this:

```
flags ¦= 1;
```

To clear the bits of interest, the number is bitwise ANDed with the one's complement of the bit mask. The "one's complement" of a number is the number with all its one bits changed to zeros and all its zero bits changed to ones. The one's complement operator in C is ~. For instance, you could clear the one's digit of flags like so:

```
flags = flags & ~1;
```

Or, equivalently, you could clear it like this:

```
flags &= ~1;
```

Sometimes it is easier to use macros to manipulate flag values. Listing X.2 shows a program that uses some macros to simplify bit manipulation.

Listing X.2. Macros that make manipulating flags easier.

```
/* Bit Masking */

/* Bit masking can be used to switch a character
   between lowercase and uppercase */

#define BIT_POS(N)            ( 1U << (N) )
#define SET_FLAG(N, F)        ( (N) |= (F) )
#define CLR_FLAG(N, F)        ( (N) &= -(F) )
#define TST_FLAG(N, F)        ( (N) & (F) )

#define BIT_RANGE(N, M)       ( BIT_POS((M)+1 - (N))-1 << (N) )
#define BIT_SHIFTL(B, N)      ( (unsigned)(B) << (N) )
#define BIT_SHIFTR(B, N)      ( (unsigned)(B) >> (N) )
#define SET_MFLAG(N, F, V)    ( CLR_FLAG(N, F), SET_FLAG(N, V) )
#define CLR_MFLAG(N, F)       ( (N) &= ~(F) )
#define GET_MFLAG(N, F)       ( (N) & (F) )

#include <stdio.h>

void main()
{

  unsigned char ascii_char = 'A';         /*  char = 8 bits only */
  int test_nbr = 10;

  printf("Starting character = %c\n", ascii_char);

  /*  The 5th bit position determines if the character is
      uppercase or lowercase.
      5th bit = 0  - Uppercase
      5th bit = 1  - Lowercase         */

  printf("\nTurn 5th bit on = %c\n", SET_FLAG(ascii_char, BIT_POS(5)) );
  printf("Turn 5th bit off = %c\n\n", CLR_FLAG(ascii_char, BIT_POS(5)) );

  printf("Look at shifting bits\n");
  printf("=====================\n");
  printf("Current value = %d\n", test_nbr);
  printf("Shifting one position left = %d\n",
         test_nbr = BIT_SHIFTL(test_nbr, 1) );
  printf("Shifting two positions right = %d\n",
         BIT_SHIFTR(test_nbr, 2) );
}
```

BIT_POS(N) takes an integer N and returns a bit mask corresponding to that single bit position (BIT_POS(0) returns a bit mask for the one's digit, BIT_POS(1) returns a bit mask for the two's digit, and so on). So instead of writing

```
#define A_FLAG   4096
#define B_FLAG   8192
```

you can write

```
#define A_FLAG  BIT_POS(12)
#define B_FLAG  BIT_POS(13)
```

which is less prone to errors.

The SET_FLAG(N, F) macro sets the bit at position F of variable N. Its opposite is CLR_FLAG(N, F), which clears the bit at position F of variable N. Finally, TST_FLAG(N, F) can be used to test the value of the bit at position F of variable N, as in

```
if (TST_FLAG(flags, A_FLAG))
        /* do something */;
```

The macro BIT_RANGE(N, M) produces a bit mask corresponding to bit positions N through M, inclusive. With this macro, instead of writing

```
#define FIRST_OCTAL_DIGIT   7         /* 111 */
#define SECOND_OCTAL_DIGIT 56         /* 111000 */
```

you can write

```
#define FIRST_OCTAL_DIGIT  BIT_RANGE(0, 2)   /* 111 */
#define SECOND_OCTAL_DIGIT BIT_RANGE(3, 5)   /* 111000 */
```

which more clearly indicates which bits are meant.

The macro BIT_SHIFT(B, N) can be used to shift value B into the proper bit range (starting with bit N). For instance, if you had a flag called C that could take on one of five possible colors, the colors might be defined like this:

```
#define C_FLAG          BIT_RANGE(8, 10)      /* 11100000000 */

/* here are all the values the C flag can take on */
#define C_BLACK         BIT_SHIFTL(0, 8)      /* 00000000000 */
#define C_RED           BIT_SHIFTL(1, 8)      /* 00100000000 */
#define C_GREEN         BIT_SHIFTL(2, 8)      /* 01000000000 */
#define C_BLUE          BIT_SHIFTL(3, 8)      /* 01100000000 */
#define C_WHITE         BIT_SHIFTL(4, 8)      /* 10000000000 */

#define C_ZERO          C_BLACK
#define C_LARGEST       C_WHITE

/* A truly paranoid programmer might do this */
#if C_LARGEST > C_FLAG
        Cause an error message. The flag C_FLAG is not
        big enough to hold all its possible values.
#endif /* C_LARGEST > C_FLAG */
```

The macro SET_MFLAG(N, F, V) sets flag F in variable N to the value V. The macro CLR_MFLAG(N, F) is identical to CLR_FLAG(N, F), except the name is changed so that all the operations on multibit flags have a similar naming convention. The macro GET_MFLAG(N, F) gets the value of flag F in variable N, so it can be tested, as in

```
if (GET_MFLAG(flags, C_FLAG) == C_BLUE)
        /* do something */;
```

NOTE

Beware that the macros `BIT_RANGE()` and `SET_MFLAG()` refer to the N argument twice, so the expression

```
SET_MFLAG(*x++, C_FLAG, C_RED);
```

will have undefined, potentially disastrous behavior.

Cross Reference:

X.1: What is the most efficient way to store flag values?

X.3: Are bit fields portable?

X.3: Are bit fields portable?

Answer:

Bit fields are not portable. Because bit fields cannot span machine words, and because the number of bits in a machine word is different on different machines, a particular program using bit fields might not even compile on a particular machine.

Assuming that your program does compile, the order in which bits are assigned to bit fields is not defined. Therefore, different compilers, or even different versions of the same compiler, could produce code that would not work properly on data generated by compiled older code. Stay away from using bit fields, except in cases in which the machine can directly address bits in memory and the compiler can generate code to take advantage of it and the increase in speed to be gained would be essential to the operation of the program.

Cross Reference:

X.1: What is the most efficient way to store flag values?

X.2: What is meant by "bit masking"?

X.4: Is it better to bitshift a value than to multiply by 2?

Answer:

Any decent optimizing compiler will generate the same code no matter which way you write it. Use whichever form is more readable in the context in which it appears. The following program's assembler code can be viewed with a tool such as CODEVIEW on DOS/Windows or the disassembler (usually called "dis") on UNIX machines:

Listing X.4. Multiplying by 2 and shifting left by 1 are often the same.

```
void main()
{

  unsigned int test_nbr = 300;
  test_nbr *= 2;

  test_nbr = 300;
  test_nbr <<= 1;

}
```

Cross Reference:

X.1: What is the most efficient way to store flag values?

X.5: What is meant by high-order and low-order bytes?
Answer:

We generally write numbers from left to right, with the most significant digit first. To understand what is meant by the "significance" of a digit, think of how much happier you would be if the first digit of your paycheck was increased by one compared to the last digit being increased by one.

The bits in a byte of computer memory can be considered digits of a number written in base 2. That means the least significant bit represents one, the next bit represents 2×1, or 2, the next bit represents 2×2×1, or 4, and so on. If you consider two bytes of memory as representing a single 16-bit number, one byte will hold the least significant 8 bits, and the other will hold the most significant 8 bits. Figure X.5 shows the bits arranged into two bytes. The byte holding the least significant 8 bits is called the least significant byte, or low-order byte. The byte containing the most significant 8 bits is the most significant byte, or high-order byte.

Figure X.5.

The bits in a two-byte integer.

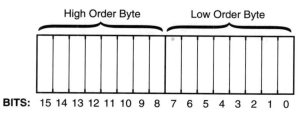

BITS: 15 14 13 12 11 10 9 8 7 6 5 4 3 2 1 0

Cross Reference:

X.6: How are 16- and 32-bit numbers stored?

X.6: How are 16- and 32-bit numbers stored?

Answer:

A 16-bit number takes two bytes of storage, a most significant byte and a least significant byte. The preceding FAQ (X.5) explains which byte is which. If you write the 16-bit number on paper, you would start with the most significant byte and end with the least significant byte. There is no convention for which order to store them in memory, however.

Let's call the most significant byte M and the least significant byte L. There are two possible ways to store these bytes in memory. You could store M first, followed by L, or L first, followed by M. Storing byte M first in memory is called "forward" or "big-endian" byte ordering. The term *big endian* comes from the fact that the "big end" of the number comes first, and it is also a reference to the book *Gulliver's Travels,* in which the term refers to people who eat their boiled eggs with the big end on top.

Storing byte L first is called "reverse" or "little-endian" byte ordering. Most machines store data in a big-endian format. Intel CPUs store data in a little-endian format, however, which can be confusing when someone is trying to connect an Intel microprocessor-based machine to anything else.

A 32-bit number takes four bytes of storage. Let's call them Mm, Ml, Lm, and Ll in decreasing order of significance. There are 4! (4 factorial, or 24) different ways in which these bytes can be ordered. Over the years, computer designers have used just about all 24 ways. The most popular two ways in use today, however, are (Mm, Ml, Lm, Ll), which is big-endian, and (Ll, Lm, Ml, Mm), which is little-endian. As with 16-bit numbers, most machines store 32-bit numbers in a big-endian format, but Intel machines store 32-bit numbers in a little-endian format.

Cross Reference:

X.5: What is meant by high-order and low-order bytes?

XI

CHAPTER

Debugging

Debugging is the process of removing problems—often called bugs—from your program. A bug can be as simple as misspelling a word or omitting a semicolon, or it can be as complex as using a pointer that contains a nonexistent address. Regardless of the complexity of the problem, knowing how to debug properly can be very beneficial to all programmers.

XI.1: My program hangs when I run it. What should I do?

Answer:

There are many reasons a program might stop working when you run it. These reasons fall into four basic categories:

The program is in an infinite loop.

The program is taking longer than expected.

The program is waiting for input from some source and will not continue until that input is correctly entered.

The program was designed to delay for an unspecified period or to halt execution.

An examination of each of these situations will follow, after a discussion of the techniques for debugging programs that hang for no apparent reason.

Debugging programs that hang for no reason can be particularly difficult. You might spend hours carefully crafting a program, trying to assure yourself that all the code is exactly as intended, or you might make one tiny modification to an existing program that had previously worked perfectly. In either case, you run the program and are rewarded with an empty screen. If you had gotten erroneous results, or even partial results, you would have something to work with. A blank screen is frustrating. You don't even know what went wrong.

To begin debugging a program like this, you should look at the listing and assure yourself that each section of the program, in the order in which the sections should be executed, is working properly. For example, say that the main program consists only of calls to three functions. We'll call them functions A(), B(), and C().

Start by verifying that function A() returns control to the main program. You can do this by placing an exit() command directly after the call to function A(), or by commenting out the calls to functions B() and C(). You then can recompile and rerun the program.

NOTE

This action could, of course, be carried out just as well with a debugger; however, this answer illustrates the classical approach to debugging. A debugger is a program that enables the programmer to observe the execution of his program, the current line it is on, the value of variables, and so forth.

What this will show is whether function A() ever returns control to the main program. If the program runs and exits, you will know that it is another part of the program that is hanging up. You can continue to test all the routines in this way until you discover the guilty routine. Then you can focus your attention on the offending function.

Sometimes the situation will be somewhat more complex. For example, the function in which your program hangs might be perfectly OK. The problem might be that that function is getting erroneous data from somewhere else. In this case, you will need to monitor the values your function is accepting and observe which ones are causing the undesired behavior.

TIP

Monitoring functions is an excellent use for a debugger.

An examination of a sample program will help illustrate the use of this technique:

```c
#include <stdio.h>
#include <stdlib.h>

/*
 *   Declare the functions that the main function is using
 */

int A() , B( int ) , C( int , int );
```

```
/*
 *  The main program
 */

int A() , B() , C(); /* These are functions in some other
                         module */

int main()
{
    int v1 , v2 , v3;

    v1 = A();
    v2 = B( v1 );
    v3 = C( v1 , v2 );
    printf( "The Result is %d.\n" , v3 );
    return(0);
}
```

After the line that invokes function A( ), you can print the value of the variable v1 to assure yourself that *it is within the range of values the function B( ) will accept.* Even if function B( ) is the one taking forever to execute, it might not be the erroneous function; rather, function A( ) might be giving B( ) values that it never expected.

Now that you've examined the method of debugging programs that simply "hang," it's time to look at some of the common errors that cause a program to hang.

Infinite Loops

When your program is in an infinite loop, it is executing a block of code an infinite number of times. This action, of course, is probably not what the programmer intended. The programmer has in some way caused the condition that keeps the program in the loop to never be false or, alternatively, has caused the condition that would make the program leave the loop to never be true. Look at a few examples of infinite loops:

```
/* initialize a double dimension array */

for( a = 0 ; a < 10 ; ++ a )
{
    for( b = 0 ; b < 10 ; ++ a )
    {
        array[ a ][ b ] = 0;
    }
}
```

The problem here is that, due to a mistake the programmer made (probably typographical in nature), the second loop, which can end only when the variable b is incremented to 10, never increments the variable b! The third part of the second for loop increments a—the wrong variable. This block of code will run forever, because b will always be less than 10.

How are you to catch such an error? Unless you notice that the variable b is never being incremented by reviewing the code, you might never catch the error. Inserting the statement

```
printf(" %d %d %d\n" , a , b , array[ a ][ b ] );
```

inside the brace of the second for loop is one action you might take while attempting to debug the code. You might expect the output from this code fragment to resemble this:

```
0 0 0
0 1 0
(and eventually reaching)
9 9 0
```

But what you would really see as output is this:

```
0 0 0
1 0 0
2 0 0
...
```

You would have a never-ending sequence, with the first number continually getting larger. Printing the variables in this fashion not only will help you catch this bug, but it also will let you know if the array did not contain the values expected. This error could conceivably be very difficult to detect otherwise! This technique of printing the contents of variables will be used again.

Other Causes of Infinite Loops

There are many other possible causes for infinite loops. Consider the following code fragment:

```
unsigned int nbr;

for( nbr = 10 ; nbr >= 0 ; -- nbr )
{
    /* do something */
}
```

This fragment of code will run forever, because nbr, as an unsigned variable, will always be greater than or equal to zero because, by definition, an unsigned variable can never be negative. When nbr reaches zero and is decremented, the result is undefined. In practice, it will become a very large positive number. Printing the value of the variable nbr inside the loop would lead you to this unusual behavior.

Yet another cause of infinite loops can be while loops in which the condition never becomes false. Here's an example:

```
int main()
{
    int a = 7;

    while( a < 10 )
    {
        ++a;
        a /= 2;
    }
    return( 0 );
}
```

Although the variable a is being incremented after every iteration of the loop, it is also being halved. With the variable being initially set to 7, it will be incremented to 8, then halved to 4. It will never climb as high as 10, and the loop will never terminate.

Taking Longer Than Expected to Execute

In some instances, you might discover that your program is not completely "locked up" but is merely taking longer than expected to execute. This situation can be frustrating, especially if you are working on a very fast computer that can perform incredibly complex tasks in minuscule amounts of time. Following are some program fragments that might take longer to execute than you would expect:

```
/*
 *  A subroutine to calculate Fibonacci numbers
 */

int fib( int i )
{
    if ( i < 3 )
        return 1;
    else
        return fib( i - 1 ) + fib( i - 2 );
}
```

A Fibonacci number is the sum of the two Fibonacci numbers that precede it, with the exception of one and two, which are set to zero. Fibonacci numbers are mathematically very interesting and have many practical applications.

NOTE

> An example of a Fibonacci number can be seen in a sunflower. A sunflower has two spirals of seeds, one of 21 seeds and one of 34 seeds. These are adjacent Fibonacci numbers.

On the face of it, the preceding code fragment is a very simple expression of the definition of Fibonacci numbers. It seems, because of its minuscule length and simplicity, that it should take very little time to execute. In reality, waiting for the computer to discover the Fibonacci value for a relatively small value, such as 100, could leave one ready to collect Social Security. The following text will examine why this is so.

Say that you want to compute the Fibonacci value for the number 40. The routine sums the Fibonacci values for 39 and 38. It has to compute these values as well, so for each of these two numbers, the routine must sum two subvalues. So, for the first step, there are two subproblems, for the next step, there are four, next, eight. The result of all of this is that an exponential number of steps end up being performed. For example, in the process of computing the Fibonacci value for the number 40, the fib() function is called more than 200 million times! Even on a relatively fast computer, this process could take several minutes.

Another problem that might take an unexpectedly long time to solve is the sorting of numbers:

```
/*
 *  Routine to sort an array of integers.
 *  Takes two parameters:
 *    ar -- The array of numbers to be sorted, and
 *    size -- the size of the array.
 */

void sort( int ar[] , int size )
{
    int i,j;
    for( i = 0 ; i < size - 1 ; ++ i )
    {
        for( j = 0 ; j < size - 1 ; ++ j )
        {
            if ( ar[ j ] > ar[ j + 1 ] )
            {
                int temp;
```

```
                        temp = ar[ j ];
                        ar[ j ] = ar[ j + 1 ];
                        ar[ j + 1 ] = temp;
                    }
                }
            }
        }
```

Upon testing this code with several short lists of numbers, you might be quite pleased; it will sort short lists of numbers very well and very quickly. But if you put it into a program and give it a very large list of numbers, the program might seem to freeze. In any case, it will take a long time to execute. Why is that?

For the answer, look at the nested for loops. There are two loops, one inside the other, both of them with the range of 0 to size - 1. This translates to the code inside of both loops being executed size*size, or *size squared times*! This code will perform acceptably on lists of 10 items; 10 squared is only 100. If, however, you try to sort a list of 5000 items, the code in the loop is executing 25 million times. And if you try to sort a list of one million numbers, which is not very uncommon in computer science, the code in the loop will be executed *one trillion times.*

In either of these cases, you need to be able to accurately assess how much work the code is actually doing. This assessment falls into the realm of algorithmic analysis, which is important for every programmer to know.

Waiting for Correct Input

Sometimes the program stops working because it is waiting for correct input from some source. This problem can manifest itself in several ways. The simplest way is if your program is waiting for information from the user, but you have forgotten to have it print a prompt of some sort. The program is waiting for input, but the user does not know this; the program appears to have locked up. This problem can also manifest itself in a slightly more insidious fashion due to buffering of output. This topic is discussed in more depth in FAQ XVII.1.

However, consider the following code fragment:

```
/*
 *  This program reads all the numbers from a file,
 *  sums them, and prints them.
 */

#include <stdio.h>

main()
{
    FILE *in = fopen( "numbers.dat" , "r" );
    int total = 0 , n;

    while( fscanf( in , " %d" , &n ) != EOF )
    {
        total += n;
    }

    printf( "The total is %d\n" , total );
    fclose( in );
}
```

This program will work perfectly well, and quickly, as long as the file NUMBERS.DAT contains integer numbers—and *only* integer numbers. If the file contains anything that is not a valid integer value, the behavior of the program will be curious. When it reaches the flawed value, it will see that the value is not an integer. It will not read the value; instead it will return an error code. However, the program hasn't reached the end of file yet, so the comparison to EOF will not be true. Therefore, the loop executes, with some undefined value for n, and tries to read from the file again. And it finds the same erroneous data there. Remember, it didn't read in the data, because it was incorrect. The program will cycle endlessly, forever trying to read in the bad data. This problem could be solved by having the while loop also test whether correct data has been read.

Of course, there are many other possible reasons that a program might hang or otherwise appear to freeze; however, generally, the cause will be in one of these three categories.

Cross Reference:

XI.2: How can I detect memory leaks?

XI.2: How can I detect memory leaks?
Answer:

A memory leak occurs when dynamically allocated memory—that is, memory that has been allocated using a form of malloc() or calloc()—is not deleted when it is no longer needed. Not freeing memory is not an error in itself; the compiler will not complain, and your program will not crash immediately when memory is not freed. The effect is that as more and more unused memory fails to be freed, the free space available to the program for new data will shrink. Eventually, when the program tries to allocate storage, it will find that none is available. This situation can cause the program to behave oddly, especially if the programmer has not accounted for the possibility of memory allocation failing.

Memory leaks are one of the most difficult errors to detect, as well as some of the most dangerous. This is because the programming error that causes the problem can be made very early on in the development of the program, but the error will not become apparent until later, when the program mysteriously runs out of memory when it is run "for real." Looking at the line that contains the failed allocation also will not help. The line of the program that allocated memory and failed to free it might be somewhere else entirely.

Unfortunately, the C language has no built-in way to detect or fix memory leaks. Aside from commercial packages that repair or detect memory leaks, detecting and repairing memory leaks requires a great deal of patience and care on the part of the programmer. It is far better to keep the possibility of memory leaks in mind while developing the program and to exercise great caution concerning them.

The simplest, and perhaps most common, cause of memory leakage is forgetting to free memory that has been allocated for use as temporary scratch space, as in the following code fragment:

```
#include <stdio.h>
#include <stdlib.h>

/*
 * Say hello to the user, and put the user's name in UPPERCASE.
 */
```

```
void SayHi( char *name )
{
    char *UpName;
    int a;

    UpName = malloc( strlen( name ) + 1 );
                        /* Allocate space for the name */
    for( a = 0 ; a < strlen( name ) ; ++ a )
        UpName[ a ] = toupper( name[ a ] );
    UpName[ a ] = '\0';

    printf( "Hello, %s!\n" , UpName );
}

int main()
{
    SayHi( "Dave" );
    return( 0 );
}
```

Of course, the problem here is easy to see—the program allocates temporary space for the storage of the uppercase version of the name but never frees it. There is a simple way to ensure that this problem will never happen. Whenever temporary space is allocated, immediately type the corresponding free statement, and insert the code that uses the temporary space in between them. This method ensures that every allocated block of memory will be cleaned up when it is no longer needed, as long as the program does not somehow leave the space in between allocation and freeing by break, continue, or the evil goto.

If this was all there was to fixing memory leaks, it would be no problem—this is a rather trivial matter to fix. In the real world of programming, however, blocks of memory are allocated and often are needed for an undetermined period; memory leakage might result if the code that handles or deletes memory blocks is in some way flawed. For example, in the process of deleting a linked list, a last node might be missed, or a pointer that is pointing to a block of memory might be overwritten. These kinds of problems can be fixed only by careful and meticulous programming or, as has already been mentioned, by packages that track memory, or by language extensions.

Cross Reference:

XI.1: My program hangs when I run it. What should I do?

XI.3: What is the best way to debug my program?
Answer:

To know which method is best for debugging a program, you have to examine all three stages of the debugging process:

- ◆ What tools should be used to debug a program?
- ◆ What methods can be used to find bugs in a program?
- ◆ How can bugs be avoided in the first place?

What Tools Should Be Used to Debug a Program?

There are many tools that the skilled programmer can use to help him debug his program. These include an array of debuggers, "lint" programs, and, last but not least, the compiler itself.

Debuggers are really wonderful for finding logic errors in programs, and consequently they are what most programmers choose as their primary debugging tools. Debuggers commonly enable the programmer to complete the following tasks:

1. Observe the program's execution.

    This capability alone would make the typical debugger invaluable. Very frequently, even with code that you have carefully written over a period of several months, it is not always clear what the program is doing at all times. Forgotten if statements, function calls, and branches might cause blocks of code to be skipped or executed when this is not what the programmer would expect. In any case, being able to see which lines of code are being executed at all times, especially during odd behavior, gives the programmer a good idea of what the program is doing and where the error lies.

2. Set breakpoints.

    By setting a breakpoint, you can cause a program to halt its execution at a certain point. This feature is useful if you know where the error in your program is. You can set the breakpoint before the questionable code, inside the code itself, or immediately after the code. When your program encounters the breakpoint and ceases execution, you can then examine the state of all the local variables, parameters, and global data. If everything is OK, the execution of the program can be resumed, until it encounters the breakpoint again or until the conditions that are causing the problem assert themselves.

3. Set watches.

    Debuggers enable the programmer to watch a variable. "Watch a variable" means that you can constantly monitor the variable's value or contents. If you are aware that a variable should never stray out of a certain range or should always have valid contents, this capability can quickly point out the source of an error. Additionally, you can cause the debugger to watch the variable for you and halt the execution of the program when a variable strays out of a predefined range, or when a condition has been met. If you are aware of what all your variables should do, this is quite easy.

Good debuggers often have additional features that are designed to ease the task of debugging. A debugger, however, is not the only tool that can be used to debug your programs. Programs such as "lint" and your compiler itself can provide valuable insight into the workings of your code.

NOTE

> Lint is a program that knows of hundreds of common programmer mistakes and points out all of them in your program. Many are not real errors, but most are worth addressing.

What these tools typically offer that a debugger cannot are *compile-time checks*. While they are compiling your code, they can look for questionable code, code that might have unintended effects, and common mistakes. Examining a few instances in which this kind of checking is used can be helpful.

Incorrect Mixing of Equality Operators

Compile-time checking can be helpful in working with the incorrect mixing of equality operators. Consider the following code fragment:

```
void foo( int a , int b )
{
    if ( a = b )
    {
        /* some code here */
    }
}
```

This kind of error can be very difficult to spot! Instead of comparing the variables, this function sets a to the value of b and executes the conditional value if b is nonzero! This action is probably not what the programmer intended (although it might be). Not only will the code be executed at the wrong times, but the value of a will be wrong when it is used later.

Uninitialized Variables

Compile-time checking can also be helpful in finding uninitialized variables. Consider the following function:

```
void average( float ar[] , int size )
{
    float total;
    int a;

    for( a = 0 ; a < size ; ++ a )
    {
        total += ar[ a ];
    }

    printf( " %f\n" , total / (float) size );
}
```

The problem here is that the variable total is never initialized; it therefore can, and probably will, contain some random garbage value. The sum of all the values in the array is added to this random garbage value (this part of the program is correct), and the average, plus the random garbage, is printed.

Implicit Casting of Variables

The C language will in some cases implicitly cast variables of one type into another. Sometimes this is a good thing (it saves the programmer from having to perform this task), but it can have unintended behavior. Perhaps the worst implicit cast is that of pointer-to-integer.

```
void sort( int ar[] , int size )
{
    /* code to sort goes here */
}

int main()
{
    int array[ 10 ];
    sort( 10 , array );
}
```

Again, this code is clearly not what the programmer intended. The results of actually executing this code, although undefined, will almost surely be catastrophic.

What Methods Can Be Used to Find Bugs in a Program?

The programmer should follow several tips during the debugging of his program.

Debug the Small Subroutines of Your Program; Move On to the Larger Ones Later

If your program is well written, it will have a number of small subsections. It is good to prove to yourself that these are correct. Despite the probability that the error in the program will not be in one of these subsections, debugging these subsections first will help give you a better understanding of the overall program structure, as well as verifying where the error is not. Furthermore, when examining the larger components of the program, you can be assured that this particular subcomponent is working properly.

Thoroughly Debug a Section of a Program Before Moving On to the Next One

This tip is very important. By proving to yourself that a section of code is correct, not only have you eliminated a possible area of error, but areas of the program that utilize this subsection can depend on its proper functioning. This also utilizes a good rule of thumb—namely, that the difficulty of debugging a section of code is equal to the square of its length. Thus, debugging a 20-line block of code is four times harder than debugging a 10-line block of code. It therefore aids in the debugging process to focus on one small segment of code at a time. This is only a general rule; use it with discretion and judgment.

Constantly Observe the Flow of Your Program and the Modification of Its Data

This is very important! If you have designed and written your program carefully, you should know, from watching the output, exactly which section of code is being executed and what the contents of the various variable are. Obviously, if your program is behaving incorrectly, this is not the case. There is little else to do but either use a debugger or fill your program with `print` statements and watch the flow of control and the contents of important variables.

Turn Compiler Warnings Up All the Way, and Attempt to Eliminate All Warnings

If you haven't been taking this action throughout the development of your program, this could be quite a job! Although many programmers consider eliminating compiler warnings to be a tedious hassle, it is quite valuable. Most code that compilers warn about is, at the very least, questionable. And it is usually worth the effort to turn it into "safer" constructs. Furthermore, by eliminating warnings, you might get to the point where the compiler is only emitting one warning—the error.

"Home In" on the Error

If you can go directly to the part of the program that has the error and search for it there, you can save yourself a lot of debugging time, as well as make hundreds of thousands of dollars as a professional debugger. In real life, we can't always go straight to the error. What we often do is eliminate parts of the program that could be in error and, by the process of elimination, arrive at the part of the program that must contain the error, no matter how difficult to see. Then all the debugging effort can be invested in this part of the code. Needless to say, it is very important to assure yourself that you really have eliminated the other blocks of code. Otherwise, you might be focusing your attention on a part of the program that is actually OK.

How Can Bugs Be Avoided in the First Place?

There's an old saying that an ounce of prevention is worth a pound of cure. This means that it's always better (easier) to ensure that a problem doesn't occur than to attempt to fix it after it has made its ugly presence felt. This is most certainly true in computer programming! A very good programmer might spend quite a long time carefully writing a program, more than a less experienced programmer might spend. But because of his patient and careful coding techniques, he might spend little, if any, time debugging his code. Furthermore, if at some time in the future his program is to develop some problem, or needs to be modified in some way, he most likely will be able to fix the bug or add the code quite quickly. On a poorly coded program, even a generally "correct" one, fixing a bug that has cropped up only after a period of time, or modifying a program, can be a nightmare.

Programs that are easy to debug and modify, generally speaking, follow the rules of structured programming. Take a look at some of the rules of structured programming.

Code Should Be Liberally Commented

Again, some programmers find commenting one's code to be a real drag. But even if you never intend to have someone else look at your code, it's a very good idea to liberally comment it. Even code that you have written that seems very clear to you now can become ugly and impossible to read after a few months. This is not to say that commenting can never be bad; too many comments can actually obscure the meaning of the code. But it can be a good idea to place a few lines of comment in each function and before each bit of code that is doing something important or something unclear. Here is an example of what might be considered well-commented code:

```
/*
 *      Compute an integer factorial value using recursion.
 *      Input : an integer number.
 *      Output : another integer
 *      Side effects : may blow up stack if input value is *Huge*
 */

int factorial( int number )
{
    if ( number <= 1 )
        return 1; /* The factorial of one is one; QED */
    else
        return n * factorial( n - 1 )/
    /* The magic! This is possible because the factorial of a
       number is the number itself times the factorial of the
       number minus one. Neat! */
}
```

Functions Should Be Concise

In light of the previously stated rule of thumb—that the difficulty of debugging a block of code is equivalent to the square of its length—this rule about keeping functions concise should make perfect sense. However, there's even more to it than that. If a function is concise, you should need a few moments of careful examination and a few careful tests to assure yourself that the function is bug free. After doing this, you can proceed to code the rest of the program, confident in the knowledge that one of your building blocks is OK. You should never have to look at it again. You are unlikely to have this level of confidence in a long, complex routine.

Another benefit of using small building-block functions is that after a small, functional bit of code has been defined, you might find it useful in other parts of your program as well. For example, if you were writing a financial program, you might need, in different parts of your program, to calculate interest by quarters, by months, by weeks, by days in a month, and so forth. If you were writing the program in an unstructured fashion, you might believe that you need separate code in each of these cases to compute the results. The program would become large and unreadable, in part due to repeated computations of compound interest. However, you could break off this task into a separate function like the one that follows:

```
/*
 *    Compute what the "real" rate of interest would be
 *    for a given flat interest rate, divided into N segments
 */

double Compute Interest( double Rate , int Segments )
{
    int a;
    double Result = 1.0;

    Rate /= (double) Segments;

    for( a = 0 ; a < Segments ; ++ a )
        Result *= Rate;

    return Result;
}
```

After you have written this function, you can use it anywhere you need to compute compound interest. You have not only possibly eliminated several errors in all the duplicated code, but considerably shortened and clarified the rest of the code. This technique might make other errors easier to find.

After this technique of breaking down a program into manageable components becomes a habit, you will see many subtler applications of its magic.

Program Flow Should Proceed "Straight Through"; gotos and Other Jumps Should Be Eliminated

This principle, although generally accepted by the computer establishment, is still hotly debated in some circles. However, it is generally agreed upon that programs with fewer statements that cause the program flow to unconditionally skip parts of the code are much easier to debug. This is because such programs are generally more straightforward and easier to understand. What many programmers do not understand is how to replace these "unstructured jumps" (which they might have learned from programming in assembly language, FORTRAN, or BASIC) with the "correct" structured constructs. Here are a few examples of how this task should be done:

```
for( a = 0 ; a < 100 ; ++ a )
{
    Func1( a );
    if ( a == 2 ) continue;
    Func2( a );
}
```

This code uses the continue statement to skip the rest of the loop if a is equal to 2. This could be recoded in the following manner:

```
for( a = 0 ; a < 100 ; ++ a )
{
    Func1( a );
    if ( a != 2 )
        Func2( a );
}
```

This code is easier to debug because you can tell what might be executed and what might not, based on the braces. How does this make your code easier to modify and debug? Suppose that you wanted to add some code that should be executed at the end of the loop every time. In the first case, if you noticed the continue, you would have to make complex changes to the code (try this; it's not intuitively obvious!). If you didn't notice the continue, you would get a hard-to-understand bug. For the second program fragment, the change would be simple. You would simply add the new function to the end of the loop.

Another possible error can arise when you are using the break statement. Suppose that you had written the following code:

```
for( a = 0 ; a < 100 ; ++ a )
{
    if ( Func1( a ) == 2 )
        break;
    Func2( a );
}
```

This loop proceeds from one to 100—assuming that the return value of Func1() is never equal to 2. If this situation ever occurs, the loop will terminate before reaching 100. If you are ever to add code to the loop, you might assume that it really does iterate from 0 to 99 based on the loop body. This assumption might cause you to make a dangerous error. Another danger could result from using the value of a; it's not guaranteed to be 100 after the loop.

C enables you to account for this situation, by writing the for loop like this:

```
for( a = 0 ; a < 100 && Func1( a ) != 2 ; ++ a )
```

This loop explicitly states to the programmer, "Iterate from 0 to 99, but halt iteration if Func1() ever equals 2." Because the entire exit condition is so apparent, it will be difficult to make a later mistake.

Function and Variable Names Should Be Descriptive

Creating function and variable names that are descriptive will make the purpose of your code much clearer—and can even be said to make your code self-documenting. This is best explained by a few examples.

Which is clearer:

```
y=p+i-c;
```

or

```
YearlySum = Principal + Interest - Charges;
```

Which is clearer:

```
p=*(l+o);
```

or

```
page = &List[ Offset ];
```

Cross Reference:

None.

XI.4: How can I debug a TSR program?

Answer:

A TSR (terminate and stay resident) program is one that, after executing, remains resident in the computer's memory and continues to carry out some task. It does so by making some element of the computer's operating system periodically invoke the code that the TSR program has caused to remain resident in the computer's memory.

The way that TSR programs operate makes them very hard to debug! This is because, to the debugger, the program only truly executes for a very short period. The debugger really has no way of knowing exactly what the program is doing, and it has no way of knowing that the TSR program continues to run after it appears to have terminated. The very "invisibility" that makes TSRs so useful can cause immense problems!

Furthermore, the process whereby the program makes itself resident in memory, by changing vectors, by changing the size of free memory, and by other methods, can catastrophically interfere with the execution of the debugging program. It is also possible that the debugger might clobber the changes that the TSR has made.

In any case, unless you have a debugger specifically developed for TSR programs, using a debugger probably will not be possible. There are, however, other methods of debugging TSR programs.

First, you can reuse a method described earlier, namely, that of using print statements to monitor the progress of a program, but with slight modifications. Whenever the TSR program is invoked by the system by whatever method is chosen (keystroke, timer interrupt, and so on), you can open a log file in append mode and print messages to it that inform the programmer about the execution of the program. This could include functions that the flow of execution encounters, the values of variables, and other information. After the TSR program is finished running (or it crashes), you can examine the log file and gain valuable insight into the problem.

Another method is to create a "dummy" TSR program. In other words, create a program that would function as a TSR, but don't make it one! Instead, make it a subroutine of a testing program. The function that would normally accept the system interrupts could easily be modified to accept function calls from the main program. The main program could contain "canned" input that it would feed to the TSR, or it could accept input dynamically from the programmer. Your code, which otherwise behaves like a TSR, never installs itself in computer memory or changes any of the operating system's vectors.

The second method has several major benefits. It enables the programmer to use his customary debugging techniques and methods, including debuggers. It also gives the programmer a better way to watch the internal operation of his program. Furthermore, real TSR programs install themselves in memory and, if they are not removed, permanently consume a section of the computer's memory. If your program is not debugged, there is, of course, a chance that it is not removing itself from computer memory properly. This would otherwise lead to complete exhaustion of computer memory (much like a memory leak).

Cross Reference:

None.

XI.5: How do you get a program to tell you when (and where) a condition fails?

Answer:

In any program, there are some conditions that should never occur. These conditions include division by zero, writing to the null pointer, and so forth. You want to be informed whenever such conditions occur in your program, and furthermore, you want know exactly where they occur.

The C language comes with such a construct, in the form of the assert() command. The assert() command tests the condition inside its parentheses, and if the condition is false, it takes these steps:

1. Prints the text of the condition that failed.
2. Prints the line number of the error.
3. Prints the source code file that contains the error.
4. Causes the program to terminate with an error condition.

Stated succinctly, the assert() command is intended to ensure that conditions that should never occur do not. Take a look at what a few of these conditions might be.

One of the most common problems is being unable to allocate memory. If the memory is absolutely needed and there is no way to free some, there is little choice but to leave the program. An assertion is a good way to do this:

```
foo()
{
    char *buffer;
    buffer = malloc( 10000 );
    assert( buffer != NULL );
}
```

This means that if buffer is ever equal to NULL, the program will terminate, informing the programmer of the error and the line. Otherwise, the program will continue.

Another use of assert() might be this:

```
float IntFrac( int Num , int Denom )
{
    assert( Denom != 0 )
    return ( ( float ) Num ) / ( ( float ) Denom );

}
```

This use prevents the program from even dividing by zero.

It should be emphasized that assert() should be used only when the falsity of the condition would indicate catastrophic failure; if possible, the programmer should attempt to create code to handle the error more gracefully. In the preceding example, a special error value might be assigned to fractions with a zero denominator. This does not, however, mean that the assert() function is useless. A well-designed program should be full of asserts. After all, it is better to know that a disastrous condition is occurring than to be blissfully unaware of it (or, perhaps, unhappily aware!).

Another benefit of assert() is that by inserting the macro NDEBUG (no debugging) at the top of a program, you can cause all the asserts to be ignored during the compile. This is important for production versions of a program, after all the bugs have been fixed. You can distribute a version without the debugging code in the binary but, by removing the definition of NDEBUG, keep it in your version for debugging value. The code without all the tedious checks runs faster, and there is no chance of a customer's program suddenly stopping because a variable has strayed slightly out of range.

Cross Reference:

XI.1: My program hangs when I run it. What should I do?

XI.3: What is the best way to debug my program?

CHAPTER XII

◆

Standard Library Functions

Half the value of working with C comes from the standard library functions. Sure, it's nice to have that sexy `for` loop, and the similarity of arrays and pointers is convenient. When the rubber meets the road, though, what counts is how convenient it is to work with strings and files and such. Some programming languages do some parts of the task better; others do other parts better. When you have to do all of it, though, there's not much that does it better than C.

A lot is missing from the standard library. There are no functions for graphics, or even full-screen text manipulation. The `signal` mechanism (see FAQ XII.10) is pretty weak. There's absolutely no support for multitasking or for using anything but conventional memory. That's the point, though; the standard library provides functionality for all programs, whether they run in a multitasking, multiple-window environment, or on a dumb terminal, or in an expensive toaster. There are some de facto standards for the rest, and you can get some from your compiler vendor or a third-party library. What *is* in the standard library, though, is a very strong base to build on.

XII.1: Why should I use standard library functions instead of writing my own?

Answer:

The standard library functions have three advantages: they work, they're efficient, and they're portable.

They work: Your compiler vendor probably got them right. More important, the vendor is likely to have done a thorough test to prove they're right, more thorough than you probably have time for. (There are expensive test suites to make that job easier.)

They're efficient: Good C programmers use the standard library functions a lot, and good compiler vendors know that. There's a competitive advantage for the vendor to provide a good implementation. When competing compilers are compared for efficiency, a good compiler implementation can make all the difference. The vendor has more motivation than you do, and probably more time, to produce a fast implementation.

They're portable: In a world where software requirements change hourly, the standard library functions do the same thing, and mean the same thing, for every compiler, on every computer. They're one of the few things you, as a C programmer, can count on.

The funny thing is, one of the most standard pieces of information about the standard library is hard to find. For every function, there's one header file (or, rarely, two) that guarantees to give you that function's prototype. (You should always include the prototype for every function you call; see FAQ VIII.2.) What's funny? That header file might not be the file that actually contains the prototype. In some (sad!) cases, it's not even the header file recommended by the compiler manual. The same is true for macros, `typedefs`, and global variables.

To get the "right" header file, look up the function in a copy of the ANSI/ISO C standard. If you don't have a copy of the standard handy, use Table XII.2, shown in the next FAQ.

Cross Reference:

VIII.2: Why should I prototype a function?

XII.2: What header files do I need in order to define the standard library functions I use?

XII.2: What header files do I need in order to define the standard library functions I use?

Answer:

You need the ones that the ANSI/ISO standard says you should use. See Table XII.2.

The funny thing is, these are not necessarily the files that define what you're looking for. Your compiler guarantees that (for example) if you want the EDOM macro, you can get it by including `<errno.h>`. EDOM might be defined in <errno.h>, or <errno.h> might just include something that defines it. Worse, the next version of your compiler might define EDOM somewhere else.

Don't look in the files for the definition and use that file. Use the file that's supposed to define the symbol you want. It'll work.

A few names are defined in multiple files: NULL, size_t, and wchar_t. If you need a definition for one of these names, use a file you need to include anyway, or pick one arbitrarily. (<stddef.h> is a reasonable choice; it's small, and it defines common macros and types.)

Table XII.2. Standard library functions' header files.

Function/Macro	Header File
abort	stdlib.h
abs	stdlib.h
acos	math.h
asctime	time.h
asin	math.h
assert	assert.h
atan	math.h
atan2	math.h
atexit	stdlib.h
atof	stdlib.h
atoi	stdlib.h
atol	stdlib.h
bsearch	stdlib.h
BUFSIZ	stdio.h
calloc	stdlib.h
ceil	math.h
clearerr	stdio.h
clock	time.h
CLOCKS_PER_SEC	time.h
clock_t	time.h
cos	math.h
cosh	math.h
ctime	time.h
difftime	time.h
div	stdlib.h
div_t	stdlib.h
EDOM	errno.h

continues

Table XII.2. continued

Function/Macro	Header File
EOF	stdio.h
ERANGE	errno.h
errno	errno.h
exit	stdlib.h
EXIT_FAILURE	stdlib.h
EXIT_SUCCESS	stdlib.h
exp	math.h
fabs	math.h
fclose	stdio.h
feof	stdio.h
ferror	stdio.h
fflush	stdio.h
fgetc	stdio.h
fgetpos	stdio.h
fgets	stdio.h
FILE	stdio.h
FILENAME_MAX	stdio.h
floor	math.h
fmod	math.h
fopen	stdio.h
FOPEN_MAX	stdio.h
fpos_t	stdio.h
fprintf	stdio.h
fputc	stdio.h
fputs	stdio.h
fread	stdio.h
free	stdlib.h
freopen	stdio.h
frexp	math.h
fscanf	stdio.h
fseek	stdio.h
fsetpos	stdio.h
ftell	stdio.h
fwrite	stdio.h
getc	stdio.h

Function/Macro	Header File
getchar	stdio.h
getenv	stdlib.h
gets	stdio.h
gmtime	time.h
HUGE_VAL	math.h
_IOFBF	stdio.h
_IOLBF	stdio.h
_IONBF	stdio.h
isalnum	ctype.h
isalpha	ctype.h
iscntrl	ctype.h
isdigit	ctype.h
isgraph	ctype.h
islower	ctype.h
isprint	ctype.h
ispunct	ctype.h
isspace	ctype.h
isupper	ctype.h
isxdigit	ctype.h
jmp_buf	setjmp.h
labs	stdlib.h
LC_ALL	locale.h
LC_COLLATE	locale.h
LC_CTYPE	locale.h
LC_MONETARY	locale.h
LC_NUMERIC	locale.h
LC_TIME	locale.h
struct lconv	locale.h
ldexp	math.h
ldiv	stdlib.h
ldiv_t	stdlib.h
localeconv	locale.h
localtime	time.h
log	math.h
log10	math.h
longjmp	setjmp.h

continues

Table XII.2. continued

Function/Macro	Header File
L_tmpnam	stdio.h
malloc	stdlib.h
mblen	stdlib.h
mbstowcs	stdlib.h
mbtowc	stdlib.h
MB_CUR_MAX	stdlib.h
memchr	string.h
memcmp	string.h
memcpy	string.h
memmove	string.h
memset	string.h
mktime	time.h
modf	math.h
NDEBUG	assert.h
NULL	locale.h, stddef.h, stdio.h, stdlib.h, string.h, time.h
offsetof	stddef.h
perror	stdio.h
pow	math.h
printf	stdio.h
ptrdiff_t	stddef.h
putc	stdio.h
putchar	stdio.h
puts	stdio.h
qsort	stdlib.h
raise	signal.h
rand	stdlib.h
RAND_MAX	stdlib.h
realloc	stdlib.h
remove	stdio.h
rename	stdio.h
rewind	stdio.h
scanf	stdio.h
SEEK_CUR	stdio.h
SEEK_END	stdio.h
SEEK_SET	stdio.h

Function/Macro	Header File
setbuf	stdio.h
setjmp	setjmp.h
setlocale	locale.h
setvbuf	stdio.h
SIGABRT	signal.h
SIGFPE	signal.h
SIGILL	signal.h
SIGINT	signal.h
signal	signal.h
SIGSEGV	signal.h
SIGTERM	signal.h
sig_atomic_t	signal.h
SIG_DFL	signal.h
SIG_ERR	signal.h
SIG_IGN	signal.h
sin	math.h
sinh	math.h
size_t	stddef.h, stdlib.h, string.h, sprintf, stdio.h
sqrt	math.h
srand	stdlib.h
sscanf	stdio.h
stderr	stdio.h
stdin	stdio.h
stdout	stdio.h
strcat	string.h
strchr	string.h
strcmp	string.h
strcoll	string.h
strcpy	string.h
strcspn	string.h
strerror	string.h
strftime	time.h
strlen	string.h
strncat	string.h
strncmp	string.h
strncpy	string.h

continues

Table XII.2. continued

Function/Macro	Header File
strpbrk	string.h
strrchr	string.h
strspn	string.h
strstr	string.h
strtod	stdlib.h
strtok	string.h
strtol	stdlib.h
strtoul	stdlib.h
strxfrm	string.h
system	stdlib.h
tan	math.h
tanh	math.h
time	time.h
time_t	time.h
struct tm	time.h
tmpfile	stdio.h
tmpnam	stdio.h
TMP_MAX	stdio.h
tolower	ctype.h
toupper	ctype.h
ungetc	stdio.h
va_arg	stdarg.h
va_end	stdarg.h
va_list	stdarg.h
va_start	stdarg.h
vfprintf	stdio.h
vprintf	stdio.h
vsprintf	stdio.h
wchar_t	stddef.h, stdlib.h
wcstombs	stdlib.h
wctomb	stdlib.h

Cross Reference:

V.12: What is the difference between #include <file> and #include "file"?

XII.1: Why should I use standard library functions instead of writing my own?

XII.3: How can I write functions that take a variable number of arguments?

Answer:

Use <stdarg.h>. This defines some macros that let your program deal with variable numbers of arguments.

 NOTE

> The "variable arguments" functions used to be in a header file known as <varargs.h> or some such. Your compiler might or might not still have a file with that name; even if it does have the file now, it might not have it in the next release. Use <stdarg.h>.

There's no portable way for a C function, with no constraints on what it might be passed, to know how many arguments it might have gotten or what their types are. If a C function doesn't take a fixed number of arguments (of fixed types), it needs some convention for what the arguments are. For example, the first argument to printf is a string, which indicates what the remaining arguments are:

```
printf("Hello, world!\n");   /* no more arguments */
printf("%s\n", "Hello, world!");   /* one more string argument */
printf("%s, %s\n", "Hello", "world!");   /* two more string arguments */
printf("%s, %d\n", "Hello", 42);   /* one string, one int */
```

Listing XII.3 shows a simple printf-like function. The first argument is the format; from the format string, the number and types of the remaining arguments can be determined. As with the real printf, if the format doesn't match the rest of the arguments, the result is undefined. There's no telling what your program will do then (but probably something bad).

Listing XII.3. A simple printf-like function.

```
#include         <stdio.h>
#include         <stdlib.h>
#include         <string.h>
#include         <stdarg.h>

static char *
int2str(int n)
{
        int     minus = (n < 0);
```

continues

Listing XII.3. continued

```c
        static char     buf[32];
        char    *p = &buf[31];

        if (minus)
                n = -n;
        *p = '\0';
        do {
                *--p = '0' + n % 10;
                n /= 10;
        } while (n > 0);
        if (minus)
                *--p = '-';
        return p;
}

/*
 * This is a simple printf-like function that handles only
 * the format specifiers %%, %s, and %d.
 */
void
simplePrintf(const char *format, ...)
{
        va_list ap; /* ap is our argument pointer. */
        int     i;
        char    *s;

        /*
         * Initialize ap to start with the argument
         * after "format"
         */
        va_start(ap, format);
        for ( ; *format; format++) {
                if (*format != '%') {
                        putchar(*format);
                        continue;
                }
                switch (*++format) {
                case 's':
                        /* Get next argument (a char*) */
                        s = va_arg(ap, char *);
                        fputs(s, stdout);
                        break;
                case 'd':
                        /* Get next argument (an int) */
                        i = va_arg(ap, int);
                        s = int2str(i);
                        fputs(s, stdout);
                        break;
                case '\0':
                        format--;
                        break;
                default:
                        putchar(*format);
                        break;
                }
```

```
        }
        /* Clean up varying arguments before returning */
        va_end(ap);
}

void
main()
{
        simplePrintf("The %s tax rate is %d%%.\n",
                "sales", 6);
}
```

Cross Reference:

XII.2: What header files do I need in order to define the standard library functions I use?

XII.4: What is the difference between a free-standing and a hosted environment?

Answer:

Not all C programmers write database management systems and word processors. Some write code for embedded systems, such as anti-lock braking systems and intelligent toasters. Embedded systems don't necessarily have any sort of file system, or much of an operating system at all. The ANSI/ISO standard calls these "free-standing" systems, and it doesn't require them to provide anything except the language itself. The alternative is a program running on a PC or a mainframe or something in-between; that's a "hosted" environment.

Even people developing for free-standing environments should pay attention to the standard library. For one thing, if a free-standing environment provides some functionality (such as a square root function), it's likely to provide it in a way that's compatible with the standard. (Reinventing the square root is like reinventing the square wheel; what's the point?) Beyond that, embedded programs are often tested on a PC before they're downloaded to a toaster (or whatever). Using the standard functions will increase the amount of code that can be identical in both the test and the real environments.

Cross Reference:

XII.1: Why should I use standard library functions instead of writing my own?

Chapter XV: Portability

XII.5: What standard functions are available to manipulate strings?

Answer:

Short answer: the functions in <string.h>.

C doesn't have a built-in string type. Instead, C programs use char arrays, terminated by the NUL ('\0') character.

C programs (and C programmers) are responsible for ensuring that the arrays are big enough to hold all that will be put in them. There are three approaches:

◆ Set aside a lot of room, assume that it will be big enough, and don't worry what happens if it's not big enough (efficient, but this method can cause big problems if there's not enough room).

◆ Always allocate and reallocate the necessary amount of room (not too inefficient if done with realloc; this method can take lots of code and lots of runtime).

◆ Set aside what should be enough room, and stop before going beyond it (efficient and safe, but you might lose data).

NOTE

C++ is moving toward a fourth approach: leave it all behind and define a string type. For various reasons, that's a lot easier to do in C++ than in C. Even in C++, it's turning out to be rather involved. Luckily, after a standard C++ string type has been defined, even if it turns out to be hard to implement, it should be very easy for C++ programmers to use.

There are two sets of functions for C string programming. One set (strcpy, strcat, and so on) works with the first and second approaches. This set copies or uses as much as it's asked to—and there had better be room for it all, or the program might be buggy. Those are the functions most C programmers use. The other set (strncpy, strncat, and so on) takes the third approach. This set needs to know how much room there is, and it never goes beyond that, ignoring everything that doesn't fit.

The "n" (third) argument means different things to these two functions:

To strncpy, it means there is room for only "n" characters, including any NUL character at the end. strncpy copies exactly "n" characters. If the second argument doesn't have that many, strncpy copies extra NUL characters. If the second argument has more characters than that, strncpy stops before it copies any NUL character. That means, when using strncpy, you should always put a NUL character at the end of the string yourself; don't count on strncpy to do it for you.

To strncat, it means to copy up to "n" characters, plus a NUL character if necessary. Because what you really know is how many characters the destination can store, you usually need to use strlen to calculate how many characters you can copy.

The difference between strncpy and strncat is "historical." (That's a technical term meaning "It made sense to somebody, once, and it might be the right way to do things, but it's not obvious why right now.")

Listing XII.5a shows a short program that uses strncpy and strncat.

NOTE

Get to know the "string-n" functions. Using them is harder but leads to more robust, less buggy software.

If you're feeling brave, try rewriting the program in Listing XII.5a with strcpy and strcat, and run it with big enough arguments that the buffer overflows. What happens? Does your computer hang? Do you get a General Protection Exception or a core dump? See FAQ VII.24 for a discussion.

Listing XII.5a. An example of the "string-n" functions.

```c
#include <stdio.h>
#include <string.h>

/*
Normally, a constant like MAXBUF would be very large, to
help ensure that the buffer doesn't overflow.  Here, it's very
small, to show how the "string-n" functions prevent it from
ever overflowing.
*/

#define MAXBUF 16

int
main(int argc, char** argv)
{
        char buf[MAXBUF];
        int i;

        buf[MAXBUF - 1] = '\0';

        strncpy(buf, argv[0], MAXBUF-1);
        for (i = 1; i < argc; ++i) {
                strncat(buf, " ",
                  MAXBUF - 1 - strlen(buf));
                strncat(buf, argv[i],
                  MAXBUF - 1 - strlen(buf));
        }

        puts(buf);
        return 0;

}
```

NOTE

Many of the string functions take at least two string arguments. It's convenient to refer to them as "the left argument" and "the right argument," rather than "the first argument" and "the second argument," for describing which one is which.

strcpy and strncpy copy a string from one array to another. The value on the right is copied to the value on the left; think of the order as being the same as that for assignment.

strcat and strncat "concatenate" one string onto the end of another. For example, if a1 is an array that holds "dog" and a2 is an array that holds "wood", after calling strcat(a1, a2), a1 would hold "dogwood".

strcmp and strncmp compare two strings. The return value is negative if the left argument is less than the right, zero if they're the same, and positive if the left argument is greater than the right. There are two common idioms for equality and inequality:

```
if (strcmp(s1, s2)) {
    /* s1 != s2 */
}
```

and

```
if (! strcmp(s1, s2)) {
    /* s1 == s2 */
}
```

This code is not incredibly readable, perhaps, but it's perfectly valid C code and quite common; learn to recognize it. If you need to take into account the current locale when comparing strings, use strcoll.

A number of functions search in a string. (In all cases, it's the "left" or first argument being searched in.) strchr and strrchr look for (respectively) the first and last occurrence of a character in a string. (memchr and memrchr are the closest functions to the "n" equivalents strchr and strrchr.) strspn, strcspn (the "c" stands for "complement"), and strpbrk look for substrings consisting of certain characters or separated by certain characters:

```
n = strspn("Iowa", "AEIOUaeiou");
/* n = 2; "Iowa" starts with 2 vowels */

n = strcspn("Hello world", " \t");
/* n = 5; white space after 5 characters */
p = strbrk("Hello world", " \t");
/* p points to blank */
```

strstr looks for one string in another:

```
p = strstr("Hello world", "or");
/* p points to the second "o" */
```

strtok breaks a string into tokens, which are separated by characters given in the second argument. strtok is "destructive"; it sticks NUL characters in the original string. (If the original string should be changed, it should be copied, and the copy should be passed to strtok.) Also, strtok is not "reentrant"; it can't be called from a signal-handling function, because it "remembers" some of its arguments between calls. strtok is an odd function, but very useful for pulling apart data separated by commas or white space. Listing XII.5b shows a simple program that uses strtok to break up the words in a sentence.

Listing XII.5b. An example of using strtok.

```
#include <stdio.h>
#include <string.h>

static char buf[] = "Now is the time for all good men ...";
```

```
int
main()
{
        char* p;
        p = strtok(buf, " ");
        while (p) {
                printf("%s\n", p);
                p = strtok(NULL, " ");
        }
        return 0;
}
```

Cross Reference:

IV.18: How can I read and write comma-delimited text?

Chapter VI: Working with Strings

VII.23: What is the difference between NULL and NUL?

IX.9: What is the difference between a string and an array?

XII.8: What is a "locale"?

XII.10: What's a signal? What do I use signals for?

XII.6: What standard functions are available to manipulate memory?

Answer:

Several functions copy, compare, and fill arbitrary memory. These functions take void* (pointers to nothing in particular); they work with pointers to anything.

There are two functions (roughly like strncpy) for copying information. One, memmove, copies memory from one place to another, even if the two places overlap. Why is that important? Say you have a buffer with some data already in it, and you want to move it "to the right" to make room at the beginning of the buffer. Listing XII.6 shows a program that tries to perform this action but doesn't do it right.

Listing XII.6. A program that tries to move data but trashes it instead.

```
static char buf[] =
   {'R', 'I', 'G', 'H', 'T', '\0', '-', '-', '-'};
int
main()
{
    int i;
    for (i=0; i<6; ++i) {
        buf[i+3] = buf[i];
    }
}
```

The idea was to change buf from being "RIGHT" to being "RIGRIGHT" so that other data could be put in the first three bytes. Unfortunately, that's not what happened. If you unroll the for loop (or run the program with a debugger to see what it's doing), you'll see that the program really acted like this:

```
buf[3] = buf[0];
buf[4] = buf[1];
buf[5] = buf[2];
buf[6] = buf[3];
buf[7] = buf[4];
buf[8] = buf[5];
buf[9] = buf[6];
```

The effect on the data is shown in Figure XII.6a (the newly copied data is shown in bold). The program trashed some of the data it was supposed to move!

Figure XII.6a.

The wrong way to "move" overlapping data.

R	I	G	H	T	\0	–	–	–
R	I	G	**R**	T	\0	–	–	–
R	I	G	**R**	**I**	\0	–	–	–
R	I	G	**R**	**I**	**G**	–	–	–
R	I	G	**R**	**I**	**G**	**R**	–	–
R	I	G	**R**	**I**	**G**	**R**	**I**	–
R	I	G	**R**	**I**	**G**	**R**	**I**	**G**

For moving or copying data that overlaps, there's a simple rule. If the source and destination areas overlap, and the source is before the destination, start at the end of the source and work backward to the beginning. If the source is after the destination, start at the beginning of the source and work to the end. See Figure XII.6b.

Figure XII.6b.

The right ways to "move" overlapping data.

R	I	G	H	T	\0	–	–	–
R	I	G	H	T	\0	–	–	**\0**
R	I	G	H	T	\0	–	**T**	**\0**
R	I	G	H	T	\0	**H**	**T**	**\0**
R	I	G	H	T	**G**	**H**	**T**	**\0**
R	I	G	H	**I**	**G**	**H**	**T**	**\0**
R	I	G	**R**	**I**	**G**	**H**	**T**	**\0**

<	<	<	L	E	F	T	\0	
L	<	<	L	E	F	T	\0	
L	**E**	<	L	E	F	T	\0	
L	**E**	**F**	L	E	F	T	\0	
L	**E**	**F**	**T**	E	F	T	\0	
L	**E**	**F**	**T**	**\0**	F	T	\0	

The purpose for explaining all that is to tell you this: the memmove function knows that rule. It is guaranteed to copy data, even overlapping data, the right way. If you're copying or moving data and you're not sure whether the source and destination overlap, use memmove. If you're sure they don't overlap, memcpy might be marginally faster.

The memcmp function is like the strncmp function, except that it doesn't stop at bytes with NUL characters ('\0'). It shouldn't be used to compare struct values, though. Say that you have the following structure:

```
struct foo {
    short s;
    long l;
}
```

And say that on the system your program will run on, a short is two bytes (16 bits) long, and a long is four bytes (32 bits) long. On a 32-bit machine, many compilers put two bytes of "junk" between s and l so that l starts on a word boundary. If your program runs on a little-endian machine (the least significant byte is stored at the lowest address), the structure might be laid out like this:

struct foo byte[0]	least significant byte of s
struct foo byte[1]	most significant byte of s
struct foo byte[2]	junk (make l start on a long boundary)
struct foo byte[3]	junk (make l start on a long boundary)
struct foo byte[4]	least significant byte of l
struct foo byte[5]	second least significant byte of lstruct
struct foo byte[6]	second most significant byte of l
struct foo byte[7]	most significant byte of l

Two struct foos with the same s and l values might not compare equal with memcmp, because the "junk" might be different.

memchr is like strchr, but it looks for a character anywhere in a specified part of memory; it won't stop at the first NUL byte.

memset is useful even for nonparanoid C programmers. It copies some byte into a specified part of memory. One common use is to initialize some structure to all zero bytes. If p is a pointer to a struct, then

```
memset(p, '\0', sizeof *p);
```

overwrites the thing p points to with zero (NUL or '\0') bytes. (This also overwrites any "junk" used to get members on word boundaries, but that's OK; it's junk, nobody cares what you write there.)

Cross Reference:

VI.1: What is the difference between a string copy (strcpy) and a memory copy (memcpy)? When should each be used?

VI.3: How can I remove the leading spaces from a string?

IX.9: What is the difference between a string and an array?

XII.7: How do I determine whether a character is numeric, alphabetic, and so on?

Answer:

The header file ctype.h defines various functions for determining what class a character belongs to. These consist of the following functions:

Function	Character Class	Returns Nonzero for Characters
isdigit()	Decimal digits	0–9
isxdigit()	Hexadecimal digits	0–9, a–f, or A–F
isalnum()	Alphanumerics	0–9, a–z, or A–Z
isalpha()	Alphabetics	a–z or A–Z
islower()	Lowercase alphabetics	a–z
isupper()	Uppercase alphabetics	A–Z
isspace()	Whitespace	Space, tab, vertical tab, newline, form feed, or carriage return
isgraph()	Nonblank characters	Any character that appears nonblank when printed (ASCII 0x21 through 0x7E)
isprint()	Printable characters	All the isgraph() characters, plus space
ispunct()	Punctuation	Any character in isgraph() that is not in isalnum()
iscntrl()	Control characters	Any character not in isprint() (ASCII 0x00 through 0x1F plus 0x7F)

There are three very good reasons for calling these macros instead of writing your own tests for character classes. They are pretty much the same reasons for using standard library functions in the first place. First, these macros are fast. Because they are generally implemented as a table lookup with some bit-masking magic, even a relatively complicated test can be performed much faster than an actual comparison of the value of the character.

Second, these macros are correct. It's all too easy to make an error in logic or typing and include a wrong character (or exclude a right one) from a test.

Third, these macros are portable. Believe it or not, not everyone uses the same ASCII character set with PC extensions. You might not care today, but when you discover that your next computer uses Unicode rather than ASCII, you'll be glad you wrote code that didn't assume the values of characters in the character set.

The header file ctype.h also defines two functions to convert characters between upper- and lowercase alphabetics. These are toupper() and tolower(). The behavior of toupper() and tolower() is undefined if their arguments are not lower- and uppercase alphabetic characters, respectively, so you must remember to check using islower() and isupper() before calling toupper() and tolower().

Cross Reference:

V.1: What is a macro, and how do you use it?

VI.2: How can I remove the trailing spaces from a string?

VI.3: How can I remove the leading spaces from a string?

XX.18: How do you tell whether a character is a letter of the alphabet?

XX.19: How do you tell whether a character is a number?

XII.8: What is a "locale"?

Answer:

A locale is a description of certain conventions your program might be expected to follow under certain circumstances. It's mostly helpful to internationalize your program.

If you were going to print an amount of money, would you always use a dollar sign? Not if your program was going to run in the United Kingdom; there, you'd use a pound sign. In some countries, the currency symbol goes before the number; in some, it goes after. Where does the sign go for a negative number? How about the decimal point? A number that would be printed 1,234.56 in the United States should appear as 1.234,56 in some other countries. Same value, different convention. How are times and dates displayed? The only short answer is, differently. These are some of the technical reasons why some programmers whose programs have to run all over the world have so many headaches.

Good news: Some of the differences have been standardized. C compilers support different "locales," different conventions for how a program acts in different places. For example, the strcoll (string collate) function is like the simpler strcmp, but it reflects how different countries and languages sort and order (collate) string values. The setlocale and localeconv functions provide this support.

Bad news: There's no standardized list of interesting locales. The only one your compiler is guaranteed to support is the "C" locale, which is a generic, American English convention that works best with ASCII characters between 32 and 127. Even so, if you need to get code that looks right, no matter where around the world it will run, thinking in terms of locales is a good first step. (Getting several locales your compiler supports, or getting your compiler to accept locales you define, is a good second step.)

Cross Reference:

None.

XII.9: Is there a way to jump out of a function or functions?

Answer:

The standard library functions setjmp() and longjmp() are used to provide a goto that can jump out of a function or functions, in the rare cases in which this action is useful. To correctly use setjmp() and longjmp(), you must apply several conditions.

You must #include the header file setjmp.h. This file provides the prototypes for setjmp() and longjmp(), and it defines the type jmp_buf. You need a variable of type jmp_buf to pass as an argument to both setjmp() and longjmp(). This variable will contain the information needed to make the jump occur.

You must call setjmp() to initialize the jmp_buf variable. If setjmp() returns 0, you have just initialized the jmp_buf. If setjmp() returns anything else, your program just jumped to that point via a call to longjmp(). In that case, the return value is whatever your program passed to longjmp().

Conceptually, longjmp() works as if when it is called, the currently executing function returns. Then the function that called *it* returns, and so on, until the function containing the call to setjmp() is executing. Then execution jumps to where setjmp() was called from, and execution continues from the return of setjmp(), but with the return value of setjmp() set to whatever argument was passed to longjmp().

In other words, if function f() calls setjmp() and later calls function g(), and function g() calls function h(), which calls longjmp(), the program behaves as if h() returned immediately, then g() returned immediately, then f() executed a goto back to the setjmp() call.

What this means is that for a call to longjmp() to work properly, the program must already have called setjmp() and must not have returned from the function that called setjmp(). If these conditions are not fulfilled, the operation of longjmp() is undefined (meaning your program will probably crash). The program in Listing XII.9 illustrates the use of setjmp() and longjmp(). It is obviously contrived, because it would be simpler to write this program without using setjmp() and longjmp(). In general, when you are tempted to use setjmp() and longjmp(), try to find a way to write the program without them, because they are easy to misuse and can make a program difficult to read and maintain.

Listing XII.9. An example of using setjmp() and longjmp().

```
#include        <setjmp.h>
#include        <stdio.h>
#include        <string.h>
#include        <stdlib.h>

#define RETRY_PROCESS 1
#define QUIT_PROCESS  2

jmp_buf env;

int     nitems;

int
procItem()
{
        char    buf[256];
        if (gets(buf) && strcmp(buf, "done")) {
                if (strcmp(buf, "quit") == 0)
                        longjmp(env, QUIT_PROCESS);
                if (strcmp(buf, "restart") == 0)
                        longjmp(env, RETRY_PROCESS);
                nitems++;
                return 1;
        }
        return 0;
}

void
```

```
process()
{
        printf("Enter items, followed by 'done'.\n");
        printf("At any time, you can type 'quit' to exit\n");
        printf("or 'restart' to start over again\n");
        nitems = 0;
        while (procItem())
                ;
}

void
main()
{
        for ( ; ; ) {
                switch (setjmp(env)) {
                case 0:
                case RETRY_PROCESS:
                        process();
                        printf("You typed in %d items.\n",
                                nitems);
                        break;
                case QUIT_PROCESS:
                default:
                        exit(0);
                }
        }
}
```

Cross Reference:

I.8: What is the difference between goto and longjmp() and setjmp()?

VII.20: What is the stack?

XII.10: What's a signal? What do I use signals for?
Answer:

A signal is an exceptional condition that occurs during the execution of your program. It might be the result of an error in your program, such as a reference to an illegal address in memory; or an error in your program's data, such as a floating-point divided by 0; or an outside event, such as the user's pressing Ctrl-Break.

The standard library function signal() enables you to specify what action is to be taken on one of these exceptional conditions (a function that performs that action is called a "signal handler"). The prototype for signal() is

```
#include        <signal.h>
void (*signal(int num, void (*func)(int)))(int);
```

which is just about the most complicated declaration you'll see in the C standard library. It is easier to understand if you define a typedef first. The type sigHandler_t, shown next, is a pointer to a function that takes an int as its argument and returns a void:

```
typedef void (*sigHandler_t)(int);
sigHandler_t signal(int num, sigHandler_t func);
```

signal() is a function that takes an int and a sigHandler_t as its two arguments, and returns a sigHandler_t as its return value. The function passed in as the func argument will be the new signal handler for the exceptional condition numbered num. The return value is the previous signal handler for signal num. This value can be used to restore the previous behavior of a program, after temporarily setting a signal handler. The possible values for num are system dependent and are listed in signal.h. The possible values for func are any function in your program, or one of the two specially defined values SIG_DFL or SIG_IGN. The SIG_DFL value refers to the system's default action, which is usually to halt the program. SIG_IGN means that the signal is ignored.

The following line of code, when executed, causes the program containing it to ignore Ctrl-Break keystrokes unless the signal is changed again. Although the signal numbers are system dependent, the signal number SIGINT is normally used to refer to an attempt by the user to interrupt the program's execution (Ctrl-C or Ctrl-Break in DOS):

```
signal(SIGINT, SIG_IGN);
```

Cross Reference:

XX.16: How do you disable Ctrl-Break?

XII.11: Why shouldn't I start variable names with underscores?
Answer:

Identifier names beginning with two underscores or an underscore followed by a capital letter are reserved for use by the compiler or standard library functions wherever they appear. In addition, all identifier names beginning with an underscore followed by anything are reserved when they appear in file scope (when they are not local to a function).

If you use a reserved identifier for a variable name, the results are undefined (your program might not compile, or it might compile but crash). Even if you are lucky enough to pick an identifier that is not currently used by your compiler or library, remember that these identifiers are reserved for possible use later. Thus, it's best to avoid using an underscore at the beginning of variable and function names.

Cross Reference:

XIX.1: Should the underscore be used in variable names?

XII.12: Why does my compiler provide two versions of *malloc()*?
Answer:

By including stdlib.h, you can use malloc() and free() in your code. This function is put in your code by the compiler from the standard C library. Some compilers have a separate library that you can ask the compiler to use (by specifying a flag such as -lmalloc on the command line) to replace the standard library's versions of malloc() and free() with a different version.

These alternative versions of malloc() and free() do the same thing as the standard ones, but they are supposedly implemented to provide better performance at the cost of being less forgiving about memory allocation errors. I have never had a reason to use these alternative routines in 15 years of C programming. But in answering this FAQ, I wrote a simple test program to heavily exercise malloc() and free() and compiled it with a well-known commercial C compiler both with and without the malloc library. I couldn't detect any significant difference in performance, and because both versions of the routines were the same size, I suspect that this particular vendor used the same code for both implementations. For this reason, I will not name the compiler vendor.

The moral of the story is that you probably don't need to bother with the other version of malloc() and probably shouldn't count on it for performance improvements. If profiling shows that your program spends a large percentage of its time in malloc() and free(), and you can't fix the problem by changing the algorithm, you might be able to improve performance by writing your own "pool" allocator.

Programs that call malloc() and free() a lot are often allocating and freeing the same type of data, which has a fixed size. When you know the size of the data to be allocated and freed, a pool allocator can be much faster than malloc() and free(). A pool allocator works by calling malloc() to allocate many structures of the same size all at once, then hands them out one at a time. It typically never calls free(), and the memory stays reserved for use by the pool allocator until the program exits. Listing XII.12 shows a pool allocator for the hypothetical type struct foo.

Listing XII.12. An example of a pool allocator.

```
#include        <stdio.h>

/* declaration of hypothetical structure "foo" */
struct foo {
        int     dummy1;
        char    dummy2;
        long    dummy3;
};

/* start of code for foo pool allocator */

#include        <stdlib.h>

/* number of foos to malloc() at a time */
#define NFOOS   64

/*
 * A union is used to provide a linked list that
 * can be overlaid on unused foos.
 */
union foo_u {
        union foo_u     *next;
        struct foo      f;
};

static union foo_u      *free_list;
```

continues

Listing XII.12. continued

```c
struct foo *
alloc_foo()
{
        struct foo      *ret = 0;
        if (!free_list) {
                int     i;
                free_list = (union foo_u *) malloc(NFOOS
                                * sizeof(union foo_u));
                if (free_list) {
                        for (i = 0; i < NFOOS - 1; i++)
                                free_list[i].next =
                                        &free_list[i + 1];
                        free_list[NFOOS - 1].next = NULL;
                }
        }
        if (free_list) {
                ret = &free_list->f;
                free_list = free_list->next;
        }
        return ret;
}

void
free_foo(struct foo *fp)
{
        union foo_u     *up = (union foo_u *) fp;
        up->next = free_list;
        free_list = up;
}

int
main(int argc, char **argv)
{
        int     i;
        int     n;
        struct foo      **a;

        if (argc < 2) {
                fprintf(stderr, "usage: %s f\n", argv[0]);
                fprintf(stderr, "where f is the number of");
                fprintf(stderr, " 'foo's to allocate\n");
                exit(1);
        }
        i = atoi(argv[1]);
        a = (struct foo **) malloc(sizeof(struct foo *) * i);
        for (n = 0; n < i; n++)
                a[n] = alloc_foo();
        for (n = 0; n < i; n++)
                free_foo(a[n]);
        return 0;
}
```

I compiled and ran this program with an argument of 300000 and compared the results to a similar program that replaced calls to alloc_foo() and free_foo() with calls to malloc() and free(). The CPU time used by the version of the program using the pool allocator was 0.46 seconds. The version of the program that used malloc() took 0.92 seconds.

Note that you should use a pool allocator only as a last resort. It might improve speed, but it can be very wasteful of memory. It also can lead to subtle memory allocation errors if you're not careful to return memory to the pool from which it came instead of calling free().

Cross Reference:

VII.21: What is the heap?

VII.26: How does free() know how much memory to release?

XII.13: What math functions are available for integers? For floating point?

Answer:

The operations +, -, *, and / (addition, subtraction, multiplication, and division) are available for both integer and floating-point arithmetic. The operator % (remainder) is available for integers only.

For floating-point math, many other functions are declared in the header file math.h. Most of these functions operate in double-precision floating point, for increased accuracy. If these functions are passed an argument outside of their domain (the domain of a function is the set of legal values for which it is defined), the function will return some unspecified value and will set the variable errno to the value EDOM. If the return value of the function is too large or small to be represented by a double (causing overflow or underflow), the function will return HUGE_VAL (for overflow) or 0 (for underflow) and will set errno to ERANGE. The values EDOM, ERANGE, and HUGE_VAL are defined in math.h.

The following list describes the functions declared in math.h:

◆ double cos(double), double sin(double), double tan(double) take a value in radians and return the cosine, sine, and tangent of the value, respectively.

◆ double acos(double), double asin(double), double atan(double) take a value and return the arc cosine, arc sine, and arc tangent of the value, respectively. The value passed to acos() and asin() must be in the range −1 to 1, inclusive.

◆ double atan2(double x, double y) returns the arc tangent of the value represented by x/y, even if x/y is not representable as a double (if y is 0, for instance).

◆ double cosh(double), double sinh(double), double tanh(double) take a value in radians and return the hyperbolic cosine, hyperbolic sine, and hyperbolic tangent of the value, respectively.

◆ double exp(double x), double log(double x), double log10(double x) take a value and return ex, the natural logarithm of x, and the logarithm base 10 of x, respectively. The two logarithm functions will cause a range error (ERANGE) if x is 0 and a domain error (EDOM) if x is negative.

◆ double sqrt(double) returns the square root of its argument. It causes a domain error (EDOM) if the value passed to it is negative.

- ◆ double ldexp(double n, int e) returns n * 2e. This is somewhat analogous to the << operator for integers.
- ◆ double pow(double b, double e) returns be. It causes a domain error (EDOM) if b is 0 and e is less than or equal to 0, or if b is less than 0 and e is not an integral value.
- ◆ double frexp(double n, int *i) returns the *mantissa* of n and sets the int pointed to by i to the *exponent* of n. The mantissa is in the range 0.5 to 1 (excluding 1 itself), and the exponent is a number such that n = *mantissa* * 2*exponent*.
- ◆ double modf(double n, int *i) returns the fractional part of n and sets the int pointed to by i to the integer part of n.
- ◆ double ceil(double), double floor(double) return the smallest integer greater than or equal to and the largest integer less than or equal to their arguments, respectively. For instance, ceil(-1.1) returns −1.0, and floor(-1.1) returns −2.0.
- ◆ double fmod(double x, double y) returns the remainder of x/y. This is similar to the % operator for integers, but it does not restrict its inputs or result to be ints. It causes a domain error (EDOM) if y is 0.
- ◆ double fabs(double) returns the absolute value of the value passed to it (a number with the same magnitude, but always positive). For instance, fabs(-3.14) returns 3.14.

Cross Reference:

II.11: Are there any problems with performing mathematical operations on different variable types?

XII.14: What are multibyte characters?
Answer:

Multibyte characters are another way to make internationalized programs easier to write. Specifically, they help support languages such as Chinese and Japanese that could never fit into eight-bit characters. If your programs will never need to deal with any language but English, you don't need to know about multibyte characters.

Inconsiderate as it might seem, in a world full of people who might want to use your software, not everybody reads English. The good news is that there are standards for fitting the various special characters of European languages into an eight-bit character set. (The bad news is that there are several such standards, and they don't agree.)

Go to Asia, and the problem gets more complicated. Some languages, such as Japanese and Chinese, have more than 256 characters. Those will never fit into any eight-bit character set. (An eight-bit character can store a number between 0 and 255, so it can have only 256 different values.)

The good news is that the standard library has the beginnings of a solution to this problem. <stddef.h> defines a type, wchar_t, that is guaranteed to be long enough to store any character in any language a C program can deal with. Based on all the agreements so far, 16 bits is enough. That's often a short, but it's better to trust that the compiler vendor got wchar_t right than to get in trouble if the size of a short changes.

The mblen, mbtowc, and wctomb functions transform byte strings into multibyte characters. See your compiler manuals for more information on these functions.

Cross Reference:

XII.15: How can I manipulate strings of multibyte characters?

XII.15: How can I manipulate strings of multibyte characters?
Answer:

Better than you might think.

Say your program sometimes deals with English text (which fits comfortably into 8-bit chars with a bit to spare) and sometimes Japanese text (which needs 16 bits to cover all the possibilities). If you use the same code to manipulate either country's text, will you need to set aside 16 bits for every character, even your English text? Maybe not. Some (but not all) ways of encoding multibyte characters can store information about whether more than one byte is necessary.

mbstowcs ("multibyte string to wide character string") and wcstombs ("wide character string to multibyte string") convert between arrays of wchar_t (in which every character takes 16 bits, or two bytes) and multibyte strings (in which individual characters are stored in one byte if possible).

There's no guarantee your compiler can store multibyte strings compactly. (There's no single agreed-upon way of doing this.) If your compiler can help you with multibyte strings, mbstowcs and wcstombs are the functions it provides for that.

Cross Reference:

XII.14: What are multibyte characters?

CHAPTER XIII

Times and Dates

Times and dates might be difficult for the beginning programmer to understand because they are not simple variables. They consist of several, perhaps many, components. To further confuse the issue, a C compiler typically comes with many different functions that all handle time differently. When should each of these be used? This chapter attempts to answer some of the frequently asked questions relating to times and dates.

XIII.1: How can I store a date in a single number? Are there any standards for this?

Answer:

You might want to convert a date to a single number for several reasons, including for efficient storage or for simple comparison. Additionally, you might want to use the resultant number as part of a coding scheme. In any case, if you want to represent a date as a single number, you need to ask yourself why you need to do this and what you intend to do with the number after you have converted it. Answering these questions will help you determine which method of conversion is superior. First, look at a simple-minded example:

```
#include <stdio.h>
#include <stdlib.h>
```

```
main()
{
    int month , day , year;
    unsigned long result;

    printf( "Enter Month, Day, Year: \n" );
    fflush( stdout );
    scanf( " %d %d %d" , &month , &day , &year );

    result = year;
    result |= month << 12;
    result |= day << 14;

    printf( "The result is: %ul.\n" , result );
}
```

This program converts three variables into a single number by bit manipulation. Here is a sample run of the program:

```
Enter Month, Day, Year:
11 22 1972
The result is: 470281.
```

Although this program does indeed work (you can test it by entering it into your computer), it contains several deficiencies. It might be a good idea to try to figure out what some of the deficiencies are before proceeding to the next paragraph.

Did you think of any defects? Here are several:

◆ The month, day, and year are not constrained. This means that the fields must be larger than is perhaps necessary, and thus efficiency is being sacrificed. Furthermore, the user could enter arbitrarily large values that would overwrite the bounds of the bit fields, resulting in a corrupted date.

◆ The numbers that are produced for the date are not in order; you cannot compare dates based on their numbers. This feature might be very convenient to have!

◆ The placement of the elements into the final number is simple, if arbitrary. Extraction is, however, not so simple. (Can you see a simple way to do it?) You might want a simpler format for storing dates that will allow for simple extraction.

These issues will be addressed one by one.

The months need to range only from 1 to 12, and the days need to range only from 1 to 31. Years, however, are another matter. You might, depending on your purpose, choose a limit on the range of years that you need to represent in the program. This range will vary, depending on the purpose of the program. Some programs might need to represent dates in the distant past, and others might need to store dates in the distant future. However, if your program needs to store only years from 1975 to 2020, you can save quite a bit of storage. You should, of course, test all the elements of the date to ensure that they are in the proper range before inserting them into the number.

NOTE

An archaeological database might be a good example of a system that would need dates in the far past.

In the C language, generally, counting (for arrays and such) begins at zero. It will help, in this case, to force all the number ranges to begin at zero. Therefore, if the earliest year you need to store is 1975, you should subtract 1975 from all the years, causing the year series to start at zero. Take a look at the program modified to work in this way:

```c
#include <stdio.h>
#include <stdlib.h>

main()
{
    int month , day , year;
    unsigned long result;

    /* prompt the user for input */
    printf( "Enter Month, Day, Year: \n" );
    fflush( stdout );
    scanf( " %d %d %d" , &month , &day , &year );

    /* Make all of the ranges begin at zero */
    --month;
    --day;
    year -= 1975;

    /* Make sure all of the date elements are in proper range */
    if (
        ( year < 0 || year > 127 ) ||  /* Keep the year in range */
        ( month < 0 || month > 11 ) || /* Keep the month in range */
        ( day < 0 || day > 31 )        /* Keep the day in range */
      )
    {
        printf( "You entered an improper date!\n" );
        exit( 1 );
    }

    result = year;
    result |= month << 7;
    result |= day << 11;

    printf( "The result is: %ul.\n" , result );
}
```

This program doesn't account for the fact that some months have fewer than 31 days, but this change is a minor addition. Note that by constraining the range of dates, you need to shift the month and date values by a lesser amount.

The numbers produced are still unsortable, however. To fix this problem, you need to make the observation that the bits farthest to the left in the integer are *more significant* than the ones to the right. What you should do, therefore, is place the most significant part of the date in the leftmost bits. To do this, you should change the part of the program that places the three variables into resultant numbers to work this way:

```c
    result = day;
    result |= month << 5;
    result |= year << 9;
```

Here's a test of this modification on some sample dates:

```
Enter Month, Day, Year:
```

```
11 22 1980
The result is: 110771.

Enter Month, Day, Year:
12 23 1980
The result is: 116211.

Enter Month, Day, Year:
8 15 1998
The result is: 74151.
```

You can now store records with their date in this format, and sort them based on this number, with full confidence that the dates will be in the proper order.

The only issues that still need to be addressed are the somewhat arbitrary nature of storage within the value, and the question of extraction. Both problems can be solved by the use of bit fields. Bit fields are explained in Chapter X. Take a look at the code without further ado:

```c
/* These are the definitions to aid in the conversion of
 * dates to integers.
 */
typedef struct
{
    unsigned int year : 7;
    unsigned int month : 4;
    unsigned int day : 5;
} YearBitF;

typedef union
{
    YearBitF date;
    unsigned long number;
} YearConverter;


/* Convert a date into an unsigned long integer. Return zero if
 * the date is invalid. This uses bit fields and a union.
 */

unsigned long DateToNumber( int month , int day , int year )
{
    YearConverter yc;
    /* Make all of the ranges begin at zero */
    --month;
    --day;
    year -= 1975;

    /* Make sure all of the date elements are in proper range */
    if (
        ( year < 0 || year > 127 ) ||    /* Keep the year in range */
        ( month < 0 || month > 11 ) ||   /* Keep the month in range */
        ( day < 0 || day > 31 )          /* Keep the day in range */
      )
      return 0;

    yc.date.day = day;
    yc.date.month = month;
    yc.date.year = year;
```

```
        return yc.number + 1;
}



/*  Take a number and return the values for day, month, and year
 *  stored therein. Very elegant due to use of bit fields.
 */

void NumberToDate( unsigned long number , int *month ,
                   int *day , int *year )
{
    YearConverter yc;

    yc.number = number - 1;
    *month = yc.date.month + 1;
    *day = yc.date.day + 1;
    *year = yc.date.year + 1975;
}

/*
 * This tests the routine and makes sure it is OK.
 */


main()
{
    unsigned long n;
    int m , d , y;
    n = DateToNumber( 11 , 22 , 1980 );
    if ( n == 0 )
    {
        printf( "The date was invalid.\n" );
        exit( 1 );
    }
    NumberToDate( n , &m , &d , &y );
    printf( "The date after transformation is : %d/%d/%d.\n" ,
            m , d , y );
}
```

There is still a certain amount of inefficiency due to the fact that some months have fewer than 31 days. Furthermore, this variance in the number of days will make it hard to increment dates and to find the difference between dates in days. The built-in C functions are best for these more complex tasks; they will save the programmer from having to rewrite a great deal of code.

Cross Reference:

XIII.2: How can I store time as a single integer? Are there any standards for this?

XIII.2: How can I store time as a single integer? Are there any standards for this?

Answer:

The question of storing a time in a single byte is similar to that of storing a date in a single byte; therefore, it will be helpful for you to have read FAQ XIII.1. Nonetheless, there are differences.

The first thing you should note is that a time of day is more "deterministic" than a date of a year. You know exactly how many seconds there will be in a minute, how many minutes there will be in an hour, and how many hours there will be in a day. This uniformity makes handling times of day somewhat easier and less prone to error.

Following is a list of features that are desirable when you are choosing a method to convert a time to a number:

◆ It should be as efficient on space as possible.

◆ It should be able to store different kinds of time (standard, military).

◆ It should enable you to advance through time quickly and efficiently.

If you've read the preceding FAQ about dates, you might decide that a good way to handle the problem is to represent time as a bit field. That is not a bad idea, and it has several salient advantages. Look at the code for representing time as an integer:

```
/*
 *  The bit field structures for representing time
 */

typedef struct
{
    unsigned int Hour : 5;
    unsigned int Minute : 6;
} TimeType;

typedef union
{
    TimeType time;
    int Number;
} TimeConverter;


/*
 *  Convert time to a number, returning zero when the values are
 *  out of range.
 */

int TimeToNumber( int Hour , int Minute )
{
    TimeConverter convert;

    if ( Hour < 1 || Hour > 24 || Minute < 1 || Minute > 60 )
        return 0;
```

```
    convert.time.Hour = Hour;
    convert.time.Minute = Minute;
    return convert.Number +1 ;
}


/*
 *  Convert a number back into the two time
 *  elements that compose it.
 */

void NumberToTime( int Number , int *Hour , int *Minute )
{
    TimeConverter convert;

    convert.Number = Number - 1;
    *Hour = convert.time.Hour;
    *Minute = convert.time.Minute;
}


/*
 *   A main routine that tests everything to
 *   ensure its proper functioning.
 */

main()
{
    int Number , Hour , Minute;
    Hour = 13;
    Minute = 13;
    Number = TimeToNumber( Hour , Minute );
    NumberToTime( Number , &Hour , &Minute );
    printf( "The time after conversion is %d:%d.\n" , Hour , Minute );
}
```

Adding seconds to the time class is relatively easy. You would need to add a seconds field to the time structure and add one extra parameter to each of the conversion functions.

Suppose, however, that you want to use this resulting number as a clock, to "tick" through the day. To carry out this task using a bit field, you would have to convert the number into a bit field, increment the seconds, and test whether the seconds value had passed 60; if it had, you would have to increment the minutes, again testing to see whether the value had passed 60, and so on. This process could be tedious!

The problem here is that the elements of the time structure do not fit evenly into bits—they are not divisible by two. It is therefore more desirable to represent time mathematically. This can be done quite simply by representing a time of day by how many seconds (or minutes) have elapsed since the start of the day. If you represent the time in this fashion, incrementing the number will move the time to the next second (or minute). Take a look at some code that represents time in this way:

```
#include <stdio.h>
#include <stdlib.h>


/*
 *  A subroutine to convert hours and minutes into an
 *  integer number. This does no checking for the sake
```

```
 *  of brevity (you've seen it done before!).
 */

int TimeToNumber( int Hours , int Minutes )
{
    return Minutes + Hours * 60;
}


/*
 *  Convert an integer to hours and minutes.
 */

void NumberToTime( int Number , int *Hours , int *Minutes)
{
    *Minutes = Number % 60;
    *Hours = Number / 60;
}

/*
 *  A quickie way to show time.
 */

void ShowTime( int Number )
{
    int Hours , Minutes;
    NumberToTime( Number , &Hours , &Minutes );
    printf( " %02d:%02d\n" , Hours , Minutes );
}



/*
 *  A main loop to test the salient features of the time class.
 */

main()
{
    int Number , a;

    Number = TimeToNumber( 9 , 32 );

    printf( "Time starts at : %d " , Number );
    ShowTime( Number );

    /*
     *  Assure yourself that minutes are added correctly.
     */

    for( a = 0 ; a < 10 ; ++ a )
    {
        printf( "After 32 minutes : " );
        Number += 32; /* Add 32 minutes to the time. */
        ShowTime( Number );
    }
}
```

This code provides a better representation of time. It is easy to manipulate and more compact, and it even allows for shorter code. Adding seconds is an exercise left to the reader.

This format is much like that used by the C functions `timelocal()` and `timegm()`. These functions count seconds from some arbitrary time/date. A slight modification of the routines presented here for both time and date should enable the programmer to utilize these functions or even his own definition of time.

Cross Reference:

XIII.1: How can I store a date in a single number? Are there any standards for this?

XIII.5: What is the best way to store the time?

XIII.3: Why are so many different time standards defined?

Answer:

Depending on the computer and compiler you are using, you might find many different time standards defined. Although having so many time standards might be convenient, it obviously took a lot of time to write all of them. And storing them all is taking up extra space on your computer's hard disk. Why bother? There are several reasons.

First, C is intended to be a portable language. Thus, a C program written on one make of computer should run on another. Often, functions that were particular to one system have had to be added to the C language when it was created on a new system. Later, when C programs need to be moved from that system to another, it is often easiest to add the specific commands to the target system. In this way, several versions of the same function could eventually be integrated into the C language. This has happened several times with the time function.

Second, there are several different possible uses for times (and dates). You might want to count time in seconds, you might want to count time as starting from a specified time and date, or you might want to count time in the smallest interval possible to ensure that your measure of time will be as accurate as possible. There is no best way to measure time. When you begin a program that involves time, you must examine the functions available to you and determine which are best suited to your purpose. If you are handling time in various ways, you might want to use several different time formats and functions. In this case, you might be glad that there are so many formats for time and that there was one to fulfill your needs.

Cross Reference:

XIII.1: How can I store a date in a single number? Are there any standards for this?

XIII.2: How can I store time as a single integer? Are there any standards for this?

XIII.4: What is the best way to store the date?

XIII.5: What is the best way to store the time?

XIII.4: What is the best way to store the date?

Answer:

To put it simply, there is no best way to store the date. The way you choose to store the date will depend on what exactly you plan to do with it. You might want to store it as an integer (perhaps counting days from a fixed time in history); as a structure containing month, day, year, and other information; or as a textual string. A textual string might seem to be impractical and difficult to handle, but as you shall see, it has its uses.

If you are merely keeping track of numerical dates, the problem is relatively simple. You should use one of the built-in formats, or represent time as an integer, and so on. You should determine whether you need to store the current date, update the date, check how far apart two dates are, and so on. There are ways to carry out many of these tasks and more using the formats and functions contained in the standard C library. However, you might be restricted if you become "locked into" one format too early in the development of your program. By keeping an open mind and by keeping your code flexible, you can use the most suited functions when the time comes.

However, you might want to represent dates in a more complex fashion. You remember dates in different ways. You don't always remember the exact date for everything; you might remember an important date in your life as "three days after my 16th birthday party" or remember a historical date as "10 years after the fall of the Ottoman Empire." Such kinds of dates cannot be stored as a simple numeric or structure. They require a more complex schema. You still might want to store such relative dates along with a reference to a known date that the computer can handle, or with a fixed date. This technique would aid in sorting and manipulating dates.

Cross Reference:

XIII.1: How can I store a date in a single number? Are there any standards for this?

XIII.5: What is the best way to store the time?

Answer:

The best way to store time depends entirely on what you need to store time for, and in what way you intend to manipulate the time values. Take a look at the different uses you might have for time, and how that might influence your choice of storage method.

Suppose that you only need to track events and that you need to track them in "real time." In other words, you want to ascertain the real-world time of when a given event occurred. The events you want to track might include the creation of a file, the start and completion of a long, complex program, or the time that a book chapter was turned in. In this case, you need to be able to retrieve and store the current time from the computer's system clock. It is better and simpler to use one of the built-in time functions to retrieve the time and to store it directly in that format. This method requires comparatively little effort on your part.

For various reasons, you might not want to store the time as formatted by the standard C functions. You might want a simpler format, for easier manipulation, or you might want to represent time differently.

In this case, it might be a good idea to represent time as an integer value, as demonstrated in the answer to FAQ XIII.2. This technique would enable you to advance through periods of time very simply and quickly and to compare different times to see which is earlier.

As with dates, you might have completely relative measures of time that will be difficult to quantify exactly. Although "half past noon" is not too hard to quantify, "after I eat lunch" is. This, however, might be not only the simplest way to track time but, in some cases, the only way! In these cases, you would simply have to store the textual string that describes the time. In this case, this is the best way to store time.

Cross Reference:

XIII.2: How can I store time as a single integer? Are there any standards for this?

CHAPTER XIV

System Calls

One of the most crucial pieces of the PC puzzle, and sometimes the most often misunderstood, is the set of system calls. The functions that the system calls represent perform practically all the rudimentary operations of the computer—screen and disk handling, keyboard and mouse handling, managing the file system, time of day, and printing are just some of the tasks performed by the system calls.

Collectively, the system calls are often referred to as the BIOS, which stands for Basic Input Output System. In reality, there are several different BIOSes. For example, the motherboard BIOS performs initial hardware detection and system booting; the VGA BIOS (if you have a VGA card) handles all the screen-manipulation functions; the fixed disk BIOS manages the hard drives; and so on. DOS is a software layer that "sits" on top of these lower-level BIOSes and provides a common access to these lower-level BIOSes. What this means is that, in general, there is a DOS system call for just about every kind of system feature you want to initiate. DOS will call one of the lower level BIOSes to actually perform the requested task. Throughout this chapter, you will find that you can call DOS to perform a task, or you can call the lower-level BIOS directly to perform the same task.

XIV.1: How can environment variable values be retrieved?

Answer:

The ANSI C language standard provides a function called getenv() that performs this very task. The getenv() function is simple—you hand it a pointer to the environment string you want to search for, and it returns a pointer to the value of that variable. The following example code illustrates how to get the PATH environment variable from C:

```
#include <stdlib.h>

main(int argc, char ** argv)
{
    char envValue[129];          /* buffer to store PATH */
    char * envPtr = envValue;    /* pointer to this buffer */

    envPtr = getenv("PATH");     /* get the PATH */

    printf("PATH=%s\n", envPtr);    /* print the PATH */

}
```

If you compile and run this example, you will see the same output that you see when you enter the PATH command at the DOS prompt. Basically, you can use getenv() to retrieve any of the environment values that you have in your AUTOEXEC.BAT file or that you have typed at the DOS prompt since booting.

Here's a cool trick. When Windows is running, Windows sets a new environment variable called WINDIR that contains the full pathname of the Windows directory. Following is sample code for retrieving this string:

```
#include <stdlib.h>

main(int argc, char ** argv)
{
    char envValue[129];
    char * envPtr = envValue;

    envPtr = getenv("windir");

    /* print the Windows directory */
    printf("The Windows Directory is %s\n", envPtr);

}
```

This is also useful for determining whether Windows is running and your DOS program is being run in a DOS shell rather than "real" DOS. Note that the windir string is lowercase—this is important because it is case-sensitive. Using WINDIR results in a NULL string (variable-not-found error) being returned.

It is also possible to *set* environment variables using the _putenv() function. Note, however, that this function is not an ANSI standard, and it might not exist by this name or even exist at all in some compilers. You can do many things with the _putenv() function. In fact, it is this function that Windows uses to create the windir environment variable in the preceding example.

Cross Reference:

XIV.2: How can I call DOS functions from my program?

XIV.3: How can I call BIOS functions from my program?

XIV.2: How can I call DOS functions from my program?
Answer:

To be honest, you are calling DOS functions whenever you call `printf()`, `fopen()`, `fclose()`, any function whose name starts with _dos, or dozens of other C functions. However, Microsoft and Borland C provide a pair of functions called `int86()` and `int86x()` that enable you to call not only DOS, but other low-level functions as well. Using these functions, you often can save time by bypassing the standard C functions and calling the DOS functions directly. The following example illustrates how to call DOS to get a character from the keyboard and print a character string, instead of calling `getch()` and `printf()` to perform the task. (This code needs to be compiled with the Large memory model.)

```c
#include <stdlib.h>
#include <dos.h>

char GetAKey(void);
void OutputString(char *);

main(int argc, char ** argv)
{
    char str[128];
    union REGS regs;
    int ch;

    /* copy argument string; if none, use "Hello World" */
    strcpy(str, (argv[1] == NULL ? "Hello World" : argv[1]));

    while((ch = GetAKey()) != 27){
        OutputString(str);
    }

}

char
GetAKey()
{
    union REGS regs;

    regs.h.ah = 1;    /* function 1 is "get keyboard character" */
    int86(0x21, &regs, &regs);

    return((char)regs.h.al);
}

void
OutputString(char * string)
```

```
{
    union REGS regs;
    struct SREGS segregs;

    /* terminate string for DOS function */
    *(string+strlen(string)) = '$';

    regs.h.ah = 9;     /* function 9 is "print a string" */
    regs.x.dx = FP_OFF(string);
    segregs.ds = FP_SEG(string);

    int86x(0x21, &regs, &regs, &segregs);
}
```

The preceding example code created two functions to replace getch() and printf(). They are GetAKey() and OutputString(). In truth, the GetAKey() function is actually more analogous to the standard C getche() function because it, like getche(), prints the key character on-screen. In both cases, DOS itself was called using the int86() function (in GetAKey()) and the int86x() function (in OutputString()) to perform the desired tasks.

DOS contains a veritable plethora of callable routines just like these two functions. Although you'll find that many of them are well covered by standard C routines, you'll also find that many are not. DOS also contains many *undocumented* functions that are quite interesting, and useful as well. An excellent example of this is the DOS Busy Flag, also called the InDos Flag. DOS function 34 hex returns a pointer to a system memory location that contains the DOS Busy Flag. This flag is set to 1 whenever DOS is busy doing something critical and doesn't want to be called (not even by itself). The flag is cleared (set to zero) when DOS is not busy. The purpose of this flag is to inform DOS when it is executing critical code. However, programmers find this flag useful as well so that they can also know when DOS is busy. Because Microsoft has recently documented this function, it is technically no longer an undocumented routine, but it has been in DOS since version 2.0. Several excellent books on documented and undocumented DOS functions are available for those who are more interested in this topic.

Cross Reference:

XIV.3: How can I call BIOS functions from my program?

XIV.3: How can I call BIOS functions from my program?
Answer:

As in the preceding example, you are quite frequently calling BIOS functions when you use standard C library routines such as _setvideomode(). In addition, even the DOS functions used previously (getch() and printf()) ultimately made calls into the BIOS to actually perform the tasks. In such cases, DOS is simply passing on your DOS request to the proper lower-level BIOS function. In fact, the following example code illustrates this fact perfectly. This code performs the same tasks that the preceding example does, except that DOS is bypassed altogether and the BIOS is called directly.

```
#include <stdlib.h>
#include <dos.h>
```

```
char GetAKey(void);
void OutputString(char *);

main(int argc, char ** argv)
{
    char str[128];
    union REGS regs;
    int ch;

    /* copy argument string; if none, use "Hello World" */
    strcpy(str, (argv[1] == NULL ? "Hello World" : argv[1]));


    while((ch = GetAKey()) != 27){
        OutputString(str);
    }

}

char
GetAKey()
{
    union REGS regs;

    regs.h.ah = 0;                  /* get character */
    int86(0x16, &regs, &regs);

    return((char)regs.h.al);
}

void
OutputString(char * string)
{
    union REGS regs;

    regs.h.ah = 0x0E;               /* print character */
    regs.h.bh = 0;

    /* loop, printing all characters */
    for(;*string != '\0'; string++){
        regs.h.al = *string;
        int86(0x10, &regs, &regs);
    }
}
```

As you can see, the only changes were in the GetAKey() and OutputString() functions themselves. The GetAKey() function bypasses DOS and calls the keyboard BIOS directly to get the character (note that in this particular call, the key is not echoed to the screen, unlike in the previous example). The OutputString() function bypasses DOS and calls the Video BIOS directly to print the string. Note the inefficiency of this particular example—the C code must sit in a loop, printing one character at a time. The Video BIOS does support a print-string function, but because C cannot access all the registers needed to set up the call to print the string, I had to default to printing one character at a time. Sigh. Regardless, you can run this example to produce the same output as is produced in the example before it.

Cross Reference:

XIV.2: How can I call DOS functions from my program?

XIV.4: How can I access important DOS memory locations from my program?

Answer:

Like the DOS and BIOS functions, there are dozens of memory locations that contain useful and interesting information about the computer. Need to know the current display mode without using an interrupt? It's in 40:49 hex (that's segment 40, offset 49). Want to find out whether the user is currently pressing the Shift, Ctrl, or Alt keys? That information is in 40:17. Want to write directly to the screen? Monochrome screens start at 0xB000:0, color text mode and 16-color graphics modes (below 640×480 16 colors) start at 0xB800:0, and all other standard graphics modes (including 640×480 16 colors and up) start at 0xA000:0. Refer to FAQ XIV.8 for more information. The following example shows how to print color text mode characters to the screen. Note that this is a slight modification to the example used in the previous few questions.

```c
#include <stdlib.h>
#include <dos.h>

char GetAKey(void);
void OutputString(int,int,unsigned int,char *);

main(int argc, char ** argv)
{
    char str[128];
    union REGS regs;
    int ch, tmp;

    /* copy argument string; if none, use "Hello World" */
    strcpy(str, (argv[1] == NULL ? "Hello World" : argv[1]));

    /* print the string in red at top of screen */
    for(tmp=0;((ch = GetAKey()) != 27); tmp+=strlen(str)){
        OutputString(0,tmp,0x400,str);
    }

}

char
GetAKey()
{
    union REGS regs;

    regs.h.ah = 0;                /* get character */
    int86(0x16, &regs, &regs);

    return((char)regs.h.al);
}
```

```c
void
OutputString(int row, int col, unsigned int videoAttribute, char *outStr)
{
    unsigned short far * videoPtr;

    videoPtr = (unsigned short far *)(0xB800L << 16);
videoPtr += (row * 80) + col;     /* Move videoPtr to cursor position */
videoAttribute &= 0xFF00;         /* Ensure integrity of attribute */

    /* print string to RAM */
    while(*outStr != '\0'){

        /* If newline was sent, move pointer to next line, column 0 */
        if( (*outStr == '\n') || (*outStr == '\r') ){
            videoPtr += (80 - ( ((int)FP_OFF(videoPtr) / 2) % 80));
            outStr++;
            continue;
        }

        /* If backspace was requested, go back one */
        if(*outStr == 8){
            videoPtr--;
            outStr++;
            continue;
        }

        /* If BELL was requested, don't beep, just print a blank
           and go on */
        if(*outStr == 7){
            videoPtr++;
            outStr++;
            continue;
        }

        /* If TAB was requested, give it eight spaces */
        if(*outStr == 9){
            *videoPtr++ = videoAttribute | ' ';
            *videoPtr++ = videoAttribute | ' ';
            *videoPtr++ = videoAttribute | ' ';
            *videoPtr++ = videoAttribute | ' ';
            *videoPtr++ = videoAttribute | ' ';
            *videoPtr++ = videoAttribute | ' ';
            *videoPtr++ = videoAttribute | ' ';
            *videoPtr++ = videoAttribute | ' ';
            outStr++;
            continue;
        }

        /* If it was a regular character, print it */
        *videoPtr = videoAttribute | (unsigned char)*outStr;
        videoPtr++;
        outStr++;
    }

    return;

}
```

Obviously, printing text characters to the screen is a bit more complicated when you have to do it yourself. I even made shortcuts by ignoring the meaning of the BELL character (to issue a beep) and a couple of other special characters (although I did implement carriage return and linefeed). Regardless, this function performs basically the same task as the previous examples, except that now you have control over the color of the character and its position when printed. This example starts printing from the top of the screen. If you want more examples of using memory locations, refer to FAQs XX.1, XX.12, and XX.17—these all use pointers to low DOS memory to find useful information about the computer.

Cross Reference:

XIV.5: What is BIOS?

XX.1: How are command-line parameters obtained?

XX.12: How can I pass data from one program to another?

XX.17: Can you disable warm boots (Ctrl-Alt-Delete)?

XIV.5: What is BIOS?
Answer:

The Basic Input Output System, or BIOS, is the foundation of the personal computer's operation. It is the program that is executed first when the computer is powered up, and it is used by DOS and other programs to access each piece of hardware inside the computer.

The bootup program, however, isn't the only code in the computer that is called BIOS. In fact, the BIOS that executes when the PC is turned on is typically called the *Motherboard BIOS*, because it is located on the motherboard. Until recently, this BIOS was fixed in a ROM chip and could not be reprogrammed to fix bugs and enhance the features. Today, the Motherboard BIOS is in an electronically reprogrammable memory chip called *Flash EPROM*, but it is still the same old BIOS. Anyway, the Motherboard BIOS walks through system memory to find other hardware in the system that also contains code foundational to its use (other BIOS code). For example, your VGA card has its own BIOS physically located on the VGA card itself—it's usually called the Video BIOS or VGA BIOS. Your hard and floppy disk controller has a BIOS that is also executed at boot time. People often will both refer to these collective programs as the BIOS and refer to a specific individual BIOS as the BIOS. Neither reference is incorrect.

With all that said, you should know that BIOS is not DOS—BIOS is the lowest-level software functionality available on the PC. DOS "sits on top of" the BIOS and calls the BIOS regularly to perform routine operations that you might mistakenly attribute to being a "DOS" function. For example, you might use DOS function 40 hex to write data to a file on the hard disk. DOS actually performs this task by ultimately calling the hard disk BIOS's function 03 to actually write the data to the disk.

Cross Reference:

XIV.6: What are interrupts?

XIV.6: What are interrupts?

Answer:

First of all, there are *hardware interrupts* and there are *software interrupts*. Interrupts provide a way for different hardware and software "pieces" of the computer to talk to each other. That is their purpose, but *what* are they, and how do they perform this communication?

The CPU (Central Processing Unit), which in the PC's case is an Intel or clone 80x86 processor, has several pins on it that are used to interrupt the CPU from its current task and make it perform some other task. Connected to each interrupt pin is some piece of hardware (a timer, for example) whose purpose is to apply a specific voltage on that CPU interrupt pin. When this event occurs, the processor stops executing the software it is currently executing, saves its current operating state, and "handles" the interrupt. The processor has already been loaded with a table that lists each interrupt number, and the program that is supposed to be executed when that particular interrupt number occurs.

Take the case of the system timer. As part of the many tasks it has to perform, the PC must maintain the time of day. Here's how it works: A hardware timer interrupts the CPU 18 times every second. The CPU stops what it is doing and looks in the interrupt table for the location of the program whose job it is to maintain the system timer data. This program is called an *interrupt handler*, because its job is to handle the interrupt that occurred. In this case, the CPU looks up interrupt eight in the table because that happens to be the system timer interrupt number. The CPU executes that program (which stores the new timer data into system memory) and then continues where it left off. When your program requests the time of day, this data is formatted into the style you requested and is passed on to you. This explanation greatly oversimplifies how the timer interrupt works, but it is an excellent example of a *hardware interrupt*.

The system timer is just one of hundreds of *events* (as interrupts are sometimes called) that occur via the interrupt mechanism. Most of the time, the hardware is not involved in the interrupt process. What I mean by that is that software frequently uses an interrupt to call another piece of software, and hardware doesn't have to be involved. DOS and the BIOS are two prime examples of this. When a program opens a file, reads or writes data to it, writes characters to the screen, gets a character from the keyboard, or even asks for the time of day, a *software interrupt* is necessary to perform each task. You might not know that this is happening because the interrupts are buried inside the innocuous little functions you call (such as getch(), fopen(), and ctime()).

In C, you can generate an interrupt using the int86() or int86x() functions. The int86() and int86x() functions require an argument that is the interrupt number you want to generate. When you call one of these functions, the CPU is interrupted as before and checks the interrupt table for the proper program to execute. In these cases, typically a DOS or BIOS program is executed. Table XIV.6 lists many of the common interrupts that you can call to set or retrieve information about the computer. Note that this is not a complete list and that each interrupt you see can service hundreds of different functions.

Table XIV.6. Common PC interrupts.

Interrupt (hex)	Description
5	Print Screen Services
10	Video Services (MDA, CGA, EGA, VGA)
11	Get Equipment List
12	Get Memory Size
13	Disk Services
14	Serial Port Services
15	Miscellaneous Function Services
16	Keyboard Services
17	Printer Services
1A	Time of Day Services
21	DOS Functions
2F	DOS Multiplex Services
33	Mouse Services
67	EMS Services

Now that you know what an interrupt is, you might realize that while your computer is just sitting idle, it is probably processing dozens of interrupts a second, and it is often processing hundreds of interrupts each second when it's working hard. FAQ XX.12 includes an example of a program that enables you to write your own interrupt handlers so that you can have two programs talk to each other through the interrupt. Check it out if you find this stuff fascinating.

Cross Reference:

XX.12: How can I pass data from one program to another?

XIV.7: Which method is better, ANSI functions or BIOS functions?

Answer:

Each method has its advantages and disadvantages. What you must do is answer a few questions to find out which method is right for the application you need to create. Do you need to get your application out quickly? Is it just a "proof of concept" or the "real thing"? Does speed matter? Do you need the approval of your inner child? OK, so maybe your inner child doesn't care, but the other questions should be answered before you decide. The following list compares the basic advantages of ANSI versus BIOS functions:

ANSI Advantages over BIOS

It requires only `printf()` statements to perform tasks
You can easily change text color and attributes
It works on every PC, regardless of configuration
You don't need to memorize BIOS functions

BIOS Advantages over ANSI

It runs faster
You can do more things using BIOS
It does not require a device driver (ANSI requires ANSI.SYS)
You don't need to memorize ANSI commands

What you will discover is that ANSI is a good place to start, and it will enable you to create some nice programs. However, you will probably find that ANSI begins to "get in your way," and you'll soon want to move on to BIOS functions. Of course, you'll also find that the BIOS gets in your way sometimes, and you'll want to go even faster. For example, FAQ XIV.4 contains an example of avoiding even the BIOS to print text to the screen. You'll probably find that this method is more fun than ANSI or BIOS.

Cross Reference:

XIV.4: How can I access important DOS memory locations from my program?

XIV.8: Can you change to a VGA graphics mode using the BIOS?

Answer:

Yes. Interrupt 10 hex, the Video BIOS, handles switching between text and graphics modes (among other things). When you execute a program that changes from text mode to graphics mode and back (even if the program is Microsoft Windows), the Video BIOS is requested to perform the change. Each different setting is called a *display mode*.

To change the display mode, you must call the Video BIOS through the "int10" services. That is, you must make interrupt calls to the interrupt handler at interrupt 10. This is just like making DOS calls (int21), except the interrupt number is different. Following is a piece of sample code that calls Video BIOS function 0 to switch from standard text mode (Mode 3) to a mode number from the command line and back:

```
#include <stdlib.h>
#include <dos.h>

main(int argc, char ** argv)
{
    union REGS regs;
    int mode;

    /* accept Mode number in hex */
    sscanf(argv[1], "%x", &mode);
```

```
        regs.h.ah = 0;              /* AH=0 means "change display mode" */
        regs.h.al = (char)mode;    /* AL=??, where ?? is the Mode number */
        regs.x.bx = 0;             /* Page number, usually zero */

        int86(0x10, &regs, &regs);  /* Call the BIOS (int10) */

        printf("Mode 0x%X now active\n", mode);
        printf("Press any key to return... ");
        getch();

        regs.h.al = 3;                 /* return to Mode 3 */
        int86(0x10, &regs, &regs);
    }
```

One interesting feature of this particular function that isn't shown here is the capability to change display modes without clearing the screen. This feature can be extremely useful in certain circumstances. To change modes without affecting screen contents, simply OR hex 80 to the display mode value you place into the AL register. For instance, if you want to switch to mode 13 (hex), you put hex 93 in AL. The remaining code stays unchanged.

Today, VGA cards also adhere to the VESA Video BIOS standard in their support of the extended display modes (see the following sidebar for an explanation). However, it requires a new "change display mode" function to support these extended modes. Per the VESA standard, you use function hex 4F rather than function 0 in the preceding example to switch VESA modes. The following example code is a modification of the preceding example to incorporate VESA mode numbers.

```
#include <stdlib.h>
#include <dos.h>

main(int argc, char ** argv)
{
    union REGS regs;
    int mode;

    /* accept Mode number in hex */
    sscanf(argv[1], "%x", &mode);

    regs.x.ax = 0x4F02;      /* change display mode */
    regs.x.bx = (short)mode; /* three-digit mode number */

    int86(0x10, &regs, &regs);  /* Call the BIOS (int10) */

    if(regs.h.al != 0x4F){
        printf("VESA modes NOT supported!\n");
    }
    else{
        printf("Mode 0x%X now active\n", mode);
        printf("Press any key to return... ");
        getch();
    }
    regs.h.al = 3;                 /* return to Mode 3 */
    int86(0x10, &regs, &regs);
}
```

Note that this now conflicts with that hex 80 "don't clear the screen" value. For VESA, it has simply moved from the high-order bit of the two-digit number to the high-order bit of the three-digit value (all VESA modes are three digits in size—again, see the sidebar for details). Therefore, to change to VESA mode 101, you make the VESA mode number 901, and the screen's contents will be preserved.

All About Display Modes

IBM created a display mode standard that attempted to define all the display modes that could ever possibly be needed. These included all the possible pixel depths (number of colors) that would ever be needed. So IBM created 19 display modes (numbered from 0 to 13 hex). Table XIV.8a shows the display mode standard.

Table XIV.8a. Standard display modes.

Mode	Resolution	Graphics or Text?	Colors
0	40×25	Text	Monochrome
1	40×25	Text	16
2	80×25	Text	Monochrome
3	80×25	Text	16
4	320×200	Graphics	4
5	320×200	Graphics	4 grays
6	640×200	Graphics	Monochrome
7	80×25	Text	Monochrome
8	160×200	Graphics	16
9	320×200	Graphics	16
A	640×200	Graphics	4
B	Reserved for EGA BIOS use		
C	Reserved for EGA BIOS use		
D	320×200	Graphics	16
E	640×200	Graphics	16
F	640×350	Graphics	Monochrome
10	640×350	Graphics	4
11	640×480	Graphics	Monochrome
12	640×480	Graphics	16
13	320×200	Graphics	256

See anything you recognize? Mode 3 is the 80×25 color text mode that you see when you turn on your PC. Mode 12 is what you get when you select "VGA" as your Microsoft Windows 3.x driver (you know, the one that comes with Windows). Note the lack of any display mode featuring more

continues

than 256 colors, or higher than 640×480 resolution. Modes 4, 9, and D for many years were the popular choice of DOS game makers, featuring a "big" resolution of 320×200 and enough colors (4 or 16) to display decent graphics. Mode 13 is the display mode used for just about all the popular action games, including DOOM (I and II), id Software's new Heretic, Apogee's Rise of the Triad, Interplay's Descent, and many others. In truth, many of these action games perform little tricks on the VGA cards that convert Mode 13 into 320×240, with more memory pages to improve graphics appearance and speed—they call it Mode X.

So where did all the other display modes, the ones you're used to, come from? They were made up by VGA card manufacturers. The other display modes you might be familiar with (800×600, 1024×768, 1280×1024, and even 1600×1200) come from a "melting pot" of sources, but regardless of their origins, the VGA card makers put them on their VGA cards to increase the cards' value. Such modes are usually called *extended display modes*. Thanks to the wonders of competition and capitalism, the card makers migrated toward these higher display modes. Others have been tried (ever heard of 1152×900?) but weren't received as well as these modes.

OK, so what is VESA, and what does it have to do with VGA cards? Although the VGA card makers all chose to support the same display modes (even the extended ones), each implemented these extended modes in its own proprietary way. Game and productivity software makers were stressed to support each proprietary method of each VGA card on the market. A group of manufacturers and other representatives formed a committee to standardize as much as possible the setup and programming of these cards. VESA (Video Electronics Standards Association) is this committee. The VESA committee adopted a standard of the extended display modes so that software could make common BIOS calls that would set up and initialize all VGA cards that adhered to this standard. It probably is safe to say that 100 percent of all VGA cards sold in the United States support the VESA standard in one form or another.

All *VESA modes* (which is what the standardized set of display modes is called) utilize mode numbers that are nine bits wide rather than the eight-bits-wide standard mode. Having a nine-bit mode number allows the VESA modes to be three hex digits long rather than two in the IBM standard (the ones from 0 to 13 hex shown in Table XIV.8a), thereby avoiding a numbering conflict. Therefore, all VESA mode values are above 100 hex. Here's how the VESA modes work: You want to program your VGA card to display 1024×768 at 256 colors, which happens to be VESA mode 105. You make a BIOS call using 105 as the display mode number. The VESA mode number is translated into the internal proprietary number by the Video BIOS (sometimes called the *VESA BIOS*) to actually perform the mode switch. VGA card manufacturers supply a VESA BIOS with each VGA card to perform these translations so that all you have to worry about is the VESA number. Table XIV.8b shows the latest list of VESA display modes (it is an ever-evolving standard).

Table XIV.8b. VESA display modes.

Resolution	Colors	VESA Mode
640×400	256	100
640×480	256	101

Resolution	Colors	VESA Mode
640×480	32,768	110
640×480	65,536	111
640×480	16.7 million	112
800×600	16	102
800×600	256	103
800×600	32,768	113
800×600	65,536	114
800×600	16.7 million	115
1024×768	16	104
1024×768	256	105
1024×768	32,768	116
1024×768	65,536	117
1024×768	16.7 million	118
1280×1024	16	106
1280×1024	256	107
1280×1024	32,768	119
1280×1024	65,536	11A
1280×1024	16.7 million	11B

Notice that these are the modes you are accustomed to seeing, especially if you use Microsoft Windows.

Cross Reference:

XIV.6: What are interrupts?

XIV.9: Does operator precedence always work (left to right, right to left)?

Answer:

If you mean "Does a right-to-left precedence operator ever go left to right, and vice versa?" the answer is no. If you mean "Can a lower-order precedence ever be risen above a higher-order precedence?" the answer is yes. Table XIV.9 lists the order of each operator from top to bottom (highest order to lowest) and shows each operator's associativity.

Table XIV.9. Operator precedence.

Operator	Associativity
() [] -> .	Left to right
! ~ ++ -- - (typecast) * & sizeof	Right to left
* / %	Left to right
+ -	Left to right
<< >>	Left to right
< <= > >=	Left to right
== !=	Left to right
&	Left to right
^	Left to right
¦	Left to right
&&	Left to right
¦¦	Left to right
?:	Right to left
= += -=	Right to left
,	Left to right

Note in the table that the != operator takes precedence over the = operator (in fact, practically everything takes precedence over the = operator). The following two source lines illustrate how precedence of one operator over another can get a programmer into trouble:

```
while(ch = getch() != 27)  printf("Got a character\n");
while((ch = getch()) != 27)  printf("Got a character\n");
```

Obviously, the purpose of this code is to get a character from the keyboard and check it against decimal 27 (the Escape key). Unfortunately, in source line one, the getch() is compared to the Escape key. The *resulting test* (which will return a TRUE or FALSE), not the character from the keyboard, is placed into ch. This is due to the precedence of the != operator over the = operator.

In the second source line, a set of parentheses was added to surround the ch = getch() operation. Because parentheses are the highest order of precedence, the keyboard character is placed into ch, then checked against the Escape key. This final check will return TRUE or FALSE to the while statement, which is exactly what is desired (while this statement is TRUE, print this sentence). As a matter of detail, it should be pointed out that ch is not checked against 27; the result of the parenthetical statement ch = getch() is checked against 27. It might not make much difference in this case, but parentheses can really change the way code is created and executed. In the case of statements with multiple parenthetical statements, the code is executed from the innermost set of parentheses to the outermost, from left to right.

Note that the associativity in each operator's individual case (left to right or right to left) does not change, but the order of precedence does.

Cross Reference:

None.

XIV.10: Should a variable's type be declared within the header of a function or immediately following? Why?

Answer:

The ANSI standard is to declare a variable's type within the header of the function. As you'll discover in Chapter XX, C was originally designed to run on the UNIX operating system back in the '70s. Naturally, this was before any sort of C ANSI standard. The declaration method for the original C compilers was to put the argument's type immediately after the function header.

Today, the ANSI standard dictates that the type be declared within the function's header. The problem with the old method was that it didn't allow for argument function type checking—the compiler could perform only return value checking. Without argument checking, there is no way to see whether the programmer is passing incorrect types to a function. By requiring arguments to be inside the function's header, and by requiring you to prototype your functions (including the argument types), the compiler can check for incorrect parameter passing in your code.

Cross Reference:

XIV.11: Should programs always include a prototype for main()?

XIV.11: Should programs always include a prototype for *main()*?

Answer:

Sure, why not? Including the prototype is not required, but it is good programming practice. Everyone knows what the argument types are for main(), but your program can define the return type. You've probably noticed in the examples in this chapter (and possibly in other chapters) that main() is not prototyped, that no explicit return type is shown in the main() body itself, and that main() does not even contain a return() statement. By writing the examples in this way, I have implied a void function that returns an int. However, because there is no return() statement, a garbage value will be returned. This is not good programming practice. Good programming practice dictates a function prototype even for main(), and a proper return value for that prototype.

Cross Reference:

XIV.12: Should main() always return a value?

XIV.12: Should *main()* always return a value?

Answer:

Your `main()` does not always have to return a value, because the calling function, which is usually COMMAND.COM, does not care much about return values. Occasionally, your program could be in a batch file that checks for a return code in the DOS `errorLevel` symbol. Therefore, return values from `main()` are purely up to you, but it is always good to return a value to the caller just in case.

Your `main()` can return void (or have no `return` statement) without problems.

Cross Reference:

XIV.11: Should programs always include a prototype for `main()`?

XIV.13: Can I control the mouse using the BIOS?

Answer:

Yes. You can communicate with mouse services by using interrupt 33 hex. Table XIV.13 lists the most common mouse services available at interrupt 33.

Table XIV.13. Mouse interrupt services.

Number	Description
0	Initialize Mouse; Hide If Currently Visible
1	Show Mouse
2	Hide Mouse
3	Get Mouse Position
4	Set Mouse Position
6	Check Whether Mouse Buttons Are Down
7	Set Horizontal Limits on Mouse
8	Set Vertical Limits on Mouse
9	Set Graphics Mode Mouse Shape
10	Set Text Mode Mouse Style
11	Get Mouse Delta Movement

The following example code uses a few of the preceding mouse routines to manipulate a text mode mouse:

```
#include <stdlib.h>
#include <dos.h>

main()
```

```
{
    union REGS regs;

    printf("Initializing Mouse...");
    regs.x.ax = 0;
    int86(0x33, &regs, &regs);

    printf("\nShowing Mouse...");
    regs.x.ax = 1;
    int86(0x33, &regs, &regs);

    printf("\nMove mouse around. Press any key to quit...");
    getch();

    printf("\nHiding Mouse...");
    regs.x.ax = 2;
    int86(0x33, &regs, &regs);

    printf("\nDone\n");
}
```

When you run this example, a flashing block cursor that you can move around will appear on-screen. Using function 3, you can query the mouse handler for the position of the mouse at any time. In fact, I wrote an entire set of mouse library routines using the functions in Table XIV.13 that are incorporated into many of my text mode DOS programs.

To access these functions, you must have a mouse driver loaded. Typically, this occurs in AUTOEXEC.BAT, where a DOS mouse driver is loaded. However, it is becoming common to have only a Windows mouse driver loaded at Windows runtime. In that case, you will have to be running in a DOS shell to access the mouse functions.

Cross Reference:

None.

CHAPTER XV

$\blacklozenge$

Portability

Portability doesn't mean writing programs that can run, unchanged, on every computer ever invented. It just means writing programs so that when things change, the programs don't have to change, much.

Don't be too quick to say, "It won't happen to me." Many MS-DOS programmers didn't worry about portability until MS-Windows came around. Then all of a sudden, their programs had to run on what looked like a different operating system. Mac programmers got to deal with a new processor when the Power PC caught on. Anyone who has maintained a program on various flavors of UNIX probably has more knowledge about portability than would fit into this whole book, let alone one chapter.

Say you're writing anti-lock braking software using Tucker C for the Anti-Lock Braking and Tire Rotation operating system (ALBATR-OS). That might sound like the ultimate in nonportable software. Even so, portability can be important. You might have to port your software from version 7.55c of Tucker C to version 8.0, or from version 3.0 to 3.2a of ALBATR-OS, to pick up some bug fixes. You might have to port it (some of it) to MS-Windows or a UNIX workstation, to be used in a simulation for testing or advertising purposes. And more likely than not, sometime between when the first line of code is written and when the last line is finally debugged, you might have to port it from one programmer to another.

Portability, in its best sense, means doing things in an unsurprising way. The goal isn't to make the job easier for the compiler. The goal is to make the job easier for the poor slobs who have to write (and rewrite!) the code. If you're the "poor slob" who gets someone else's code, every surprise in the original code will cost you time, leave the potential for making subtle bugs, or both. If you're the original coder, you still want to make the code unsurprising for the next poor slob. You'll want the code to be easy enough to understand that no one will come complaining to you that they don't understand it. Besides, more than likely, the next "poor slob" will be *you*, several months after you've forgotten why you wrote that for loop in such a tricky way.

The essence of making your code portable is simple: *If there's a simple, standard way of doing something, do it that way!*

The first step in making your code portable is to use the standard library functions, and to use them with the header files defined in the ANSI/ISO C standard. See Chapter XII, "Standard Library Functions," for details.

The second step is to, whenever possible, write code that you expect will work with all compilers, rather than code that appears to work with your current compiler. If your manual warns about a feature or a function being specific to your compiler, or certain compilers, be wary of using it. Many good books on C programming have advice on what you can depend on working portably. In particular, if you don't know whether something will work, don't immediately write a test program and see whether your compiler accepts it. Just because your compiler does, in this version, doesn't mean that code is very portable. (This is more of a problem for C++ programmers than for C programmers.) Besides, small test programs have a tendency to miss some aspects of the feature or problem they were intended to test.

The third step is to isolate any nonportable code. If you're not sure whether part of your program is portable, add a comment to that effect as soon as you can! If large parts of your program (whole functions or more) depend on where they run or how they're compiled, put the different nonportable implementations in separate .c files. If small parts of your program have portability issues, use #ifdefs. For example, filenames in MS-DOS look like \tools\readme, but under UNIX, they look like /tools/readme. If your code needs to break down such filenames into their separate parts, you need to look for the right separator. With code like

```
#ifdef unix
#define FILE_SEP_CHAR '/'
#endif
#ifdef __MSDOS__
#define FILE_SEP_CHAR '\\'
#endif
```

you can use FILE_SEP_CHAR as an argument to strchr or strtok to find the "path" of directories that lead to the file. That step won't find the drive name of an MS-DOS file, but it's a start.

Finally, one of the best ways to find potential portability problems (and ways to fix them) is to have someone else find them! Seriously, if you can, have someone else look over your code. He or she might know something you don't, or might see something you never thought of. (Some tools, often with the word "lint" in their names, and some compiler options can help find some problems. Don't expect them to find big ones.)

XV.1: Should C++ additions to a compiler be used in a C program?

Answer:

Not unless your "C program" is really a C++ program.

Some features of C++ were so nifty that they were accepted by the ANSI/ISO C standards committees. They're no longer "C++ additions"; they're part of C. Function prototypes and the const keyword were added to C because they were really good ideas.

A few features of C++, such as inline functions and ways of using const to replace #define, are sometimes called "better C" features. There have been a few partly C++ compilers with a few of these features. Should you use them?

Here's one programmer's opinion: If you want to write C code, write C code. Write code that all C compilers will accept. If you want to take advantage of C++ features, move to C++. You can take baby steps, a few new tricks at a time, or you can go all out and create templated pure abstract base classes with lots of inlines and exceptions and conversion operators. After you've crossed the line, though, you've crossed it; your program is now a C++ program, and you shouldn't expect a C compiler to accept it.

Now let me say this. Work has started on a new C standard, one that will include some C++ features and some brand new features. Over the next few years, some of those new features will be implemented by some compiler vendors. That doesn't guarantee they will be implemented by all compilers, or make it into the next C standard. Keep your ears open. When it sounds as if a new feature has really caught on, not just in the compiler you use but in all the ones you might use, then think about using it yourself. It didn't make sense to wait until 1989 to start using function prototypes. On the other hand, it turns out there was no good time to start using the noalias keyword if you wanted your code to be portable.

Cross Reference:

XV.2. What is the difference between C++ and C?

XV.2: What is the difference between C++ and C?

Answer:

There are two perspectives to consider: the C programmer's, and the C++ programmer's.

To a C programmer, C++ is a quirky language that's hard to deal with. Most C++ libraries can't be linked into a C program by a C compiler. (There's no support of templates or "virtual tables," which the compiler has to create at link time.) Even if you link your program with a C++ compiler, a lot of C++ functions can't be called at all from C code. C++ programs, unless they're very carefully designed, can be somewhat slower and a lot bigger than similar C programs. C++ compilers have more bugs than C compilers. C++ programs are much harder to port from one compiler to another. Finally, C++ is a big language, hard to learn. The definitive (for 1990) book was more than 400 pages long, and more has been added every year since then.

C, on the other hand, is a nice, simple language. No changes have been made to the language in years. (That won't last forever; see FAQ XV.1.) The compilers are good and getting better. Good C code is trivial to port between good C compilers. Object-oriented design isn't easy to do in C, but it's not that hard. You can (almost) always build your C code with C++ compilers if you want.

To a C++ programmer, C is a good beginning. There are many mistakes you can make in C that you'll never make in C++; the compiler won't let you. Some of the tricks of the C trade can be very dangerous if just slightly misused.

C++, on the other hand, is a great language. With a little discipline and up-front design work, C++ programs can be safe, efficient, and very easy to understand and maintain. There are ways of writing C++ programs so that they will be faster and smaller than the equivalent C programs. Object-oriented design is very easy in C++, but you're not forced to work that way. The compilers are getting better every day, and the standards are firming up. You can (almost) always drop down to the C level if you want to.

What, specifically, is different between C and C++? There are a few C constructs that C++ doesn't allow, such as old-style function definitions. Mostly, C++ is C with new features:

◆ A new comment convention (see FAQ XV.3).

◆ A new "Boolean" type with real `true` and `false` values, compatible with existing C and C++ code. (You can throw away that piece of paper taped to your monitor, the one that says, "0 = false, 1 = true." It's still valid, but it's just not as necessary.)

◆ Inline functions, safer than `#define` macros and more powerful, but just as fast.

◆ Guaranteed initialization of variables, if you want it. Automatic cleanup of variables when they go away.

◆ Better, safer, stronger type checking and memory management.

◆ Encapsulation, so new types can be defined with all their operations. C++ has a `complex` type, with the same operations and syntax as `float` or `double`. It's not built into the compiler; it's implemented in C++, using features every C++ programmer can use.

◆ Access control, so the only way to use a new type is through the operations it allows.

◆ Inheritance and templates, two complementary ways of writing code that can be reused more ways than just calling functions.

◆ Exceptions, a way for a function to report a problem further than just the function that called it.

◆ A new approach to I/O, safer and more powerful than `printf`, that separates formatting from the kind of file being written to.

◆ A rich library of data types. You'll never have to write a linked list or a binary tree again. (This time for sure, honest. Really!)

Which is better, C or C++? That depends on who you are, who you're working with, how much time you have to learn, and what tools you need and want and can use. It depends. There are C++ programmers who will never go back to C, and C programmers who have gone back from C++ and love it. There are programmers who are using some C++ features and a C++ compiler, but who have never really understood C++, who are "writing C programs in C++." Hey, there are people writing FORTRAN programs in C (and C++); they never caught on either.

Great programming languages don't make great programs. Great programmers understand the language they're programming in, whatever language it is, and use it to make great programs.

Cross Reference:

XV.1: Should C++ additions to a compiler be used in a C program?

XV.3: Is it valid to use // for comments in a C program?
Answer:

No. Some C compilers might be able to support the use of //, but that doesn't make it C.

In C, a comment starts with /* and ends with */. C-style comments are still valid in C++, but there's another convention as well. Everything after (and including) //, up to the end of a line, is considered a comment. For example, in C you could write this:

```
i += 1; /* add one to i */
```

That's valid C++, but so is the following line:

```
i += 1; // add one to i
```

The advantage of the new C++ comments is that you can't forget to close it, as you can with a C-style comment:

```
i += 1; /* add one to i
printf("Don't worry, nothing will be "); /* oops */
printf("lost\n);
```

In this example, there's only one comment. It starts on the first line and ends at the end of the second line. The "don't worry" printf is commented out.

Why is this C++ feature more likely than any other to creep into C compilers? Some compilers use a separate program for a preprocessor. If the same preprocessor is used for C and C++ compilers, there might be a way for the C compiler to get the preprocessor to handle the new C++ comments.

C++-style comments are very likely to be adopted into C, eventually. If, one day, you notice that all the C compilers you might use support // comments, feel free to use them in your programs. Until then, use C comments for C code.

Cross Reference:

Introduction to Chapter V: Working with the Preprocessor

V.2: What will the preprocessor do for a program?

XV.1: Should C++ additions to a compiler be used in a C program?

XV.4: How big is a *char*? A *short*? An *int*? A *long*?
Answer:

One byte, at least two bytes, at least two bytes, and at least four bytes. Other than that, don't count on anything.

A char is defined as being one eight-bit byte long. That's easy.

A short is at least two bytes long. It might be four bytes, on some machines, with some compilers. It could be even longer.

An int is the "natural" size of an integer, as long as that's at least two bytes long and at least as big as a short. On a 16-bit machine, an int is probably two bytes long. On a 32-bit machine, an int is probably four bytes long. When 64-bit machines become common, their ints will probably be eight bytes long. The operative word is "probably." For example, the original Motorola 68000 was a hybrid 16/32-bit machine. One 68000 compiler generated either two-byte ints or four-byte ints, depending on a command-line option.

A long is at least as big as an int (and thus, at least as big as a short). A long must be at least four bytes long. Compilers for 32-bit machines might make shorts, ints, and longs all be four bytes long—or they might not.

If you need some integral variable to be four bytes long, don't assume that an int or a long will do. Instead, have a typedef to some built-in type (one probably exists), and surround it with #ifdefs:

```
#ifdef FOUR_BYTE_LONG
typedef long int4;
#endif
```

You might use such a type if you need to write an integer variable as a stream of bytes, to a file or to a network, to be read by a different machine. (If you do, you should see the next FAQ as well.)

If you need some integral variable to be two bytes long, you might be in trouble! There's no guarantee such a beast exists. You can always squeeze a small value into a two-char array; see the next FAQ for details.

Cross Reference:

X.6: How are 16- and 32-bit numbers stored?

XV.5. What's the difference between big-endian and little-endian machines?

XV.5: What's the difference between big-endian and little-endian machines?

Answer:

The difference between big-endian and little-endian is in which end of a word has the most significant byte. Looked at another way, it's a difference of whether you like to count from left to right, or right to left. Neither method is better than the other. A portable C program needs to be able to handle both kinds of machines.

Say that your program is running on a machine on which a short is two bytes long, and you're storing the value 258 (decimal) in a short value at address 0x3000. Because the value is two bytes long, one byte will be stored at 0x3000, and one will be stored at 0x3001. The value 258 (decimal) is 0x0102, so one byte will be 1, and one will be 2. Which byte is which?

That answer varies from machine to machine. On a big-endian machine, the most significant byte is the one with the lower address. (The "most significant byte" or "high-order byte" is the one that will make the biggest change if you add something to it. For example, in the value 0x0102, 0x01 is the most significant byte, and 0x02 is the least significant byte.) On a big-endian machine, the bytes are stored as shown here:

address	0x2FFE	0x2FFF	0x3000	0x3001	0x3002	0x3003
value	0x01	0x02				

That makes sense; addresses are like numbers on a ruler, with the smaller addresses on the left and the larger addresses on the right.

On a little-endian machine, however, the bytes are stored as shown here:

address	0x3003	0x3002	0x3001	0x3000	0x2FFF	0x2FFE
value	0x01	0x02				

That makes sense, too. The smaller (in the sense of less significant) part is at the lower address.

Bad news: some machines store the bytes one way; some, the other. For example, an IBM compatible handles the bytes differently than a Macintosh.

Why does that difference matter? What happens if you use `fwrite` to store a `short` directly, as two bytes, into a file or over a network, not formatted and readable but compact and binary? If a big-endian machine stores it and a little-endian reads it (or vice versa), what goes in as 0x0102 (258) comes out as 0x0201 (513). Oops.

The solution is, instead of storing `short`s and `int`s the way they're stored in memory, pick one method of storing (and loading) them, and stick to it. For example, several standards specify "network byte order," which is big-endian (most significant byte in the lower address). For example, if s is a short and a is an array of two `char`s, then the code

```
a[0] = (s >> 4) & 0xf;
a[1] = s & 0xf;
```

stores the value of s in the two bytes of a, in network byte order. This will happen if the program is running on a little-endian machine or on a big-endian machine.

You'll notice I haven't mentioned which machines are big-endian and which are little-endian. That's deliberate. If portability is important, you should write code that works either way. If efficiency is important, you usually should *still* write code that works either way. For example, there's a better way to implement the preceding code fragment on big-endian machines. However, a good compiler will generate machine code that takes advantage of that implementation, even for the portable C code it's given.

NOTE

The names "big-endian" and "little-endian" come from *Gulliver's Travels* by Jonathan Swift. On his third voyage, Gulliver meets people who can't agree how to eat hard-boiled eggs: big end first, or little end first.

"Network byte order" applies only to `int`, `short`, and `long` values. `char` values are, by definition, only one byte long, so there's no issue with them. There's no standard way to store `float` or `double` values.

Cross Reference:

X.5: What is meant by high-order and low-order bytes?

X.6: How are 16- and 32-bit numbers stored?

CHAPTER XVI

◆

ANSI/ISO Standards

If you don't appreciate the value of the C language standards, you probably don't know how lucky you are.

A C programmer can expect to take a C program developed anywhere, drop it into another compiler, and have it compile. That's not entirely true; many header files and function libraries are particular to specific compilers or specific platforms. There are a (very!) few language extensions, such as the near and far keywords and register pseudo-variables for Intel-based compilers, but even they've become standard across vendors for that platform.

If this seems to you to be the normal state of affairs, like having the accelerator pedal on the left and brakes on the right, you've lived a sheltered life. There are two different standards for BASIC, but no widespread implementation for either. The most popular Pascal compiler in the world doesn't conform to either official standard. The C++ standard that's being developed has changed so fast that it has never been backed up by a widely distributed implementation. There's a rigorous Ada standard that several implementations conform to, but Ada hasn't exactly taken the world by storm.

There are technically two C standards, one from the ANSI (American National Standards Institute) X3J11 committee and one from ISO (International Standards Organization) 9899-1990. Because the few changes ISO made supersede the ANSI document, and ANSI itself accepts the international version, it's correct to talk about "the ANSI/ISO standard."

So, how does that help you? A copy of the standard, covering both the language and the library, with commentary, is available commercially: Herbert Schildt's *The Annotated ANSI C Standard* (Osborne McGraw-Hill, ISBN 0-07-881952-0). It's a lot cheaper than most official standards, which ANSI and ISO sell to help cover the costs of establishing standards. Not every C programmer needs a copy, but nothing's more definitive than this.

The bottom line is that the ANSI/ISO standard is *the* definitive answer to the question "What is C?" If your compiler vendor does something that doesn't follow the standard, you can report it as a bug and expect little argument.

The standard doesn't cover everything. In particular, it doesn't cover a lot of interesting things a C program might do, such as graphics or multitasking. There are many competing (read "incompatible") standards to cover these areas. Maybe some will be recognized as definitive. Don't hold your breath.

By the way, there are ANSI standards for a lot of things besides programming languages. One of the many things ANSI has written a standard for is a set of escape sequences for full-screen text manipulation. That's what the MS-DOS "ANSI driver" refers to in Chapter XVII, "User Interface." (Ironically, the MS-DOS ANSI.SYS implements only a fraction of the ANSI standard sequences.)

XVI.1: Does operator precedence always work?
Answer:

The rules for operator precedence are a little complicated. In most cases, they're set up to do what you need. Arguably, a few of the rules could have been done better.

Quick review: "Operator precedence" is the collection of rules about which "operators" (such as + and = and such) take "precedence," that is, which are calculated first. In mathematics, an expression such as 2×3+4×5 is the same as (2×3)+(4×5); the multiplication happens before the addition. That means that multiplication "takes precedence over" addition, or multiplication "has higher precedence than" addition.

There are no fewer than 16 levels of operator precedence in C. It turns out having that many rules can make C programs slightly harder to read sometimes, but much easier to write. That's not the only way to make that tradeoff, but it's the C way. The levels of operator precedence are summarized in Table XVI.1.

Table XVI.1. Summary of operator precedence (highest to lowest).

Level	Operators
1	x[y] (subscript)
	x(y) (function call)
	x.y (member access)
	x->y (member pointer access)
	x++ (postincrement)
	x-- (postdecrement)
2	++x (increment)
	--x (decrement)
	&x (address-of)
	*x (pointer indirection)

Level	Operators
	+x (same as x, just as in mathematics)
	-x (mathematical negation)
	!x (logical negation)
	~x (bitwise negation)
	sizeof x and sizeof(x_t) (size in bytes)
3	(x_t)y (type cast)
4	x*y (multiplication)
	x/y (division)
	x%y (remainder)
5	x+y (addition)
	x-y (subtraction)
6	x<<y (bitwise left shift)
	x>>y (bitwise right shift)
7	x<y, x>y, x<=y, x>=y (relation comparisons)
8	x==y, x!=y (equality comparisons)
9	x&y (bitwise AND)
10	x^y (bitwise exclusive OR)
11	x¦y (bitwise OR)
12	x&&y (logical AND)
13	x¦¦y (logical OR)
14	x?y:z (conditional)
15	x=y, x*=y, x/=y, x+=y, x-=y, <<=, >>=, &=, ^=, ¦= (assignment; right associative!)
16	x,y (comma)

The highest level of precedence is postfix expressions, things that go after an expression. The next highest level is prefix or unary expressions, things that go before an expression. The next highest level after that is type cast.

NOTE

The most important thing to know about operator precedence is that *p++ means the same thing as *(p++); that is, the ++ operates on the pointer, not the pointed-to thing. Code such as *p++ = *q++ is very common in C. The precedence is the same as that for (*(p++)) = (*(q++)). In English, that means, "Increment q by one but use its old value, find the thing q points to, decrement p by one but use its old value, and assign the thing pointed to by q to the thing pointed to by p." The value of the whole expression is the value of the thing originally pointed to by q. You'll see code like this again and again in C, and you'll have many opportunities to write code like this. You can look up the other operator precedence rules when you can't remember them. To be a good C programmer, though, you'll have to know what *p++ means without much conscious thought.

continues

The original C compiler was written for a computer that had instructions to handle constructs such as *p++ and *p++ = *q++ incredibly efficiently. As a result, a lot of C code is written that way. As a further result, because there's so much C code like that, people who design new computers make sure that there are very efficient instructions to handle these C constructs.

The next level of precedence is multiplication, division, and division remainder (also known as modulus). After that comes addition and subtraction. Just as in mathematical expressions, 2*3+4*5 means the same thing as (2*3)+(4*5).

The next level of precedence is bitwise shifting.

The next levels are the relational comparisons (such as x<y) and then the equality comparisons (x==y and x!=y).

The next three levels are bitwise AND, exclusive OR, and OR, respectively.

NOTE

The third most important thing to know about operator precedence (after what *p++ and x=y=z mean) is that x&y==z is *not* the same as (x&y)==z. Because the precedence of the bitwise operators is lower than that of the comparison operators, x&y==z is the same as x&(y==z). That means "See whether y and z are equal (1 if they are, 0 if they aren't), then bitwise AND x and the result of the comparison." This is a far less likely thing to do than "bitwise AND x and y and see whether the result is equal to z." One might argue that the precedence of the bitwise operators should be higher than that of the comparison operators. It's about 20 years too late to do anything about it. If you want to compare the results of a bitwise operation with something else, you need parentheses.

The next levels are the logical operators, such as x&&y and x||y. Note that logical AND has higher precedence than logical OR. That reflects the way we speak in English. For example, consider this:

```
if (have_ticket && have_reservation
 || have_money && standby_ok) {
    goto_airport();
}
```

In English, you would say, "If you have a ticket and you have a reservation, or if you have money and it's OK to fly standby, go to the airport." If you override the precedence with parentheses, you have a very different condition:

```
/* not a recommended algorithm! */
if (have_ticket
  && (have_reservation || have_money)
  && standby_ok) {
    goto_airport();
}
```

In English, you would say, "If you have a ticket, and if you have a reservation or you have money, and it's OK to fly standby, go to the airport."

The next level of precedence is the conditional expression, x?y:z. This is an if-then-else construct that's an expression, not a statement. Sometimes conditional expressions make code much simpler; sometimes they're obscure. Conditional expressions are right associative, which means that

```
a ? b : c ? d : e
```

means the same thing as this:

```
a ? b : (c ? d : e)
```

This is very much like an else-if construct.

The next level of precedence is assignment. All the assignment operators have the same precedence. Unlike all the other C binary operators, assignment is "right associative"; it's done right to left, not left to right. x+y+z is the same as (x+y)+z, and x*y*z is the same as (x*y)*z, but x=y=z is the same as x=(y=z).

> **NOTE**
>
> The second most important thing to know about operator precedence (after what *p++ means) is what x=y=z means. Because assignment is right associative, it means x=(y=z), or in English, "Assign the value of z to y, and then assign that value to x." It's very common to see code such as this:
>
> ```
> a = b = c = d = 0;
> ```
>
> This assigns zero to d, then c, then b, and finally a, right to left.

The lowest level of precedence in C is the comma operator. The comma operator takes two expressions, evaluates the first one, throws it away, and evaluates the second one. This makes sense only if the first expression has a side effect, such as assignment or a function call. The comma and assignment operators are often used in for statements:

```
for (i=0, count=0; i < MAX; ++i) {
    if (interesting(a[i]) {
        ++count;
    }
}
```

Cross Reference:

I.6: Other than in a for statement, when is the comma operator used?

I.12: Is left-to-right or right-to-left order guaranteed for operator precedence?

I.13: What is the difference between ++var and var++?

I.14: What does the modulus operator do?

II.13: When should a type cast be used?

II.14: When should a type cast not be used?

VII.1: What is indirection?

XVI.2: Should function arguments' types be declared in the argument list of a function or immediately following?

Answer:

Function arguments should be declared in the argument list, unless you're dealing with an out-of-date compiler. In that case, you should use an #ifdef to do it both ways.

There are two ways to define a function. Consider two functions, foo1 and foo2, that take one char* argument and return an integer. Say they're defined in the following way:

```
/* old style */
int
foo1(p)
char* p;
{
    /* body of function goes here */
}

/* new style */
int
foo2(char* p)
{
    /* body of function goes here */
}
```

The only advantage of the old style is that it's prettier for long argument lists.

The advantage of the new style is that it provides a function prototype as well as a function definition. Thus, if any call to foo2 is made in the same .c file in which foo2 is defined, after foo2 is defined, the compiler will check the arguments in the call with the arguments in the definition. If the arguments don't match, the compiler will probably inform you that something is terribly wrong. (The standard doesn't require this step, but it occurs with most compilers.) If the arguments in the call can be converted to the arguments in the definition, they will be. That happens only if the function is defined in the new style, or if a function prototype is seen. If the function is defined in the old style and no prototype was seen, no argument conversion will be performed; probably, little or no argument checking will be done either.

The only disadvantage of the new style is that there are still compilers that don't support it. (These are mostly UNIX-based compilers that are bundled, at no extra charge, with the operating system. On the other hand, many versions of UNIX come standard with ANSI-compliant C compilers.)

If you might need to deal with non-ANSI C compilers, your best bet is to pick a macro that will be defined when prototypes and new style function definitions are supported. A header file for this macro can define it automatically, for cases in which prototypes are known to be supported:

```
#ifdef __ANSI__
#ifndef USE_PROTOS
#define USE_PROTOS 1
#endif
#endif
```

Function declarations might look like this:

```
#ifdef USE_PROTOS
int foo1(char*);
int foo2(char*);
#else
int foo1();
int foo2();
#endif
```

A function definition might look like this:

```
int
#ifdef USE_PROTOS
foo1(char* p)
#else
foo1(p)
char* p;
#endif
{
    /* body of function goes here */
}
```

If your software runs only on MS-DOS, MS-Windows, or Macintosh personal computers, don't worry about the old style; always use the new style.

Cross Reference:

VIII.1: When should I declare a function?

VIII.2: Why should I prototype a function?

XVI.3: Should programs include a prototype for *main()*?
Answer:

Programs should never include a prototype for `main`.

`main()` is a function, mostly the same as any other function. However, `main()` can be defined with at least two possible parameter lists:

```
int main(void)
```

(taking no arguments) or

```
int main(int argc, char** argv);
```

NOTE

> The arguments to `main()` don't have to be called `argc` and `argv`, but they almost always are. There are better ways and places to be creative than making up new names for `main()`'s arguments.

In the second case,

> argc is the number of arguments passed to the program at runtime,
>
> argv[0] is the name of the program,
>
> argv[1] through argv[argc-1] are the arguments passed to the program, and
>
> argv[argc] is a null pointer.

There might be other legitimate definitions, such as this one:

```c
int main(int argc, char** argv, char** envp);
```

envp is an environment list, like the one used by getenv(). It's terminated by a null pointer the same way argv is.

There's no prototype that can match all the legal definitions of main(). The standard says no compiler will provide a prototype for main(); in my opinion, you shouldn't either.

Without a prototype, your program can't explicitly call main() and still do argument checking. Such a call isn't forbidden by the standard, but it's probably not a good idea.

NOTE

C++ programs are explicitly forbidden from calling main(). (Some compilers enable you to do this; they're wrong.) The C++ compiler adds some magical code to main() so initialization ("construction") of global variables happens. If a C++ program could run main() twice, this initialization could happen twice, which would be a Bad Thing.

Cross Reference:

VIII.2: Why should I prototype a function?

XVI.4: Should *main()* always return a value?

Answer:

Yes, unless it calls exit().

When a program runs, it usually terminates with some indication of success or some error code. A C program controls this indication in one (or both) of two ways, which have exactly the same effect:

> It returns a value (the success or failure code) from main().
>
> It calls exit(), passing the success or failure code as an argument.

If the program "drops off the end of main()" without taking either of these actions, there's no guarantee what the success or failure code will be. This is a Bad Thing.

Whenever you write a C program, quickly check the main() function. The last statement should always be either a return statement or a call to the exit() function. (The only exception is when the last statement will never finish, such as an infinite for loop with no break statement. In that case, your compiler will probably complain about adding another statement that can never be reached.)

Cross Reference:

VIII.9: Is using exit() the same as using return?

CHAPTER XVII

◆

User Interface—
Screen and
Keyboard

For a program to be useful, it must have some way of communicating the results, or its needs, to the user. To accomplish communication with the user of the program, the C language comes with a robust library of routines known collectively as the standard input/output library. This chapter looks closely at these routines and answers some frequently asked questions about them.

XVII.1: Why don't I see my screen output until the program ends?

Answer:

Sometimes, depending on the compiler and operating system you are working on, output will be buffered. "Buffered" means that any output you send to a device, whether the screen, the disk, or the printer, is saved until there is a large enough amount to be written efficiently. When enough output has been saved, it is written to the device as one block.

This process can cause two problems for the programmer unaware of its effects. First, output might not be displayed on-screen until sometime after your program sends it. This effect might be a problem if the programmer is trying to keep track of exactly what his program is doing, and when.

The second, and more insidious, problem can occur when your program prints some prompt for the user and waits for input. There is no guarantee in the ANSI C standard that attempting to get input from the user will flush the output buffer. Therefore, the message you sent to the screen might not be displayed before your program tries to get input. The user thus does not know that he is being prompted for input; as far as he can tell, your lovely program has just suddenly stopped working.

How can this problem be fixed? There are two ways. The first way to fix the problem is to insert the line

```
setvbuf( stdout , NULL , _IONBF , 0 );
```

at the start of the program, before any output has been printed. This code has the effect of completely unbuffering output to the screen. After this command is executed, every character that is sent to the screen is printed immediately as it is sent.

This method is a convenient way to solve the problem, but it is not ideal. Without getting into a technical discussion of screen input and output, I'll just state that there are good reasons why screen output is buffered, and that you might want to leave it so.

This brings us to the other way of solving the output-buffering problem. The command fflush(), when invoked on an output buffer, causes it to empty itself even if it is not full. Therefore, to solve the screen buffering problem, you can simply insert the command

```
fflush( stdout );
```

whenever you want the output buffer to be flushed. It would be appropriate to flush the output buffer before requesting input from the user, or before the program goes into an extensive computation that will delay it for a time. This way, whenever the program pauses, you'll know why.

Cross Reference:

None.

XVII.2: How do I position the cursor on the screen?
Answer:

There is no method in the C standard for positioning the cursor on the screen. There are many reasons for this omission. C is designed to work across a broad range of computers, many of which have different screen types. On a line terminal, for example, it is impossible to move the cursor up. An embedded system might even be written in C, in which case there might not be a screen at all!

That being said, there is still a use for positioning the cursor on the screen in your own programs. You might want to give the user an attractive visual that is possible to display only by moving the cursor around. Or you might even want to attempt a little animation using the print commands. Despite the lack of standards for this action, there are several ways the problem can be addressed.

First, the writer of the compiler can supply a library of routines that handle screen output specific to that compiler. One of these routines will certainly be the positioning of the cursor. This is arguably the worst solution, because every manufacturer is free to make his own implementation. Therefore, a program written with one compiler will almost certainly need to be rewritten if it moves to another compiler, much less another machine.

Second, a standard set of library functions can be defined that the compiler writer can implement for his compiler. This is the root of the popular curses package. Curses is available for most machines and compilers. Therefore, a program written to use curses for screen output works on most other computers and compilers.

Third, you can use the fact that the device to which you are printing can interpret the characters you are sending in a particular way. There is a standard way in which terminals (or screens) should be made to interpret characters sent to them, the ANSI standard. If you assume that your computer is ANSI compliant, you can print the right characters to manipulate your screen into positioning the cursor in the places you want, among other actions.

Cross Reference:

None.

XVII.3: What is the easiest way to write data to the screen?
Answer:

The C programming language contains literally hundreds of functions designed to write data to the screen. It can be difficult to decide which of them might be "best" for writing to the screen at a particular time. Many programmers simply pick one or two of the printing functions and use them exclusively. This is an acceptable practice, although it means that the programmer might not always produce the best possible code.

What a programmer should do is review what each printing function is designed for, and what it does best. Thereafter, whenever he needs to print something to the screen, he can use the function that best suits his needs. He might even create some printing functions of his own.

Learning to correctly use the printing functions contained in the standard C library is part of the first step to becoming a truly proficient programmer. Let's examine some of the functions in detail.

```
printf( <format string> , variables );
```

`printf` is the most widely used printing function. Some programmers use it exclusively to send text to the screen. Despite this fact, the function was designed only to print formatted text to the screen. In fact, `printf` is short for "print formatted." Formatted text is text that contains not just the character string that you placed into your code, but also numbers, characters, and other data dynamically created by your program. Additionally, it can make these appear in a particular way. For instance, it can make real numbers appear with a specific number of digits on either side of the decimal point. For this purpose, the `printf` function simply cannot be beat!

Why, then, might one choose not to use `printf`? There are several reasons.

The first reason is that the programmer might want to make what he is doing more clear. Perhaps the programmer is interested only in performing a small subset of the actions provided by the `printf` function. In this case, he might want to use a specific function that provides just that subset, such as

```
putchar( char );
```

This function is designed to send one character to the screen. It is great if this is what you want to do, but it's not really good for anything else. However, by using this function, you are making it exceedingly clear that what this section of code is doing is sending single characters to the screen.

```
puts( char * );
```

This function writes a string of characters to the screen. It does not attempt to accept extra data, as printf does, and it does not process the string that has been passed to it. Again, by using this function, you make it abundantly clear what your code is doing.

The second reason the programmer might choose not to use printf is that he might want to make his code more efficient. The printf function has a lot of overhead; what this means is that it needs to do a great deal of work to perform even a simple operation. It needs to search the string that has been passed to it for format specifiers, it needs to check how many arguments were passed to it, and so forth. The two functions already presented here do not have such overhead. They have the potential for being substantially faster. This fact is not very important for most programs that write data to the screen. It can become an important issue, however, if you are handling large amounts of data from a disk file.

The third reason not to use printf is that the programmer wants to reduce the size of his executable. When you use a standard C function in your program, it must be "linked in." This means that it must be included into the executable file you are producing. Whereas the code for the simple printing functions, such as putch or puts, is quite small, the code for printf is substantially larger—especially because it might include the other two as a matter of course!

This consideration is probably the least important of those presented so far. Still, if you are using a static linker and you want to keep your executable files small, this can be an important trick. For example, it is very desirable to keep the size of TSRs and some other programs to a minimum.

In any case, the programmer should decide which functions he needs to use based on his purposes.

Cross Reference:

None.

XVII.4: What is the fastest way to write text to the screen?

Answer:

Usually, you are not overly concerned with the speed with which your program writes to the screen. In some applications, however, you need to be able to write to the screen as quickly as possible. Such programs might include these:

◆ Text editors. If you cannot draw to the screen very quickly, scrolling of the screen due to the user entering text, as well as other actions, might be too slow.

◆ Animated text. It is common to print characters quickly over the same area to achieve animation. If you cannot print text to the screen very quickly, this animation will be too slow and will not look very good.

◆ Monitor programs. Such a program might continually monitor the system, another program, or some hardware device. It might need to print status updates to the screen many times a second. It is quite possible that the printing to the screen allowed by the standard C library might be too slow for such a program.

What are you to do in such a case? There are three ways you might try to increase the speed with which your program writes to the screen: by choosing print functions with a lower overhead, by using a package or library with faster print features, and by bypassing the operating system and writing directly to the screen. These methods will be examined from the least involved solution to the most complex.

Choosing Print Functions with a Lower Overhead

Some print functions have more overhead than others. "Overhead" refers to extra work that function must do compared to other functions. For example, printf has much more overhead than a function such as puts. Why is that?

The puts function is simple. It accepts a string of characters and writes them to the display. The printf function, of course, will do the same thing, but it does a lot more. It examines the string of characters you have sent to it, looking for special codes which indicate that internal data is to be printed.

Perhaps your code doesn't have internal characters, and you aren't passing anything to it. Unfortunately, the function has no way of knowing that, and it must scan the string for special characters every time.

There is a smaller difference between the functions putch and puts, with putch being better (having less overhead) if you plan to write only a single character.

Unfortunately, the overhead incurred by these C functions is minuscule compared to the overhead of actually drawing the characters onto your display. Thus, this method will probably not gain the programmer very much, except in peculiar circumstances.

Using a Package or Library with Faster Print Features

This is probably the easiest option that will result in real speed gains. You can get a package that will either replace the built-in printing functions in your compiler with faster versions or provide you with faster alternatives.

This option makes life pretty easy on the programmer because he will have to change his code very little, and he can use code that someone else has already spent a great deal of time optimizing. The downside is that the code might be owned by another programmer, and including it in your code might be expensive; or, if you decide to move your code to another platform, it might not exist for that machine.

Nonetheless, this can be a very practical and workable decision for the programmer to make.

Bypassing the Operating System and Writing Directly to the Screen

This action is somewhat frowned on, for many reasons. In fact, it is impossible to perform on some machines and under some operating systems. Furthermore, it is likely to be different for different machines, or even between different compilers on the same computer!

Nonetheless, for speed of video output, you simply cannot beat writing bytes directly to the screen. With full-screen text, you might be able to write hundreds of screens per second. If you need this kind of performance (perhaps for a video game), this method of output is probably worth the effort.

Because each computer and operating system handles this concept differently, it is impractical to give code for every operating system here. Instead, you shall see exactly how this concept is carried out under MS-DOS with Borland C. Even if you are not using these systems, you should be able to learn the correct methods from the following text, enabling you to write similar routines for your computer and operating system.

First of all, you need some method to write data to the screen. You can do this by creating a pointer that "points" to the screen memory. Under Borland C for MS-DOS, this task can be accomplished with this line of code:

```
char far *Screen = MK_FP( 0xb8000 , 0x0000 );
```

A "far" pointer is one that is not limited to the small data segment that has been reserved for your program; it can point anywhere in memory. MK_FP generates a far pointer to a specific location. Some other compilers and computers will not require the pointer type differentiation, or they might not have a similar function. You should look in your compiler's manual for the appropriate information.

Now, you have a pointer that points to the upper-left corner of the screen. You can write bytes to the location of this pointer, and you will see the characters you are writing appear there, as in the following program:

```
#include <dos.h>

main()
{
   int a;
   char far *Screen = MK_FP( 0xb800 , 0x0000 );
   for( a = 0 ; a < 26 ; ++ a )
       Screen[ a * 2 ] = 'a' + a;
   return( 0 );
}
```

After running this program, you should see the alphabet printed across the top of your monitor, in lowercase letters.

You will notice that instead of being written to consecutive locations in video memory, the characters were written only to every other byte of screen memory. Why is that? It is because even though a character occupies only a single byte, a byte is stored immediately after it to hold its color value. Therefore, each character as displayed on-screen is represented by two bytes in the computer's memory: one byte for the character itself and another byte for its color value.

This means two things: First, you must write characters only into every other byte of memory, or else you will see only every other character, as well as having bizarrely colored text. Second, you need to write the color bytes yourself if you plan to have colored text or overwrite the color that already exists at a location. Unless you do this, your text will be written with the color of what was already there. Every color byte must describe not only the color of the character, but also the color of the background it is written over. There are 16 foreground colors and 16 background colors. The lower four bits of the byte are reserved for the foreground color, and the high four bits are reserved for the background color.

This topic might seem a little complex for the inexperienced programmer, but it is actually pretty easy to understand. Just remember that there are 16 colors, ranging from 0 to 16, and that to get the screen byte value, you add the foreground color to the value of the background color times 16. This is shown by the following program:

```
#include <stdio.h>

main()
{
   int fc , bc , c;
   scanf( " %d %d" , &fc , &bc );
   printf( " Foreground = %d , Background = %d , Color = %d\n" ,
           fc , bc , fc + bc * 16 );
   return( 0 );
}
```

I think the reader will agree that it is impractical in most cases for the programmer to have to explicitly write bytes to the screen throughout his program. Instead, it is better to write a routine for writing text to the display quickly, and reuse it frequently. Let's examine the construction of such a routine.

First, you need to ask yourself, "What information will I need to pass to my general-purpose printing function?" For starters, you want to be able to specify

The text to be written to the screen

The location of the text (two numbers)

The color of the text, as well as the background (also two numbers)

Now that you know what data you need to pass to your function, you can declare it in the following fashion:

```
void PrintAt( char *Text , int x , int y , int bc , int fc )
{
```

Now you want to calculate the byte value for the color of the text you will print:

```
int Color = fc + bc * 16;
```

You also need to calculate the starting position for the text pointer:

```
char far *Addr = &Screen[ ( x + y * 80 ) * 2 ];
```

Pay special attention to the fact that you must multiply the offset by two to write into the correct place. Also, note that this line assumes that somewhere in your code you have already defined the Screen variable. If you haven't, just insert the line

```
char far *Screen = MK_FP( 0xb800 , 0x0000 );
```

somewhere in your code.

Now that the preliminaries are out of the way, it's time to actually copy the bytes onto the screen. Look at the code that will carry out this task:

```
while( *Text )
{
   *( Addr++ ) = *( Text++ );
   *( Addr++ ) = Color;
}
```

This code loops while there are still characters left to copy, copying each character to the screen along with its corresponding color.

Take a look at this code in its entirety along with a corresponding test program:

```
#include <dos.h>
/* This is needed for the MK_FP function */
char far *Screen = MK_FP( 0xb800 , 0x0000 );

void PrintAt( char *Text , int x , int y , int bc , int fc )
{
        int Color = fc + bc * 16;
        char far *Addr = &Screen[ ( x + y * 80 ) * 2 ];
        while( *Text )
        {
                *( Addr++ ) = *( Text++ );
                *( Addr++ ) = Color;
        }
}

main()
{
        int a;
        for( a = 1 ; a < 16 ; ++ a )
           PrintAt( "This is a test" , a , a , a + 1 , a );
        return( 0 );
}
```

If you time this function as compared to the built-in printing functions, you should find it to be much faster. If you are using some other hardware platform, you might be able to use the concepts presented here to write a similarly quick printing function for your computer and operating system.

Cross Reference:

None.

XVII.5: How can I prevent the user from breaking my program with Ctrl-Break?

Answer:

MS-DOS, by default, enables the user of a program to stop its execution by pressing Ctrl-Break. This is, in most cases, a useful feature. It enables the user to exit in places from which a program might not allow exit, or from a program that has ceased to execute properly.

In some cases, however, this action might prove to be very dangerous. Some programs might carry out "secure" actions that, if broken, would give the user access to a private area. Furthermore, if the program is halted while updating a data file on disk, it might destroy the data file, perhaps destroying valuable data.

For these reasons, it might be useful to disable the Break key in some programs. A word of warning: delay placing this code in your program until you are 100 percent sure it will work! Otherwise, if your code malfunctions and your program gets stuck, you might be forced to reboot the computer, perhaps destroying updates to the program.

Now I'll show you how to disable the Break key. This is something of a special operation. It can't be done on some machines, some do not have a Break key, and so on. There is therefore no special command in the C language for turning off the Break key. Furthermore, there is not even a standard way to do this on MS-DOS machines. On most machines, you must issue a special machine-language command. Here is a subroutine for turning off the Break key under MS-DOS:

```
#include <dos.h>

void StopBreak()
{
    union REGS in , out;
    in.x.ax = 0x3301;
    in.x.dx = 0;
    int86( 0x21 , &in , &out );
}
```

This subroutine creates a set of registers, setting the ax register to hexadecimal 3301, and the dx register to 0. It then calls interrupt hexadecimal 21 with these registers. This calls MS-DOS and informs it that it no longer wants programs to be stopped by the Break key.

Here's a program to test this function:

```
#include <stdio.h>
#include <dos.h>

void StopBreak()
{
    union REGS in , out;
    in.x.ax = 0x3301;
    in.x.dx = 0;
    int86( 0x21 , &in , &out );
}

int main()
{
    int a;
    long b;
    StopBreak();
    for( a = 0 ; a < 100 ; ++ a )
    {
        StopBreak();
        printf( "Line %d.\n" , a );
        for( b = 0 ; b < 500000L ; ++ b );
    }
    return 0;
}
```

Cross Reference:

None.

XVII.6: How can you get data of only a certain type, for example, only characters?

Answer:

As with almost all computer science questions, the answer is, it depends on exactly what you're doing. If, for example, you are trying to read characters from the keyboard, you can use scanf:

```
scanf( " %c" , &c );
```

Alternatively, you can do this with some of the built-in C library functions:

```
c = getchar();
```

These options will produce basically the same results, with the use of scanf providing more safety checking for the programmer.

If you want to receive data of other types, you can use two methods. You can get the data character by character, always making sure that the correct thing is being entered. The other method is to use scanf, checking its return value to make sure that all fields were entered correctly.

You can use the second method to simply and efficiently extract a stream of records, verifying all of them to be correct. Here is an example program that carries out this maneuver:

```
#include <stdio.h>

main()
{
    int i,a,b;
    char c;
    void ProcessRecord( int, int, char );

    for( i = 0 ; i < 100 ; ++ a ) /* Read 100 records */
    {
        if ( scanf( " %d %d %c" , &a , &b , &c ) != 3 )
            printf( "data line %d is in error.\n" );
        else
            ProcessRecord( a , b , c );
    }
    return( 0 );
}
```

Cross Reference:

None.

XVII.7: Why shouldn't *scanf* be used to accept data?

Answer:

Although scanf is generally the most-used function for keyboard input, there are times when it is best not to use scanf. These situations can be broken down into various cases:

◆ Cases in which the user's keystrokes must be processed immediately when entered.

If you are writing a program in which keystrokes must be acted on immediately after the key is pressed, scanf is useless. scanf waits at least until Enter is pressed. You don't know whether the user will press Enter one second, one minute, or one century after the key is pressed.

Although this use is obviously bad in a real-time program, such as a computer game, it can also be bad in common utility programs. If you have a lettered menu, the user will probably prefer to press the letter *a* by itself, rather than pressing *a* followed by the Enter key.

Unfortunately, the standard C library has no functions designed to carry out this action. You must rely on supplementary libraries or special functions included with your compiler.

◆ Cases in which you need things that scanf might parse away.

scanf is a very smart function—in some cases, too smart. It will cross lines, throw away bad data, and ignore white space to attempt to satisfy the programmer's request for input data.

Sometimes, however, you do not need this degree of cleverness! Sometimes you want to see the input exactly as the user typed it, even if there is not enough of it, too much of it, or such. A case of a program that is not suitable for scanf is one that must accept textual commands from the user. You don't know ahead of time how many words will be in the sentence that the user will type, nor do you have any way of knowing when the user will press Enter if you are using scanf!

◆ Cases in which you do not know ahead of time what data type the user will be entering.

Sometimes, you are prepared to accept input from the user, but you do not know whether he will be entering a number, a word, or some special character. In these cases, you must get the data from the user in some neutral format, such as a character string, and decide what exactly the input is before continuing.

Additionally, scanf has the problem of preserving bad input in the input buffer. For example, if you are attempting to read in a number, and the user enters a character string, the code might loop endlessly trying to parse the character string as a number. This point can be demonstrated by the following program:

```
#include <stdio.h>

main()
{
    int i;
    while( scanf( " %d" , &i ) ==0 )
    {
        printf( "Still looping.\n" );
    }
     return( 0 );
}
```

The program works fine if you enter a number as it expects, but if you enter a character string, it loops endlessly.

Cross Reference:

None.

XVII.8: How do I use function keys and arrow keys in my programs?

Answer:

The use of function keys and arrow keys in a program can make the program much easier to use. The arrow can be allowed to move the cursor, and the function keys can enable users to do special things, or they can replace commonly typed sequences of characters.

However, as is often the case with "special" features, there is no standard way to access them from within the C language. Using scanf to try to access these special characters will do you no good, and getchar cannot be depended on for this sort of operation. You need to write a small routing to query DOS for the value of the key being pressed. This method is shown in the following code:

```
#include <dos.h>

int GetKey()
{
    union REGS in , out;
    in.h.ah = 0x8;
    int86( 0x21 , &in , &out );
    return out.h.al;
}
```

This method bypasses the C input/output library and reads the next key from the key buffer. It has the advantage that special codes are not lost, and that keys can be acted on as soon as they are pressed, instead of being stored in a buffer until Enter is pressed.

Using this function, you can get the integer function of keys when they are pressed. If you write a test program like

```
#include <stdio.h>
#include <dos.h>

int GetKey()
{
    union REGS in , out;
    in.h.ah = 0x8;
    int86( 0x21 , &in , &out );
    return out.h.al;
}

int main()
{
    int c;
    while( ( c = GetKey() ) != 27 )
            /* Loop until escape is pressed */
    {
        printf( "Key = %d.\n" , c );
    }
    return 0;
}
```

you might get output like this for a typed string:

```
Key = 66.
Key = 111.
Key = 98.
Key = 32.
Key = 68.
Key = 111.
Key = 98.
Key = 98.
Key = 115.
```

When you press function keys or arrows, something different will happen; you will see a zero followed by a character value. This is the way special keys are represented: as a zero value followed by another, special value.

You therefore can take two actions. First, you can watch for zeros and, whenever one is pressed, treat the next character in a special fashion. Second, in the key press function, you can check for zeros and, when one is pressed, get the next value, modify it in some way, and return it. This second option is probably the better of the two options. Here's an efficient way of getting this task done:

```
/*
 New improved key-getting function.
*/

int GetKey()
{
    union REGS in , out;
    in.h.ah = 0x8;
    int86( 0x21 , &in , &out );
    if ( out.h.al == 0 )
        return GetKey()+128;
    else
        return out.h.al;

}
```

This is the most efficient and clean of the two solutions. It will save a lot of work on the programmer's part by saving him from having to check for special cases. Special keys have values over 128.

Cross Reference:

None.

XVII.9: How do I prevent the user from typing too many characters in a field?

Answer:

There are two reasons to prevent a user from typing too many characters in a field. The first reason is that you might want to deal with only a fixed number of characters in your code. The second, and perhaps more important, reason is that if the user types more characters than your buffer can handle, it will overflow your buffer and corrupt memory. This potential danger is often overlooked in C tutoring books. For example, the following code is very dangerous if the user types more than 50 characters:

```
char buf[ 50 ];
scanf( " %s" , buf );
```

The way to fix the problem is by specifying in your scanning statement the maximum size of the string you want to scan. This task is accomplished by inserting a number between the % and the s, like so:

```
" %50s"
```

This specification will accept, at most, 50 characters from the user. Any extra characters the user types will remain in the input buffer and can be retrieved by another scanning command.

It is important to note that a string also needs a null terminator. Therefore, if you want to accept 50 characters from the user, your string must be of length 51. This is 50 characters for the real string data, plus a byte for the null terminator.

The following example program tests this technique:

```
#include <stdio.h>

/*
   Program to show how to stop the
   user from typing too many characters in
   a field.
*/

int main()
{
    char str[ 50 ]; /* This is larger than you really need */

    /*
      Now, accept only TEN characters from the user. You can test
      this by typing more than ten characters here and seeing
      what is printed.
    */

    scanf( " %10s" , str );

    /*
      Print the string, verifying that it is, at most, ten characters.
    */

    printf( "The output is : %s.\n" , str );
    return( 0 );
}
```

And here's a sample run of the program. With the input

```
supercalifragilisticexpialidocious
```

the output is

```
supercalif.
```

Cross Reference:

None.

XVII.10: How do you zero-pad a number?

Answer:

To zero-pad a number, insert a number, preceded by a zero, after the % in the format specifier. This matter is best explained by direct example:

```
/* Print a five-character integer, padded with zeros. */

printf( "%05d" , i );

/* Print a floating point, padded left of the zero out to
   seven characters. */

printf( "%07f" , f );
```

If you fail to include the zero prefix on the number, it will be padded with spaces and not zeros.

Here is a sample program demonstrating this technique:

```
#include <stdio.h>

int main()
{
   int i = 123;
   printf( "%d\n" , i );
   printf( "%05d\n" , i );
   printf( "%07d\n" , i );
   return( 0 );
}
```

And here is its output:

```
123
00123
0000123
```

Cross Reference:

None.

XVII.11: How do you print a dollars-and-cents value?

Answer:

The C language does not have any built-in facility for printing dollars-and-cents values. However, this omission does not present the programmer who is trying to print monetary values with an insurmountable problem. It is quite easy to create a function that prints monetary values for you. After you create such a function, you can use it in any program you want.

Such a function is short and easy to write, and it will be presented here with a short explanation of how it works. The routine is broken into small, easy-to-write segments, making it easier to understand. The reason for breaking a program into smaller segments is discussed in Chapter XI, "Debugging."

These routines need to use some of the standard C routines. Therefore, you need to include some header files. Make sure that any program that uses this routine includes these header files at the start:

```
#include <stdio.h>
#include <stdlib.h>
#include <math.h>
#include <string.h>
```

With the proper header files included, you can create a function that will accept a dollar value and print it with commas:

```
void PrintDollars( double Dollars )
{
    char buf[ 20 ];
    int l , a;
    sprintf( buf , "%01f" , Dollars );

    l = strchr( buf , '.' ) - buf;
    for( a = ( Dollars < 0.0 ) ; a < l ; ++ a )
    {
        printf( "%c" , buf[ a ] );
        if ( ( ( ( l - a ) % 3 ) == 1 ) && ( a != l - 1 ) )
            printf( "," );
    }
}
```

Perhaps you're used to seeing real numbers represented as floats. This is commonplace. Floats, however, are generally not suited for monetary work, because they suffer from a large degree of inaccuracy, such as rounding errors. Doubles are far more accurate than floats and therefore are much better suited for true numerical work.

You can easily test this routine yourself by writing a program that passes it integer numbers. This routine will not, however, print decimals or "change." To perform this task, you need to write another function specifically dedicated to this purpose:

```
void PrintCents( double Cents )
{
    char buf[ 10 ];
    sprintf( buf , "%-.02f" , Cents );
    printf( "%s\n" , buf + 1 + ( Cents <= 0 ) );
}
```

This routine takes a decimal value and prints it correctly. Again, you can test this routine by writing a small program that passes it values.

Now you have two routines: one that prints the dollars part of a monetary value, and one that prints the cents. You certainly don't want to have to separate each number into two parts and call each function separately!

Instead, you can make one function that accepts a monetary value, divides it into its dollars and cents components, and calls the two routines you already have. Here is that function:

```
void DollarsAndCents( double Amount )
{
   double Dollars = Amount >= 0.0 ? floor( Amount ) : ceil( Amount
);
   double Cents = Amount - (double) Dollars;

   if ( Dollars < 0.0 ) printf( "-" );
   printf( "$" );
   PrintDollars( Dollars );
   PrintCents( Cents );
}
```

There you have it! The DollarsAndCents routine accepts a real number (a double) and prints it to the screen in dollars-and-cents format. You probably want to test the routine. To do this, you can make a main function that attempts to print many dollars-and-cents values. Here is such a routine:

```
int main()
{
  double num = .0123456789;
  int a;
  for( a = 0 ; a < 12 ; ++ a )
  {
      DollarsAndCents( num );
      num *= 10.0;
  }
  return( 0 );
}
```

The output of the preceding program should look like this:

```
$0.01
$0.12
$1.23
$12.35
$123.46
$1,234.57
$12,345.68
$123,456.79
$1,234,567.89
$12,345,678.90
$123,456,789.00
$1,234,567,890.00
```

If you want to print monetary values differently, it is quite easy to modify this program to print numbers in a different format.

Cross Reference:

None.

XVII.12: How do I print a number in scientific notation?

Answer:

To print a number in scientific notation, you must use the %e format specifier with the printf function, like so:

```
float f = 123456.78;
printf( " %e is in scientific\n" , f );
```

Of course, if you are to do this with integers, you must convert them to floating point first:

```
int i = 10000;
printf( " %e a scientific integer.\n" , (float) i );
```

Here is an example program demonstrating the %e format specifier:

```
#include <stdio.h>

main()
{
    double f = 1.0 / 1000000.0;
    int i;

    for( i = 0 ; i < 14 ; ++ i )
    {
        printf( "%f = %e\n" , f , f );
        f *= 10.0;
    }
    return( 0 );
}
```

Cross Reference:

None.

XVII.13: What is the ANSI driver?

Answer:

Each computer has its own way of handling the screen. This is a necessary evil; if we became locked into a certain standard, the industry would stagnate. However, this difference causes great problems when you are attempting to write programs for different computers, as well as programs that must communicate over the phone line. To help alleviate this problem, the ANSI standard was introduced.

The ANSI standard attempts to lay a basic outline of how programs can cause the video terminal to perform certain standard tasks, such as printing text in different colors, moving the cursor, and clearing the screen. It does this by defining special character sequences that, when sent to the screen, affect it in specified ways.

Now, when you print these character sequences to the screen normally on some computers, you see the characters themselves, not the effect they were intended to produce. To fix this problem, you need to load a program that will observe every character being printed to the screen, remove any special characters from the screen (so that they do not get printed), and carry out the desired action.

On MS-DOS machines, this program is called ANSI.SYS, and it must be loaded when the machine is booted up. This can be done by adding the line

```
DRIVER=ANSI.SYS
```

to your CONFIG.SYS file. The actual ANSI.SYS driver might be somewhere else in your directory tree; if so, it must be specified explicitly (with the full path). Here's an example:

```
driver=c:\sys\dos\ansi.sys
```

Cross Reference:

None.

XVII.14: How do you clear the screen with the ANSI driver?
Answer:

This action can be accomplished with <esc>[2J. Here is a program that demonstrates this point:

```
#include <stdio.h>

main()
{
   printf( "%c[2JNice to have an empty screen.\n" , 27 );
    return( 0 );
}
```

Cross Reference:

None.

XVII.15: How do you save the cursor's position with the ANSI driver?
Answer:

This maneuver can be accomplished with <esc>[s. Here is a program that demonstrates this action:

```
#include <stdio.h>

main()
{
   printf( "Cursor position is %c[s \n" , 27 );
   printf( "Interrupted!\n" );
```

```
    printf( "%c[uSAVED!!\n" , 27 );
    return( 0 );
}
```

Cross Reference:

None.

XVII.16: How do you restore the cursor's position with the ANSI driver?

Answer:

This action can be accomplished with <esc>[u. Refer to the preceding FAQ for an example.

Cross Reference:

None.

XVII.17: How do you change the screen color with the ANSI driver?

Answer:

The way to carry out this task is to change the current text background color, then clear the screen. The following program serves as an example:

```
#include <stdio.h>

int main()
{
    printf( "%c[43;32m%c[2JOhh, pretty colors!\n" , 27 , 27 );
    return( 0 );
}
```

Cross Reference:

None.

XVII.18: How do you write text in color with the ANSI driver?

Answer:

The color of text is one of the text's attributes you can change. You can change the attributes of text with <esc>[<attr>m. In the case of ANSI sequences, these attributes are represented by numerical values. You can set multiple attributes with one command by separating them with semicolons, like this: <esc>[<*attr*>;<*attr*>m. The following program demonstrates this action:

```
#include <stdio.h>

main()
{
    printf( "%c[32;44mPsychedelic, man.\n" , 27 );
    return( 0 );
}
```

Here is a list of attributes supported by the ANSI driver. Your particular monitor might not support some of the options.

```
1. High Intensity.
2. Low Intensity.
3. Italic.
4. Underline.
5. Blinking.
6. Fast Blinking.
7. Reverse.
8. Invisible.
```

Foreground colors:

```
30. Black.
31. Red.
32. Green.
33. Yellow.
34. Blue.
35. Magenta.
36. Cyan.
37. White.
```

Background colors:

```
40. Black.
41. Red.
42. Green.
43. Yellow.
44. Blue.
45. Magenta.
46. Cyan.
47. White.
```

Cross Reference:

None.

XVII.19: How do I move the cursor with the ANSI driver?

Answer:

There are two ways to move the cursor, relative motion and absolute motion. Relative motion is measured from the place where the cursor currently is; for example, "Move the cursor up two spaces." Absolute placement is measured from the upper-left corner of the screen; for example, "Move the cursor to the 10th row, column 5."

Relative motion is carried out in the following fashion:

> `<esc>[#a` in which # is the number of spaces to move up.
> `<esc>[#b` in which # is the number of spaces to move down.
> `<esc>[#c` in which # is the number of spaces to move right.
> `<esc>[#d` in which # is the number of spaces to move left.

To move the cursor to an absolute location, you do this:

> `<esc>[<row>;<col>H` in which *row* and *col* are the row and column at which you want the cursor to be positioned.

Cross Reference:

None.

CHAPTER

Writing and Compiling Your Programs

This chapter presents techniques to use when writing and compiling programs. You will learn several techniques used by professional C programmers in their everyday programs. In this chapter, you will learn that separating your source code into several files can be helpful in small and large projects alike, especially when you are creating function libraries. You will learn which memory models are available and which you will need to use for the different projects you work on. If you have several source files that make up your application, you will benefit from learning about a utility called MAKE that can help manage your project. You will learn what the difference between a .COM file and an .EXE file is, and a possible advantage to using .COM files.

Additionally, you will learn techniques to use to overcome a typical DOS problem: not enough memory to run your program. Usage of expanded memory, extended memory, disk swapping, overlay managers, and DOS extenders is discussed in an attempt to provide you with several options to remedy the "RAM cram" problem—choose the method that's best for you.

XVIII.1: Should my program be written in one source file or several source files?

Answer:

If your program is extremely small and focused, it is perfectly OK to contain all the source code within one .c file. If, however, you find yourself creating a lot of functions (especially general-purpose functions), you will want to split your program into separate source files (also known as modules).

The process of splitting your source code into several source files is known as *modular programming*. Modular programming techniques advocate the use of several different focused modules working together to make up a complete program. For instance, if your program has several utility functions, screen functions, and database functions, you might want to separate the functions into three source files that make up the utility module, screen module, and database module.

By putting your functions in separate files, you can easily reuse your general-purpose functions in other programs. If you have several functions that can be used by other programmers, you might want to create a function library that can be shared with others (see FAQ XVIII.9).

You can never have "too many" modules—you can create as many for your program as you see fit. A good rule of thumb is to keep your modules focused. Include only functions that are logically related to the same subject in the same source file. If you find yourself writing several nonrelated functions and putting them in the same file, you might want to pause to look at your program's source code structure and try to create a logical breakdown of modules. For example, if you are creating a contact management database, you might want to have a structure like this:

Module Name	Contains
Main.c	The main() function
Screen.c	Screen management functions
Menus.c	Menu management functions
Database.c	Database management functions
Utility.c	General-purpose utility functions
Contact.c	Functions for handling contacts
Import.c	Record import functions
Export.c	Record export functions
Help.c	On-line help support functions

Cross Reference:

XVIII.10: My program has several files in it. How do I keep them all straight?

XVIII.2: What are the differences between the memory models?

Answer:

DOS uses a segmented architecture to address your computer's memory. For each physical memory location, it has an associated address that can be accessed using a segment-offset method. To support this segmented architecture, most C compilers enable you to create your programs using any of the six memory models listed in the following table:

Memory Model	Limits	Pointer Usage
Tiny	Code, data, and stack—64KB	Near
Small	Code—64KB	Near
	Data and stack—64KB	Near
Medium	Code—1 megabyte	Far
	Data and stack—64KB	Near
Compact	Code—64KB	Near
	Data and stack—1 megabyte	Far
Large	Code—1 megabyte	Far
	Data and stack—1 megabyte	Far
Huge*	Code—1 megabyte	Far
	Data and stack—1 megabyte	Far

* Note that in the Huge memory model, static data (such as an array) can be larger than 64KB. This is not true in all the rest of the memory models.

The Tiny memory model is extremely limited (all code, data, and stack must fit in 64KB); it is most often used for the creation of .COM files. The Huge memory model imposes a significant performance penalty because of the way it has to "fix up" memory addresses; it is rarely used.

Cross Reference:

XVIII.3: What are the most commonly used memory models?

XVIII.4: Which memory model should be used?

XVIII.3: What are the most commonly used memory models?

Answer:

The most common are the Small, Medium, and Large memory models. The Tiny memory model is typically used only for creation of .COM files, which is somewhat rare in today's world of high-powered machines. The Compact memory model allows your program to have very little code and a lot of data. This, too, is uncommon in today's business place, because very often you will find significant amounts of code where there are significant amounts of data. The Huge memory model is somewhat inefficient because of the memory addressing scheme it imposes, and it is also a rarity.

Typically, you should use the Small, Medium, or Large memory models, depending on the size of your program. For a small utility program, the Small memory model might be suitable. This memory model enables you to have 64KB of code and 64KB for your data and stack. If your program has slightly larger data requirements than this, you might want to use the Medium memory model, which enables you to have up to 1 megabyte of addressable data space. For larger programs, you will want to use the Large memory model, which enables you to have 1 megabyte of code and 1 megabyte of data and stack space.

If you are writing a Windows program or using a 32-bit compiler, you will use the Small memory model. This is because such environments are not restricted to the segmented architecture of DOS programs.

Cross Reference:

XVIII.2: What are the differences between the memory models?

XVIII.4: Which memory model should be used?

XVIII.4: Which memory model should be used?
Answer:

If you are going to create a .COM file, the Tiny memory model must be used. All code, data, and stack space must fit in 64KB. This memory model is popular among small utility programs. The Small memory model is also used for relatively small programs, except that you are not limited to a total of 64KB for your entire program. In the Small memory model, you can have 64KB for your code space and 64KB for data and stack usage. Besides being used for small programs, the Small memory model is also used in environments such as Windows and for 32-bit compilers because memory addressing is not limited to DOS's 16-bit constraints.

If your program has a relatively large amount of code but relatively small amounts of static data, you can choose to write your program with the Medium memory model. If your program is extremely large (requiring many modules, code, and data), you might want to use the Large memory model. This memory model is most often used for writing business applications in DOS.

Use of the Compact and Huge memory models is much less common than use of the Small, Medium, and Large memory models. The Compact memory model enables you to have a large amount of static data but a relatively small (64KB or less) amount of code. Programs that fit this model are rare and are typically restricted to conversion programs that have large amounts of static translation tables that must be stored in memory. The Huge memory model is identical to the large memory model, except that the Huge memory model allows static data to be larger than 64KB. Like the Compact memory model, the Huge memory model is rare, primarily because its usage imposes a significant performance hit. Because of its relatively inefficient performance, you should avoid using the Huge memory model unless you absolutely must have an array or some other static data that is larger than 64KB. Keep in mind that arrays and other programming constructs can be allocated dynamically at runtime by using functions such as `malloc()` and `calloc()`, and they do not necessarily have to be static in nature.

Cross Reference:

XVIII.2: What are the differences between the memory models?

XVIII.3: What are the most commonly used memory models?

XVIII.5: How do you create a .COM file?
Answer:

Creating a .COM file is accomplished by compiling your program with the Tiny memory model and using special linker commands to make the output extension .COM rather than the normal .EXE extension. Keep in mind that for your program to qualify for a .COM file, all code, data, and stack must be able to fit in 64KB. This memory model is typically restricted to only the smallest of programs, usually programs such as TSRs and small utility programs.

Each compiler has a different method of creating .COM files. You should refer to your compiler's documentation for information regarding which compiler or linker switches you need to use to create a .COM file rather than an .EXE file.

Cross Reference:

XVIII.6: What is the benefit of a .COM file over an .EXE file?

XVIII.6: What is the benefit of a .COM file over an .EXE file?
Answer:

A .COM file is limited to 64KB for all code, data, and stack storage and therefore is limited to small applications such as utility programs and TSRs (terminate-and-stay-resident programs). One distinct advantage of a .COM file over an .EXE file is that .COM files load faster than .EXE files.

A .COM file is also known as a "memory image" file because it is loaded directly into memory with no required "fixups." An .EXE file contains special fix-up instructions inserted by the linker into the file's header. These instructions include a relocation table used to manage the different parts of the executable program. A .COM file does not contain any of these instructions or a relocation table, because the entire program can fit into 64KB. Thus, DOS does not need to parse through any fix-up code, and the .COM file loads faster than an .EXE file.

.COM files are usually simplistic and are somewhat limited in what they can accomplish. For instance, you cannot allocate memory from the far heap from a .COM file.

Cross Reference:

XVIII.5: How do you create a .COM file?

XVIII.7: Are all the functions in a library added to an .EXE file when the library is linked to the objects?

Answer:

No. When the linker is invoked, it will look for "unresolved externals." This means that it will poll your library files for functions that were not defined in your source code files. After it finds an unresolved external function, it pulls in the object code (.obj) which contains that function's definition. Unfortunately, if this function was compiled with a source file that contained other function definitions, those functions are included also. You therefore might have unwanted and unneeded code unnecessarily pulled into your executable information. This is why it is important to keep your library functions contained within their own source file—otherwise, you might be wasting precious program space. Some compilers contain special "smart" linkers that can detect unneeded functions such as these and discard them so that they don't make their way into your program.

Here is an example: Suppose that you have two source files, libfunc1.c and libfunc2.c. Each contains functions you want to put in a library.

The source file libfunc1.c contains the following two functions:

```
void func_one()
{
    ...
}

void func_two()
{
    ...
}
```

The source file libfunc2.c contains the following function:

```
void func_three()
{
    ...
}
```

Now suppose that you have compiled these two source code files into a library named myfuncs.lib. Suppose that a program linked with myfuncs.lib contains a call to func_one(). The linker will search the myfuncs library to pull in the object code that contains the definition of the func_one() function. Unfortunately, the func_one() function was compiled with the same source file that contains the definition for the func_two() function, and the linker will be forced to pull in the func_two() function even though your program doesn't use it. Of course, this assumes that func_one() does not contain a call to func_two(). If a program were to contain a call to func_three(), only the object code for func_three() would be pulled in because it was compiled in its own source file.

Generally, you should keep library functions contained within their own source files. This organization helps your programs to be more efficient because they will be linked only with the functions they really need, and not other functions they don't need. This also helps in a team development situation in which source code files are continually checked in and checked out. If a programmer is going to perform maintenance on a function that is contained within its own source file, they can focus on that one function. If the source file were to contain several other function definitions that needed maintenance, other programmers would not be able to check out the other functions because they are contained in one source file.

Cross Reference:

XVIII.8: Can multiple library functions be included in the same source file?

XVIII.9: Why should I create a library?

XVIII.8: Can multiple library functions be included in the same source file?

Answer:

You can define as many functions as you want in the same source file and still include them in a library—however, this technique has serious disadvantages when it comes to linking your programs and sharing source files in a team development environment.

When you include more than one library function in the same source file, the functions are compiled into the same object (.obj) file. When the linker links one of these functions into your program, all the functions in the object file are pulled in—whether or not they are used in your program. If these functions are unrelated (do not have calls to each other within their definitions), you will be wasting precious program space by pulling unneeded code. See FAQ XVIII.7 for an example. This is one reason why it is better to put library functions in their own separate source files.

Another good reason to put library functions in their own source files is for code sharing in a team development environment. Using separate source files enables programmers to check out and check in individual functions, instead of locking others out of being able to make changes to several functions contained in one source file.

Cross Reference:

XVIII.7: Are all the functions in a library added to an .EXE file when the library is linked to the objects?

XVIII.9: Why should I create a library?

XVIII.9: Why should I create a library?

Answer:

Creating a function library enables you to put reusable functions in a place where they can be shared with other programmers and programs. For instance, you might have several general-purpose utility functions that are used in several of your programs. Instead of duplicating the source code for all of these different programs, you can put these functions in a centralized function library and then link them into your program when the linker is invoked. This method is better for program maintenance, because you can maintain your functions in one centralized place rather than several places.

If you are working in a team environment, putting your reusable functions in a library allows other programmers to link your functions into their programs, saving them from having to duplicate your effort and write similar functions from scratch. Additionally, in large projects that involve several modules, a function library can be used to contain "framework" support functions that are used throughout the application.

Your compiler includes a library manager (typically named LIB.EXE or something similar) that can be used to add and delete object code modules (.obj's) from function libraries. Some compilers enable you to maintain your libraries from within their integrated development environments without having to invoke a library manager manually. In any case, you should refer to the answers to FAQ XVIII.7 and XVIII.8 for important information regarding the creation of libraries and good techniques to adhere to.

Cross Reference:

XVIII.7: Are all the functions in a library added to an .EXE file when the library is linked to the objects?

XVIII.8: Can multiple library functions be included in the same source file?

XVIII.10: My program has several files in it. How do I keep them all straight?

Answer:

Your compiler includes a MAKE utility (typically called MAKE.EXE, NMAKE.EXE, or something similar) that is used to keep track of projects and the dependencies of source files that make up those projects. Here is an example of a typical MAKE file:

```
myapp.obj:     myapp.c              myapp.h
               cl -c myapp.c

utility.obj:   utility.c            myapp.h
               cl -c utility.c

myapp.exe:     myapp.obj            utility.obj
               cl myapp.obj         utility.obj
```

This example shows that myapp.obj is dependent on myapp.c and myapp.h. Similarly, utility.obj is dependent on utility.c and myapp.h, and myapp.exe is dependent on myapp.obj and utility.obj. Below each dependency line, the compiler command to recompile or relink the dependent object is included. For instance, myapp.obj is re-created by invoking the following command line:

```
cl -c myapp.c
```

In the preceding example, myapp.obj is recompiled only if myapp.c or myapp.h has a time stamp later than myapp.obj's time stamp. Similarly, utility.obj is recompiled only when utility.c or myapp.h has a time stamp later than utility.obj's time stamp. The myapp.exe program is relinked only when myapp.obj or utility.obj has a later time stamp than myapp.exe.

MAKE files are extremely handy for handling large projects with many source file dependencies. MAKE utilities and their associated commands and implementations vary from compiler to compiler—see your compiler's documentation for instructions on how to use your MAKE utility.

Most of today's compilers come with an integrated development environment, in which you can use project files to keep track of several source files in your application. Having an integrated development environment frees you from having to know the intricacies of a MAKE utility and enables you to easily manage the source files in your project. The integrated development environment automatically keeps track of all dependencies for you.

Cross Reference:

XVIII.1: Should my program be written in one source file or several source files?

XVIII.11: I get the message *DGROUP: group exceeds 64K* during my link. What's wrong?

Answer:

If you see this error message while linking your program, the linker is indicating that you have more than 64KB of near data (static data elements, global variables, and so on) in your data (DGROUP) segment. You can remedy this situation in a few ways:

◆ Eliminate some of your global variables.

◆ Decrease your program's stack size.

◆ Use dynamic memory allocation techniques to dynamically allocate data elements instead of defining them as static or global.

◆ Declare data elements specifically as far rather than near.

Eliminating some of your global variables will probably require some rework on your part as to the inherent design of your program, but it will be worth it when all is said and done. Global variables by nature tend to be somewhat of a maintenance nightmare and should be used only when absolutely necessary. If you have allocated a lot of space to be used as stack space, you might want to experiment with lowering the stack space size to see whether you can gain memory that way. If you are using a lot of static data in your program, try to think of a way you could possibly rework your static data and allocate it dynamically rather than statically. This technique will free up the near heap and enable you to allocate data from the far heap instead (see FAQ XVIII.15 for a discussion on near and far heap space).

Cross Reference:

XVIII.12: How can I keep my program from running out of memory?

XVIII.12: How can I keep my program from running out of memory?

Answer:

If you are using a lot of static data, you might want to think about using dynamic memory allocation instead. By using dynamic memory allocation (with the `malloc()` and `calloc()` functions), you can dynamically allocate memory when you need it and release it (via the `free()` function) when it is no longer needed. This helps in a couple of ways. First, dynamic memory allocation allows your program to be more efficient because your program uses memory only when necessary and uses only the memory it really needs. You don't have a lot of unused memory unnecessarily being taken up by static and global variables. Second, you can check the return value of the `malloc()` and `calloc()` functions to trap for situations in which you might not have enough memory.

If your program is extremely large, you might want to use an overlay manager or a DOS extender, or you might want to use alternative memory allocation schemes such as EMS or XMS (see FAQs XVIII.13 and XVIII.14 for further discussion on these topics).

Cross Reference:

XVIII.11: I get the message `DGROUP: group exceeds 64KB` during my link. What's wrong?

XVIII.13: My program is too big to run under DOS. How can I make it fit?

XVIII.14: How can I get more than 640KB of memory available to my DOS program?

XVIII.15: What is the difference between near and far?

XVIII.13: My program is too big to run under DOS. How can I make it fit?

Answer:

When your application has grown too large for DOS (over 640KB), there are two good ways to give your program more memory. One way is to use an *overlay manager.* An overlay manager will manage the modules (.obj files) of your program and read them in from disk and discard them as needed. This way, your program can be several megabytes in size and still fit in a computer that has only 640KB of memory available. Some advanced overlay managers enable you to determine module "groups" that you would like to be read in and discarded all together. This helps you fine-tune your application for performance reasons. Other less advanced overlay managers do not have this feature and do not enable you to fine-tune which overlaid modules should be treated as a group.

Another way to get more memory for your application is to use a *DOS extender*. A DOS extender is a special application that uses the protected mode features of 386, 486, and newer computers to access several megabytes of memory in one flat address space. When your program is linked with a DOS extender, the DOS extender code becomes a part of your program's start-up code. When your program is invoked, the DOS extender is loaded and your program falls under the control of the DOS extender. All memory allocation calls are routed through the DOS extender, thereby enabling you to bypass DOS and let the extender handle the intricacies of allocating memory above the 640KB threshold.

Unfortunately, DOS extenders have some definite disadvantages. One disadvantage is that most DOS extenders have runtime royalty fees that apply when you distribute your programs. This can be quite costly, especially if you have many users. A few compilers come with royalty-free DOS extenders, but this feature is typically the exception rather than the norm. Another disadvantage of using a DOS extender is that its operation typically requires you to change your source code to access the extender's application program interface (API) instead of using DOS calls.

Overlay managers do not typically require runtime fees, so they are more cost efficient and less expensive than DOS extenders. Additionally, you rarely need to change your source code to use an overlay manager. Most of the time, the use of an overlay manager is transparent to the program.

Cross Reference:

XVIII.11: I get the message `DGROUP: group exceeds 64KB` during my link. What's wrong?

XVIII.12: How can I keep my program from running out of memory?

XVIII.14: How can I get more than 640KB of memory available to my DOS program?

XVIII.15: What is the difference between near and far?

XVIII.14: How can I get more than 640KB of memory available to my DOS program?
Answer:

When you find yourself in a memory-crunch situation, needing to use more than 640KB of memory in a DOS program, you can use a few good methods of getting more memory available. One way is to use *disk swapping*. Disk swapping means that you write data elements that are stored in memory to disk when you do not need them. After writing a data element (variable, array, structure, and so forth) to disk, you can free up the memory that was used by that data element (by using the `free()` function) and thus have more memory available to your program. When you need to use the data element that was swapped to disk, you can swap out another data element from memory to disk and read the previously swapped variable back in from disk. Unfortunately, this method requires a lot of coding and can be quite tedious to implement.

Another good way to get more than 640KB of memory available to your DOS program is to use an alternative memory source—EMS (expanded memory) or XMS (extended memory). EMS and XMS, which refer to two ways of allocating memory above the 640KB region, are explained in separate paragraphs in the following text.

EMS stands for Expanded Memory Specification. This is a method developed by Lotus, Intel, and Microsoft for accessing memory above the 1 megabyte region on IBM-compatible machines. Currently, two versions of this specification are used: LIM 3.2 and LIM 4.0. The newer version, LIM 4.0, overcomes some of the limitations of LIM 3.2. Expanded memory is enabled by the installation of an expanded memory manager (such as EMM386.EXE included with DOS). Your program makes calls to the expanded memory manager to request blocks of expanded memory. The expanded memory manager uses a technique called bank switching to move memory temporarily from above the 1 megabyte region to an empty region in the upper memory area between 640KB and 1 megabyte. Bank switching involves taking a memory allocation request from the application program and allocating 16KB of upper memory area at a time to keep track of memory that is addressed above the 1 megabyte region.

Extended memory is enabled by the installation of an extended memory manager (such as HIMEM.SYS included with DOS). Your program makes calls to the extended memory manager to request extended memory blocks (EMBs). No "bank switching" technique is used for requesting extended memory. Your program simply makes a function call to the extended memory manager to request a block of memory above the 1 megabyte region. Unfortunately, code cannot be executed above the 1 megabyte region under DOS; therefore, you cannot execute code stored in extended memory. Similarly, you cannot directly address data stored in extended memory, so many programmers like to set up a "buffer area" in conventional memory (below 640KB) to provide a swap area between conventional and extended memory.

The techniques used for expanded memory are older and somewhat outdated. Expanded memory was popular when DOS-based machines first came out that had add-on expanded memory boards attached. Using expanded memory techniques is somewhat slower than using extended memory techniques. In fact, many of today's PC configurations eliminate expanded memory altogether by including the NOEMS flag in the EMM386.EXE entry of the config.sys file. Most modern programs have abandoned the older expanded memory techniques for the newer extended memory techniques.

If your program needs to address above the 1 megabyte region, you should use extended memory rather than expanded memory. When you use extended memory, your programs will have greater stability and perform faster than if you had chosen to use expanded memory.

The specific steps of implementing extended and expanded memory are beyond the scope of this book. Explaining how to address memory with these techniques would probably require a separate chapter. Instead, you can obtain the EMS (Expanded Memory Specification) and XMS (Extended Memory Specification) documents directly from Microsoft or download them from a network service such as CompuServe. These documents detail the EMS and XMS application programming interface (API) and show you in detail how to use each technique.

Cross Reference:

XVIII.11: I get the message DGROUP: group exceeds 64KB during my link. What's wrong?

XVIII.12: How can I keep my program from running out of memory?

XVIII.13: My program is too big to run under DOS. How can I make it fit?

XVIII.15: What is the difference between near and far?

XVIII.15: What is the difference between near and far?

Answer:

DOS uses a segmented architecture to address your computer's memory. For each physical memory location, it has an associated address that can be accessed using a segment-offset method. For instance, here is a typical segmented address:

`A000:1234`

The portion on the left side of the colon represents the segment (A000), and the portion on the right side of the colon represents the offset from that segment. Every program under DOS accesses memory in this manner—although the intricacies of addressing with the segment-offset method are often hidden from the casual C programmer.

When your program is executed, it is assigned a default data segment that is put in the data segment (DS) register. This default data segment points to a 64KB area of memory commonly referred to as near data. Within this near data area of memory, you will find your program's stack, static data, and the near heap. The near heap is used for allocating global variables and other data elements you need at program start-up. Any data allocated from this area is called near data. For instance, consider the following program, which allocates 32KB of near data from the near heap at program start-up:

```
/* Note: Program uses the Medium memory model... */

#include <stdio.h>
#include <alloc.h>
#include <string.h>
#include <stdlib.h>
#include <dos.h>

void main(void);

void main(void)
{

    char* near_data;

    near_data = (char*) malloc((32 * 1024) * sizeof(char));

    if (near_data == (char*) NULL)
    {
        printf("Whoopsie! Malloc failed!\n");
        exit(1);
    }

    strcpy(near_data,
           "This string is going to be stored in the near heap");

    printf("Address of near_data: %p\n", &near_data);

    free(near_data);

}
```

In the preceding example, near_data is a character pointer that is assigned a 32KB block of memory. By default, the 32KB block of memory is allocated from the near heap, and the resulting 16-bit address is stored in the character pointer near_data.

Now that you are aware of what near data is, you are probably wondering what far data is. Quite simply, it is any data that resides outside of the default data segment (the first 64KB of data memory). Here is an example program that allocates 32KB from the far data area (or far heap, as it is commonly called):

```
/* Note: Program uses the Medium memory model... */

#include <stdio.h>
#include <alloc.h>
#include <string.h>
#include <stdlib.h>
#include <dos.h>

void main(void);

void main(void)
{
    char far* far_data;

    far_data = (char far*) farmalloc((32 * 1024) * sizeof(char));

    if (far_data == (char far*) NULL)
    {
        printf("Whoopsie! Far malloc failed!\n");
        exit(1);
    }

    _fstrcpy(far_data,
            "This string is going to be stored in the far heap");

    printf("Address of far_data: %Fp\n", &far_data);

    farfree(far_data);

}
```

In this example, the far character pointer is assigned a 32-bit address reflecting a 32KB area of free memory in the far heap. Notice that to explicitly allocate from the far heap, a far pointer must be used, and hence the far modifier is added to the character pointer definition. Also note that some of the functions (farcoreleft(), farmalloc(), farfree()) are different for allocating from the far heap as opposed to the near heap.

The far heap usually contains much more free memory than the near heap, because the near heap is limited to 64KB. If you compile and run the previous examples on your computer, you will find that the first example (which allocates from the near heap) has approximately 63KB of memory available. The second example (which allocates from the far heap) has approximately 400KB to 600KB (depending on your computer's configuration) of memory available. Thus, if your program requires a lot of memory for data storage, you should use the far heap rather than the near heap.

Whatever memory model you use (with the exception of the Tiny memory model), you can use the near and far modifiers and their corresponding near and far functions to explicitly allocate memory from the near and far heap. Using near and far data wisely will help your programs run more efficiently and have less risk of running out of memory.

Note that the concept of near and far data is unique to personal computers running DOS because of the segmented architecture scheme used by DOS. Other operating systems such as UNIX or Windows NT use flat memory models, which impose no near or far limitations.

Cross Reference:

XVIII.11: I get the message DGROUP: group exceeds 64KB during my link. What's wrong?

XVIII.12: How can I keep my program from running out of memory?

XVIII.13: My program is too big to run under DOS. How can I make it fit?

XVIII.14: How can I get more than 640KB of memory available to my DOS program?

CHAPTER

Programming Style and Standards

This chapter focuses primarily on the layout of your code. Usage of comments, white space, variable and function naming standards, and bracing techniques are covered. In this chapter, you will learn that the use of comments and white space do not affect your program's speed, size, or efficiency. You will also learn three standards of putting braces in your code. When it comes to naming your variables and functions, you will learn two notation styles ("camel" and "Hungarian") and will learn that putting underscores in your variable and function names makes them more readable. You will also learn how to name your functions and how long your function and variable names should be.

In addition to naming conventions and standards, several general programming topics are covered, such as recursion (what it is and how to use it); null loops; infinite loops; iterative processing via the `while`, `do...while`, and `for` loops; the difference between the `continue` and `break` statements; and the best way to represent true and false in your programs.

This chapter has many topics to cover, so hold on tight—and be sure to pay attention to the naming styles and conventions. They could help make your programs much more readable and understandable.

XIX.1: Should the underscore be used in variable names?

Answer:

Using the underscore in variable names is a matter of style. There is nothing wrong with using underscores or avoiding them altogether. The important thing to remember is to be consistent—use the same naming conventions throughout your application. This means that if you are programming in a team environment, you and your team members should decide on a naming convention and stick with it. If not everyone uses the same convention, your program integration will be horrible and hard to read. Additionally, you should adhere to the style used by the third-party libraries (if any) that are used in your program. If at all possible, use the same naming convention as the third-party library. Doing so will make your programs more readable and consistent.

Many C programmers find the underscore method of variable naming to be convenient. Perhaps this is because the underscore method tends to be very readable. For instance, the following two function names are similar, but one could argue that the underscored function name is more readable:

```
check_disk_space_available(selected_disk_drive);
```

```
CheckDiskSpaceAvailable(SelectedDiskDrive);
```

The second notation used here is called camel notation—see FAQ XIX.5 for an explanation of camel notation.

Cross Reference:

XIX.2: Can a variable's name be used to indicate its data type?

XIX.5: What is camel notation?

XIX.6: Do longer variable names affect the speed, executable size, or efficiency of a program?

XIX.9: How many letters long should variable names be? What is the ANSI standard for significance?

XIX.10: What is Hungarian notation, and should I use it?

XIX.2: Can a variable's name be used to indicate its data type?

Answer:

Yes, indicating the data type in a variable's name has become a very popular convention in today's world of large, complex systems. Usually, the variable's type is represented by one or two characters, and the variable name is prefixed with these characters. A well-known naming convention that uses this technique is called *Hungarian* notation, named after Microsoft programmer Charles Simonyi. Table XIX.2 contains some common prefixes.

Table XIX.2. Some common Hungarian notation prefixes.

Data Type	Prefix	Example
char	c	cInChar
int	i	iReturnValue
long	l	lNumRecs
string	sz	szInputString (terminated by zero byte)
int array	ai	aiErrorNumbers
char*	psz	pszInputString

Environments such as Microsoft Windows make heavy use of Hungarian notation or some derivative. Other fourth-generation environments, such as Visual Basic and Access, have also adopted a variation of the Hungarian notation.

You don't have to stick exactly to a particular notation when writing your programs—it is perfectly OK to create your own customized derivative. This is especially true when you are creating notations for your own typedefs. For instance, if you have a typedef named SOURCEFILE that keeps information such as the source filename, handle, number of lines, last compile date and time, number of errors, and so on, you might want to create a prefix notation such as "sf" (source file). This way, when you see a variable named sfBuffer, you know that it refers to a variable that holds the contents of your SOURCEFILE structure.

Whatever the case may be, it is a good idea to adopt some form of naming convention for your variables and functions. This is especially true when you are working on large projects with many different programmers or when you are working in environments such as Microsoft Windows. Adopting a well-thought-out naming convention might help you make your programs more readable, especially if your code is extremely complex.

Cross Reference:

XIX.1: Should the underscore be used in variable names?

XIX.5: What is camel notation?

XIX.6: Do longer variable names affect the speed, executable size, or efficiency of a program?

XIX.9: How many letters long should variable names be? What is the ANSI standard for significance?

XIX.10: What is Hungarian notation, and should I use it?

XIX.3: Does the use of comments affect program speed, executable size, or efficiency?

Answer:

No. When your program is compiled, all comments are ignored by the compiler, and only executable statements are parsed and eventually put into the final compiled version of the program.

Because comments have no bearing on your program's speed, size, or efficiency, you should use comments as often as possible. Each of your program modules should have a header that explains the purpose of the module and any special considerations. Similarly, each function you write should have information such as author name, date written, modification dates and reasons, parameter usage guidelines, description of the function, and so forth. This information will help other programmers understand your programs better, or it might help you remember some key ideas of implementation later.

You also should use comments in your source code (in-between programming statements). For instance, if you have a particular portion of code that is complex or if you feel that something needs a bit more clarity, do not hesitate to put a comment in the code. Doing so might take a little more time up front, but you or someone else might be able to save several hours of valuable time by glancing at the comment and immediately knowing what the programmer had in mind.

See FAQ XIX.4 for an example program that shows how using comments, white space, and the underscore naming convention can make your code much cleaner and much more understandable by others.

Cross Reference:

XIX.4: Does the use of white space affect program speed, executable size, or efficiency?

XIX.6: Do longer variable names affect the speed, executable size, or efficiency of a program?

XIX.4: Does the use of white space affect program speed, executable size, or efficiency?
Answer:

No. As with comments, all white space is ignored by the compiler. When your program is compiled, all white space and comments are ignored, and only the executable statements are parsed and eventually put into the final compiled version of the program.

The use of white space in your C programs can help make your programs more readable and improve clarity by separating out your executable statements, functions, comments, and so forth. Many times, you improve your program's readability by simply adding blank lines between statements. For instance, consider the following portion of code:

```
/* clcpy by GBlansten */

void clcpy(EMP* e, int rh, int ot)
{ e->grspy=(e->rt*rh)+(e->rt*ot*1.5);
e->txamt=e->grspy*e->txrt;
e->ntpy=e->grspy-e->txamt;
updacctdata(e);
if (e->dd==false) cutpyck(e);
else prtstb(e); }
```

As you can see, this function is quite a mess. Sure, it works, but no programmer in the world would like to maintain this type of code. Consider what the function would look like if you were to apply some of the naming conventions used in this chapter (such as using underscores and eliminating short cryptic names), use some bracing techniques (such as Allman's technique), and add some white space and comments:

```
/************************************************************************

Function Name: calc_pay
Parameters:     emp       - EMPLOYEE pointer that points to employee data
                reg_hours - The number of regular hours (<= 40) employee
                            has worked
                ot_hours  - The number of overtime hours (> 40) employee
                            has worked
Author:         Gern Blansten
Date Written:   13 dec 1993
Modifications:  04 sep 1994 by Lloyd E. Work
                - Rewrote function to make it readable by human beings.

Description:    This function calculates an employee's gross pay, tax
                amount, and net pay, and either prints a paycheck for the
                employee or (in the case of those who have direct deposit)
                prints a paycheck stub.

*************************************************************************/

void calc_pay(EMPLOYEE* emp, int reg_hours, int ot_hours)
{
    /* gross pay = (employee rate * regular hours) +
                   (employee rate * overtime hours * 1.5) */

    emp->gross_pay = (emp->rate * reg_hours) +
                     (emp->rate * ot_hours * 1.5);

    /* tax amount = gross pay * employee's tax rate */

    emp->tax_amount = emp->gross_pay * emp->tax_rate;

    /* net pay = gross pay - tax amount */

    emp->net_pay = emp->gross_pay - emp->tax_amount;

    /* update the accounting data */

    update_accounting_data(emp);

    /* check for direct deposit */

    if (emp->direct_deposit == false)

        cut_paycheck(emp);            /* print a paycheck */

    else

        print_paystub(emp);           /* print a paycheck stub */

}
```

As you can see, Lloyd's version (the one with liberal use of comments, white space, descriptive variable names, and so on) is much more readable than Gern's ill-fated version. Chances are that good 'ol Gern has been (or soon will be) replaced....

You should use white space (and comments, for that matter) as much as you see fit. Doing so will help your programs to be much more readable—and possibly lengthen your job expectancy.

Cross Reference:

XIX.3: Does the use of comments affect program speed, executable size, or efficiency?

XIX.6: Do longer variable names affect the speed, executable size, or efficiency of a program?

XIX.5: What is camel notation?
Answer:

Camel notation, as it has come to be known, involves using mixed upper- and lowercase letters to form variable and function names. For instance, here is the same function named using the camel notation method and the underscore method:

```
PrintEmployeePaychecks();
```

```
print_employee_paychecks();
```

The first version of this function uses the camel notation—each logical break in the function name is accentuated by the use of a capital letter. The second version of the function uses the underscore method— each logical break in the function name is accentuated by the use of an underscore.

Camel notation has gained in popularity over the years, and it is used quite a bit in many newer libraries and environments such as Microsoft Windows. The underscore method, on the other hand, has been around since C's first years and is very popular in older programs and environments such as UNIX.

Cross Reference:

XIX.1: Should the underscore be used in variable names?

XIX.2: Can a variable's name be used to indicate its data type?

XIX.6: Do longer variable names affect the speed, executable size, or efficiency of a program?

XIX.9: How many letters long should variable names be? What is the ANSI standard for significance?

XIX.10: What is Hungarian notation, and should I use it?

XIX.6: Do longer variable names affect the speed, executable size, or efficiency of a program?
Answer:

No. When you compile your program, each variable and function name is converted to a "symbol"—that is, a smaller, symbolic representation of the original function. So, whether you have a function named

```
PrintOutAllOfTheClientsMonthEndReports();
```

or

```
prt_rpts();
```

the results are the same. Generally, you should use descriptive function and variable names so that your programs will be more readable. Check your compiler's documentation to see how many characters of significance are allowed—most ANSI compilers allow at least 31 characters of significance. In other words, only the first 31 characters of a variable or function name are checked for their uniqueness—the rest of the characters are ignored.

A good rule of thumb is to make your function and variable names read just like the English language, as if you were reading a book. You should be able to read the function or variable name and easily recognize it and know generally what its function is.

Cross Reference:

XIX.1: Should the underscore be used in variable names?

XIX.2: Can a variable's name be used to indicate its data type?

XIX.3: Does the use of comments affect program speed, executable size, or efficiency?

XIX.4: Does the use of white space affect program speed, executable size, or efficiency?

XIX.5: What is camel notation?

XIX.9: How many letters long should variable names be? What is the ANSI standard for significance?

XIX.10: What is Hungarian notation, and should I use it?

XIX.7: What is the correct way to name a function?
Answer:

Functions should generally begin with a verb and end with a noun. This practice follows the general convention used by the English language. Here are some examples of properly named functions:

```
PrintReports();
SpawnUtilityProgram();
ExitSystem();
InitializeDisk();
```

Notice that in all of these examples, a verb is used to begin the function name, and a noun is used to complete the function name. If you were to read these in English, you might recognize these functions as

print the reports

spawn the utility program

exit the system

initialize the disk

Using the verb-noun convention (especially in English-language countries) makes your programs immediately more readable and familiar to the programmer who is reading your code.

Cross Reference:

XIX.5: What is camel notation?

XIX.8: What is the correct way to use braces?

XIX.10: What is Hungarian notation, and should I use it?

XIX.8: What is the correct way to use braces?
Answer:

In C, there is no right and wrong way to use braces—as long as you have a closing brace for every opening brace, you will not have brace problems in your programs. However, three prominent bracing styles are commonly used: Kernighan and Ritchie, Allman, and Whitesmiths. These three styles will be discussed next.

In the book *The C Programming Language,* Brian Kernighan and Dennis Ritchie introduced their style of implementing braces. The style looks like this:

```
if (argc < 3) {
    printf("Error! Not enough arguments. Correct usage is:\n");
    printf("C:>copyfile <source_file> <destination_file>\n");
    exit(1);
}
else {
    open_files();
    while (!feof(infile)) {
        read_data();
        write_data();
    }
    close_files();
}
```

Notice that with the K&R style, the opening brace is placed on the same line as the statement it is used with, and the closing brace is aligned below the statement it closes. For instance, in the preceding example, the `if` statement has its opening brace on the same line, and its closing brace is aligned below it. The same is true of the `if` statement's corresponding `else` condition and of the `while` statement that occurs later in the program.

Here is the same example, except this time the Allman brace style is used:

```
if (argc < 3)
{
    printf("Error! Not enough arguments. Correct usage is:\n");
    printf("C:>copyfile <source_file> <destination_file>\n");
    exit(1);
}
else
{
    open_files();
    while (!feof(infile))
```

```
    {
        read_data();
        write_data();
    }
    close_files();
}
```

Notice that with the Allman style, each brace is placed on its own line. Both the opening and the closing braces are aligned with the statement that is used.

Here is the same example with the Whitesmiths style of bracing:

```
if (argc < 3)
    {
    printf("Error! Not enough arguments. Correct usage is:\n");
    printf("C:>copyfile <source_file> <destination_file>\n");
    exit(1);
    }
else
    {
    open_files();
    while (!feof(infile))
        {
        read_data();
        write_data();
        }
    close_files();
    }
```

As with the Allman style, the Whitesmiths style calls for putting braces on their own lines. However, the braces are indented to be aligned with the statements the braces contain. For instance, in the preceding example, the opening brace of the if statement is aligned with the first printf() function call.

Whatever method you choose to use, *be consistent*—and you will help yourself and others read your programs more easily.

Cross Reference:

XIX.5: What is camel notation?

XIX.7: What is the correct way to name a function?

XIX.10: What is Hungarian notation, and should I use it?

XIX.9: How many letters long should variable names be? What is the ANSI standard for significance?

Answer:

Generally, your variable names should be long enough to effectively describe the variable or function you are naming. Short, cryptic names should be avoided, because they often cause problems when other programmers try to interpret your code. Instead of using a short, cryptic function name such as

```
opndatfls();
```

you should use a longer name such as

```
open_data_files();
```

or

```
OpenDataFiles();
```

The same is true of variable names. Instead of using a cryptic variable name such as

```
fmem
```

why not expand it to its full definition:

```
free_memory_available
```

Using expanded names will help make your code much easier to read and understand. Most ANSI compilers allow at least 31 characters of significance—that is, only the first 31 characters are checked for uniqueness.

A good rule of thumb is to make your function and variable names read just like the English language, as if you were reading a book. You should be able to read the function or variable name and easily recognize it and know generally what its function is.

Cross Reference:

XIX.1: Should the underscore be used in variable names?

XIX.2: Can a variable's name be used to indicate its data type?

XIX.5: What is camel notation?

XIX.6: Do longer variable names affect the speed, executable size, or efficiency of a program?

XIX.10: What is Hungarian notation, and should I use it?

XIX.10: What is Hungarian notation, and should I use it?
Answer:

Hungarian notation was originally created by Microsoft programmer Charles Simonyi (no doubt of Hungarian descent). With this notation, the names of your variables or functions are prefixed with one or two characters that represent the data type of the variable or function.

This kind of notation has many advantages. It is used extensively in environments such as Microsoft Windows. See FAQ XIX.2 for a full explanation of Hungarian notation and some example notation standards you might want to adopt.

Cross Reference:

XIX.1: Should the underscore be used in variable names?

XIX.2: Can a variable's name be used to indicate its data type?

XIX.5: What is camel notation?

XIX.6: Do longer variable names affect the speed, executable size, or efficiency of a program?

XIX.9: How many letters long should variable names be? What is the ANSI standard for significance?

XIX.11: What is iterative processing?

Answer:

Iterative processing involves executing the same programming statements repetitively, possibly breaking at a point when a condition occurs. The C language provides some built-in constructs for iterative processing, such as while loops, do...while loops, and for loops. With each of these, a predefined number of statements is executed repetitively while a certain condition remains true. Here is an example of iterative processing:

```
while (x < 100)
{

    y = 0;

    do {

        for(z=0; z<100; z++)
            y++;

    } while (y < 1000);

    x++;

}
```

In this example, the statements included in the while loop are executed 100 times. Within the while loop is a do...while loop. In the do...while loop is a for loop that is executed 10 times. Within the for loop, the variable y is incremented 100 times. Therefore, the statement

```
y++;
```

is executed 100,000 times (100 whiles × 10 do...whiles × 100 fors). y will not be 100,000 when the while loop is complete, however, because y is reset to 0 each 1000 iterations.

Iterative processing is used tremendously throughout C programs. Often, you will use iterative processing to read from and write to arrays and files. For example, here is a program that uses iterative processing to read in your AUTOEXEC.BAT file and print its contents on-screen:

```
#include <stdio.h>
#include <stdlib.h>

int main(void);

int main(void)
{
    FILE* autoexec_file;
    char  buffer[250];
```

```
if ((autoexec_file = fopen("C:\\AUTOEXEC.BAT", "rt")) == NULL)
{
    fprintf(stderr, "Cannot open AUTOEXEC.BAT file.\n");
    exit(1);
}

printf("Contents of AUTOEXEC.BAT file:\n\n");

while (!feof(autoexec_file))
{
    fgets(buffer, 200, autoexec_file);
    printf("%s", buffer);
}

fclose(autoexec_file);

return(0);

}
```

Notice that this example uses a while statement to repeatedly call the fgets() and printf() functions to read in lines from the AUTOEXEC.BAT file and print them to the screen. This is just one example of how iterative processing can be used.

Cross Reference:

XIX.12: What is recursion, and how do you use it?

XIX.12: What is recursion, and how do you use it?
Answer:

In C, a function that calls itself (either directly or indirectly) is said to be *recursive*. You might be wondering why on earth a function would want to call itself. Perhaps this situation is best explained by an example. One classic case of recursion coming in handy is when a number's *factorial* is being calculated. To calculate a number's factorial value, you multiply that number (x) by its predecessor (x−1) and keep going until you've reached 1. For instance, the factorial of 5 can be calculated as shown here:

```
5 * 4 * 3 * 2 * 1
```

If x were 5, you could transform this calculation into an equation:

```
x! = x * (x-1) * (x-2) * (x-3) * (x-4) * 1
```

To perform this calculation using C, you could write a function called calc_factorial() that would repeatedly call itself, each time decrementing the number being calculated, until you have reached 1. Here is an example of how you might write the calc_factorial() function:

```
#include <stdio.h>

void main(void);
```

```
unsigned long calc_factorial(unsigned long x);

void main(void)
{
    int x = 5;

    printf("The factorial of %d is %ld.\n", x, calc_factorial(x));

}

unsigned long calc_factorial(unsigned long x)
{
    if (!x)
        return 1L;

    return(x * calc_factorial(x-1L));

}
```

In the preceding example, the `calc_factorial()` calls itself after decrementing the value of x. If x is equal to 0, the `if` statement will evaluate to true, and `calc_factorial()` is not recursively called. Hence, when 0 is reached, the function exits for one last time, returning the value 1. It returns 1 because you can safely multiply any value by 1 and still retain its original value. If your program contained the statement

```
x = calc_factorial(5);
```

it would expand out to this:

```
x = 5 * (5-1) * (4-1) * (3-1) * (2-1) * 1;
```

Hence, x would evaluate to the factorial of 5, which is 120.

Recursion is a neat concept and can be a great source for experimentation, but it does not come without cost. Recursive functions tend to take longer than straightforward programming statements (that is, `while` loops), and they also consume valuable stack space. Each time a recursive function calls itself, its state needs to be saved on the stack so that the program can return to it when it is done calling itself. Invariably, recursive functions can be trouble if they are not carefully thought out.

If possible, you should avoid writing recursive functions. For instance, the previous factorial function could have been written this way:

```
#include <stdio.h>

void main(void);
unsigned long calc_factorial(unsigned long x);

void main(void)
{
    int x = 5;

    printf("The factorial of %d is %ld.\n", x, calc_factorial(x));

}
```

```
unsigned long calc_factorial(unsigned long x)
{
    unsigned long factorial;

    factorial = x;

    while (x > 1L)
    {
        factorial *= --x;
    }

    return(factorial);

}
```

This version of the calc_factorial() function uses a while loop to calculate a value's factorial. Not only is it much faster than the recursive version, but it also consumes a minimal amount of stack space.

Cross Reference:

XIX.11: What is iterative processing?

XIX.13: What is the best way to represent true and false in C?
Answer:

In C, anything that evaluates to 0 is evaluated to be false, and anything that evaluates to a nonzero value is true. Therefore, the most common definition for false is 0, and the most common definition for true is 1. Many programs include header files that define this:

```
#define FALSE   0
#define TRUE    1
```

If you are writing a Windows program, you should note that this exact definition of TRUE and FALSE appears in the windows.h header file. This form of defining true and false is very common and perfectly acceptable. There are, however, a few other ways of defining true and false. For instance, consider this definition:

```
#define FALSE   0
#define TRUE    !FALSE
```

This simply says that FALSE is 0 and TRUE is anything but 0. Note that even negative numbers, such as −1, are nonzero and therefore evaluate to true.

Another popular way to define true and false is to create your own *enumerated* type, such as Boolean (or BOOL), like this:

```
enum BOOL {
    FALSE,
    TRUE
};
```

As you might already know, the first element of an enumerated type is assigned the value 0 by default.

Therefore, with the preceding enum definition, FALSE is assigned 0 and TRUE is assigned 1. Using an enumerated type has some benefits over using the more common symbolic constant (#define). See FAQ V.6 and FAQ V.7 for an explanation of the benefit of using enum.

Which method is best? There is no single answer to this question. If you are writing a Windows program, TRUE and FALSE are already defined for you, so there is no need to create your own definition of TRUE and FALSE. Otherwise, you can choose your own way from the methods described previously.

Cross Reference:

V.6: What is the benefit of using enum to declare a constant?

V.7: What is the benefit of using an enum rather than a #define constant?

XIX.14: What is the difference between a null loop and an infinite loop?

Answer:

A null loop does not continue indefinitely—it has a predefined number of iterations before exiting the loop. An infinite loop, on the other hand, continues without end and never exits the loop. This is best illustrated by comparing a null loop to an infinite loop.

Here is an example of a null loop:

```
for (x=0; x<500000; x++);
```

Notice that in this example, a semicolon is placed directly after the closing parenthesis of the for loop. As you might already know, C does not require semicolons to follow for loops. Usually, only the statements within the for loop are appended with semicolons. Putting the semicolon directly after the for loop (and using *no* braces) creates a null loop—literally, a loop that contains no programming statements. In the preceding example, when the for loop executes, the variable x will be incremented 500,000 times with no processing occurring between increments.

You might be wondering what null loops are used for. Most often, they are used for putting a pause in your program. The preceding example will make your program "pause" for however long it takes your computer to count to 500,000. However, there are many more uses for null loops. Consider the next example:

```
while (!kbhit());
```

This example uses a null loop to wait for a key to be pressed on the keyboard. This can be useful when your program needs to display a message such as Press Any Key To Continue or something similar (let's hope your users are smart enough to avoid an endless search for the "Any Key"!).

An infinite loop, unlike a null loop, can *never* be terminated. Here is an example of an infinite loop:

```
while (1);
```

In this example, the while statement contains a constant that is nonzero. Therefore, the while condition will always evaluate to true and will never terminate. Notice that a semicolon is appended directly to the end of the closing parenthesis, and thus the while statement contains no other programming statements. Therefore, there is no way that this loop can terminate (unless, of course, the program is terminated).

Cross Reference:

XIX.15: What is the difference between continue and break?

XIX.15: What is the difference between *continue* and *break*?
Answer:

A continue statement is used to return to the beginning of a loop. The break statement is used to exit from a loop. For example, here is a typical continue statement:

```
while (!feof(infile)
{
    fread(inbuffer, 80, 1, infile); /* read in a line from input file */
    if (!strncmpi(inbuffer, "REM", 3))  /* check if it is
                                            a comment line */
        continue;      /* it's a comment, so jump back to the while() */
    else
        parse_line();                  /* not a comment--parse this line */
}
```

In this example, a file is being read and parsed. The letters "REM" (short for "remark") are used to denote a comment line in the file that is being processed. Because a comment line means nothing to the program, it is skipped. As each line is read in from the input file, the first three letters of the line are compared with the letters "REM." If there is a match, the input line contains a comment, and the continue statement is used to jump back to the while statement to continue reading in lines from the input file. Otherwise, the line must contain a valid statement, so the parse_line() function is called.

A break statement, on the other hand, is used to exit a loop. Here is an example of a break statement:

```
while (!feof(infile)
{
    fread(inbuffer, 80, 1, infile); /* read in a line from input file */
    if (!strncmpi(inbuffer, "REM", 3))  /* check if it is
                                            a comment line */
        continue;      /* it's a comment, so jump back to the while() */
    else
    {
        if (parse_line() == FATAL_ERROR)  /* attempt to parse
                                              this line */
            break;         /* fatal error occurred, so exit the loop */
    }
}
```

This example builds on the example presented for the continue statement. Notice that in this example, the return value of the parse_line() function is checked. If the parse_line() function returns the value FATAL_ERROR, the while loop is immediately exited by use of the break statement. The break statement causes the loop to be exited, and control is passed to the first statement immediately following the loop.

Cross Reference:

XIX.14: What is the difference between a null loop and an infinite loop?

CHAPTER XX

◆

Miscellaneous

This book has attempted to cover every major topic of C programming, and hopefully the information was useful and understandable. It is impossible, however, to cover every possible aspect of something as complex as the computer in a book as succinct as this. Therefore, this chapter is devoted to providing a mixed bag of questions and answers covering areas that might have fallen through the cracks.

XX.1: How are command-line parameters obtained?

Answer:

Every time you run a DOS or Windows program, a Program Segment Prefix, or PSP, is created. When the DOS program loader copies the program into RAM to execute it, it first allocates 256 bytes for the PSP, then places the executable in the memory immediately after the PSP. The PSP contains all kinds of information that DOS needs in order to facilitate the execution of the program, most of which do not apply to this FAQ. However, there is at least one piece of data in the PSP that does apply here: the command line. At offset 128 in the PSP is a single byte that contains the number of characters of the command line. The next 127 bytes contain the command line itself. Coincidentally, that is why DOS limits your typing at the DOS prompt to 127 characters—it allocates only that much to hold the command line. Unfortunately, the command-line buffer in the PSP does not contain the name of the executable—it contains only the characters you typed after the executable's name (including the spaces).

For example, if you type

```
XCOPY AUTOEXEC.BAT AUTOEXEC.BAK
```

at the DOS prompt, XCOPY.EXE's PSP command-line buffer will contain

```
AUTOEXEC.BAT AUTOEXEC.BAK
```

assuming that the xcopy program resides in the DOS directory of drive C. It's difficult to see in print, but you should note that the space character immediately after the XCOPY word on the command line is also copied into the PSP's buffer.

Another negative side to the PSP is that, in addition to the fact that you cannot find your own program's name, any redirection of output or input noted on the command line is not shown in the PSP's command-line buffer. This means that you also cannot know (from the PSP, anyway) that your program's input or output was redirected.

By now you are familiar with using the argc and argv argument parameters in your C programs to retrieve the information. But how does the information get from the DOS program loader to the argv pointer in your program? It does this in the start-up code, which is executed before the first line of code in your main() function. During the initial program execution, a function called _setargv() is called. This function copies the program name and command line from the PSP and DOS environment into the buffer pointed to by your main() function's argv pointer. The _setargv() function is found in the xLIBCE.LIB file, x being S for Small memory model, M for Medium memory model, and L for Large memory model. This library file is automatically linked to your executable program when you build it. Copying the argument parameters isn't the only thing the C start-up code does. When the start-up code is completed, the code you wrote in your main() function starts being executed.

OK, that's fine for DOS, but what about Windows? Actually, most of the preceding description applies to Windows programs as well. When a Windows program is executed, the Windows program loader creates a PSP just like the DOS program loader, containing the same information. The major difference is that the command line is copied into the lpszCmdLine argument, which is the third (next-to-last) argument in your WinMain() function's parameter list. The Windows C library file xLIBCEW.LIB contains the start-up function _setargv(), which copies the command-line information into this lpszCmdLine buffer. Again, the x represents the memory model you are using with your program. If you are using QuickC, the start-up code is contained in the xLIBCEWQ.LIB library file.

Although the command-line information between DOS and Windows programs is managed in basically the same way, the *format* of the command line arrives in your C program in slightly different arrangements. In DOS, the start-up code takes the command line, which is delimited by spaces, and turns each argument into its own NULL-terminated string. You therefore could prototype argv as an array of pointers (char * argv[]) and access each argument using an index value of 0 to *n*, in which *n* is the number of arguments in the command line minus one. On the other hand, you could prototype argv as a pointer to pointers (char ** argv) and access each argument by incrementing or decrementing argv.

In Windows, the command line arrives as an LPSTR, or char _far *. Each argument in the command line is delimited by *spaces*, just as they would appear at the DOS prompt had you actually typed the characters yourself (which is unlikely, considering that this is Windows and they want you to think you are using a Macintosh by double-clicking the application's icon). To access the different arguments of the Windows command line, you must manually walk across the memory pointed to by lpszCmdLine, separating the arguments, or use a standard C function such as strtok() to hand you each argument one at a time.

If you are adventurous enough, you could peruse the PSP itself to retrieve the command-line information. To do so, use DOS interrupt 21 as follows (using Microsoft C):

```
#include <stdio.h>
#include <dos.h>

main(int argc, char ** argv)
{
    union REGS regs;                    /* DOS register access struct */
    char far * pspPtr;                  /* pointer to PSP */
    int cmdLineCnt;                     /* num of chars in cmd line */

    regs.h.ah = 0x62;                   /* use DOS interrupt 62 */
    int86(0x21, &regs, &regs);          /* call DOS */
    FP_SEG(pspPtr) = regs.x.bx;         /* save PSP segment */
    FP_OFF(pspPtr) = 0x80;              /* set pointer offset */

    /* *pspPtr now points to the command-line count byte */
    cmdLineCnt = *pspPtr;
}
```

It should be noted that in the Small memory model, or in assembly language programs with only one code segment, the segment value returned by DOS into the BX register is your program's code segment. In the case of Large memory model C programs, or assembly programs with multiple code segments, the value returned is the code segment of your program that contains the PSP. After you have set up a pointer to this data, you can use this data in your program.

Cross Reference:

XX.2: Should programs always assume that command-line parameters can be used?

XX.2: Should programs always assume that command-line parameters can be used?

Answer:

These days, you can usually assume that the command-line parameters can be used by your program. Before DOS 2.0, the command-line information stored in the PSP was slightly different (it *didn't* strip input and output redirection data from the command line). In addition, the data pointed to by argv[0] did not reliably contain the executable's pathname until DOS 2.0. The DOS interrupt 62 that retrieves the PSP segment wasn't available (or at least documented) until DOS 3.0. You therefore can at least assume that you can get consistent command-line information on PCs running DOS 3.0 or newer.

After you have determined that you are running DOS 3.0 or greater, you can basically do whatever you want to the command-line data, because the information is placed on the stack for you to play with (via argv). Of course, normal data manipulation rules apply to command-line data as they do to all data arriving on the stack. The real problems arise when you don't have argv provided by your compiler. For example, you could write your program in assembly language, or in some archaic compiler that does not provide argc and argv. In these cases, you will have to find some method of retrieving the command-line information yourself. That is where the DOS interrupt 62 comes in handy.

If you use DOS interrupt 62 to retrieve a pointer to the command line, you must be aware that you are pointing to data that is used by DOS and for DOS. Although the data is there for you to see, you should not assume that the data is there for you to alter. If you need to use the command-line information to make decisions at various times throughout your program, you should copy the data into a local buffer before actually using the data. This technique enables you to have complete control of the data without worrying about stepping on DOS's toes. In fact, this applies also to C programs that supply argv. It is not uncommon for a function outside main() to need access to the command-line data. For it to get access to the data, your main() must save it globally, or pass it (once again) on the stack to the function that needs it. It is therefore good programming practice to save the command-line information into a local buffer if you intend to use it.

Cross Reference:

XX.1: How are command-line parameters obtained?

XX.3: What is the difference between "exception handling" and "structured exception handling"?

Answer:

Generally speaking, the difference between a structured exception and exception handling is Microsoft's implementation of exception handlers themselves. So-called "ordinary" C++ exception handling uses three statements added to the C++ language: try, catch, and throw. The purpose of these statements is to allow a piece of software (the exception handler) to attempt a safe bailout of the application that was running when the exception occurred. The exception handler can trap exceptions on any data type, including a C++ class. The implementation of the three statements is based on the ISO WG21/ANSI X3J16 C++ standard for exception handling. Microsoft C++ supports exception handling based on this standard. Note that this standard applies only to C++ and not to C.

On the other hand, structured exception handling is an extension to the Microsoft C/C++ compiler. Its single largest advantage is that it works with either C or C++. Microsoft's structured exception handling design uses two new constructs: try-except and try-finally. These two constructs are not a subset or superset of the ANSI C++ standard; instead, they are a different implementation of exception handling (leave it to Microsoft to forge ahead on its own). The try-except construct is known as *exception handling*, and try-finally is known as *termination handling*. The try-except statement allows an application to retrieve the state of the machine when the exception occurred. This is very handy for displaying information about the error to the user, or for use while you are debugging your code. The try-finally statement enables applications to guarantee execution of cleanup code when normal code execution is interrupted. Although structured exception handling has its advantages, it also has its drawbacks. Because this is not an ANSI standard, code using structured exception handling is not as portable as code using ANSI exception handling. A good rule of thumb is if your application is going to be a C++ program, you are advised to stick to ANSI exception handling (use the try, catch, and throw statements).

Cross Reference:

None.

XX.4: How do you create a delay timer in a DOS program?

Answer:

Fortunately for us programmers, the folks at Microsoft thought it would be a good idea to create a hardware-independent delay timer. The purpose, of course, is to allow a delay of a fixed amount of time, regardless of the speed of the computer on which the program is being run. The following example code demonstrates how to create a delay timer in DOS:

```c
#include <stdio.h>
#include <dos.h>
#include <stdlib.h>


void main(int argc, char ** argv)
{
    union REGS regs;
    unsigned long delay;

    delay = atol(argv[1]);      /* assume that there is an argument */

    /* multiply by 1 for microsecond-granularity delay */
    /* multiply by 1000 for millisecond-granularity delay */
    /* multiply by 1000000 for second-granularity delay */
    delay *= 1000000;

    regs.x.ax = 0x8600;
    regs.x.cx = (unsigned int)((delay & 0xFFFF0000L) >> 16);
    regs.x.dx = (unsigned int)(delay & 0xFFFF);

    int86(0x15, &regs, &regs);
}
```

The example uses DOS interrupt 0x15, function 0x86, to perform the delay. The amount of delay is in microseconds. Due to this, the delay function assumes that you might want a really big number, so it expects the high-order 16 bits of the delay value in CX, and the low-order 16 bits of the delay value in DX. At its maximum, the delay function can stall for more than 4 billion microseconds, or about 1.2 hours.

The example assumes that the delay value will be in microseconds. This version of the example multiplies the delay by one million so that the delay entered on the command line will be turned into seconds. Therefore, a "delay 10" command will delay for 10 seconds.

Cross Reference:

XXI.2: How do you create a delay timer in a Windows program?

XX.5: Who are Kernighan and Ritchie?

Answer:

Kernighan and Ritchie are Brian W. Kernighan and Dennis M. Ritchie, authors of *The C Programming Language*. This book is known affectionately throughout the world as the "K&R Manual," the "white book," the "K&R Bible," and other similar names. The book was originally published by Prentice-Hall in 1978. Dennis developed the C programming language for the UNIX operating system running on the DEC PDP-11 mainframe computer. He and Brian were working for AT&T Bell Laboratories in the early 1970s when both C and the K&R Manual were developed. C was modeled somewhat after the B programming language, written by Ken Thompson in 1970, and BCPL, written by Martin Richards in 1969.

Cross Reference:

None.

XX.6: How do you create random numbers?
Answer:

Well, actually, there's no such thing as a truly random number generator on a computer. However, a point can be reached where the number repetition pattern is so large that the number appears to be random. That is the ultimate goal of a random number generator. Such a device is called a *pseudo-random number generator*.

There is a lot of theory about how to generate random numbers. I will not discuss in this section the theory and mathematics behind creating random number generators. Entire books have been written dealing with this subject alone. What can be said about any random number generator is that no matter which implementation you use, you must provide the algorithm some value to get it "started." It helps if this number is also random, or at least pseudo-random. Fast counting registers or shift registers are often used to create this initial number, called a *seed*, that is fed into the generator.

For this book, I will demonstrate the use of the random number generator provided by the C language. Modern C compilers include a pseudo-random number generator function to help you produce a random number, based on an ANSI standard. Both Microsoft and Borland support this standard via the `rand()` and `srand()` functions. Here's how they work: You provide the seed for the `srand()` function; this seed is an `unsigned int`, so the range is 0 to 65,535. After you have fed the seed to `srand()`, you call `rand()`, which returns a random number (in the range of 0 to 32,767) based on the seed value provided to `srand()`. You can call `rand()` as many times as you want after seeding `srand()`, and you'll continue to get back random numbers. You can, at any time, seed `srand()` with a different value to further "randomize" the output of `rand()`.

This process sounds simple enough. The problem is that if you feed `srand()` the same seed value each time you call it, you will get back the same series of "random" numbers. For example, you call `srand()` with a seed value of 17. When you call `rand()`, you get the random number 94. Call `rand()` again, and you get 26,602. Call `rand()` a third time, and you get 30,017. Seems fairly random (although this is a painfully small set of data points). If, however, you call `srand()` again, seeding it with 17 again, `rand()` will return 94, 26,602, and 30,017 on its first three calls, along with all the remaining numbers you got back in the first series of calls to `rand()`. Therefore, you still need to seed `srand()` with a random number so that it can produce a random number.

The following example shows a simple, but quite effective, method for generating a fairly random seed value—the time of day.

```
#include <stdlib.h>
#include <stdio.h>
#include <sys/types.h>
#include <sys/timeb.h>

void main( void )
{
    int i;
    unsigned int seedVal;
    struct _timeb timeBuf;

    _ftime(&timeBuf);

    seedVal = ((((((unsigned int)timeBuf.time & 0xFFFF) +
                (unsigned int)timeBuf.millitm)) ^
                (unsigned int)timeBuf.millitm));

    srand((unsigned int)seedVal);

    for(i = 0; i < 10; ++i)
        printf("%6d\n", rand());
}
```

The function calls _ftime() to retrieve the current time of day in seconds elapsed since January 1, 1970 (no kidding), placed into the timeBuf.time structure member. After the call, the timeBuf structure also contains the number of milliseconds that have elapsed in the current second in the millitm member. Note that in DOS, millitm actually holds the number of *hundredths* of a second that have elapsed in the current second. The number of milliseconds is added to the elapsed time in seconds, and the total is XORed with the millisecond count. You could apply many more logical mathematical functions to these two structure members to control the range of seedVal and further its apparent randomness, but this example is sufficient.

Note that in the preceding example, the output of rand() has not been scaled to a specific range. Suppose that you want to pretend to create a lottery number-picking machine whose values ranged from 1 to 44. You could simply ignore any output from rand() that did not fall into this range, but it could take a long time before you acquired the necessary six lottery numbers. Instead, you can scale the output from rand() to any numeric range you want. Assume that you have produced a satisfactory random number generator that provides a random number in the range of 0 to 32,767 (as in the case of the earlier example) and that you want to scale the output down to 1 to 44. The following example shows how to accomplish this task:

```
int i, k, range;
int min, max;
double j;

min = 1;            /* 1 is the minimum number allowed */
max = 44;           /* 44 is the maximum number allowed */
range = max - min;    /* r is the range allowed: 1 to 44 */

i = rand();    /* use the above example in this slot */

/* Normalize the rand() output (scale to 0 to 1) */
/* RAND_MAX is defined in stdlib.h */
j = ((double)i / (double)RAND_MAX);

/* Scale the output to 1 to 44 */
i = (int)(j * (double)range);
i += min;
```

This example places a restriction on the random output to a range from 1 to 44. Here's what the function does: It gets a random number whose range is from 0 to RAND_MAX (32,767) and divides that random number by RAND_MAX. This process produces a *normalized* value—that is, a value whose range is 0 to 1. Next, the normalized value is scaled up by the range of allowed values (43 in this case—44 minus 1). This produces a value from 0 to 43. Next, the minimum amount allowed is added to this number to place the scaled value in the proper range—1 to 44. To experiment, replace the min and max numbers with different values, and you'll see that the example properly scales the random number to the new min and max values.

Cross Reference:

None.

XX.7: When should a 32-bit compiler be used?

Answer:

A 32-bit compiler should be used on a 32-bit operating system. The 32-bit compiler creates 32-bit programs that run your PC much faster than 16-bit programs—which is why 32-bit *anything* is hot.

With all the different versions of Microsoft Windows out there, which compiler is best for which operating system? This passage looks at what Microsoft offers, and assigns the correct compiler to the correct operating system. Windows 3.1 and Windows for Workgroups 3.11 are 16-bit operating systems; Microsoft Visual C++ 1.x is a 16-bit compiler. The compiler produces code that will run on Windows 3.1. Microsoft Windows NT and Windows 95 are 32-bit operating systems; Visual C++ 2.0, the latest compiler from Microsoft, is a 32-bit compiler created to produce 32-bit code for these operating systems. The 16-bit programs that Visual 1.x produces will run on Windows NT and Windows 95 as well as Windows 3.1.

The opposite is *not* true, however—32-bit code produced by Visual 2.0 will not run on Windows 3.1. This fact presents a problem for Microsoft, which wants everyone to use its 32-bit compiler but has 60 million PCs out there running a version of Windows that can't run these new 32-bit programs. To get around this obstacle, Microsoft created a translation library called *Win32s* that performs the 32- to 16-bit "thunking," as it is called, to allow 32-bit programs produced by Visual C++ 2.0 to run on Windows 3.1 and Windows for Workgroups. Win32s is specifically designed to run on Windows 3.1 (and WFW)—it is not meant for Windows 95 and NT because they do not need to "thunk" to run 32-bit code. Using Win32s, it is possible to produce a single program using Visual C++ 2.0 that will run on Windows 3.1 (and WFW) as well as Windows NT.

The only remaining gotcha is the compilers themselves. Visual C++ 1.x is a 16-bit Windows program—it will run on Windows 95 and NT and will produce the same 16-bit program as if it were running on Windows 3.1. However, Visual C++ 2.0, being a 32-bit Windows program, will not run on Windows 3.1. It won't even run if you install Win32s, because Microsoft conveniently makes sure you are running Windows 95 or NT before Visual 2.0 will start.

To summarize, run Visual C++ 1.x (version 1.51 is the latest) on Windows 3.1, Windows for Workgroups, Windows NT, or Windows 95 to create 16-bit programs that will run on all versions of Windows; run Visual C++ 2.0 to create 32-bit programs that will run fastest on Windows 95 and NT but will also run very well on Windows 3.1 (and WFW).

For you Borland C/C++ users, Borland's Turbo C++ Version 3.1 is the latest 16-bit compiler, and Borland C++ Version 4.5 is the 32-bit Windows compiler (note that the 32-bit compiler doesn't have the "Turbo" moniker). Both compilers contain the compiler, Borland's OWL C++ classes, and an excellent integrated debugger.

Cross Reference:

None.

XX.8: How do you interrupt a Windows program?

Answer:

There is no trivial way to interrupt a Windows application so that you can perform a necessary task (if that is your goal). Windows 3.x is a nonpreemptive multitasking operating system. Put another way, it is a *cooperative* multitasking operating system. It is cooperative partly because there is no way to simply steal time away from a Windows program that is currently in control of the processor. If you look at the Windows API, you'll see functions such as PeekMessage() and WaitMessage(). As the Microsoft help documentation says concerning these functions:

> The GetMessage, PeekMessage, and WaitMessage functions yield control to other applications. Using these functions is the only way to allow other applications to run. Applications that do not call any of these functions for long periods prevent other applications from running.

All that having been said, it still can be done. One method is to create a timer in your Windows program that "goes off" every so often. As long as your program is alive, you will get time to perform whatever task you want to when the timer goes off. However, this action is not technically *interrupting* a program in process—it is simply using the cooperative multitasking features of Windows. If you need to interrupt a Windows program, you can do so with a *filter function* (also called a *hook function*). A filter function in Windows is analogous to an interrupt service routine in DOS (see FAQs XX.12 and XX.17). Using a filter function, you can hook certain Windows events and perform tasks when that event occurs. In fact, you can use a filter function to monitor nearly every message that exists in Windows using one or more of the available hooks. This example, however, uses the keyboard hook because it enables you to interrupt a program at will by entering a specific key combination. The following example hooks the keyboard event chain and puts up a message box when the Ctrl-Alt-F6 key is pressed. This method works regardless of the application that is currently running.

```
#include <dos.h>
#include <windows.h>

DWORD FAR PASCAL __loadds KeyBoardProc(int, WORD, DWORD);
static FARPROC nextKeyboardFilter = NULL;

BOOL shiftKeyDown, ctrlKeyDown;

#define REPEAT_COUNT    0x000000FF    /* test key repeat */
#define KEY_WAS_UP      0x80000000    /* test WM_KEYUP */
#define ALT_KEY_DOWN    0x20000000    /* test Alt key state */

#define EAT_THE_KEY     1             /* swallow keystroke */
```

```
#define SEND_KEY_ON          0                /* act on keystroke */

BOOL useAltKey = TRUE;                       /* use Alt key in sequence */
BOOL useCtrlKey = TRUE;                      /* also use Ctrl key */
BOOL useShiftKey = FALSE;                    /* don't use Shift key */

/* Entry point into the DLL. Do all necessary initialization here */

int FAR PASCAL LibMain(hModule, wDataSeg, cbHeapSize, lpszCmdLine)
HANDLE  hModule;
WORD    wDataSeg;
WORD    cbHeapSize;
LPSTR   lpszCmdLine;
{

    /* initialize key state variables to zero */
    shiftKeyDown = 0;
    ctrlKeyDown = 0;

    return 1;
}

/* The keyboard filter searches for the hotkey key sequence.
   If it gets it, it eats the key and displays a message box.
   Any other key is sent on to Windows. */

DWORD FAR PASCAL __loadds
KeyBoardProc(int nCode, WORD wParam, DWORD lParam)
{
    BOOL fCallDefProc;
    DWORD dwResult = 0;

    dwResult = SEND_KEY_ON;     /* default to send key on */
    fCallDefProc = TRUE;              /* default to calling DefProc */

switch(nCode){
    case HC_ACTION:
    case HC_NOREMOVE:

        /* If key is Shift, save it */
        if(wParam == (WORD)VK_SHIFT){
            shiftKeyDown = ((lParam & KEY_WAS_UP) ? 0 : 1);
            break;
        }

        /* If key is Ctrl, save it */
        else if(wParam == (WORD)VK_CONTROL){
            ctrlKeyDown = ((lParam & KEY_WAS_UP) ? 0 : 1);
            break;
        }

        /* If key is the F6 key, act on it */
        else if(wParam == (WORD)VK_F6){

            /* Leave if the F6 key was a key release and not press */
            if(lParam & KEY_WAS_UP) break;

            /* Make sure Alt key is in desired state, else leave */
            if( (useAltKey) && !(lParam & ALT_KEY_DOWN) ){
```

```
                        break;
                    }
                else if( (!useAltKey) && (lParam & ALT_KEY_DOWN) ){
                        break;
                    }

                    /* Make sure Shift key is in desired state, else leave */
                    if(useShiftKey && !shiftKeyDown){
                        break;
                    }
                else if(!useShiftKey && shiftKeyDown){
                        break;
                    }

                    /* Make sure Ctrl key is in desired state, else leave */
                    if(useCtrlKey && !ctrlKeyDown){
                        break;
                    }
                else if(!useCtrlKey && ctrlKeyDown){
                        break;
                    }

                    /* Eat the keystroke, and don't call DefProc */
                    dwResult = EAT_THE_KEY;
                    fCallDefProc = FALSE;

                    /* We made it, so Ctrl-Alt-F6 was pressed! */
                    MessageBox(NULL, (LPSTR)"You pressed Ctrl-Alt-F6!",
                                    (LPSTR)"Keyboard Hook", MB_OK);
                    break;
                    }

            default:
                    fCallDefProc = TRUE;
                    break;
        }

    if( (nCode < 0) || (fCallDefProc && (nextKeyboardFilter != NULL)))
        dwResult = DefHookProc(nCode, wParam, lParam,
                                            &nextKeyboardFilter);

        return(dwResult);
    }

/* This function is called by the application to set up or tear
   down the filter function hooks. */

void FAR PASCAL
SetupFilters(BOOL install)
{
    if(install){
        nextKeyboardFilter = SetWindowsHook(WH_KEYBOARD,
                                        (FARPROC)KeyBoardProc);
    }
    else{
        UnhookWindowsHook(WH_KEYBOARD, (FARPROC)KeyBoardProc);
        nextKeyboardFilter = NULL;
    }
}
```

Microsoft strongly recommends placing filter functions in a DLL rather than your application (notice the presence of a LibMain() and the lack of a WinMain()). To complete this application, you need to write an ordinary Windows application that calls the SetupFilters() function with TRUE as the argument to start monitoring keystrokes, and FALSE as the argument to stop monitoring keystrokes. While your application is alive and you have called SetupFilters(TRUE), the callback function KeyBoardProc() is receiving all keystrokes, even while you are running other Windows applications. If you press Ctrl-Alt-F6, a small message box appears on-screen informing you that you pressed those keys. Presto, you have just interrupted whatever Windows application was running at the time you pressed those keys!

Note that the keyboard filter function will not receive keystrokes while in a DOS shell. However, the filter function will receive, and can interrupt, a system modal dialog box like the one that asks whether you really want to exit Windows.

Cross Reference:

XX.12: How can I pass data from one program to another?

XX.17: Can you disable warm boots (Ctrl-Alt-Del)?

XXI.10: What is dynamic linking?

XX.9: Why should I use static variables?
Answer:

Static variables are excellent for use as a local variable that does not lose its value when the function exits. For example, you might have a function that gets called numerous times, and that part of the function's job is to count how many times it gets called. You cannot accomplish this task with a simple local variable because it will be uninitialized each time the function is entered. If you declare your counter variable as static, its current value will be maintained, just as with a global variable.

So why not just use a global variable instead? You could, and there's nothing wrong with using a global variable. The problem with using global variables is that maintaining a program with lots of global variables becomes cumbersome, particularly if you have numerous functions that uniquely access one global variable. Again, there's nothing wrong with doing it that way—the issue simply becomes one of good code design and readability. By declaring such variables as static, you are informing yourself (or another person who might be reading your code) that this variable is local but is treated like a global (maintains its value). If the static variable was instead declared as a global, the person reading the code must assume that the global is accessed in many places when in fact it might not be.

In summary, the reason you should use static variables is that it is good programming practice when you need a localized variable that maintains its state.

Cross Reference:

II.17: Can static variables be declared in a header file?

XX.10: How can I run another program after mine?

Answer:

Of course, the easiest way to run another program after yours is to put them both in a batch file, one after the other. When you run the batch file, the programs listed will execute in order. But you already knew that.

There is no specific method for performing a "when my program is finished, run this one" function call in C or in DOS. However, C provides two sets of functions that will allow a program at any time to run another program that basically ends the first program upon execution of the second. If you were to put such a call at the end of your first application, you could do exactly what you need. The two functions provided are exec() and spawn(). In reality, each function is actually a family of functions, each function allowing a unique twist over the other functions in the family. The exec family of functions is execl(), execle(), execlp(), execlpe(), execv(), execve(), execvp(), and execvpe(). The following list shows what the e, l, p, and v additions mean to the function:

e	An array of pointers to environment parameters is explicitly passed to the child process.
l	Command-line arguments are passed individually to the executable.
p	Uses the PATH environment variable to find the file to be executed.
v	Command-line arguments are passed to the executable as an array of pointers.

Which combination of options you choose in your application is entirely up to you and the needs of the application you want to launch. Following is an example of a program that calls another application whose name is specified on the command line:

```c
#include <stdio.h>
#include <process.h>

char *envString[] = {            /* environment for the app */
    "COMM_VECTOR=0x63",          /* communications vector */
    "PARENT=LAUNCH.EXE",         /* name of this app */
    "EXEC=EDIT.COM",             /* name of app to exec */
    NULL};                       /* must be NULL-terminated */

void
main(int argc, char ** argv)
{

    /* Call the one with variable arguments and an environment */
    _execvpe("EDIT.COM", argv, envString);

    printf("If you can read this sentence, the exec didn't happen!\n");
}
```

In the preceding short example, _execvpe() is called to execute EDIT.COM, the DOS file editor. The arguments to EDIT come from the command line to the example. After the exec has occurred, the original application has gone away; when EDIT exits, you are returned to the DOS prompt. If the printf() statement is displayed on-screen, something went awry in the exec attempt, because you will not get there if the exec succeeds. Note that the environment variables for EDIT.COM are completely meaningless. However, if you *did* exec a program that needed the environment variables, they would be available for use by the application.

There is a second way to accomplish this same task—spawn(). The spawn function family is spawnl(), spawnle(), spawnlp(), spawnlpe(), spawnv(), spawnve(), spawnvp(), and spawnvpe(). The e, l, p, and v appendages mean the same as they do with exec. In fact, this function family is identical to exec except for one small difference—spawn can either launch another application while killing the original, or launch another application and return to the original when the second application is complete. The argument list for the spawn functions is identical to that for exec except that one additional argument is required: you must use _P_OVERLAY (original application dies) or _P_WAIT (return to original when finished) as the first argument to the spawn functions. The following example demonstrates the same task as the preceding example:

```
#include <stdio.h>
#include <process.h>

char *envString[] = {          /* environment for the app */
"COMM_VECTOR=0x63",            /* communications vector */
"PARENT=LAUNCH.EXE",           /* name of this app */
"EXEC=EDIT.COM",               /* name of app to exec */
NULL};                         /* must be NULL-terminated */

void
main(int argc, char ** argv)
{

    /* Call the one with variable arguments and an environment */
    _spawnvpe(_P_OVERLAY, "EDIT.COM", argv, envString);

    printf("If you can read this sentence, the exec didn't happen!\n");

}
```

The only difference here is the name change from exec to spawn, and the additional *mode* argument. What is nice about spawn's capability to overlay versus wait is the ability to make a runtime decision regarding waiting or leaving during the spawn. In fact, the _P_WAIT argument answers the next FAQ.

Cross Reference:

XX.11: How can I run another program during my program's execution?

XX.11: How can I run another program during my program's execution?

Answer:

As seen in the preceding example, the spawn family of functions allows one application to start another application, then return to the original application when the first one is finished. Read FAQ XX.10 for a good background dose of spawn and for example code (all you have to do is change _P_OVERLAY to _P_WAIT and you're done).

However, there is another way to accomplish this task that needs to be mentioned. This other method involves the system() call. The system() function is similar to, but still different from, the exec or spawn functions. In addition to suspending the current application to execute the new one (instead of killing it), `system()` launches the COMMAND.COM command interpreter (or whatever command interpreter is running on your machine) to run the application. If COMMAND.COM or its equivalent cannot be found, the application is not executed (this is not the case with exec and spawn). The following example is yet another version of a call to EDIT.COM to open a file, whose name arrives from the example program's command line:

```c
#include <stdio.h>
#include <process.h>
#include <stdlib.h>

char argStr[255];

void
main(int argc, char ** argv)
{
    int ret;

    /* Have EDIT open a file called HELLO if no arg given */
    sprintf(argStr, "EDIT %s", (argv[1] == NULL ? "HELLO" : argv[1]));

    /* Call the one with variable arguments and an environment */
    ret = system(argStr);

    printf("system() returned %d\n", ret);
}
```

As it was with the earlier example (using _P_WAIT), the `printf()` statement after the `system()` call is executed because the initial program was merely suspended and not killed. In every case, `system()` returns a value that signifies success or failure to run the specified application. It does *not* return the return code from the application itself.

Cross Reference:

XX.10: How can I run another program after mine?

XX.12: How can I pass data from one program to another?
Answer:

You can accomplish this task in a couple of basic ways—you can pass the data via a file or via memory. The steps for any of the methods are fairly straightforward: you define where the data is to be placed, how to get it there, and how to notify the other program to get or set the data; then you get or set the data in that location. Although the file technique is simple to define and create, it can easily become slow (and noisy). This answer will therefore concentrate on the memory data-transfer technique. The parts of the process will be detailed one at a time:

Define where the data is to be placed. When you write the two applications (it takes two to share), you must build into them a way to know where the data is going to be when you need to retrieve it. Again, there are several ways you can solve this part. You can have a fixed data buffer internal to one (or each of the programs) and pass a pointer to the buffer back and forth. You could dynamically allocate the memory and pass a pointer to the data back and forth. If the data is small enough, you could pass the information through the CPU's general purpose registers (this possibility is unlikely due to the pitifully few number of registers in the x86 architecture). The most flexible and modular method is to dynamically allocate the memory.

Define how to get the data there. This part is straightforward—you use _fmemcpy() or an equivalent memory copy routine. This naturally applies for both getting and setting the data.

Define how to notify the other program. Because DOS is not a multitasking operating system, it is obvious that one (or both) of the programs must have some part of the software already resident in memory that can accept the call from the other program. Again, several choices are available. The first application could be a device driver that is referenced in CONFIG.SYS and loaded at boot time. Or it could be a TSR (terminate-and-stay-resident) application that leaves the inter-application part of the program resident in memory when it exits. Another option is to use the system() or spawn() calls (see FAQ XX.11) to start the second application from within the first one. Which option you select depends on your needs. Because data passing to and from a DOS device driver is already well documented, and system() and spawn() calls were documented earlier, I'll describe the TSR method.

The following example code is a complete program but is admittedly thin for the purposes of grasping only the critical pieces of the process (see FAQ XX.15 regarding example code). The following example shows a TSR that installs an interrupt service routine at interrupt 0x63, then calls the terminate-and-stay-resident exit function. Next, another program is executed that simply initiates an interrupt call to 0x63 (much like you make DOS int21 calls) and passes "Hello World" to that program.

```
#include <stdlib.h>
#include <dos.h>
#include <string.h>

void SetupPointers(void);
void OutputString(char *);

#define STACKSIZE       4096

unsigned int _near OldStackPtr;
unsigned int _near OldStackSeg;
unsigned int _near MyStackOff;
unsigned int _near MyStackSeg;
unsigned char _near MyStack[STACKSIZE];
unsigned char _far * MyStackPtr = (unsigned char _far *) MyStack;

unsigned short AX, BX, CX, DX, ES;

/* My interrupt handler */
void _interrupt _far _cdecl NewCommVector(
        unsigned short es, unsigned short ds, unsigned short di,
        unsigned short si, unsigned short bp, unsigned short sp,
        unsigned short bx, unsigned short dx, unsigned short cx,
        unsigned short ax, unsigned short ip, unsigned short cs,
        unsigned short flags);

/* Pointers to the previous interrupt handler */
void (_interrupt _far _cdecl * comm_vector)();

union REGS regs;
struct SREGS segregs;

#define COMM_VECTOR         0x63    /* Software interrupt vector */

/* This is where the data gets passed into the TSR */
```

```
char _far * callerBufPtr;
char localBuffer[255];                  /* Limit of 255 bytes to transfer */
char _far * localBufPtr = (char _far *)localBuffer;

unsigned int ProgSize = 276;      /* Size of the program in paragraphs */

void
main(int argc, char ** argv)
{
    int i, idx;

    /* Set up all far pointers */
    SetupPointers();

    /* Use a cheap hack to see if the TSR is already loaded
       If it is, exit, doing nothing */
    comm_vector = _dos_getvect(COMM_VECTOR);
    if(((long)comm_vector & 0xFFFFL) ==
                             ((long)NewCommVector & 0xFFFFL)){
        OutputString("Error: TSR appears to already be loaded.\n");
        return;
    }

    /* If everything's set, then chain in the ISR */
    _dos_setvect(COMM_VECTOR, NewCommVector);

    /* Say we are loaded */
    OutputString("TSR is now loaded at 0x63\n");

    /* Terminate, stay resident */
    _dos_keep(0, ProgSize);
}

/* Initializes all the pointers the program will use */

void
SetupPointers()
{
    int idx;

    /* Save segment and offset of MyStackPtr for stack switching */
    MyStackSeg = FP_SEG(MyStackPtr);
    MyStackOff = FP_OFF(MyStackPtr);

    /* Initialize my stack to hex 55 so I can see its footprint
       if I need to do debugging */
    for(idx=0;idx<STACKSIZE; idx++){
        MyStack[idx] = 0x55;
    }

}
void _interrupt _far _cdecl NewCommVector(
        unsigned short es, unsigned short ds, unsigned short di,
        unsigned short si, unsigned short bp, unsigned short sp,
        unsigned short bx, unsigned short dx, unsigned short cx,
        unsigned short ax, unsigned short ip, unsigned short cs,
        unsigned short flags)
{

    AX = ax;
```

```
            BX = bx;
            CX = cx;
            DX = dx;
            ES = es;

            /* Switch to our stack so we won't run on somebody else's */

            _asm{
                                        ; set up a local stack
                cli                     ; stop interrupts
                mov     OldStackSeg,ss  ; save stack segment
                mov     OldStackPtr,sp  ; save stack pointer (offset)
                mov     ax,ds           ; replace with my stack s
                mov     ss,ax           ; ditto
                mov     ax,MyStackOff   ; replace with my stack ptr
                add     ax,STACKSIZE - 2 ; add in my stack size
                mov     sp,ax           ; ditto
                sti                     ; OK for interrupts again
            }

        switch(AX){
            case 0x10:      /* print string found in ES:BX */
                /* Copy data from other application locally */
                FP_SEG(callerBufPtr) = ES;
                FP_OFF(callerBufPtr) = BX;
                _fstrcpy(localBufPtr, callerBufPtr);

                /* print buffer 'CX' number of times */
                for(; CX>0; CX--)
                    OutputString(localBufPtr);
                AX = 1;     /* show success */
                break;

            case 0x30:      /* unload; stop processing interrupts */
                _dos_setvect(COMM_VECTOR, comm_vector);
                AX = 2;     /* show success */
                break;
default:
                OutputString("Unknown command\r\n");
                AX = 0xFFFF;         /* unknown command -1 */
                break;
        }

        /* Switch back to the caller's stack */

        _asm{
            cli                         ; turn off interrupts
            mov     ss,OldStackSeg      ; reset old stack segment
            mov     sp,OldStackPtr      ; reset old stack pointer
            sti                         ; back on again
        }

        ax = AX;                /* use return value from switch() */

}

/* avoids calling DOS to print characters */
void
OutputString(char * str)
```

```
{
int i;

    regs.h.ah = 0x0E;
    regs.x.bx = 0;

    for(i=strlen(str); i>0; i--, str++){
        regs.h.al = *str;
        int86(0x10, &regs, &regs);
    }
}
```

The preceding section is the TSR portion of the application pair. It has a function, NewCommVector(), installed at interrupt 0x63 (0x63 is typically an available vector). After it is installed, it is ready to receive commands. The switch statement is where the incoming commands are processed and actions are taken. I arbitrarily chose 0x10 to be the command "copy data from ES:BX and print that data to the screen CX number of times." I chose 0x30 to be "unhook yourself from 0x63 and stop taking commands." The next piece of code is the other program—the one that sends the commands to 0x63. (Note that it must be compiled in the Large memory model.)

```
#include <stdlib.h>
#include <dos.h>

#define COMM_VECTOR     0x63

union REGS regs;
struct SREGS segregs;

char buffer[80];
char _far * buf = (char _far *)buffer;

main(int argc, char ** argv)
{
    int cnt;

    cnt = (argc == 1 ? 1 : atoi(argv[1]));

    strcpy(buf, "Hello There\r\n");

    regs.x.ax = 0x10;
    regs.x.cx = cnt;
    regs.x.bx = FP_OFF(buf);
    segregs.es = FP_SEG(buf);

    int86x(COMM_VECTOR, &regs, &regs, &segregs);

    printf("ISR returned %d\n", regs.x.ax);

}
```

You might think that this short program looks just like other programs that call int21 or int10 to set or retrieve information from DOS. If you did think that, you would be right. The only real difference is that you use 0x63 rather than 0x21 or 0x10 as the interrupt number. This program simply calls the TSR and requests it to print the string pointed to by es:bx on-screen. Lastly, it prints the return value from the interrupt handler (the TSR).

By printing the string "Hello There" on-screen, I have achieved all the necessary steps for communicating between two applications. What is so cool about this method is that I have only scratched the surface of possibilities for this method. It would be quite easy to write a third application that sends a command such as "give me the last string that you were asked to print." All you have to do is add that command to the switch statement in the TSR and write another tiny program that makes the call. In addition, you could use the system() or spawn() calls shown in FAQ XX.11 to launch the TSR from within the second example program. Because the TSR checks to see whether it is already loaded, you can run the second program as often as you want, and only one copy of the TSR will be installed. You can use this in all your programs that "talk" to the TSR.

Several assumptions were made during the creation of the TSR. One assumption is that there is no important interrupt service routine already handling interrupt 0x63. For example, I first ran the program using interrupt 0x67. It loaded and worked, but I could no longer compile my programs because interrupt 0x67 is also hooked by the DOS extender used by Microsoft to run the C compiler. After I sent command 0x30 (unload yourself), the compiler ran flawlessly again because the DOS extender's interrupt handler was restored by the TSR.

Another assumption was in the residency check. I assumed that there will never be another interrupt handler with the same near address as NewCommVector(). The odds of this occurring are extremely small, but you should know this method is not foolproof. Although I switched stacks in NewCommVector() to avoid running on the calling program's stack, I assume that it is safe to call any function I want. Note that I avoided calling printf because it is a memory hog and it calls DOS (int21) to print the characters. At the time of the interrupt, I do not know whether DOS is available to be called, so I can't assume that I can make DOS calls. Note that I *can* make calls (like the one to OutputString()) that do not use the DOS int21 services to perform the desired task. If you must use a DOS service, you can check a DOS busy flag to see whether DOS is callable at the time. A note about _dos_keep(). It requires you to tell it how many paragraphs (16-byte chunks) of data to keep in memory when exiting. For this program, I give it the size of the entire executable in paragraphs, rounded up a bit (276). As your program grows, you must also grow this value, or strange things will happen.

Cross Reference:

XX.10: How can I run another program after mine?

XX.11: How can I run another program during my program's execution?

XX.15: Some of your examples are not very efficient. Why did you write them so badly?

XX.13: How can I determine which directory my program is running from?

Answer:

Fortunately for us DOS programmers, the DOS program loader provides the full pathname of the executable file when it is run. This full pathname is provided via the argv[0] pointer, which is pointed to by the argv variable in your main() function. Simply strip off the name of your program, and you have the directory from which your application is running. A bit of example code demonstrates this:

```c
#include <stdio.h>
#include <stdlib.h>
#include <string.h>

void main(int argc, char ** argv)
{
    char execDir[80];
    int i, t;

    /* set index into argv[0] to slash character prior to appname */
    for(i = (strlen(argv[0]) - 1);
            ( (argv[0][i] != '/') && (argv[0][i] != '\\') ); --i);

    /* temporarily truncate argv[] */
    t = argv[0][i];
    argv[0][i] = 0;

    /* copy directory path into local buffer */
    strcpy(execDir, argv[0]);

    /* put back original character for sanity's sake */
    argv[0][i] = t;
}
```

Cross Reference:

XX.1: How are command-line parameters obtained?

XX.14: How can I locate my program's important files (databases, configuration files, and such)?

Answer:

DOS provides a pair of functions that enable you to search a directory for a file of any type. You can search for files that are normal, archive, hidden, system, read-only, directories, and even volume labels. Following is a short example of how to search for a particular file in the current directory:

```c
#include <stdio.h>
#include <dos.h>

void main( void )
{
    struct _find_t  myFile;

    _dos_findfirst( "MYFILE.INI", _A_NORMAL, &myFile );

    while(_dos_findnext(&myFile) == 0)
        printf("Found file %s of size %s\n", myFile.name,
                                             myFile.size);
}
```

This example demonstrates how the `_dos_findfirst()` and `_dos_findnext()` functions work. You can go into a directory and use these two functions as shown to find a file of a particular name. These functions also allow the * and ? wildcards. They will return every file in a directory if you use *.* as the filename. To find every file on the hard drive, place the preceding example code in a recursive function that will go into subdirectories to search for the specified file.

Cross Reference:

None.

XX.15: Some of your examples are not very efficient. Why did you write them so badly?

Answer:

Although some of the examples are complete programs because they are tiny, it is not necessary, nor is it practical, to display complete, fully documented programs. They are distracting in that they break up the flow of the book, and they do not help you in your basic goal, which I hope is to attain specific, informative, but brief answers to your questions.

Cross Reference:

XX.12: How can I pass data from one program to another?

XX.14: How can I locate my program's important files (databases, configuration files, and such)?

XX.16: How do you disable Ctrl-Break?

Answer:

There are several ways to disable the Ctrl-Break function. I will discuss two popular techniques for accomplishing this task.

The first technique is to use DOS to disable Ctrl-Break. DOS interrupt 0x21, function 0x33 enables you to get and set the Ctrl-Break check flag, that is, the flag that tells DOS whether to process the Ctrl-Break keys when they are pressed. The following example illustrates this method:

```c
#include <stdio.h>
#include <dos.h>


void main(int argc, char ** argv)
{
    union REGS regs;
    int ctrlBreakFlag;

    /* find out the current state of the flag */
    regs.x.ax = 0x3300;              /* subfunction 0 gets flag state */
    int86(0x21, &regs, &regs);
    ctrlBreakFlag = regs.h.dl;    /* save flag value from DL */

    /* set the state of the flag to disable Ctrl-Break */
```

```
    regs.x.ax = 0x3301;
    regs.h.dl = 0;                  /* disable checking */
    int86(0x21, &regs, &regs);      /* subfunction 1 sets flag state */

}
```

In the preceding example, DOS was called to query the current state of the Ctrl-Break check flag, which was saved into `ctrlBreakFlag`. The return value from the DOS call, found in DL, will be 0 if Ctrl-Break checking is disabled, and 1 if checking is enabled. Next, the code clears DL and calls the DOS Set Ctrl-Break flag function to disable Ctrl-Break checking. This will be true until it is reset again by another call to this function. Not shown in the preceding example is subfunction 02 (AX = 0x3302), which simultaneously gets and sets the state of the Ctrl-Break flag. To perform this task, put 0x3302 into AX, put the desired Ctrl-Break state in DL, do the interrupt, and save the previous state from DL into `ctrlBreakFlag`.

The second major method is to use a *signal*. A signal is a carryover from the old UNIX days (hey, I'm not that old!). The purpose of the signal function is to allow the programmer to be called when certain events occur. One of these events is the user interruption, or Ctrl-Break in DOS-land. The next example demonstrates how to use the Microsoft `signal()` function to trap and act on the Ctrl-Break event (assume that Ctrl-Break checking is enabled):

```c
#include   <stdio.h>
#include   <signal.h>

int exitHandler(void);

int main(int argc, char ** argv)
{
    int   quitFlag = 0;

    /* Trap all Ctrl-Breaks */
    signal(SIGINT, (void (__cdecl *)(int))exitHandler);

    /* Sit in infinite loop until user presses Ctrl-Break */
    while(quitFlag == 0)
        printf("%s\n", (argc > 1) ? argv[1] : "Waiting for Ctrl-Break");
}

/* Ctrl-Break event handler function */

int exitHandler()
{
    char   ch;

    /* Disable Ctrl-Break handling while inside the handler */
    signal(SIGINT, SIG_IGN);

    /* Since it was an "interrupt," clear keyboard input buffer */
    fflush( stdin );

    /* Ask if user really wants to quit program */
    printf("\nCtrl-Break occurred. Do you wish to exit this program?
    ➥(Y or N) ");

    /* Flush output buffer as well */
    fflush(stdout);

    /* Get input from user, print character and newline */
```

```
    ch = getche();
    printf("\n");

    /* If user said yes, leave program */
    if(toupper(ch) == 'Y')
        exit(0);

    /* Reenable Ctrl-Break handling */
    signal(SIGINT, (void (__cdecl *)(int))exitHandler);

    return(0);
}
```

The beauty of this example is that you have a function that gets called every time Ctrl-Break is pressed. This means you have the choice of what you want to do. You can ignore the event, which is essentially "disabling" Ctrl-Break. Or you can act on it in any way you want. Another advantage to this method is that when your program exits, normal operation of Ctrl-Break resumes without manual intervention.

Cross Reference:

XX.17: Can you disable warm boots (Ctrl-Alt-Delete)?

XX.17: Can you disable warm boots (Ctrl-Alt-Delete)?
Answer:

Yes. Disabling warm boots is not particularly easy to figure out, but it is not difficult to actually code. To trap a Ctrl-Alt-Delete key sequence, you must trap the keyboard's *interrupt service routine* (ISR). From a high-level perspective, it works like this: You monitor (trap) all keystrokes, waiting for the dreaded Ctrl-Alt-Delete combination. If the keystroke is not Ctrl-Alt-Delete, you pass the keystroke on to the "computer" (remember, I'm speaking in high-level terms). When you see the Ctrl-Alt-Delete combination, you can swallow it (remove it from the keyboard's character buffer) or change it to some other keystroke (one that your program might be expecting to mean that the user just tried to reboot the machine). When your program is finished, it stops monitoring the keystrokes and resumes normal operation. This is how TSRs work—they chain themselves to the keyboard and other interrupts so that they can know when to pop up and do that voodoo that they do so well.

"So how do you do this?" you might ask. With a C program, of course. The next example shows a simplified form of trapping all Ctrl-Alt-Delete keystrokes and doing "nothing" when that combination is pressed:

```
#include <stdlib.h>
#include <dos.h>

/* function prototypes */
void (_interrupt _far _cdecl KbIntProc)(
        unsigned short es, unsigned short ds, unsigned short di,
        unsigned short si, unsigned short bp, unsigned short sp,
        unsigned short bx, unsigned short dx, unsigned short cx,
        unsigned short ax, unsigned short ip, unsigned short cs,
        unsigned short flags);

void (_interrupt _far _cdecl * OldKbIntProc)(void);
```

```c
unsigned char far * kbFlags;      /* pointer to keyboard flags */

int key_char, junk;               /* miscellaneous variables */

/* keyboard scancode values */
#define ALT         0x8
#define CTRL        0x4
#define KEY_MASK    0x0F

#define DELETE      0x53

void
main(int argc, char ** argv)
{
    int i, idx;

    /* Save old interrupt vectors */
    OldKbIntProc = _dos_getvect(0x9);

    /* Set pointer to keyboard flags */
    FP_SEG(kbFlags) = 0;
    FP_OFF(kbFlags) = 0x417;

    /* Add my ISR to the chain */
    _dos_setvect(0x9, KbIntProc);

    /* Print something while user presses keys... */
    /* Until ESCAPE is pressed, then leave */
    while(getch() != 27){
        printf("Disallowing Ctrl-Alt-Delete...\n");
    }

    /* Remove myself from the chain */
    _dos_setvect(0x9, OldKbIntProc);

}


void _interrupt _far _cdecl KbIntProc(
        unsigned short es, unsigned short ds, unsigned short di,
        unsigned short si, unsigned short bp, unsigned short sp,
        unsigned short bx, unsigned short dx, unsigned short cx,
        unsigned short ax, unsigned short ip, unsigned short cs,
        unsigned short flags)
{

    /* Get keystroke input from keyboard port */
    key_char = inp(0x60);

    if( ((*kbFlags & KEY_MASK) == (CTRL | ALT))
                        && (key_char == DELETE) ){

        /* Reset the keyboard */
        junk = inp(0x61);
        outp(0x61, (junk | 0x80));
        outp(0x61, junk);
        outp(0x60, (key_char | 0x80));
        outp(0x60, 0x9C);
```

```
}

/* Reset the interrupt counter */
outp(0x20, 0x20);


/* Now call the next ISR in line */
(*OldKbIntProc)();

}
```

There are only two sections to this program: the main() body and the keyboard interrupt service routine KbIntProc(). The main() uses _dos_getvect() to retrieve the address of the function (ISR) that is currently servicing keystrokes from the keyboard. Next, it uses _dos_setvect() to replace the keyboard servicing function with your own—KbIntProc(). A while loop that constantly gets keystrokes prints the same message repeatedly until the Escape key (decimal 27) is pressed. When that event occurs, the program calls _dos_setvect() to restore the original keyboard servicing program into place.

However, KbIntProc() is where all the fun takes place. When installed (by the _dos_setvect() call described previously), it gets to look at all keystrokes before anyone else. Therefore, it has the first crack at manipulating or entirely removing the keystroke that came in. When a keystroke arrives, the keyboard is checked to see whether the Ctrl and Alt keys are down. Also, the keystroke itself is checked to see whether it is the Delete key (hex 53). If both cases are true, the Delete key is removed by resetting the keyboard. Regardless of whether the keystroke was ignored, manipulated, or removed by you, the ISR always calls the original keyboard interrupt service routine (OldKbIntProc()). Otherwise, the machine immediately grinds to a halt.

When this example program is executed, it prints "Disallowing Ctrl-Alt-Delete..." each time you press any key. When you do press Ctrl-Alt-Delete, nothing happens, because the keystroke is removed and the computer has no idea you are pressing those three keys. Exiting the program restores the state of the machine to normal operation.

If you think about it, you will realize that this program can trap any keystroke or key combination, including Ctrl-C and Ctrl-Break. You therefore could legitimately consider this method for trapping the Ctrl-Break key sequence. I should point out that this method is quite intrusive—the tiniest of bugs can quickly halt the machine. But don't let that stop you from learning or having fun.

Cross Reference:

XX.16: How do you disable Ctrl-Break?

XX.18: How do you tell whether a character is a letter of the alphabet?

Answer:

All letters of the alphabet (including all keys on a computer keyboard) have an assigned number. Together, these characters and their associated numbers compose the ASCII character set, which is used throughout North America, Europe, and much of the English-speaking world.

The alphabet characters are conveniently grouped into lowercase and uppercase, in numerical order. This arrangement makes it easy to check whether a value is a letter of the alphabet, and also whether the value is uppercase or lowercase. The following example code demonstrates checking a character to see whether it is an alphabet character:

```
int ch;

ch = getche();

if( (ch >= 97) && (ch <= 122) )
    printf("%c is a lowercase letter\n", ch);
else if( (ch >= 65) && (ch <= 90) )
    print("%c is an uppercase letter\n", ch);
else
    printf("%c is not an alphabet letter\n", ch);
```

The values that the variable ch is being checked against are decimal values. Of course, you could always check against the character itself, because the ASCII characters are defined in alphabetical order as well as numerical order, as shown in the following code example:

```
int ch;

ch = getche();

if( (ch >= 'a') && (ch <= 'z') )
    printf("%c is a lowercase letter\n", ch);
else if( (ch >= 'A') && (ch <= 'Z') )
    print("%c is an uppercase letter\n", ch);
else
    printf("%c is not an alphabet letter\n", ch);
```

The method you choose to use in your code is arbitrary. On the other hand, because it is hard to remember every character in the ASCII chart by its decimal equivalent, the latter code example lends itself better to code readability.

Cross Reference:

XX.19: How do you tell whether a character is a number?

XX.19: How do you tell whether a character is a number?
Answer:

As shown in the ASCII chart in FAQ XX.18, character numbers are defined to be in the range of decimal 48 to 57, inclusive (refer to FAQ XX.18 for more information on the ASCII chart). Therefore, to check a character to see whether it is a number, see the following example code:

```
int ch;

ch = getche();

if( (ch >= 48) && (ch <= 57) )
    printf("%c is a number character between 0 and 9\n", ch);
```

```
else
    printf("%c is not a number\n", ch);
```

As in the preceding FAQ, you can check the variable against the number character range itself, as shown here:

```
int ch;

ch = getche();

if( (ch >= '0') && (ch <= '9') )
    printf("%c is a number character between 0 and 9\n", ch);
else
    printf("%c is not a number\n", ch);
```

As before, which method you choose is up to you, but the second code example is easier to understand.

Cross Reference:

XX.18: How do you tell whether a character is a letter of the alphabet?

XX.20: How do you assign a hexadecimal value to a variable?
Answer:

The C language supports binary, octal, decimal, and hexadecimal number systems. In each case, it is necessary to assign some sort of special character to each numbering system to differentiate them. To denote a binary number, use b at the end of the number (1101b). To denote an octal number, use the backslash character (\014). To denote a hexadecimal number, use the 0x character sequence (0x34). Of course, decimal is the default numbering system, and it requires no identifier.

To assign a hexadecimal value to a variable, you would do as shown here:

```
int x;

x = 0x20;     /* put hex 20 (32 in decimal) into x
x = '0x20';   /* put the ASCII character whose value is
                 hex 20 into x */
```

You must know the hexadecimal numbering system in order to know what numbers to assign. Refer to FAQ XX.24 for detailed information on the hexadecimal numbering system.

Cross Reference:

XX.24: What is hexadecimal?

XX.21: How do you assign an octal value to a number?
Answer:

Assigning an octal value to a variable is as easy as assigning a hexadecimal value to a variable, except that you need to know the octal numbering system in order to know which numbers to assign.

```
int x;

x = \033;        /* put octal 33 (decimal 27) into x */
x = '\033';      /* put the ASCII character whose value is
                    octal 33 into x */
```

Refer to FAQ XX.23 for detailed information on the octal numbering system.

Cross Reference:

XX.23: What is octal?

XX.22: What is binary?
Answer:

The binary numbering system is the lowest common denominator in computing. Binary is base 2. Do you remember being taught different numbering systems in elementary or high school? In one of my math classes in grade school, I was taught base 6. You count 1, 2, 3, 4, 5, then 10, 11, 12, 13, 14, 15, then 20, and so on. At least that's the way I was taught. In truth, you should count 0, 1, 2, 3, 4, 5, then 10, 11, 12, 13, 14, 15, and so on. By starting with 0, it becomes slightly easier to see the groupings of six digits—hence the *six* in base 6. Notice that you count from 0 to the number that is one less than the base (you count from 0 to 5 because 6 is the base). After you have counted to 5, you move to two decimal places. If you think about it, our base 10 (decimal) system is similar—you count up to one less than the base (9), and then you go to two digits and resume counting.

In computers, the numbering system is base 2—binary. With base 2, you count 0, 1, then 10, 11, then 100, 101, 110, 111, then 1000, 1001, 1010, 1011, 1100, 1101, 1110, 1111, and so on. Contrast base 2 with base 6; in base 2, you count from 0 to 1 before going to two decimal places.

Of course, the next question is "Why is base 2 used?" The reason is the transistor. The transistor is what makes modern-day computers possible. A transistor is like a light switch. A light switch has two positions (or states), *on* and *off*. So does a transistor. You could also say that off equals 0, and on equals 1. By doing so, you can count from 0 to 1 using a transistor (or a light switch if you want). It doesn't seem as though you can do any serious computing with only two numbers (0 and 1), but we're not finished yet. Suppose that you had a light switch panel that contained four light switches. Although each switch still has only two states, the four switches, when treated in combination, can have 16 unique positions, or 2^4 (four switches, two states each). Therefore, you can count from 0 to 15 with just four switches, as shown in Table XX.22.

Table XX.22. Binary counting.

Switches	Decimal Value	Power
0	0	
1	1	2^0
10	2	2^1
11	3	
100	4	2^2
101	5	
110	6	
111	7	
1000	8	2^3
1001	9	
1010	10	
1011	11	
1100	12	
1101	13	
1110	14	
1111	15	

The table demonstrates three important points: (1) By placing the switches side by side, you can count with them—up to 15 in this case (16 total counts); (2) You can consider each switch as a decimal place, or rather a *binary* place, just as you can with the decimal system; (3) When each switch is considered to represent a binary place, that switch also happens to be a *power* of two (2^0, 2^1, 2^2, 2^3, and so on).

Further, notice that in the table where a power of two is shown, the count had to add another binary place. This is the same as the decimal system, in which each time you increase another decimal place, that new decimal place is a power of 10 ($1 = 10^0$, $10 = 10^1$, $100 = 10^2$, and so on). Knowing this, you can convert binary numbers to decimal with minimal effort. For example, the binary number 10111 would be $(1 \times 2^4) + (0 \times 2^3) + (1 \times 2^2) + (1 \times 2^1) + (1 \times 2^0)$, which equals $(16 + 0 + 4 + 2 + 1)$, or 23 in decimal. A much larger binary number, 10 1110 1011, would be $(1 \times 2^9) + (0 \times 2^8) + (1 \times 2^7) + (1 \times 2^6) + (1 \times 2^5) + (0 \times 2^4) + (1 \times 2^3) + (0 \times 2^2) + (1 \times 2^1) + (1 \times 2^0)$, which equals $(512 + 0 + 128 + 64 + 32 + 0 + 4 + 2 + 1)$, or 743 in decimal.

So what does all this nonsense get us? In the realm of computers, there are *bits*, *nibbles*, and *bytes*. A nibble is four bits, and a byte is eight bits. Do you know what a bit is? It's a transistor. Therefore, a byte is eight transistors, side by side, just like the four switches in Table XX.22. Remember that if you had four switches (or transistors) grouped together, you could count to 2^4, or 16. You could have called that a *nibble* of switches. If a nibble is four transistors grouped together, a byte is eight transistors grouped together. With eight transistors, you can count to 2^8, or 256. Looking at it another way, this means that a byte (with eight transistors) can contain 256 unique numbers (from 0 to 255). Continue this a little further. The Intel 386, 486, and Pentium processors are called 32-bit processors. This means that each operation taken by the Intel chip is 32 bits wide, or 32 transistors wide. Thirty-two transistors, or bits, in parallel is 2^{32}, or 4,294,967,296. That's more than 4 billion unique numbers!

Of course, this description does not explain how a computer uses those numbers to produce the fantastic computing power that occurs, but it does explain why and how the binary numbering system is used by the computer.

Cross Reference:

XX.23: What is octal?

XX.24: What is hexadecimal?

XX.23: What is octal?

Answer:

Octal is base 8. Oh, no, another numbering system? Unfortunately, yes. But there is no need to describe base 8 to the level of detail that was described for base 2. To count in octal, you count 0, 1, 2, 3, 4, 5, 6, 7, 10, 11, 12, 13, and so on. The following two lines count in base 8 and in base 10 side by side for comparison purposes (base 10 is on top):

```
0, 1, 2, 3, 4, 5, 6, 7,  8,  9, 10, 11, 12, 13, 14, 15, 16
0, 1, 2, 3, 4, 5, 6, 7, 10, 11, 12, 13, 14, 15, 16, 17, 20
```

Notice that in base 8 (on bottom), you had to increase to two decimal, I mean octal, places after you reached 7. The second octal place is of course 8^1 (which is equal to 8 in the decimal system). If you were to continue counting to three octal places (100 in octal), that would be 8^2, or 64 in decimal. Therefore, 100 in octal is equal to 64 in decimal.

Octal is not as frequently used these days as it once was. The major reason is that today's computers are 8-, 16-, 32-, or 64-bit processors, and the numbering system that best fits those is binary or hexadecimal (see FAQ XX.24 for more information on the hexadecimal numbering system).

The C language supports octal character sets, which are designated by the backslash character (\). For example, it is not uncommon to see C code that has the following statement in it:

```
if(x == '\007') break;
```

The \007 happens to also be decimal seven; the code is checking for the terminal beep character in this case. Another common number denoted in octal is \033, which is the Escape character (it's usually seen in code as \033). However, today you won't see much of octal—hexadecimal is where it's at.

Cross Reference:

XX.22: What is binary?

XX.24: What is hexadecimal?

XX.24: What is hexadecimal?

Answer:

Hexadecimal is the base 16 numbering system. It is the most commonly used numbering system in computers. In hexadecimal, or hex for short, you count 0, 1, 2, 3, 4, 5, 6, 7, 8, 9, A, B, C, D, E, F, 10, 11, 12, 13, 14, 15, 16, 17, 18, 19, 1A, 1B, 1C, 1D, 1E, 1F, and so on. Don't get too bothered by the letters—they are merely single-digit placeholders that represent (in decimal) 10 through 15. Remember the rule of counting in different bases—count from 0 to the number that is one less than the base. In this case, it is 15. Because our Western numbers do not contain single-digit values representing numbers above 9, we use A, B, C, D, E, and F to represent 10 to 15. After reaching 15, or F, you can move to two decimal, rather hexadecimal, places—in other words, 10. As with octal and binary, compare hex counting to decimal counting (once again, decimal is on top):

```
1, 2, 3, 4, 5, 6, 7, 8, 9, 10, 11, 12, 13, 14, 15, 16, ...
1, 2, 3, 4, 5, 6, 7, 8, 9, A,  B,  C,  D,  E,  F,  10, ...
```

Note that "10", what we historically have called ten, in decimal is equal to "A" in hex. As with the previously discussed numbering systems, when you increase to two or three or more hexadecimal places, you are increasing by a power of 16. 1 is 16^0, 16 is 16^1, 256 is 16^2, 4096 is 16^3, and so on. Therefore, a hex number such as 3F can be converted to decimal by taking $(3 \times 16^1) + (F \times 16^0)$, which equals $(48 + 15)$, or 63 in decimal (remember, F is 15 in decimal). A number such as 13F is $(1 \times 16^2) + (3 \times 16^1) + (F \times 16^0)$, which equals $(256 + 48 + 15)$, or 319 in decimal. In C source code, you will see these numbers shown as 0x3F or 0x13F. The "0x" is used to show the compiler (and the programmer) that the number being referenced should be treated as a hexadecimal number. Otherwise, how could you tell whether the value "16" were decimal or hex (or even octal, for that matter)?

A slight modification can be made to Table XX.22 by adding hex counting to that table (see Table XX.24).

Table XX.24. Binary, decimal, hexadecimal conversion table.

Binary	Decimal Value	Binary Power	Hex	Hex Power
0000	0		0	
0001	1	2^0	1	16^0
0010	2	2^1	2	
0011	3		3	
0100	4	2^2	4	
0101	5		5	
0110	6		6	
0111	7		7	
1000	8	2^3	8	
1001	9		9	
1010	10		A	
1011	11		B	

Binary	Decimal Value	Binary Power	Hex	Hex Power
1100	12		C	
1101	13		D	
1110	14		E	
1111	15		F	
1 0000	16	2^4	10	16^1

I added one more count at the bottom, taking the total to decimal 16. By comparing binary to decimal to hex, you can see that, for example, ten is "1010" in binary, "10" in decimal, and "A" in hex. In the last line, sixteen is "1 0000" or "10000" in binary, "16" in decimal, and "10" in hex. What does all this mean? Because today's 16-, 32-, and 64-bit processors all have bit widths that happen to be multiples of 16, hexadecimal fits very nicely as the numbering system for those types of computers.

Another added quality is that hex is also a multiple of binary. Note that the last line of Table XX.24 shows the binary value broken into two sections (1 0000). Four binary digits (or four bits) can count up to 15 (16 unique numbers when you include zero). Four bits also equals a nibble. By looking at the table, you can see that one digit of hex can also count up to 15 (16 unique numbers because we include zero). Therefore, one hex digit can represent four binary digits. A good example is (decimal) 15 and 16. Fifteen is shown as 1111 in binary, the highest number four binary digits can count. It is also shown as F, the highest number one hex digit can count. After you go to 16, it takes five binary digits (1 0000) and two hex digits (10). The following lines convert the same numbers used earlier (0x3F and 0x13F) to binary:

    3F   111111
    13F   100111111

If you replace the leading spaces with zeros and break the binary digits into groups of four, it might become a little clearer:

    03F   0 0011 1111
    13F   1 0011 1111

You are not required to break binary numbers into groups of four—it's simply easier to count when you know that every four binary digits equal one hex digit. To prove that the numbers are equal, I'll convert the binary representations to decimal (because the hex values were already converted in a previous paragraph). 111111 would be $(1 \times 2^5) + (1 \times 2^4) + (1 \times 2^3) + (1 \times 2^2) + (1 \times 2^1) + (1 \times 2^0)$, which equals $(32 + 16 + 8 + 4 + 2 + 1)$, or 63 in decimal, just as before. The number 1 0011 1111 would be $+ (1 \times 2^8) + (0 \times 2^7) + (0 \times 2^6) + (1 \times 2^5) + (1 \times 2^4) + (1 \times 2^3) + (1 \times 2^2) + (1 \times 2^1) + (1 \times 2^0)$, which equals $(256 + 32 + 16 + 8 + 4 + 2 + 1)$, or 319 in decimal. Hexadecimal and binary fit together like hand and glove.

Cross Reference:

XX.22: What is binary?

XX.23: What is octal?

XX.25: What are escape characters?

Answer:

Escape characters are characters designed to perform a command or task instead of being printed on the computer screen. For example, an escape character could be a character sent to a device that tells the computer screen to draw the next line in red rather than the normal white. The escape character is sent to the device that draws the red line along with the actual characters the device is supposed to draw in red. So how does the device know that the character is an escape character? Typically, the Escape key (decimal 27, octal /033) is sent just before the escape character so that the device knows that an escape character is next to arrive. After the device has the escape character, it acts on the command that the escape character represents, then resumes normal operation—taking characters and printing them on-screen. Because it usually takes two or more characters to pull off the desired command (the Escape key plus the command character itself), this is often referred to as an escape sequence.

I know that this sounds confusing (the Escape key, followed by the escape character), but that is precisely why these are called escape characters. The Escape key is used to inform whoever wants to know that the next character is a command, not an ordinary character. The escape character itself (the one that comes *after* the Escape key) can be any character—it could even be another Escape key. The actual character that represents the desired command to occur is up to the program that is reading these characters and waiting for such commands.

An example of this is the ANSI.SYS device driver. This driver, loaded in your CONFIG.SYS file, intercepted all characters that were printed on-screen and processed these characters for escape sequences. The purpose of ANSI.SYS was to provide a way to print colored, underlined, or blinking text, or to perform higher-level commands such as clear the screen. The advantage to ANSI.SYS was that you didn't have to know what type of monitor or display card you had—ANSI.SYS took care of that for you. All you had to do was embed the escape characters into the appropriate places in the character strings you displayed on-screen, and ANSI.SYS would take care of the rest. For example, if you printed "\033H4Hello there" ANSI.SYS would print "Hello there" on-screen in red. ANSI.SYS would see the Escape key (\033), read the command (which in this case is H4—print remaining characters in red), and print what was left ("Hello there").

Before ANSI.SYS, escape characters were used in the old centralized computing environments (one mainframe computer with a bunch of dumb terminals connected to it). Back in those days, the terminals had no computing power of their own and could not display graphics, and many were monochrome, unable to display color. However, each monitor did have a series of escape characters that the mainframe could send to the monitor to make it do such things as clear the screen, underline, or blink. Programmers would embed the escape characters into their character strings just as you do with ANSI.SYS, and the monitor would perform the desired command.

Today, this type of escape sequence usage has all but died out. On the other hand, many other types of character sequences could be described as escape characters that have been around for just as long, and they are still used heavily today. For example, in the section where I describe how to assign an octal or a hex value to a variable, I am using an escape character (the pair "0x" in the case of hex, and the single \ character in octal). Note that these characters do not actually use the Escape key as the "hey, here comes something special" notifier, but nonetheless they are used to denote something special about what is to immediately follow. In fact, the backslash character (\) is used quite frequently as an escape character. In C, you use \n to tell the computer to "perform a linefeed operation here." You can use \t to perform a tab advance, and so on.

Cross Reference:

CHAPTER

XXI

◆

Windows

Microsoft Windows is a graphical environment that runs atop MS-DOS on IBM-compatible PCs. Since the introduction of version 3.0 in 1990, Windows has boomed as a standard for PC programs.

As a C programmer writing applications under Windows, you will face many challenges because it is unlike any environment you have ever encountered. This chapter will present several questions you might have regarding programming in the Windows environment and will attempt to provide concise answers to these questions. However, you should not rely on this chapter alone for your technical information when working with Windows.

Instead, if you haven't done so already, you should rush out and get a copy of *Programming Windows 3.1* by Charles Petzold. This is the definitive reference and tutorial regarding Windows programming. Petzold starts the book with brief discussions regarding the background of Windows and then takes you step-by-step through the details of Windows programming. If you really want to learn how to write Microsoft Windows programs in C, you need this book. Another good book is *Teach Yourself Windows Programming in 21 Days*, from Sams Publishing.

Another reference that will come in handy when you're learning Windows programming is the *Microsoft Developer Network CD*. This is a CD-ROM that comes packed with samples from all sources. Many of the sample programs can be cut and pasted directly into your compiler.

If you have briefly studied Windows, this chapter should help answer some of your recurring questions.

XXI.1: Can *printf()* be used in a Windows program?

Answer:

The standard C function printf() can be used in a Microsoft Windows program; however, it has no usefulness to the Windows environment, and it does not produce the same result as in a DOS environment. The printf() function directs program output to stdout, the standard output device. Under DOS, the standard output device is the user's screen, and the output of a printf() statement under a DOS program is immediately displayed.

Conversely, Microsoft Windows is an *operating environment* that runs on top of DOS, and it has its own mechanism for displaying program output to the screen. This mechanism comes in the form of what is called a *device context*. A device context is simply a handle to a portion of the screen that is handled by your program. The only way to display output on-screen in the Microsoft Windows environment is for your program to obtain a handle to a device context. This task can be accomplished with several of the Windows SDK (Software Development Kit) functions. For instance, if you were to display the string "Hello from Windows!" in a windows program, you would need the following portion of code:

```
void print_output(void)
{
    ...
    hdcDeviceContext = BeginPaint(hwndWindow, psPaintStruct);

    DrawText(hdcDeviceContext, "Hello from Windows!", -1,
            &rectClientRect, DT_SINGLELINE);
    ...
}
```

Put simply, all output from a Windows program must be funnelled through functions provided by the Windows API. If you were to put the line

```
printf("Hello from Windows!");
```

into the preceding example, the output would simply be ignored by Windows, and your program would appear to print nothing. The output is ignored because printf() outputs to stdout, which is not defined under Windows. Therefore, any C function such as printf() (or any other function that outputs to stdout) under the Windows environment is rendered useless and should ultimately be avoided.

Note, however, that the standard C function sprintf(), which prints formatted output to a string, is permissible under the Windows environment. This is because all output from the sprintf() function goes directly to the string and not to stdout.

Cross Reference:

XXI.9: What is the difference between Windows functions and standard DOS functions?

XXI.2: How do you create a delay timer in a Windows program?

Answer:

You can create a delay timer in a Windows program by using the Windows API function SetTimer(). The SetTimer() function sets up a timer event in Windows to be triggered periodically at an interval that you specify. To create a timer, put the following code in your WinMain() function:

```
SetTimer(hwnd, 1, 1000, NULL);
```

This code sets up a timer in Windows. Now, every 1000 clock ticks (1 second), your program receives a WM_TIMER message. This message can be trapped in your WndProc (message loop) function as shown here:

```
switch (message)
{

        case WM_TIMER :

                /* this code is called in one-second intervals */

                return 0 ;

}
```

You can put whatever you like in the WM_TIMER section of your program. For instance, FAQ XXI.23 shows how you might display the date and time in a window's title bar every second to give your users a constant update on the current day and time. Or perhaps you would like your program to periodically remind you to save your work to a file. Whatever the case, a delay timer under Windows can be very handy.

To remove the timer, call the KillTimer() function. When you call this function, pass it the handle to the window the timer is attached to and your own timer identifier. In the preceding SetTimer() example, the number 1 is used as the timer identifier. To stop this particular timer, you would issue the following function call:

```
KillTimer(hwnd, 1);
```

Cross Reference:

None.

XXI.3: What is a handle?

Answer:

A handle under Windows is much like a handle used to refer to a file in C. It is simply a numeric representation of an object. Under Windows, a handle can refer to a brush (the object that paints the screen), a cursor, an icon, a window, a device context (the object that is used to output to your screen or printer), and many other objects. The handle assigned to an object is used to reference it when calling other Windows functions.

Handle numbers are assigned by Windows, usually when a Windows API function call is made in your program. Typically, variables that represent handles are prefixed with the letter h and a mnemonic representation of the object they refer to. For instance, to create a window, you might make the following Windows API call:

```
hwndSample =
    CreateWindow(szApplicationName,    /* Window class name */
                 "FAQ Sample Program", /* Caption for title bar */
                 WS_OVERLAPPEDWINDOW,  /* Style of window */
                 CW_USEDEFAULT,        /* Initial x position */
                 CW_USEDEFAULT,        /* Initial y position */
                 CW_USEDEFAULT,        /* Initial x size */
                 CW_USEDEFAULT,        /* Initial y size */
                 NULL,        /* Window handle of parent window */
                 NULL,        /* Menu handle for this window */
                 hInstance,   /* Instance handle */
                 NULL) ;      /* Other window parameters */
```

The Windows API function CreateWindow() is used to create an instance of a window on the screen. As you can see from the preceding example, it returns a handle to the window that is created. Whenever this window is referenced from this point on, the handle variable hwndSample is used. Windows keeps track of handle numbers internally, so it can dereference the handle number whenever you make a Windows API function call.

Cross Reference:

None.

XXI.4: How do you interrupt a Windows program?

Answer:

As a user of Microsoft Windows, you might already know that you can terminate a Windows program in many ways. Here are just a few methods:

◆ Choose **File** | **Exit** from the pull-down menu.

◆ Choose **Close** from the control box menu (-) located to the left of the title bar.

◆ Double-click the mouse on the control box.

◆ Press Ctrl-Alt-Delete.

◆ Choose **End** Task from the Windows Task Manager.

◆ Exit Windows.

This list includes the more typical ways users exit their Windows programs. As a Windows developer, how can you provide a way for users to interrupt your program?

If you have used many DOS programs, you might remember the key combination Ctrl-Break. This combination was often used to break out of programs that were hung up or that you could not figure a way to get out of. Often, DOS programs would not trap the Ctrl-Break combination, and the program would be aborted. DOS programs could optionally check for this key combination and prevent users from breaking out of programs by pressing Ctrl-Break.

Under Windows, the Ctrl-Break sequence is translated into the virtual key VK_CANCEL (see FAQ XXI.17 for an explanation of virtual keys). One way you can trap for the Ctrl-Break sequence in your Windows program is to insert the following code into your event (message) loop:

```
...

switch (message)
{

    case WM_KEYDOWN:

        if (wParam == VK_CANCEL)
        {

            /* perform code to cancel or
               interrupt the current process */

        }

}

...
```

In the preceding example program, if the wParam parameter is equal to the virtual key code VK_CANCEL, you know that the user has pressed Ctrl-Break. This way, you can query the user as to whether he wants to cancel the current operation. This feature comes in handy when you are doing long batch processes such as printing reports.

Cross Reference:

None.

XXI.5: What is the GDI and how is it accessed?
Answer:

GDI stands for Graphic Device Interface. The GDI is a set of functions located in a dynamic link library (named GDI.EXE, in your Windows system directory) that are used to support device-independent graphics output on your screen or printer. Through the GDI, your program can be run on any PC that supports Windows. The GDI is implemented at a high level, so your programs are sheltered from the complexities of dealing with different output devices. You simply make GDI calls, and Windows works with your graphics or printer driver to ensure that the output is what you intended.

The gateway to the GDI is through something called a Device Context. A device context handle is simply a numeric representation of a device context (that is, a GDI-supported object). By using the device context handle, you can instruct Windows to manipulate and draw objects on-screen. For instance, the following portion of code is used to obtain a device context handle from Windows and draw a rectangle on-screen:

```
long FAR PASCAL _export WndProc (HWND hwnd, UINT message,
                                 UINT wParam, LONG lParam)
{

    HDC             hdcOutput;
```

```
        PAINTSTRUCT     psPaint;
        HPEN            hpenDraw;

        ...

        switch(message)
        {

            ...

            case WM_PAINT:

                hdcOutput = BeginPaint(hwndMyWindow, &psPaint);

                hpenDraw = CreatePen(PS_SOLID, 3, 0L);

                SelectObject(hdcOutput, hpenDraw);

                Rectangle(hdcOutput, 0, 0, 150, 150);

                TextOut(hdcOutput, 200, 200,
                        "Just the FAQ's, Ma'am...", 24);

            ...

        }

    ...

    }
```

In the preceding program, the BeginPaint() function prepares the current window to be painted with graphics objects. The CreatePen() function creates a pen object of a specified style, width, and color. The pen is used to paint objects on-screen. The SelectObject() function selects the GDI object you want to work with. After these setup functions are called, the Rectangle() function is called to create a rectangle in the window, and the TextOut() function is called to print text to the window.

Cross Reference:

None.

XXI.6: Why is windows.h important?
Answer:

The windows.h header file contains all the definitions and declarations used within the Windows environment. For instance, all system color constants (see FAQ XXI.25) are defined in this header file. Additionally, all Windows-based structures are defined here. Each Windows API function is also declared in this header.

No Windows program can be created without the inclusion of the windows.h header file. This is because all Windows API functions have their declarations in this file, and without this file, your program will probably receive a warning or error message that there is no declaration for the Windows function you are calling. All Windows-based structures, such as HDC and PAINTSTRUCT, are defined in the windows.h header file. You therefore will get compiler errors when you try to use any Windows-based structures in your program without including the windows.h file. Additionally, Windows contains numerous symbolic constants that are used throughout Windows programs. Each of these constants is defined in the windows.h header file.

Thus, the windows.h header file is extremely important, and no Windows program can exist without it. It is roughly equivalent (regarding the rules of inclusion) to the standard stdio.h file that you always include in any DOS-based C program. Not including the file can bring several compiler warnings and errors.

Cross Reference:

XXI.7: What is the Windows SDK?

XXI.8: Do you need Microsoft's Windows SDK to write Windows programs?

XXI.7: What is the Windows SDK?

Answer:

The Windows SDK (Software Development Kit) is a set of resources (software and manuals) that are available to the C programmer to construct Windows programs with. The Windows SDK includes all the Windows API function libraries, thus enabling you to link your C programs with the Windows API functions. It also includes a handful of useful utilities such as the Image Editor (for creating and modifying icons, bitmaps, and so on). It includes the executable file WINSTUB.EXE, which is linked with each Windows program to notify users that the executable is a Windows program. For instance, if you have ever tried running a Windows program from the DOS prompt, you probably have seen one of the following messages (or something similar):

```
This program requires Microsoft Windows.

This program must be run under Microsoft Windows.
```

The WINSTUB.EXE program automatically prints this message every time someone tries to run a Windows executable from a non-Windows environment. Note that the WINSTUB.EXE program is not separated, but rather is embedded into your Windows executable. It is transparent to you and the users of your programs.

The Windows SDK also includes extensive printed documentation of each Windows API function call. This documentation comes in handy when you are writing Windows programs. The *Programmer's Reference Guide* details how to use each Windows API function.

With all the utilities, libraries, and documentation included with the Windows SDK, you might be inclined to think that the Windows SDK is required in order to produce Windows-based programs. See the next FAQ for a response.

Cross Reference:

XXI.6: Why is windows.h important?

XXI.8: Do you need Microsoft's Windows SDK to write Windows programs?

XXI.8: Do you need Microsoft's Windows SDK to write Windows programs?

Answer:

No. You do not need to purchase the Windows SDK from Microsoft to produce Windows programs—instead, most of today's compilers include the Windows libraries, utilities, and online documentation that is replicated in the SDK.

When Windows was first introduced, Microsoft was the only vendor that had a C compiler capable of producing Windows programs. Simply purchasing the Microsoft C compiler did not enable you to create Windows programs, however. Instead, you were required to purchase the Windows SDK from Microsoft to allow your Microsoft C compiler to create your Windows programs.

With the advent of Borland C++ in 1990, the SDK was no longer required. This is because Borland licensed the Windows libraries from Microsoft so that the developers who used Borland C++ did not need to purchase the Windows SDK. Borland also included its own Windows utilities and documentation so that a developer would be fully equipped to write Windows applications. This, in effect, started a revolution. From this point on, compiler vendors typically licensed the Windows API libraries and included them in their compilers. Even Microsoft, pressured by competition, dropped the SDK "requirement" with the introduction of Microsoft C/C++ 7.0.

Today, you can purchase pretty much any compiler that is Windows-capable without having to spend hundreds of extra dollars to buy the Windows SDK. Instead, you will find that your Windows-based compiler comes with all the necessary libraries, utilities, and documentation. In most cases, the Windows API documentation is provided online and not in hard copy to save distribution expenses.

Cross Reference:

XXI.6: Why is windows.h important?
XXI.7: What is the Windows SDK?

XXI.9: What is the difference between Windows functions and standard DOS functions?

Answer:

Unlike most DOS functions, Windows functions are always declared as FAR PASCAL. The FAR keyword signifies that the Windows API function is located in a different code segment than your program. All Windows API function calls are declared as FAR, because all the Windows functions are located in dynamic link libraries and must be loaded at runtime into a different code segment than the one you are running your program in.

The PASCAL keyword signifies that the pascal calling convention is used. The pascal calling convention is slightly more efficient than the default C calling convention. With regular non-pascal function calls, the parameters are pushed on the stack from right to left beginning with the last parameter. The code calling the function is responsible for adjusting the stack pointer after the function returns. With the pascal calling sequence, the parameters are pushed on the stack from left to right, and the called function cleans up the stack. This method results in greater efficiency.

Note that the capitalized words FAR and PASCAL are really uppercase representations of their lowercase keywords, far and pascal. Windows simply #defines them as uppercase to comply with notation rules. Also note that DOS functions can optionally be declared as far pascal—this is perfectly legal. However, under Windows, all API functions are FAR PASCAL. This is not an option, but a mandatory requirement of the Windows environment.

Cross Reference:

XXI.1: Can printf() be used in a Windows program?

XXI.10: What is dynamic linking?
Answer:

All Windows programs communicate with the Windows kernel through a process known as dynamic linking. Normally, with DOS programs, your programs are linked statically. This means that your linker resolves all unresolved external function calls by pulling in the necessary object code modules (.OBJs) to form an executable file (.EXE) that contains the executable code for all functions called within your program.

The Windows environment, on the other hand, provides too many functions to be linked statically into one executable program. A statically linked program under Windows would probably be several megabytes in size and horribly inefficient. Instead, Windows makes extensive use of dynamic link libraries. Dynamic link libraries (.DLLs) are somewhat like the C libraries you create under DOS, with the exception that DLLs can be loaded dynamically at runtime and do not have to be linked in statically at link time. This method has several advantages. First, your Windows executables are typically small, relying on calls to DLLs to provide runtime support. Second, Windows can load and discard DLLs on demand—which allows Windows to fine-tune its environment at runtime. Windows can make room for more programs if it can dynamically discard functions that are not being used currently.

How does dynamic linking work? It is not an easy process by any means. First of all, when you link your Windows program, your compiler creates a table in your executable file that contains the name of the dynamic link library referenced and an ordinal number or name that represents that function in that dynamic link library. At runtime, when you reference a function call that is located in a dynamic link library, that DLL is loaded into memory, and the function's entry point is retrieved from your executable's DLL table. When the DLL is no longer needed, it is unloaded to make room for other programs.

Dynamic link libraries are typically used for large programs with many functions. You can create a DLL with your compiler—see your compiler's documentation for specific instructions on how to carry out this task.

Cross Reference:

None.

XXI.11: What are the differences among *HANDLE*, *HWND*, and *HDC*?

Answer:

Under Windows, the symbolic names HANDLE, HWND, and HDC have different meanings, as presented in Table XXI.11.

Table XXI.11. Symbolic names and their meanings.

Symbolic Name	Meaning
HANDLE	Generic symbolic name for a handle
HWND	Handle to a window
HDC	Handle to a device context

It is a Windows standard to make symbolic names uppercase. As FAQ XXI.3 explains, a handle under Windows is simply a numeric reference to an object. Windows keeps track of all objects through the use of handles. Because window objects and device context objects are used quite often under Windows, they have their own handle identifier names (HWND for window and HDC for device context). Many other standard handle names exist under Windows, such as HBRUSH (handle to a brush), HCURSOR (handle to a cursor), and HICON (handle to an icon).

Cross Reference:

None.

XXI.12: Are Windows programs compatible from one compiler to the next?

Answer:

All compilers available for development of Microsoft Windows programs *must* support the Microsoft Windows SDK (Software Development Kit), and therefore the Windows functions you use in your programs are compatible across compilers. A typical Windows program developed in standard C using only Windows API calls should compile cleanly for all Windows-compatible compilers. The functions provided in the Windows API are compiler-independent and easy to port between compilers such as Borland C++, Microsoft Visual C++, and Symantec C++.

Most of the Windows-based programs on the market today, however, use C++ class libraries to augment and simplify the complexity of using the Windows SDK. Some class libraries, such as Microsoft's Foundation Class Library (MFC) and Borland's ObjectWindows Library (OWL), are *compiler-specific*. This means that you cannot take a Windows program developed with MFC using Microsoft's Visual C++ and port it to

Borland C++, nor can you take a Windows program developed with OWL using Borland C++ and port it to Visual C++. Some class libraries, such as zApp and Zinc, are compiler-independent and are thus safer to use when multiple compilers must be supported.

Note that if you are using C++ for your Windows development, you should pay close attention to your compiler's adherence to ANSI-standard C++, because there are different levels of support for ANSI C++ between compilers. For instance, some compilers have full support for C++ *templates*, whereas others do not. If you were to write a Windows program using templates, you might have a hard time porting your code from one compiler to another.

Typically, though, if you are developing with ANSI-standard C and the Microsoft Windows API, your code should be 100 percent portable to any other Windows-compatible compiler.

Cross Reference:

None.

XXI.13: Will Windows always save and refresh your program's windows?

Answer:

No. Windows itself is not responsible for saving and restoring your program's windows. Instead, Windows sends a message to your program—the WM_PAINT message—that notifies your program that its client area needs repainting.

The client area refers to the portion of the screen that your program is in control of—that is, the portion of the screen occupied by your program's windows. Whenever another program overlays your program with another window, your client area is covered by that application's window. When that application's window is removed, Windows sends a WM_PAINT message to your program. Your Windows program should contain an event loop that looks for and responds to such messages. When your program receives the WM_PAINT message, you are responsible for initiating the appropriate code to repaint your application's window.

The WM_PAINT message is generated by Windows when one of the following events occurs:

◆ A previously hidden portion of your program's client area is uncovered.

◆ Your application's window is moved or resized.

◆ Your application's window is scrolled by the use of a scrollbar.

◆ A pull-down or pop-up menu is invoked.

Additionally, you can force your program to repaint the screen (thus generating a WM_PAINT message to your own program) by calling the Windows API function InvalidateRect().

Your program should contain an event loop that captures incoming messages and responds to them. Here is an example of a typical event loop that responds to a WM_PAINT message:

```
switch(message)
{
```

```
    ...

case WM_PAINT:

    hdcOutput = BeginPaint(hwndMyWindow, &psPaint);

    hpenDraw = CreatePen(PS_SOLID, 3, 0L);

    SelectObject(hdcOutput, hpenDraw);

    Rectangle(hdcOutput, 0, 0, 150, 150);

    TextOut(hdcOutput, 200, 200, "Just the FAQ's, Ma'am...", 24);

    ...

}
```

When the preceding program is run, a WM_PAINT message is generated by Windows on program start-up and any time the client area is moved, resized, or scrolled.

It should be noted that actions such as cursor movement and drag-and-drop operations do not require a WM_PAINT message to be generated. In these cases, Windows saves and restores the portion of the screen that has been covered with the cursor or icon.

Cross Reference:

XXI.14: How do you determine a Windows program's client area size?

XXI.14: How do you determine a Windows program's client area size?

Answer:

Your program's client area size is defined as the height and width of your program's window that is displayed on-screen. The client area size can be determined by processing the WM_SIZE message in your program's event loop. The WM_SIZE message contains three parameters, two of which can be used to determine your client area size. Your program's event loop (window procedure) is passed a parameter named lParam that can be evaluated when a WM_SIZE message is received. The low-order word of the lParam variable contains your program's client area width, and the high-order word of the lParam variable contains your program's client area height. Here is an example of determining client area size:

```
switch (message)
{

    ...

case WM_SIZE:

    nProgramWidth = LOWORD(lParam);
```

```
        nProgramHeight = HIWORD(lParam);

    ...

}
```

LOWORD and HIWORD are actually macros defined in windows.h that extract the low-order and high-order words, respectively.

Cross Reference:

XXI.20: Can a mouse click be captured in an area outside your program's client area?

XXI.15: What are OEM key codes?
Answer:

The OEM (Original Equipment Manufacturer) key codes refer to the original 255 characters preprogrammed into all IBM-compatible ROMs—everything from hex 00 to hex FF. These characters not only represent the uppercase and lowercase characters of the alphabet, but also contain several nonprintable characters (tab, bell, carriage return, linefeed, and such) and several "graphical" characters used for line drawing. This character set also contains some symbols for representing fractions, pi, infinity, and others. Many DOS-based programs use this character set to print graphics on-screen, because these 255 characters are the only ones available for DOS to use.

Cross Reference:

XXI.16: Should a Windows program care about the OEM key codes?

XXI.17: What are virtual key codes?

XXI.18: What is a dead key?

XXI.16: Should a Windows program care about the OEM key codes?
Answer:

No. As FAQ XXI.15 explains, OEM key codes refer to the original 255 characters of the IBM character set that comes preprogrammed into every 80x86 ROM.

Many of these characters were used in older DOS-based programs to represent characters that normally would have required graphics. Because Windows is a graphical environment that contains hundreds of functions for creating graphical objects, these characters are no longer needed. Instead of writing Windows functions to use the OEM character set to draw a rectangle, for instance, you can simply call the Windows API function Rectangle(). Thus, the OEM character codes are not needed in Windows, and you can effectively ignore them when writing your Windows programs.

Note that although you can ignore these key codes, Windows cannot. For instance, you probably already know that many of your DOS programs can be run in a window under Windows. When this is the case, Windows must "interpret" the DOS program's use of the OEM character set and map it accordingly on-screen.

Cross Reference:

XXI.15: What are OEM key codes?

XXI.17: What are virtual key codes?

XXI.18: What is a dead key?

XXI.17: What are virtual key codes?

Answer:

When your program receives a `WM_KEYUP`, `WM_KEYDOWN`, `WM_SYSKEYUP`, or `WM_SYSKEYDOWN` message, the `wParam` parameter will contain the keystroke's virtual key code. This virtual key code can be used to reference what key on the keyboard was pressed. The key code does not map to any physical character set (such as the OEM key codes—see FAQ XXI.16), but rather it originates from a "virtual" table (set forth in windows.h) of key codes. Table XXI.17 lists some available virtual key codes.

Table XXI.17. Some of the virtual key codes available in Windows programs.

Hex	Symbolic Name	Key
01	VK_LBUTTON	N/A
02	VK_RBUTTON	N/A
03	VK_CANCEL	Ctrl-Break
04	VK_MBUTTON	N/A
08	VK_BACK	Backspace
09	VK_TAB	Tab
0C	VK_CLEAR	Numeric keypad 5 (Num Lock off)
0D	VK_RETURN	Enter
10	VK_SHIFT	Shift
11	VK_CONTROL	Ctrl
12	VK_MENU	Alt
13	VK_PAUSE	Pause
14	VK_CAPITAL	Caps Lock
1B	VK_ESCAPE	Esc
20	VK_SPACE	Spacebar
21	VK_PRIOR	Page Up
22	VK_NEXT	Page Down

Hex	Symbolic Name	Key
23	VK_END	End
24	VK_HOME	Home
25	VK_LEFT	Left arrow
26	VK_UP	Up arrow
27	VK_RIGHT	Right arrow
28	VK_DOWN	Down arrow
29	VK_SELECT	N/A
2A	VK_PRINT	N/A
2B	VK_EXECUTE	N/A
2C	VK_SNAPSHOT	Print Screen
2D	VK_INSERT	Insert
2E	VK_DELETE	Delete
2F	VK_HELP	N/A
30–39		0 through 9 on main keyboard
41–5A		A through Z
60	VK_NUMPAD0	Numeric keypad 0
61	VK_NUMPAD1	Numeric keypad 1
62	VK_NUMPAD2	Numeric keypad 2
63	VK_NUMPAD3	Numeric keypad 3
64	VK_NUMPAD4	Numeric keypad 4
65	VK_NUMPAD5	Numeric keypad 5
66	VK_NUMPAD6	Numeric keypad 6
67	VK_NUMPAD7	Numeric keypad 7
68	VK_NUMPAD8	Numeric keypad 8
69	VK_NUMPAD9	Numeric keypad 9
6A	VK_MULTIPLY	Numeric keypad *
6B	VK_ADD	Numeric keypad +
6C	VK_SEPARATOR	N/A
6D	VK_SUBTRACT	Numeric keypad –
6E	VK_DECIMAL	Numeric keypad
6F	VK_DIVIDE	Numeric keypad /
70	VK_F1	F1
71	VK_F2	F2
72	VK_F3	F3
73	VK_F4	F4

continues

Table XXI.17. continued

Hex	Symbolic Name	Key
74	VK_F5	F5
75	VK_F6	F6
76	VK_F7	F7
77	VK_F8	F8
78	VK_F9	F9
79	VK_F10	F10
7A	VK_F11	F11
7B	VK_F12	F12
7C	VK_F13	N/A
7D	VK_F14	N/A
7E	VK_F15	N/A
7F	VK_F16	N/A
90	VK_NUMLOCK	Num Lock
91	VK_SCROLL	Scroll Lock

Many more virtual keys are available, but most of them depend on which international settings you have set up for your Windows configuration.

Note that besides being able to obtain the keystroke from Windows, you can also obtain the state of the Shift, Ctrl (Control), and Alt keys. You can do so by using the function GetKeyState(). For instance, the function call

```
GetKeyState(VK_SHIFT);
```

returns a negative value if the Shift key is down (pressed). If the Shift key is not pressed, the return value is positive.

Cross Reference:

XXI.15: What are OEM key codes?

XXI.16: Should a Windows program care about the OEM key codes?

XXI.18: What is a dead key?

XXI.18: What is a dead key?

Answer:

A dead key is a keystroke that is not recognizable by Windows. On some international keyboards, it is impossible to translate certain characters into keystrokes. In this case, Windows sends either a WM_DEADCHAR or a WM_SYSDEADCHAR message to your program, indicating that Windows cannot interpret the character code of the incoming keystroke.

You can, however, manually reference the actual ASCII character code of the incoming character. When your program receives one of these two messages, you can inspect the value of the wParam parameter and determine which key was pressed. You therefore can manually customize your programs for internationalization by determining ahead of time which foreign characters your program needs to handle.

Cross Reference:

XXI.15: What are OEM key codes?

XXI.16: Should a Windows program care about the OEM key codes?

XXI.17: What are virtual key codes?

XXI.19: What is the difference between the caret and the cursor?
Answer:

In Windows, the cursor represents the mouse position on the screen. The caret represents the current editing position. If you look at the Windows program Notepad, for example, you'll notice that as you move the mouse around, you see the familiar arrow move. This arrow is the cursor; it represents the current position of the mouse.

If you type some text into the Notepad program, you'll notice that the next available edit position in the Notepad window has a blinking vertical bar in it. This is the caret; it represents the current editing position. You can control the caret's blink rate by invoking the Windows control panel.

In Windows programs, five functions are available to control the caret. These functions are listed in Table XXI.19.

Table XXI.19. Functions to control the caret.

Function Name	Purpose
CreateCaret	Creates a caret
SetCaretPos	Sets the position of the caret
ShowCaret	Shows the caret
HideCaret	Hides the caret
DestroyCaret	Destroys the caret

If you're a die-hard DOS programmer moving into Windows programming, you might think it odd that the "cursor" position actually represents the mouse position and not the editing position. This is just one little caveat you must get used to when joining the ranks of Windows programmers who now have to refer to the "cursor" position as the "caret" position.

Cross Reference:

None.

XXI.20: Can a mouse click be captured in an area outside your program's client area?

Answer:

In Windows, the client area of your program includes all the space within the border of your window, with the exception of the following areas:

◆ The title bar
◆ The scrollbars
◆ The pull-down menu

Can a mouse click be captured within any of these three regions? Yes. When the mouse is clicked in these regions, Windows sends a "nonclient area" message to your program. This way, you can trap for these events when they occur.

Trapping for these events is unusual, however. This is because Windows has prebuilt functionality to handle mouse clicks in these regions. For instance, if you double-click on a window's title bar, the window resizes itself (maximized or restored). If you click on a scrollbar, the window scrolls. If you click on a pull-down menu, the menu is shown on-screen. None of these events requires any code to be written—they are automatically handled by Windows.

Most of the time, you will want to pass these messages to what is called the `DefWindowProc()` function. The `DefWindowProc()` calls the default window procedure (that is, it implements the window's built-in functionality). You very rarely would need to trap for a nonclient mouse hit. Nonetheless, Table XXI.20 presents some of the messages you can trap for.

Table XXI.20. Nonclient area mouse events.

Nonclient Message	Meaning
WM_NCLBUTTONDOWN	Nonclient left mouse button down
WM_NCMBUTTONDOWN	Nonclient middle mouse button down
WM_NCRBUTTONDOWN	Nonclient right mouse button down
WM_NCLBUTTONUP	Nonclient left mouse button up
WM_NCMBUTTONUP	Nonclient middle mouse button up
WM_NCRBUTTONUP	Nonclient right mouse button up
WM_NCLBUTTONDBLCLK	Nonclient left mouse button double-click
WM_NCMBUTTONDBLCLK	Nonclient middle mouse button double-click
WM_NCRBUTTONDBLCLK	Nonclient right mouse button double-click

Cross Reference:

XXI.14: How do you determine a Windows program's client area size?

XXI.21: How do you create an animated bitmap?
Answer:

Sometimes you will run across a Windows program that entertains you with an animated bitmap. How is this task accomplished? One method is to set up a timer event that switches the bitmap every second or two, thus making the bitmap "appear" to be animated. In fact, it is not animated, but rather several versions of the same bitmap are switched fast enough to make it appear as though the bitmap is moving.

The first step is to insert the following code into your WinMain() function:

```
SetTimer(hwnd, 1, 1000, NULL);
```

This code sets up a timer event that will be invoked every 1000 clock ticks (1 second). In your event (message) loop, you can then trap the timer event, as shown here:

```
switch(message)
{

    case WM_TIMER:

        /* trapped timer event; perform something here */

}
```

Now, when the WM_CREATE message comes through, you can load the original bitmap:

```
case WM_CREATE:

    hBitmap = LoadBitmap(hInstance, BMP_ButterflyWingsDown);
```

In this case, BMP_ButterflyWingsDown is a bitmap resource bound to the executable through the use of a resource editor. Every time a WM_TIMER event is triggered, the following code is performed:

```
case WM_TIMER:

    if (bWingsUp)
        hBitmap = LoadBitmap(hInstance, BMP_ButterflyWingsDown);
    else
        hBitmap = LoadBitmap(hInstance, BMP_ButterflyWingsUp);
```

This way, by using the boolean flag bWingsUp, you can determine whether the butterfly bitmap's wings are up or down. If they are up, you display the bitmap with the wings down. If they are down, you display the bitmap with the wings up. This technique gives the illusion that the butterfly is flying.

Cross Reference:

None.

XXI.22: How do you get the date and time in a Windows program?

Answer:

To get the date and time in a Windows program, you should call the standard C library functions `time()` and `localtime()` or some derivative (`asctime()`, `ctime()`, `_ftime()`, `gmttime()`). These functions are compatible with both DOS and Windows. You should never attempt to call a DOS-only or a ROM BIOS function directly. You should always use either Windows API function calls or standard C library routines. Here is an example of code that can be used to print the current date and time in a Windows program:

```
char*        szAmPm = "PM";
char         szCurrTime[128];
char         szCurrDate[128];
struct tm*   tmToday;
time_t       lTime;

time(&lTime);

tmToday = localtime(lTime);

wsprintf(szCurrDate, "Current Date: %02d/%02d/%02d",
                     tmToday->tm_month, tmToday->tm_mday,
                     tmToday->tm_year);

if (tmToday->tm_hour < 12 )
    strcpy(szAmPm, "AM" );

if (tmToday->tm_hour > 12 )
    tmToday->tm_hour -= 12;

wsprintf(szCurrTime, "Current Time: %02d:%02d:%02d %s",
                     tmToday->tm_hour, tmToday->tm_min,
                     tmToday->tm_sec, szAmPm);

TextOut(50, 50, szCurrDate, strlen(szCurrDate));

TextOut(200, 50, szCurrTime, strlen(szCurrTime));

}
```

The `time()` and `localtime()` functions are used to get the current local time (according to the Windows timer, which gets its time from MS-DOS). The `time()` function returns a `time_t` variable, and the `localtime()` function returns a tm structure. The tm structure can easily be used to put the current date and time into a readable format. After this task is completed, the `wsprintf()` function is used to format the date and time into two strings, szCurrDate and szCurrTime, which are then printed in the current window via the `TextOut()` Windows API function call.

Cross Reference:

None.

XXI.23: How do you update the title bar in a Windows program?

Answer:

The title bar (or caption bar, as it is often called) can be updated in a Windows program by using the Windows API function `SetWindowText()`. The `SetWindowText()` function takes two parameters. The first parameter is the handle to the window, and the second parameter is the new title you want to display on the window.

One reason you might want to take this action is to provide your users with the current date and time on the title bar. This task can be accomplished with the following code:

```
char*       szAmPm = "PM";
char        szNewCaption[200];
struct tm*  tmToday;
time_t      lTime;

time(&lTime);

tmToday = localtime(lTime);

wsprintf(szNewCaption,
        "My Application - %02d/%02d/%02d   %02d:%02d:%02d %s",
        tmToday->tm_month, tmToday->tm_mday,  tmToday->tm_year,
        tmToday->tm_hour, tmToday->tm_min,
        tmToday->tm_sec, szAmPm);

SetWindowText(hwnd, szNewCaption);
```

Of course, you probably will want to set up this code in some sort of timer event loop so that the title is updated every second (or minute).

Cross Reference:

None.

XXI.24: How do you access the system colors in a Windows program?

Answer:

You can obtain the system colors by calling the Windows API function `GetSysColor()`. The `GetSysColor()` function takes one parameter, which signifies which color element you want to obtain. The color elements are represented by color constants defined in the windows.h header file. The Windows system color constants are listed in the following FAQ (XXI.25).

For instance, to obtain the color for the window's active border, you might make the following function call:

```
rgbColor = GetSysColor(COLOR_ACTIVEBORDER);
```

The GetSysColor() function returns an RGB value. The RGB value represents the intensity of the colors red, green, and blue that are present in the returned color. An RGB value of 0 signifies black, and an RGB value of 255 signifies white. You can extract the individual red, green, and blue values from the RGB value by calling the GetRValue(), GetGValue(), and GetBValue() Windows API functions.

The Windows API function SetSysColors() can be used to set system colors. Here is an example of some code that sets the color of the active border to red:

```
int         aiColorElements[1];
DWORD       argbColor[1];

aiColorElements[0] = COLOR_ACTIVEBORDER;

argbColor[0] = RGB(0xFF, 0x00, 0x00);

SetSysColors(1, aiColorElements, argbColor);
```

The SetSysColors() function takes three arguments. The first argument is the number of elements to set color for, the second is an array of integers holding the system color constants to set color for, and the third is an array of RGB values that correspond to the colors you want to invoke for the elements represented by the second argument.

Cross Reference:

XXI.25: What are the system color constants?

XXI.25: What are the system color constants?
Answer:

The system color constants are used by Windows to control the colors of various objects included in the Windows environment. Table XXI.25 lists the system color constants (as defined in windows.h).

Table XXI.25. The system color constants.

Color Constant	Target Object
COLOR_SCROLLBAR	Scrollbar
COLOR_BACKGROUND	Windows desktop
COLOR_ACTIVECAPTION	Active title
COLOR_INACTIVECAPTION	Inactive title
COLOR_MENU	Menu bar
COLOR_WINDOW	Window
COLOR_WINDOWFRAME	Window frame
COLOR_MENUTEXT	Menu text
COLOR_WINDOWTEXT	Window text

Color Constant	Target Object
COLOR_CAPTIONTEXT	Title text
COLOR_ACTIVEBORDER	Active border
COLOR_INACTIVEBORDER	Inactive border
COLOR_APPWORKSPACE	Application workspace
COLOR_HIGHLIGHT	Highlight
COLOR_HIGHLIGHTTEXT	Highlight text
COLOR_BTNFACE	Button face
COLOR_BTNSHADOW	Button shadow
COLOR_GRAYTEXT	Grayed-out text
COLOR_BTNTEXT	Button text

You can change the system colors from within your Windows programs by calling the GetSysColor() and SetSysColor() functions. You can also set these colors by altering the [colors] section of your WIN.INI (Windows initialization) file, or you can interactively set them by using the Windows control panel.

Cross Reference:

XXI.24: How do you access the system colors in a Windows program?

XXI.26: How do you create your own buttons or controls?
Answer:

Controls such as buttons are typically created with a resource editor. With a resource editor, you can interactively design your windows and place pushbuttons, check boxes, radio buttons, and other controls in your window. You can then access them from within your Windows program by referring to each resource's unique resource id (which you define).

This is not the only way, however, to create controls such as buttons. Buttons and other controls are called "child window controls." Each child window control has the capability to trap incoming messages (such as the WM_COMMAND message) and pass them on to the parent window control. A child window control such as a pushbutton can be created by using the Windows API function CreateWindow(). It might seem odd to call the function CreateWindow() to create a pushbutton, but a control is, in effect, its own "virtual" window, and thus it needs to have its own handle. Here is some sample code that shows how this task is performed:

```
...

switch (message)
{

  ...

  case WM_CREATE:
```

```
                 hwndCloseButton =
                   CreateWindow("button",    /* Windows registered class name */
                                "Close",     /* Window text (title) */
                                WS_CHILD | WS_VISIBLE | PUSHBUTTON,    /* Style */
                                50,           /* Horizontal position */
                                50,           /* Vertical position */
                                100,          /* Width */
                                100,          /* Height */
                                hwndParent, /* Handle of parent window */
                                0,            /* Child-window identifier */
                                ((LPCREATESTRUCT) lParam)->hInstance,
                                NULL);  /* Window creation options */

       ...

     }
```

Cross Reference:

None.

XXI.27: What is a static child window?

Answer:

A static child window is a window control that does not accept mouse or keyboard input. Typical examples of static child windows are rectangles, frames, a window's background or border, and static text (labels) that appear on-screen. Typically, it makes no sense to process mouse or keyboard events when dealing with static controls.

A static control can be created by specifying the "static" class in the Windows API CreateWindow() function call. Here is an example of a field label that is created by invoking the CreateWindow() function:

```
hwndNameLabel = CreateWindow ("static", "Customer Name:",
                              WS_CHILD | WS_VISIBLE | SS_LEFT,
                              0, 0, 0, 0,
                              hwnd,
                              50,
                              hInstance, NULL) ;
```

This example creates a field label in the window with the caption "Customer Name:." This field label would probably coincide with a window of the edit class that would accept the user's input of the customer's name.

Cross Reference:

XXI.28: What is window subclassing?

XXI.28: What is window subclassing?

Answer:

Windows subclassing refers to a technique whereby you can "tap" into a built-in Windows function and add your own functionality without disturbing or abandoning the original Windows functionality. For example, the Windows procedure for a check box control is coded deep within the system internals of Windows, and the source code is not readily available. However, through the use of two Windows API functions, you can tap into this code and build your own functionality into it.

The two Windows API functions that accomplish this task are called `GetWindowLong()` and `SetWindowLong()`. The `GetWindowLong()` function returns the address of the Windows procedure you want to subclass. The `SetWindowLong()` function can be used to override the default Windows procedure and point to your own custom-made version. Note that you do not have to replicate all functionality by doing this—when you need to reference the original procedure's functionality, you can pass the messages through to it.

You can save the old procedure's address by including the following code in your program:

```
lpfnOldCheckBoxProc = (FARPROC) GetWindowLong(hwndCheckBox, GWL_WNDPROC);
```

Your new custom check box procedure can replace the old procedure by including the following code in your program:

```
SetWindowLong(hwndCheckBox, GWL_WNDPROC, (LONG) lpfnCustomCheckBoxProc);
```

In this example, the `GetWindowLong()` function is used to save the old procedure's address. The `GWL_WNDPROC` identifier tells the `GetWindowLong()` function to return a pointer to the check box's procedure. After this is saved, a new procedure (named `lpfnCustomCheckBoxProc`) is invoked by a call to the `SetWindowLong()` function. Now, whenever Windows would normally call `hwndCheckBox`'s default procedure, your custom check box procedure will be called instead.

In your custom check box procedure, you can always pass messages through to the original procedure. This is done by using the Windows API function `CallWindowProc()` as shown here:

```
CallWindowProc(lpfnOldCheckBoxProc, hwnd, message, wParam, lParam);
```

This way, you do not have to replicate all functionality that was in the original procedure. Instead, you can trap for only the messages you want to customize. For instance, if you have ever seen a variation of a check box (such as Borland's custom check box), you know that it does not look like the default check box you would normally see in Windows programs. This variation is accomplished through Windows subclassing. The `WM_PAINT` message is simply subclassed out, and a new customized version of the check box rather than the original version is painted.

Cross Reference:

XXI.27: What is a static child window?

XXI.29: What is the edit class?

Answer:

Windows contains many classes of windows that can be created by using the `CreateWindow()` function. One of these classes is the edit class, which creates a rectangular region in the window that is editable. When this editable region receives the focus, you can edit the text in any way you want—select it; cut, copy, or paste it to the clipboard; or delete it.

A window created with the edit class is called an edit control. Edit controls can be single-line or multiline. Here is an example of a portion of code that creates a multiline scrollable edit control in a window:

```
...

switch (message)
{

   ...

   case WM_CREATE:

       hwndEdit = CreateWindow ("edit",
                                NULL,
                                WS_CHILD ¦ WS_VISIBLE ¦
                                WS_HSCROLL ¦ WS_VSCROLL ¦
                                WS_BORDER ¦ ES_LEFT ¦ ES_MULTILINE ¦
                                ES_AUTOHSCROLL ¦ ES_AUTOVSCROLL,
                                0, 0, 0, 0,
                                hwnd, 1,
                                ((LPCREATESTRUCT) lParam) -> hInstance,
                                NULL) ;

   ...

}
```

The edit class is very powerful. It has a lot of built-in functionality that does not need to be programmed into it. For instance, all the clipboard commands (cut, copy, paste, delete) are automatically active when focus is switched to an edit control. You do not need to write any code for this functionality to be included.

As you can see from the preceding example, an edit control has many options that can make it totally customizable to your needs. An edit control also carries with it several associated events (messages) that you can trap for. Table XXI.29 lists these events.

Table XXI.29. Events associated with an edit control.

Message	Meaning
EN_SETFOCUS	Received input focus
EN_KILLFOCUS	Lost input focus
EN_CHANGE	Contents are about to change
EN_UPDATE	Contents have changed
EN_HSCROLL	Horizontal scrollbar clicked

Message	Meaning
EN_VSCROLL	Vertical scrollbar clicked
EN_ERRSPACE	No space left in buffer
EN_MAXTEXT	No space left while in insert mode

Cross Reference:

XXI.30: What is the listbox class?

XXI.30: What is the listbox class?
Answer:

One of the predefined classes available when you are calling the CreateWindow() function is the listbox class. This class provides a vertically scrollable list of items enclosed in a rectangular region. This list of items can be modified—you can add items to and delete items from the list at runtime. A listbox control can be a single-selection listbox (only one item at a time can be selected) or a multiselection listbox (more than one item at a time can be selected).

As with the edit class, the listbox class comes with a tremendous amount of predefined functionality. You do not need to program in many of the listbox class's functions. For instance, in a single-selection listbox, you can move the arrow keys up and down, and the selection changes with the movement. If the listbox is scrollable, the list automatically scrolls. The Page Up and Page Down keys scroll the listbox region one page up or down. You can even perform an "auto-search" within the listbox: when you press a letter on the keyboard, the listbox "jumps" to the first item that begins with that letter. When you press the spacebar, the current item is selected. The multiselectable listbox control has all of this functionality and more. Plus, each of these listbox styles is automatically mouse-enabled.

You can create a new listbox control in a window by using the CreateWindow() function like this:

```
...

switch (message)
{

  ...

  case WM_CREATE :

       hwndList = CreateWindow ("listbox", NULL,
                               WS_CHILD ¦ WS_VISIBLE ¦ LBS_STANDARD,
                               100,
                               200 + GetSystemMetrics (SM_CXVSCROLL),
                               200,
                               hwnd, 1,
                               GetWindowWord (hwnd, GWW_HINSTANCE),
                               NULL) ;

  ...
```

```
}
...
```

Like the edit class, the listbox class comes with many associated attributes and events (messages). Table XXI.30 presents some messages available for the listbox class.

Table XXI.30. Some of the available messages for the listbox class.

Message	Meaning
LBN_SETFOCUS	The listbox received input focus
LBN_KILLFOCUS	The listbox lost input focus
LBN_SELCHANGE	The current selection has changed
LBN_DBLCLK	The user double-clicked the mouse on a selection
LBN_SELCANCEL	The user deselected an item
LBN_ERRSPACE	The listbox control has run out of space

Cross Reference:

XXI.29: What is the edit class?

XXI.31: How is memory organized in Windows?
Answer:

Windows organizes its memory into two "heaps": the local heap and the global heap. The local heap is much like the local heap of a DOS program. It contains room for static data, some stack space, and any free memory up to 64K. You can access memory in this area in the same manner as you would access a DOS program's memory (by using the `malloc()` or `calloc()` functions).

The global heap, however, is totally different from anything available under DOS. The global heap is controlled by Windows, and you cannot use standard C function calls to allocate memory from the global heap. Instead, you must use Windows API function calls to allocate global memory. Global memory segments can be classified as either fixed or movable. A fixed segment in the global heap cannot be moved in memory. Its address remains the same throughout the life of the program. On the other hand, a movable segment in the global heap can be "moved" to another location in memory to make more contiguous room for global allocation. Windows is smart enough to move memory when it needs to allocate more for Windows programs. This action is roughly equivalent to an "automatic" `realloc()` function call.

Generally, you should make every effort to ensure that the code and data segments of your Windows programs are marked as movable. You should do so because movable segments can be handled at runtime by Windows. Fixed segments, on the other hand, always reside in memory, and Windows can never reclaim this space. Heavy use of fixed segments might make Windows perform acrobatic "disk thrashing" with your hard drive, because Windows attempts to shuffle things in memory to make more room.

Using movable segments allows Windows to have more control at runtime, and your programs will generally be better liked by your users. Movable segments can also be marked as discardable. This means that when Windows needs additional memory space, it can free up the area occupied by the segment. Windows uses a "least recently used" (LRU) algorithm to determine which segments to discard when attempting to free up memory. Code, data, and resources can be discarded and later read back in from your program's .EXE file.

Cross Reference:

XXI.32: How is memory allocated in a Windows program?

XXI.32: How is memory allocated in a Windows program?
Answer:

FAQ XXI.31 explained how memory was organized under Windows. For allocating memory from the local heap, typical C functions such as malloc() or calloc() can be used. However, to allocate memory from the global heap, you must use one of the Windows API functions, such as GlobalAlloc(). The GlobalAlloc() function allocates memory from the global heap and marks it as fixed, movable, or discardable (see FAQ XXI.31 for an explanation of these three terms).

Here is an example of a Windows program code snippet that allocates 32K of global memory:

```
GLOBALHANDLE        hGlobalBlock;
LPSTR               lpGlobalBlock;

hGlobalBlock = GlobalAlloc(GMEM_MOVEABLE | GMEM_ZEROINIT, 0x8000L);

... /* various program statements */

lpGlobalBlock = GlobalLock(hGlobalBlock);

... /* various program statements */

GlobalUnlock(hGlobalBlock);

... /* various program statements */

GlobalFree(hGlobalBlock);
```

Take a look at how the preceding portion of code works. First, two variables are declared. The first variable is hGlobalBlock, which is of type GLOBALHANDLE. This is simply defined as a 16-bit integer to hold the handle of the block returned by Windows. Notice that, unlike DOS, Windows returns a handle to an allocated portion of memory. It does so because portions of memory can be moved or discarded, thus invalidating pointer usage. If you use pointers in your program, you can't be sure that Windows has not moved the portion of memory you were working with—that is, unless you call the GlobalLock() function (which is explained in the next paragraph).

The first function call, GlobalAlloc(), is used to allocate a 32K portion of global heap memory that is flagged as movable and is automatically zero-initialized. After calling this function, hGlobalBlock will contain a handle to this portion of memory. Using this handle, you can reference the memory as much as you want in your program. It makes no difference to you if the memory is moved by Windows—the handle will remain the same. However, if you need to work with a pointer to this memory rather than a handle (for accessing memory directly), you need to call the `GlobalLock()` function. This function is used to "lock" (that is, mark as nonmovable) the portion of memory that you have allocated. When memory is locked like this, Windows will not move the memory, and thus the pointer returned from the `GlobalLock()` function will remain valid until you explicitly unlock the memory by using the `GlobalUnlock()` function.

When you are finished working with the allocated global heap memory, you can free it up and return its space to Windows by calling the `GlobalFree()` Windows API function.

Cross Reference:

XXI.31: How is memory organized in Windows?

XXI.33: What is the difference between modal and modeless dialog boxes?

Answer:

Windows dialog boxes can be either "modal" or "modeless." When your program displays a modal dialog box, the user cannot switch between the dialog box and another window in your program. The user must explicitly end the dialog box, usually by clicking a pushbutton marked OK or Cancel. The user can, however, generally switch to another program while the dialog box is still displayed. Some dialog boxes (called "system modal") do not allow even this movement. System modal dialog boxes must be ended before the user does anything else in Windows. A common use of modal dialog boxes is to create an "About" box that displays information regarding your program.

Modeless dialog boxes enable the user to switch between the dialog box and the window that created it as well as between the dialog box and other programs. Modeless dialog boxes are preferred when the user would find it convenient to keep the dialog box displayed awhile. Many word processing programs such as Microsoft Word use modeless dialog boxes for utilities such as the spell checker—the dialog box remains displayed on-screen, enabling you to make changes to your text and return immediately to your spell checker.

Modeless dialog boxes are created by using the `CreateDialog()` function:

```
hdlgModeless = CreateDialog(hInstance, lpszTemplate,
                            hwndParent, lpfnDialogProc) ;
```

The `CreateDialog()` function returns immediately with the window handle of the dialog box. Modal dialog boxes are created by using the `DialogBox()` function:

```
DialogBox(hInstance, "About My Application", hwnd, lpfnAboutProc);
```

The `DialogBox()` function returns when the user closes the dialog box.

Cross Reference:

None.

I

Index

G

Add to Your Sams Library Today with the Best Books for Programming, Operating Systems, and New Technologies

The easiest way to order is to pick up the phone and call

1-800-428-5331

between 9:00 a.m. and 5:00 p.m. EST.

For faster service please have your credit card available.

ISBN	Quantity	Description of Item	Unit Cost	Total Cost
0-672-30441-4		Borland C++ 4 Developer's Guide (Book/Disk)	$39.95	
0-672-30279-9		C++ Programming PowerPack (Book/Disk)	$24.95	
0-672-30177-6		Windows Programmer's Guide to Borland C++ Tools (Book/Disk)	$39.95	
0-672-30030-3		Windows Programmer's Guide to Serial Communications (Book/Disk)	$39.95	
0-672-30097-4		Windows Programmer's Guide to Resources (Book/Disk)	$34.95	
0-672-30226-8		Windows Programmer's Guide to OLE/DDE (Book/Disk)	$34.95	
0-672-30364-7		Win32 API Desktop Reference (Book/CD)	$49.95	
0-672-30236-5		Windows Programmer's Guide to DLLs and Memory Management (Book/Disk)	$34.95	
0-672-30295-0		Moving into Windows NT Programming (Book/Disk)	$39.95	
0-672-30338-8		Inside Windows File Formats (Book/Disk)	$29.95	
0-672-30299-3		Uncharted Windows Programming (Book/Disk)	$44.95	
0-672-30239-X		Windows Developer's Guide to Application Design (Book/Disk)	$34.95	

❏ 3½" Disk

❏ 5¼" Disk

Shipping and Handling: see information below.	
TOTAL	

Shipping and Handling: $4.00 for the first book, and $1.75 for each additional book. Floppy disk: add $1.75 for shipping and handling. If you need to have it NOW, we can ship product to you in 24 hours for an additional charge of approximately $18.00, and you will receive your item overnight or in two days. Overseas shipping and handling adds $2.00 per book and $8.00 for up to three disks. Prices subject to change. Call for availability and pricing information on latest editions.

201 W. 103rd Street, Indianapolis, Indiana 46290

1-800-428-5331 — Orders   1-800-835-3202 — FAX   1-800-858-7674 — Customer Service

Book ISBN 0-672-30561-5

Standard library functions' header files.

function/macro	zxheader file	function/macro	zxheader file
abort	stdlib.h	free	stdlib.h
abs	stdlib.h	freopen	stdio.h
acos	math.h	frexp	math.h
asctime	time.h	fscanf	stdio.h
asin	math.h	fseek	stdio.h
assert	assert.h	fsetpos	stdio.h
atan	math.h	ftell	stdio.h
atan2	math.h	fwrite	stdio.h
atexit	stdlib.h	getc	stdio.h
atof	stdlib.h	getchar	stdio.h
atoi	stdlib.h	getenv	stdlib.h
atol	stdlib.h	gets	stdio.h
bsearch	stdlib.h	gmtime	time.h
BUFSIZ	stdio.h	HUGE_VAL	math.h
calloc	stdlib.h	_IOFBF	stdio.h
ceil	math.h	_IOLBF	stdio.h
clearerr	stdio.h	_IONBF	stdio.h
clock	time.h	isalnum	ctype.h
CLOCKS_PER_SEC	time.h	isalpha	ctype.h
clock_t	time.h	iscntrl	ctype.h
cos	math.h	isdigit	ctype.h
cosh	math.h	isgraph	ctype.h
ctime	time.h	islower	ctype.h
difftime	time.h	isprint	ctype.h
div	stdlib.h	ispunct	ctype.h
div_t	stdlib.h	isspace	ctype.h
EDOM	errno.h	isupper	ctype.h
EOF	stdio.h	isxdigit	ctype.h
ERANGE	errno.h	jmp_buf	setjmp.h
errno	errno.h	labs	stdlib.h
exit	stdlib.h	LC_ALL	locale.h
EXIT_FAILURE	stdlib.h	LC_COLLATE	locale.h
EXIT_SUCCESS	stdlib.h	LC_CTYPE	locale.h
exp	math.h	LC_MONETARY	locale.h
fabs	math.h	LC_NUMERIC	locale.h
fclose	stdio.h	LC_TIME	locale.h
feof	stdio.h	struct lconv	locale.h
ferror	stdio.h	ldexp	math.h
fflush	stdio.h	ldiv	stdlib.h
fgetc	stdio.h	ldiv_t	stdlib.h
fgetpos	stdio.h	localeconv	locale.h
fgets	stdio.h	localtime	time.h
FILE	stdio.h	log	math.h
FILENAME_MAX	stdio.h	log10	math.h
floor	math.h	longjmp	setjmp.h
fmod	math.h	L_tmpnam	stdio.h
fopen	stdio.h	malloc	stdlib.h
FOPEN_MAX	stdio.h	mblen	stdlib.h
fpos_t	stdio.h	mbstowcs	stdlib.h
fprintf	stdio.h	mbtowc	stdlib.h
fputc	stdio.h	MB_CUR_MAX	stdlib.h
fputs	stdio.h	memchr	string.h
fread	stdio.h	memcmp	string.h